CRAIGO,
THANKS FOR ALL YOUR
INCREDIBLE SUPPORT AND
LE MASTERS FRIENDSHIP!

Sport: Greed & Betrayal

By

Graeme Joffe

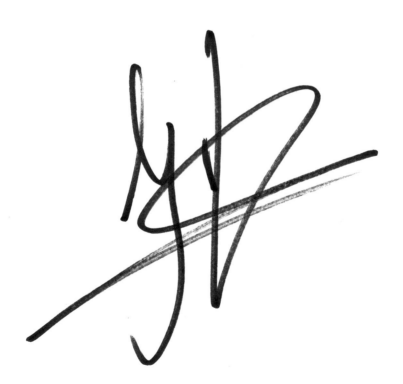

Cover design: Lila McLaurin Konecny

ISBN: 9781798747599

First Edition

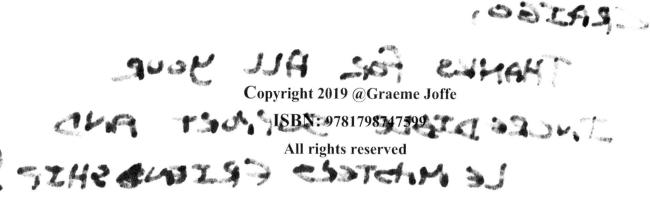

I take my hat off to Graeme Joffe, the lone South African sports journalist in the wilderness with courage to expose corruption and cronyism as a South African version of David Walsh. He might not get many invites to the cocktail parties, but this guy deserves the support - and tip offs - of decent minded people who want change for the better. If there was a Pulitzer Prize for courageous sports journalism in SA, Joffe would be the only candidate. What many of his don't touch rivals don't realise, is that he is the only go to man from sources wanting to blow open stories. It's only a matter of time before he drops a bombshell. The system in South African sport is all about sports administrators co-opting journos and then rewarding them with cocktail party invites and dropping the odd little scoop story. It's an easy life if that is the mediocrity that you aspire to. If however, you want to speak truth to power, it is another story altogether. I don't like to comment excessively on SA living 7000km over the pond, but can tell you the Stockholm syndrome is a malignant tumour that needs to be chemotherapied fast. South Africa has produced world class achievements across the spectrum, sport included, and deserves nothing less than the highest standards of excellence in its support structure. - (Dale Granger, former SA rugby journalist)

Email from Craig Wapnick (former World Squash top 50 ranked player)

22 July 2015

Dear Joffers

I have been pondering the state of our sporting nation. As an ex sports person I am angry. I want to fight like you are fighting. When you told me not to get involved as I have a family I thought you were overreacting a bit.

Now I know you were serious.

So, I have decided I am going to let you fight the corruption within administration and the extravagant spending on themselves while I will concentrate on drawing attention to the actual success of SA Sport in the hope of showing people just how bad our leadership is.

We are sporting nobodies in the world.

Australians are sports mad with 80% of funding going to athletes we are the opposite we are actually an embarrassment for all our wealth and facilities. Our football is the biggest mess of all. So it's not like this an elitist sport issue. This is across the board. A few individuals carry our flag in selected sports but for the most part we are nowhere in almost all Olympic sports and others. We live in the greatest climate for sport in the world and we have one top twenty tennis player who trains and lives in the US, I can go on and on about mediocrity.

Where does it come from? Where is the inspiration? The funding? The excitement?

People in charge are not true sports people. They have no idea what it takes. They want the glory but they don't really care. So, let's judge the minister of sport (and SASCOC) on results like any CEO would be judged. They should be fired on performance.

The SA sports awards for what? To reward who? As a sporting nation we don't deserve to pat ourselves on the back. This lavish banquet is like me winning my local club champs and holding a banquet to reward myself. I would run SA sport and drive a beetle like the president of Uruguay before taking for myself ahead athletes. Why because I want young people to compete and to win internationally where it really counts.

When we were allowed back into international sport we had a chance to play against the best. We have abused that privilege. I would make sure my team earn their BMW's and their perk if any - they would all do this for passion reasons first. I would never go to the Commonwealth Games ahead of any deserving athlete.

I am going to write a job description for the person and people running sport and you will see that they are not qualified because of one thing and thing only - athletes must come first at all times. Anyone who qualifies for Olympics deserves to go whether medal contenders or not. I would never fly business class to games I should not be at and be able to look at myself in the mirror.

I would be nobody until our athletes perform.

The business of sport is not money, the business of sport is competing to win the rest will come. If I was a sponsor of SASCOC or other I would put in a performance clause and I would insist that 80% of all sponsorship money goes to athletes with a serious audit.

So, Joffers, perhaps in a few years-time, you will run SA Sport with me on your side (no quotas, 100% transparency pure passion mixed with sensible business acumen and 100% performance based) - we will make sure our athletes, from the top to development come first and then maybe some will start coming first.

Keep up the fight.

Any sports journalist who goes along for the ride is not a sports journalist they are fair weather reporters. It is their choice as many don't want to miss free lunch in the box. But then again you get reporters who love a free lunch and you get journalists who truly honor free speech.

You are not a reporter my mate, you are a proper sports journalist.

Cheers

Wappo

Chapters

1: First whistle-blow
2: Olympic spin
3: Unhealthy State of SA sport
4: London 2012
5: Oscar Pistorius
6: The fix is in …
7: Press Ombudsman
8: SASCOC sues for R21 million
9: By George: More legal threats
10: Commonwealth Games
11: Reporting without fear or favour
12: Dirt of the Day
13: Wanted!
14: The Missing Police File
15: Private Eye
16: "They're coming to get you"
17: WhatsApp
18: SA Sports Awards
19: Meeting with the FBI
20: "Tata My Chance"
21: Conflicted media
22: No Sochi, No Rio
23: The political mix
24: Township TV: Making a difference
25: Breaking my silence
26: Forensic linguistics
27: Defamation insurance
28: Joining the dots (Part 1)
29: Joining the dots (Part 2)
30: New beginnings

Abbreviations

International:

CGF - Commonwealth Games Federation
FIFA - Fédération Internationale de Football Association
FIH - International Hockey Federation
FINA - International Swimming Federation
IAAF - International Association of Athletics Federations
ICC - International Cricket Council
IOC- International Olympic Committee
WADA - World Anti-Doping Agency

South Africa:

ANC - African National Congress
ASA - Athletics South Africa
BSA - Basketball South Africa
CSA - Cycling South Africa
CSA - Cricket South Africa
DA - Democratic Alliance
DStv - Digital Satellite Television
GLRU - Golden Lions Rugby Union
HSM - Highbury Safika Media
KSA - Karate South Africa
MTN - Mobile telecommunication company
NLC - National Lotteries Commission
NLDA - National Lottery Distribution Agency
NLDTF - National Lottery Distribution Trust Fund
NOCSA - National Olympic Committee of South Africa
NSA - Netball South Africa
OPEX - Operation Excellence Programme
PAIA - Promotion of Access to Information Act
PSA - Powerboat South Africa
PSL - Premier Soccer League
SABC - South African Broadcasting Corporation
SAEF - South African Equestrian Federation
SAFA - South African Football Association
SAGF - South African Gymnastics Federation
SAHA - South African Hockey Association
SAIDS - South African Institute for Drug-free Sport
SAPS - South African Police Service
SARS - South African Revenue Service
SARU - South African Rugby Union
SASCOC - South African Sports Confederation and Olympic Committee
SATTB - South African Table Tennis Board
SRSA - Sport and Recreation South Africa
VSA - Volleyball South Africa

* The South African Rand (ZAR) trading at R14.85 to the US dollar ($) - (March 2019)
* Numerous sources are anonymous on request

Introduction

'Everyone deserves a fair chance'

Sport has been my life.

"Graeme Joffe was born with a cricket bat in one hand and a ball in the other."

The quote was from my very first interview as a sports mad 10 year old in the North Eastern Tribune, a knock and drop newspaper for our residential area, growing up in Highlands North, Johannesburg.

I wanted to bat like South African cricket legend, Graeme Pollock and bowl like the great, Clive Rice.

It's good to dream but I became a jack of all trades, master of none.

At Fairways Primary School, I played cricket, soccer, squash and tennis. We were extremely fortunate to have the former SA cricketer and Wits soccer player, Jimmy Cook as a coach and mentor.

Fairways is a five minute walk to the iconic Wanderers cricket stadium in Johannesburg and it was always a race to see who could get there first after the school bell.

Watching cricket during those "Mean Machine" days were unforgettable. Hard to forget the likes of Cook, Fotheringham, Kallicharan, Pollock, Rice, McKenzie, Page, Kourie, Jennings, McMillan, Radford and Hanley.

Jimmy was not only a very special coach but also a firm believer in giving everyone a fair chance. You may have batted three one week but if it was weaker opposition the next week, you could find yourself batting at 10 or 11 to give someone else a chance.

Try explaining that to a 10 year-old who was hungry for runs and wickets every week.

But it resonated with what my late father instilled in us kids at a very young age - 'everyone deserves a fair chance in life'. I miss him and those words.

My dad was a true gentleman who spent hours and hours on the tennis and squash courts with all his kids except for one daughter who was given almost all the musical genes in the family and was nicknamed by her high school field hockey coach as the 'gutless wonder'. Sorry Mands!

Balfour Park was our junior sports stomping ground. It was a 30 minute walk from our house in 10th Avenue, Highlands North and sometimes it was 40 minutes if we had 10 cents for one game of pinball at the Rocket Cafe.

I can still smell the salt and vinegar hot chips (slap chips) from the little club kitchen which was easily digested with a Fanta Grape.

No better way than to spend a Saturday afternoon sitting the behind the goals at the Balfour stadium shouting for our professional team, Highlands Park. Eugene Kleynans, Des Backos,

Martin Cohen, Jimmy Joubert, Jerry Sadike just to name a few – they were my soccer playing idols.

And not forgetting all those dads who volunteered their invaluable time to coach us through the junior soccer ranks. They played a big role in our lives.

I attended Highlands North Boys High School, graduating in 1986. Sport was my everything! I would walk six blocks to school at 7am every morning and not come home until after 5pm. Whatever sport was on that afternoon, I was partaking.

If only all kids in SA had that opportunity today.

Rugby is synonymous with most boys schools in South Africa and I gave it my best shot but wasn't the bravest fullback. I was in the team more for my kicking but that too let me down at the biggest moment.

It was the big high school rivalry between Highlands North and King Edwards (KES) in 1986. The score was was 15-13 to KES with a minute to go and we got a potential game winning penalty between the 25 and 10 metre line. I like to add that it was near the touchline but have been reminded more than often that the penalty was in fact in the middle of the field.

In other words, a fairly straight forward kick to win the game.

I set up for the kick in front of the 5,000 strong crowd with the Highlands supporters ready to run onto the field to celebrate a famous win on the road.

I was going to be the school hero -- instead I was the school zero.

The penalty kick never got off the ground and rolled gently between the middle of the poles.

KES held on for the 15-13 win.

It was a tough pill to swallow at age 17 but it taught me more about life than anything else. It was just a game and the sun will come up tomorrow. 33 years later, it's still a standing joke amongst my KES friends who played in the same game.

Don't worry Joffers, we gave you one point for the 'grubber goal' - so, you only lost 15-14.

Thanks Michael Faber and Johnny Gerber!

The Highlands boys remember it differently and I was nicknamed, "Costas" for cost-us the match!

I managed to play provincial U14 cricket before my bowling action went into a steady decline and squeezed into a couple of provincial squash teams before my high school career came to an end.

But not before one more 'standout' athletics performance.

I wasn't built for track but our headmaster, the late Russel Kitto wasn't having any of it and tried to turn me into a 3000m runner. What was he thinking?

Days and weeks of training, climbing koppies (hills) until the big season finale - the boys Inter-High Track and Field meet at Parktown in 1986. I was left behind at the starting gun and saw the heels of all the runners for the remainder of the race. Needless to say, I was lapped by the winner and got a standing ovation when I finally crossed the finish line. I felt like a winner only because I was given the opportunity to compete.

Russel Kitto was a gem of a headmaster, a disciplinarian, a no nonsense educator with a big heart. Above all, he was an advocate of fair play.

As if I wasn't doing enough school sport, I also had to play club cricket and soccer for Balfour and Jeppe respectively. Those were special times as an 17-year-old. Nothing like a team sport where age didn't matter.

What to do after high school is no easy decision unless you have a clear career path in mind.

I wanted to be like the South African sports broadcaster, Trevor Quirk who commentated on just about everything from cricket to tiddlywinks.

Sorry Quirky!

Undecided about my studies, I applied to be an American Field Scholar (AFS) exchange student, hoping to be sent to the United States as the older of my two sisters was living in Chicago. The application came back as successful - Switzerland.

Where's that? It wasn't even one of my top three choices. Very smart of AFS getting you to list your top three choices and then sending you somewhere out of your comfort zone.

I had a bit of a flair for languages (got a distinction for Zulu in matric thanks mainly to a great teacher, Sue Scott-Dobie) but don't ask me about my other grades.

I took a quick crash course in High German before heading to Zurich, Switzerland as an AFS exchange student.

What a year, a year of growing, a year of meeting students from around the world, learning new cultures and getting to see a little of Europe. Expanding my horizons!

I attended the Ramibuhl Gymnasium in Zurich which will always have a special place in my heart. I was nicknamed 'der graham-brotli' (a swiss bread) as you won' t find too many that go by the name of Graeme in Switzerland.

The school trips to Milan, the Netherlands and skiing were unforgettable. I wasn't a natural on the ski slopes but managed to stay in one piece.Trying to understand chemistry and maths taught in German was tougher than any black ski slope. I think I wrote a lot of postcards back home during those school lessons but was high up in the English class.

Love the fact that the Swiss can speak so many languages.

I lived in a small town called Esslingen which was a ten minute bus ride to the Squash Club Oetwil am See. The president of the club was Peter Frieden and I owe him and the members a huge debt of gratitude.

They couldn't have been more welcoming. Danke schoen!

Before I left for Switzerland, I got a little taste of print journalism as I started a school sport column for a major SA daily newspaper, "The Star" and also did a little sub editing.

I'll never forget my first headline after Spanish soccer giants, Real Madrid beat a side 8-nil.

"Was it Real?"

Not bad huh? Well, I thought it was pretty sharp for an 18 year-old and proud to see it in the paper the next morning in black and white without being edited.

I was given my start by the then sports editor, Julian Kearns and the banter in the newsroom was fun and lively.

Great people all with a die-hard passion for sport.

Studying Journalism at Rhodes University in Grahamstown was going to be a natural fit for me and was undeniably three of the best years of my life. It was only three as I don't think my liver could have taken any more but it was enough to get my Bachelor of Arts degree with majors in Journalism and German.

I played cricket, soccer and squash for Rhodes and was proudly part of the soccer unification process, which resulted in the first mixed race team on campus. Hard to describe the feeling, experience and immense satisfaction of playing a game in Zwide Township (Port Elizabeth) and touring Mdantsane (East London) with a unified Rhodes soccer team.

Apartheid had divided us but sport had now brought us together.

To assist my parents with the expense of my Rhodes education, I took on the responsibility of being an assistant housemaster at St Andrews Preparatory School in Grahamstown. It was free board and lodging at the school in return for some dormitory duties and coaching sport. A real learning curve and a very worthwhile experience to be able to give back at a young age.

And believe it or not, my long-distance running career was resurrected at Rhodes thanks to a 'quiet' drinks night at the good old Victoria (the Vic) hotel. With soccer team-mates, Greg Farrell, Craig Neave, Ant Hudson we got into a bet which involved running the Two Oceans Marathon (56km ultra-marathon) in Cape Town.

Two against two and the winners buy dinner after the race. Not the smartest bet in the world!

I won't bore you with the training schedule and how we qualified to run the Two Oceans but needless to say, I was the weakest of the four but managed to pick them off one by one in the race to win the dinner.

You're welcome Ant!

I couldn't feel my legs for the last 15km and my appetite was also gone that night but I still ordered as much as possible to take advantage of the free dinner.

After three great years at Rhodes (1989-1991), it was time to graduate to the real world and seek gainful employment.

Staying in South Africa would have meant doing one year in the military first but after going to a cadet camp in high school, I knew eating sardines for breakfast, lunch and supper and waking up at 5am every morning wasn't for me.

I decided to give the military a miss and to try my luck in the United States. I stayed with my sister and brother-in-law in Chicago and proceeded to send out 100s of CV's/resumes to TV, Radio and Print media across the country.

The response was a little depressing as I didn't have much work experience or vast knowledge of the US sports (basketball, baseball, football and ice hockey).

But it didn't take long for basketball legend, Michael Jordan to become my new sporting hero. Going to the old Chicago stadium to watch Jordan and the Bulls was a sports treat. Goose bump stuff when the lights were dimmed before the game and "player number 23, Michael Jordan" is welcomed onto the court.

Today, if people ask me who is the greatest athlete in the world - my answer would have be Michael Jordan for the way in which he could dominate a team sport. Tiger Woods would be a close second.

Trying to find a job in the US was becoming a challenge and I had almost resigned myself to going back to South Africa after four months.

Then came the call from a Bill MacPhail at CNN in Atlanta.

At first, I thought it was my brother-in-law playing a telephone prank on me until the voice on the other end said 'you're welcome to hang up and call me back on this 404 number and speak to my secretary, Elizabeth Bakos.'

I thought quickly and wisely enough not to hang up.

My heart was racing and I don't remember much of the conversation apart from Bill saying my resume landed on his desk a couple days ago and they'd like to interview me for a CNN International Sports anchor position.

What? With no TV experience? Maybe it was a prank after all?

One week later, I arrived in Atlanta.

First stop, the CNN Center. I had a couple hours to kill before my interview. The CNN Center was packed but not with anyone who even looked vaguely familiar. I guess I had never been to a Grateful Dead concert before. The "dead fans" were there in numbers for the concert that night at the Omni, which is next to the CNN Center.

The secondary smoke from the Dead fans didn't even help and I was still as nervous as anything for my first real job interview, at CNN of all places.

Bill MacPhail was one of the most respected men in the industry and made me feel at ease. I think I sold him on my cricket knowledge but he couldn't believe a game could take five days and still end in a draw.

That is still too much for most American sports fans to comprehend.

I was given the tour of CNN and sold on the bright lights. Bill promised to let me know one way or another in a couple weeks if I had the job.

Jackpot!

My first real job was going to be an International Sports Anchor at CNN. Never in my wildest dreams. I was in the right place at the right time as CNN International was ready for lift off with the Gulf war.

The first few months were very tough as the sports segments were recorded and we had to do it all. Write the script, voice it to camera, source the footage, get all the scores made up and edit the package for air. I was drowning and paying the price for not having done a television course at Rhodes University. I did Radio instead as the TV course was on a Friday afternoon which clashed with my social golf.

Priorities Graeme, priorities!

Over time, like anything else, it became easier. Nothing like hands on experience!

CNN International was being broadcast back to South Africa and my mother kept telling me I was doing a great job. She was my biggest fan. Truth be told, I wasn't very good. I knew my sport but wasn't a natural in front of the camera.

I needed some help.

The help came the way of a speech coach who told me I was doing too much "head dancing" which was distracting for viewers and I needed to slow down my delivery as CNN International was going to over 100 countries where English was not necessarily the mother tongue.

I was yanked off air for a few months, a very bitter pill to swallow but worked tirelessly to earn back my stripes. It worked!

A few years down the road and our short-recorded segments turned into a half hour live show, "World Sport".

Live TV, what a thrill and nothing quite like it but once you've said it, it's said. Being a perfectionist, I had to learn to let it go when I made a mistake.

With CNN being a 24 hour news network, my shift was mostly from 7pm-3am, which meant getting home at 3.30am, having something to eat, watching re-runs of Jerry Springer and then falling asleep around 5am.

It felt like celebrating New Year's Eve every day without drinking but CNN set me up for life.

Seven great years of learning the A-Z of television and from some of the most talented people in the industry. Indebted to the late Jim Huber who took me under his wing for my first big reporting gig at the Masters.

Some will hate me for this but I also got to play Augusta National in 1997.

They have a media lottery every year and some members of the press get to play the course on the Monday after the Masters. I won the Lottery and proceeded to shoot 92. I remember all 92 shots like it was yesterday.

Yes, I played Augusta National but don't have a green jacket to show for it! More about that later in the book.

I returned to South Africa at the end of 1999. As a sports journalist, I always wanted to work in my home country. Africa stays in your blood and having learned the ropes at CNN, I felt I could make a difference.

I teamed up with an old acquaintance, Darren Scott who owned a TV production company and worked on a number of shows that we produced for the pay TV channel, SuperSport. The highlight was a two week trip to Sydney for the Olympic Games in 2000.

I had a full media accreditation and got to see a lot of the tennis, swimming, hockey and track and field.

It was my Olympic dream but no medals for my opening TV stand-up segment in front of the main stadium. I was a one man band and had set the camera up on the tripod to do my 30 second opening when a big gust of wind took over. I was helpless from 15 feet away as the tripod and camera went *(&%^$#$@$((&*. Needless to say I had to buy a new camera.

Sydney was the host with the most and if I never get to another Olympic Games, I think I got to witness one of the best ever.

In 2001, I embarked on a six week trip through Africa to film a TV documentary series called 'Africa's Sporting Heroes'.

It started in Kenya where I caught up with running legend, Kip Keino who rose to world fame by winning gold in the 1500m at the Summer Olympic Games in 1968. His story is truly amazing and what he and his wife have done for orphans in the Kenyan town of Eldoret is of epic humanitarian proportions.

My travels took me through Namibia, Zambia, Uganda, Tanzania, Malawi, Rwanda, Ethiopia, Ghana, Ivory Coast, Nigeria and Egypt.

I kicked the ball around with Ghanian soccer legend, Abedi Pele and his sons at their home in Accra, Ethiopian track star, Kenenisa Bekele hosted me in Addis Ababa, filmed cricket in Uganda, boxing in Tanzania, tennis in Rwanda, basketball in Nigeria and saw the biggest rivalry in Egyptian football between Al Ahly and Zamalek.

The stories were heart warming, poverty in the extreme but millions of smiles that made me smile. Africa has its own unique heartbeat. I love the continent and the people!

In 2004, I joined 94.7 Highveld Stereo as the sports presenter on the biggest breakfast radio show in Johannesburg, "The Rude Awakening".

It was rude having to wake up every morning at 4.30am but we had a lot of good times and laughs. Radio felt more natural to me and many said I had a face for radio. Ouch!

The nickname "Joffers my boy" became a household name thanks to radio show host, Jeremy Mansfield. At that point in my career, I was still the 'happy go lucky' reporter Joffers.

Graeme Joffe is a familiar voice on 94.7 Highveld Stereo's The Rude Awakening. "Joffers" is probably best known for his stupid sport joke of the day.

And boy, the jokes were stupid!

Most of the listeners only used to laugh when I would laugh hysterically at the end of every joke, making as though it was always my best ever.

The standing joke though, was why Joffers was still single?

The station even created programming content, something similar to the reality TV series, "The Bachelor" called "Joffers My Girl".

I was the bachelor! I have to be the only guy in the world to have a three week long radio competition to find him a wife and he's still single.

Final Four in the Joffers My Girl competition

Yes, I was the thorn among the roses.

I recall all my friends telling me I was luckiest guy in the world, living with four girls in a penthouse for three weeks. It wasn't that easy boys, you can relax. In fact, it scarred me for life and that's why I'm probably still not married.

That's my story and I'm sticking to it!

The winner of "Joffers My Girl" and I would spend a week at a resort on the island of Madagascar.

I am a romantic Scorpio (born 1 November) but what would happen if the winner and I had no love connection?

After all, the listeners were doing the voting and I had no say.

I asked good friend, Paddy Brearley who was managing director of the Legacy Hotel Group which put the winning prize together, what one does at this island resort as I was never much of a water baby.

His reply was not what I wanted to hear.

Rock climbing, walks and watch turtles make love.

I was in trouble. No TV's to watch sport and no golf!

But it all ended well as Jeremy gave the winner, Nicole the option to "bullet" me and go with someone else. She did exactly that and took her neighbour who had recently lost her husband.

I was now the butt of the joke.

Ha, ha – Joffers got dumped!

2010 was an exciting time to be a sports journalist in South Africa with the FIFA 2010 World Cup in our own backyard. I went to the opening game at Ellis Park where Bafana Bafana (the South Africa Men's National Team) and Mexico played to a 1-all draw.

But throughout the tournament, I always felt there was something missing or not right.

I guess I was right!

In 2011, I became a freelance journalist, which led me down the dark, lonely road of investigative sports journalism.

Investigative purely by default and it became an addiction!

Chapter 1: The First Whistle-Blow

During the 2012 Super Rugby tournament between provincial teams from Australia, New Zealand and South Africa, there were a number of negative local press articles and social media posts about one of the five South African sides, the Golden Lions.

The critique was accompanied by a pro agenda for another team from South Africa (SA), the Southern Kings to replace the Lions in the tournament from 2013.

As a die-hard Lions fan and foremost a journalist, it sparked an interest.

One SA team had to be relegated for the 2013 season and the South African Rugby Union (SARU) had failed to implement a promotion/relegation system.

It had become a free for all.

On initial investigation, I found the main media source of the 'Lions bashing' to be Cape Town based journalist, Mark Keohane and some of his fellow bloggers from Highbury Safika Media (HSM).

HSM is a media house, which also publishes the SA Rugby Magazine.

But what Keohane failed to make public was his serious conflict of interests. For one, he was an 'unaccredited player agent' for the Southern Kings captain, Luke Watson.

When I confronted Keohane on the conflict and that he was not being objective as a journalist, he was quick to go into denial mode. He then tried to blackmail me on twitter with the aid of his fellow HSM employees, Ryan Vrede and Simon Borchardt.

Keohane: I am not Luke's agent. HSM has never done any work related 2 Kings or Nelson Mandela.

Keohane: Ask Joffers why he left CNN.

Vrede: What I've heard about the story you wouldn't want it all out. Just behave or the dossier will come out.

Keohane: Surprised by your lack of homework. I am not Luke's agent. HSM has never done any work related to Kings or Nelson Mandela.

Borchardt: Another emotional rant from Joffersmyboy. How can Mark Keohane be representing Luke Watson when he resigned from HSM three months ago?

The pathetic tweets were a blatant attempt to divert attention from their unethical journalism and behaviour and there was definitely no 'lack of homework'. I had already been forwarded some email correspondence between Keohane, the then CEO of Eastern Province (EP) rugby/Southern Kings, Anele Pamba and Luke Watson, highlighting the irregular and unethical dealings.

The provinces have their own rugby unions and the officials are elected by the clubs in the respective regions. Luke's father, Cheeky Watson was the president of Eastern Province Rugby. It was a grave conflict of interests, which would later come back to haunt the province as Luke would be paid more than they could afford.

Keohane's email to Pamba on Thursday 25 November 2010, the subject "Player contracts" included the following:

With regards to Luke (Watson) the proposal from our side was an incentive of R1million should the Kings win promotion and stay in the Currie Cup Premier Division the following year. Your response has been to commit to R500 000, payable at the end of the respective financial years relevant to the respective seasons. Given that Luke will sign for three years and that we will re-enter into an extension after the second year, you will appreciate that Luke certainly sees his short- and long-term future with the Kings and has the ambition to make the Kings the strongest provincial and regional entity in the Southern Hemisphere, and a side that attracts the best players in the world to the province and region.

As the incentive is all performance based, the counter proposal would be an additional R250 000 if the Kings finish in the top four of the Currie Cup Premier Division in Luke's third year. I would request you look favourably at this counter proposal, given the payout of the final R250 000 would only be payable at the end of the 2013 season, in which time Luke will have proven his worth to the squad, the province and the region.

Should the team achieve the success Luke believes will happen, the R250 000 incentive in the third year would be justified because of the performance because the Kings would be a top four team in South Africa. I believe this shows intent and ambition from the player and equal intent and ambition from the Kings in the pursuit of creating something magical in the Eastern Cape. There is no risk to the Kings and the reward would not be out of the ordinary if the Kings in three years are ranked in the top four in the country.

Anele and Cheeky, once again thank you for the professionalism and I trust we will be in a position to positively conclude the detail today.

Pamba's response to Keohane …

Herewith confirmation of the offer to Luke Watson:

R3 million per annum from 1 June 2011 – 31 May 2013
R4 million from 1 June 2013 – 31 May 2014
R150 000 relocation costs, payable 1 month before arrival in South Africa.
R500 000 incentive as bonus if team wins promotion to the Premier Division of the Absa Currie Cup in 2011 and retains its status in 2012. This amount will be paid in equal instalments after qualifying, as agreed between the Union and the player.

Keohane had worked his 'unaccredited magic' and sent an email to Luke Watson on 3 December 2010 stating:

I want to keep our professional working relationship uncomplicated and prefer to see my role as that of managing you rather than being an agent, and that the relationship is between you and me. Should we see the need to grow this and develop it further into a business as discussed then we cross that bridge when we get there.

I get a straight 7 and a half percent of whatever you get and in return I do all your negotiations, all your endorsements, prepare your media, marketing and professional plan and implement and manage that plan.

So much for Keohane (Keo) not being Luke's agent and HSM having never done any work related to the Kings. The first whistle had been blown!

Watson signs with Keo

Luke Watson arrived back in South Africa last week after a successful playing stint in Bath, and after a quiet few days spent catching up with family, friends and former players, he was presented to the media in Cape Town by Highbury Safika Media. (HSM - publishers of SA Rugby magazine and www.keo.co.za amongst others). - (sport24, 17 May 2011)

The Super Rugby expansion was a big bone of contention already back in 2006. The then Southern Spears (Kings) was assured of a place in the 2007 and 2008 competitions but SARU failed to deliver on that promise. Millions of rand were wasted in the process. The Lions/Kings saga became an ugly spat built up over years and it didn't need journalists with hidden agendas to misinform the public and twist the facts.

The HSM spin machine was in full force and they nailed their colours to the mast with client, Luke Watson on the front cover of the SA Rugby magazine in June 2011.

(SA Rugby Magazine, June 2011)

Keohane and company were pumping up their client big time.

I approached SA Rugby (SARU) to find out if they would be taking any disciplinary action against Keohane for acting as an unaccredited agent but the SARU CEO, Jurie Roux simply said:

We have no direct knowledge of which agent is acting for which player and can only act if a complaint is laid.

I then asked the South African Rugby Players Association (SARPA) if they knew that Keohane was acting as an unaccredited agent for Watson.

SARPA CEO, Piet Heymans: *Yes, SARPA was aware and this was reported to SARU.*

Who wasn't telling the truth?

After I had exposed Keohane, his brother, Shane was quickly given a temporary SARU agent accreditation. He was supposed to attend a workshop and write the exam. Accredited SARU agent, Jason Smith said of the temporary accreditation:

I assume it entitles you to act as a fully accredited agent until you pass your exam but if he doesn't pass then he will most probably lose his temporary accreditation. Mark was not accredited when he acted on behalf of Luke. Did anything happen? No. Do SARU bend the rules? Yes. Is the entire system crooked? Yes.

SARU then try to sell me another story in an effort to cover their dirty tracks.

The player agent regulations are designed to regulate who can negotiate a playing contract with a union. In other spheres of activity anyone can represent a player (father/mother/brother/lawyer etc.) HSM was the commercial agent of Luke Watson at the time of his return. HSM has subsequently established a rugby division with Gert van der Merwe as their accredited agent.

SARU was often very economical with the truth and I would expose them time after time for serious unethical processes and financial irregularities.

But they were an untouchable boys club linked to government.

The Lions were eventually relegated and the Kings promoted for the 2013 Super 15 season by virtue of a "dirty vote" by the SARU General Council. In addition, there would be a promotion/relegation playoff between the bottom SA side and the Lions the following season.

One season too late!

Two months before the dirty vote, Roux said:

Everyone has agreed that we must secure a solution that does not damage any of the existing franchises.

And he told the Parliamentary Portfolio Committee on Sport:

The Kings will play in the competition in 2013, but not at the expense of one of the other franchises.

He lied!

When making the announcement that the Kings were in and Lions were out, SARU president, Oregan Hoskins said:

Promotion/relegation is a worldwide phenomenon for under achieving teams.

Wow!

The Currie Cup is South Africa's premier domestic rugby competition and the Kings were not even playing in the top tier in 2012. There was no justification for their sudden promotion to an international competition.

Hoskins was a presidential puppet figure in SA Rugby whilst also studying for his SuperSport sponsored MBA (a conflict of interests) and Roux was running the ship.

SARU had violated its own constitution and was a shareholder in the Kings. They had ploughed millions into the ailing franchise and thought the Super 15 would be a quick fix to get their money back. The Lions, one of the biggest franchises in SA rugby was now facing an uncertain future but the players were resilient.

Lions winger, Deon van Rensburg sent me this email on 5 October 2012.

Just want to say thanks for the openness in your article in news 24. Thank you for supporting honesty and integrity. Thank you for speaking your mind and support for the Lions. We as players now how much work is going in behind the scenes by management trying to keep players here at the Lions as well as putting a good competitive competition together for next year. I believe that the Lions will be the top union in SA within the next 5 years. The values of management and players is of such high standard that nothing will get us down. Please keep on supporting the Lions.

Deon was spot on.

The Lions were the top SA team in Super Rugby in the 2016, 2017 and 2018 seasons only to lose in the respective finals to the Hurricanes (2016) and Crusaders (2017/2018).

It was an amazing turnaround!

Back in 2010, the Golden Lions Rugby Union was having its own financial woes. The Guma TAC group of companies came to the rescue with a cash injection but just a year later, they terminated all shareholding negotiations and took steps to liquidate the union to recoup their investment, declaring the Lions were bankrupt.

It was all very messy and the supporters wanted answers.

Graeme, I would like to thank you for your straight-talking column on News24 today. As a Lions supporter and season ticket holder this whole mess surrounding the Lions has been extremely difficult to process and it seems as if most media/writers have sided with SARU and the Kings. Frankly I find this ridiculous! Columnists like Tank Lanning and Mark Keohane have been blurring the boundaries between journalism and simply going along with the stream to protect their own self interests. I understand that the idea of a column is to express your opinion (like you did today) but it seems as if Keohane and Lanning are just waiting for their Kings-cheerleader outfits to arrive in the mail. I don't know which union you support when simply being a supporter, but I thank you for at least contributing some form of sense and a different opinion to the Kings-Cheerleaders out there. - Andries Combrinck

The Kings surprised most in the 2013 Super Rugby season with some real gutsy performances and they ended up winning three games but still finished bottom of the combined log. The Lions were left to play some meaningless friendlies as they had no back up plan for their untimely relegation. The promotion/relegation playoff loomed for the 2014 season and had the Lions lost, it was the end of the road for one of SA's major rugby unions.

The Lions won the two leg playoff by the narrowest of margins and two years later, the Eastern Province Kings had become a bankrupt franchise with players not getting paid salaries and having to sell off assets to make a living.

An anonymous Kings player shared the heartache and turmoil in an email on 1 December 2015.

Yes I am a player, and yes I'm keeping my name anonymous, not because I'm a coward, but because I know the Kings is run by a "family mafia"and I'm afraid of the consequences people close to me may be subjected too. Judging by threatening messages my team mates and staff members have received from father and son, I'm making the right decision to remain anonymous. Earlier today a team mate cried out for help, I'm joining that train, however I'm not asking for money, I'm asking for action, people to stand up against the atrocities of this dictatorship, get rid of Hitler and everyone that comes along with him, and this Union will flourish. However, all I see in the country is a rugby board and union (SARU and unions) driven by agendas, rotten to the core. I pray God will not only help the Kings, but help South Africa. Rugby in this country is burning and falling. People don't understand how toxic and poisonous this environment is, it's sickening and dysfunctional , and please supporters of the Kings and everyone out there must understand , this is no joke, players and employees are suffering, being kicked out of their homes, cars being taken away, electricity being cut off and living on bowls of rice. This is a tragedy. Players are suffering and the blood is on the hands of the man at the helm.

The man at the helm was Cheeky Watson who was an anti-apartheid activist and because of his ANC political connections, he had become very powerful in SA sport. SARU and SARPA are joined at the hip and they allowed the situation to become untenable as the rugby storm brewed long into 2016.

From living the high life with annual salaries of up to R1.85-million to selling their assets to survive – the drastic change in lifestyle has left unpaid EP Kings players battling to put food on the table. A total of 36 rugby players now want the beleaguered franchise to be wound up. The liquidation application, filed with the Port Elizabeth High Court on January 29, initially saw 18 professional rugby players highlight their plight with claims that the EP Kings owed them close to R1.3-million in salary arrears. (EP Herald, 22 February 2016)

AN R80-million cash injection promised to the Eastern Province Rugby Union (EPRU) by a mystery sponsor saved the beleaguered franchise from final liquidation yesterday. But as EPRU was given another lifeline, with the court proceedings postponed to May 31 for it to apply for business rescue, role-players were tight-lipped about where the money was coming from. (EP Herald, 11 May 2016)

A mystery sponsor for R80 million? The mystery sponsor turned out to be Integrated Sports Limited, based in London and proposed by Chris Wishlade.

Ejikeme Ukposi, a Nigerian, is the only listed Officer at Integrated Sports. No office in London. If you call the number, you get a 24 hour concierge answering service for the company and they confirmed they work 24/7 answering phone for Integrated Sports who don't have a physical address. The company website gives the impression that they are based in Kensington and they list their clients amongst others as the FA and SA rugby. Who is allowing this outfit to get involved with a member union of SARU? Chris Wishlade owes a friend of a friend a proper amount of money. Did Jurie Roux approve this crowd? Perhaps he thinks this is normal?

The English rugby club, Saracens had also filed a petition for the bankruptcy of Wishlade in 2014.

Kings saviour's web of lies: A BANKRUPT businessman with an unregistered UK firm and false business address is the "saviour" Eastern Province rugby is relying on to bail it out of an ongoing crisis. (EP Herald, 14 June 2016)

Surprise!

The 'bailout' fell through and on 4 August 2016, the Eastern Province Rugby Union was liquidated but most of its assets had already been moved into another company.

According to my sources:

Jurie used SA Rugby Travel Pty Ltd to steal Super rugby from EP Rugby and didn't consider that the company would be scrutinised and questions asked about it - if an audit is done on that company, you will find something in my opinion. The fact that government money is being channelled into various people's pockets - this is easy to expose. The key individual is Louis Von Zeuner. He is best mates with Sports Minister, Fikile Mbalula and Jurie brought him into the fray. Fikile and Von Zeuner are always sitting next to each other at rugby. And now Von Zeuner is running SA Cricket. He is Fikile's guy. Von Zeuner is one of the most powerful white men in SA sport.

Jurie Roux as a Director of EP Rugby allegedly took the EP Rugby TV Rights fees of R28m and the players into SA Rugby Travel of which he is the sole director and shareholder and used his office as SARU CEO to rubber stamp his daylight heist in an unconscionable act of white-collar crime.

It was business as usual and if all of this wasn't enough of a big red flag, how about the injection of R90 million from SARU into a company called, "MyPlayers" to stop the exodus of SA players to overseas clubs.

The key man in the entire process is Louis von Zeuner. Jurie brought him in a Chairman of MY PLAYERS. He then authorised the payment of R90m to MY PLAYERS per annum for something called 'Collective Image Rights of the Players'. The rights are supposedly controlled by Sarpa, a trade union, but the R90m pa for 5 years is paid to a PTY LTD. Apparently the players are the shareholders but should any player ask for the financials, their curiosity is 'controlled'.

The question here is how does SARU see fit to pay R90m a year for 5 years to My Players Fund for image rights of players valuing the "image rights higher than any super model in Milan NY London or Paris? This is a heist of extraordinary proportions perpetuated by a corrupt band of administrators.

And stopping the exodus?

No fewer than 45 top players left South African shores for overseas clubs after the Super Rugby season in 2016 and the player drain continued in 2017 and 2018 taking the number to over 300.

Where is the rugby money really going?

Watson's under hand dealings finally caught up with him in 2017.

Hawks arrest former EP rugby president Cheeky Watson

The Hawks have arrested former EP rugby president Cheeky Watson, along with Nadia Gerwel, Andrea Wessels, and Mandisa Mkaza on charges of fraud or corruption. It is believed to be linked to the Nelson Mandela Bay Municipality's IPTS funds of R200 million. (Timeslive, 31 March 2017)

The Hawks are South Africa's Directorate for Priority Crime Investigation which targets crime and corruption referred to it by the President or the South African Police Service (SAPS).

It was set up by the Zuma administration in 2008 and replaced the Scorpions which was independent of the SAPS structures.

The State alleges Gerwel and Wessels used an events management company as a vehicle to launder money. But when that company was no longer viable, they allegedly turned to Access Management, a company operating at the Nelson Mandela Bay stadium, and then to EP Rugby. According to court papers, close to R3 million was allegedly laundered into the bank accounts of Access, EP Rugby and Zeranza – by means of Watson, Gerwel and Wessels acting in concert with one another. (IOL, 20 August 2018)

Access Management is another 'very interesting player' in the market.

The managing director of Access Management just happens to the former SA Rugby MD, Rian Oberholzer. Access were 'awarded' the contract by the municipality in Port Elizabeth to manage operations at the Nelson Mandela Bay Stadium, which was built for the 2010 FIFA World Cup.

The deal was a sweet one. Reports suggesting Access got R600 000 a month plus millions in performance-based bonuses.

But they seemed to be scoring from a lot of offside positions.

The Nelson Mandela Bay Ratepayers Association (NMBRA) and AfriForum Port Elizabeth announced that they had conducted an investigation into Access Management, the operator of the Nelson Mandela Bay Stadium, and discovered that the Nelson Mandela Bay Metropolitan Municipality was channeling ratepayers monies through Access to pay the running costs of the EP Kings and the players - and that this been ongoing for a number of years. (RNews, 9 November 2015)

Chippa United have been drawn into the case of fraud, corruption and theft charges brought last Friday against the Nelson Mandela Bay Municipality by the Nelson Mandela Bay Ratepayers Association. The Premier Soccer League club allegedly illegally benefitted from a R750000 loan made out to them, through Nelson Mandela Bay Stadium managers Access Management, to help them stage their league game against Kaizer Chiefs in August last year. According to the Municipal Finance Management Act, municipalities are prohibited from making out loans to members of the public, councillors or municipal officials. (Sowetan, 3 February 2016)

Stadium operator Access Management, a municipal official and a Uitenhage businesswoman are at the centre of a secret Treasury report claiming they are part of "one big conspiracy to siphon money from the Nelson Mandela Bay municipality". The hard-hitting draft report, compiled by auditing firm Deloitte, accuses Access of being a gateway through which millions of rands meant for the city's notorious bus system were funnelled in 2012 to pay businesswoman Andrea Wessels to organise a music concert ... (Times Live, 30 November 2015)

Details of how Access Management served as the gateway for the Nelson Mandela Bay Municipality to filter millions of rands to the EP Kings and Chippa United have been spelt out in documents before the Port Elizabeth High Court. Rian Oberholzer, the director of Access Management – the official operator of the Nelson Mandela Bay Stadium – said he was unsure of whether or not the loans were approved by council. (Herald Live, 15 August 2016)

The Nelson Mandela Bay Municipality and stadium management company Access Management are the latest to go head-to-head in court. This comes at the end of a year that saw the South African Rugby Union take control of the Southern Kings (to avoid a multi-million Rand lawsuit), the Eastern Province Kings being declared bankrupt and stripped of all its player assets, while SARU also pulled the plug on its funding of the EP Rugby Academy (which may result in the institution having to close its doors because of a lack of funding). In an unprecedented step, Access Management broke its silence in the long-standing dispute with the municipality and trade union – issuing a statement after the NMB municipality has dragged them to court, claiming the stadium operators forced them to pay out ZAR200-million more than they should have in a six-year period. (Rugby365, 25 November 2016)

In May 2012, avid rugby fan, Francois Bonthuys posted a blog titled, 'The Keo Connection: He is the wolf in sheep's clothing'.

It exposed the cosy relationship between the Nelson Mandela Bay municipality, Oberholzer, Watson, EP Kings, Keohane and Highbury Safika Media. The threats came thick and fast.

Oberholzer was the leader in chief of the threats, warning Bonthuys that he was 'playing with the Lions balls'.

Bonthuys reluctantly took the blog down, fearing for his safety.The Highbury Safika Media boys celebrated the disappearance of the blog, which I had shared on twitter and they poked the bear again.

Vrede copied in Keohane and Borchardt in his tweet:

Joffers, where's your article? Joffers, you there? Joffers, why did you leave CNN? Tell us son?

Vrede was Keohane's lap dog and they were desperately trying to divert attention with their attempted blackmail.

They had to be hiding more in the HSM kennel!

Chapter 2: Olympic Spin

I started to dig a little deeper.

Mark Keohane had also quietly become a spokesperson/consultant for the South African Sports Confederation and Olympic Committee (SASCOC) and the country's Olympic athletes.

How was this possible?

As for SASCOC. ....they are so naive they can be spun around in small circles. As the in-house line goes, 'just push a plate of muffins in front of Tubby (Reddy) (SASCOC CEO) and he'll say yes to everything.' - Gary Lemke, Highbury Safika Media employee

Highbury Safika Media (HSM) had gotten a multi-million rand contract and renewal to manage the media, marketing and public relations of SASCOC. Was it put out to tender as is should have been as per government procedure?

Of course not!

I interviewed the SASCOC president, Gideon Sam on my radio talk show, SportsFire in 2012 and he blatantly lied about the 'tender'.

They did, they did. You know what happened in 2008 I said to the board ... guys, I think one of the biggest drawbacks for this organisation is that nobody knows what this SASCOC is all about. I went to Mpumalanga, you know, that shocked me, because I was addressing the sports people in Mpumalanga, Nelspruit and the guys said to me: 'Gee, I thought this SASCOC was a factory somewhere in Jo'burg.' I said: 'But how can you say that, are you not a sports person?' 'No I don't know this SASCOC. So I said ... guys ... we have to spend money and go out there and make sure. So yes they tendered, they put their proposals forward, we looked at it as a board and management and we were happy. - Gideon Sam, SASCOC president

SASCOC tender that wasn't

South Africa's Olympic president Gideon Sam misled the public about a lucrative communications contract awarded to media firm Highbury Safika Media (HSM). In April, Sam, president of the South African Sports Confederation and Olympic Committee (Sascoc), said on Radio Today and DStv that HSM had tendered for the contract, speculated to be worth more than R12 million, but this month Sascoc admitted after an access to information request by Media24 Investigations the contract did not go out to tender. (The Witness, 23 June 2012)

June 2012: Response by SASCOC to Media24 Investigations

Kindly note that this matter was not put out to tender and we are not obliged to do so, but we conducted our own investigations and were satisfied with the good track-record of the company concerned, and thereafter arrived to an agreement to the satisfaction of both parties.

On whether other companies had tendered for the contract: Gideon Sam's on-air response to Graeme Joffe:

We had ... what is this ... Maggie something. But if you just call Vinesh (Maharaj) at our office, he normally works with those things. But we had people who wanted to do that account for us.

Response by Sam to Media24 Investigations

It is correct that other names and other companies were under consideration, and I do not feel the necessity to name the unsuccessful companies.

Asked to clarify why he said on-air HSM tendered when they hadn't, Sam said:

At the outset please be aware that I cannot recollect the exact words uttered by me in regard to the interview with Mr Joffe, but would clearly state that it is not now, nor has it ever been my intention or desire to mislead or misrepresent any facts. My understanding and recollection of the matter was that I was asked numerous questions around the gentleman Mr Keohane, and the procedure.

Sam was the Springbok team manager when Keohane was the SA Rugby communications manager until 2003. There was no need to 'ask numerous questions around this gentleman'. They knew each other very well and Keohane continued to spin it for his SASCOC 'business buddies' with tweets like this when the Olympic Committee was under scrutiny.

Gideon & Tubby. I had pleasure of seeing the work put in over 4 yrs. Stay strong, stay united. There's not a better Pres/CEO combo

Ironically, this tweet was three months after Keohane had resigned in disgrace as the SASCOC spokesperson.

Sports writer's hedonistic ways may end his career

Celebrity rugby writer Mark Keohane resigned suddenly on Friday as spokesperson of South Africa's Olympic team – hours after City Press confronted him with allegations of drug abuse and sexual harassment. (City Press, 2 June 2012)

The allegations were well documented in a Commission for Conciliation, Mediation and Arbitration (CCMA) statement from a former female staff member at HSM.

These excerpts from the statement make for some very sad and sickening reading …

For the past 2.5 years Mark Keohane has had a sad gross cocaine addiction, which has affected any guidance of me or my team. I have suffered from his addiction including:

Having to apologise to female bar staff at the Newlands private suite after he sexually verbally harassed them whilst on cocaine. He also sent sexually harassing text messages which the bar staff's mother found on her phone;

The resignation of my marketing assistant due to initially being sexually harassed by Mark Keohane and then blatantly being victimized by Shane Keohane (brother).

Having to attend meetings that Mark Keohane has initiated after hours and then not bothered to attend as he had been 'out' the night before.

Being blamed for poor decisions that he has made on a whim.

Having to tell the Director of Marketing from HSM's biggest client, the Foschini Group, goodbye on behalf of Mark Keohane, in full knowledge that Mark Keohane was using cocaine down the passage in the toilets, often returning to the private suite in a state.

Having Mark Keohane be so gone on cocaine and alcohol that he talked to me, who was sober, about his 6 year old daughter's private parts and when she will have sex, of which made me sick.

In October 2009 Mark Keohane suffered a huge car crash from a 2 day cocaine fuelled binge, of which he was sent to the Cape Town Medi-Clinic psych-ward. I had no guidance or any real contact from him for over two months. Upon his return he seemed change, however approximately 1 month afterwards seemed to be going down the same direction again. Rizqah Jakoet is the HR Manager at Highbury Safika Media.

It is common knowledge in the company that nothing told to Rizqah is private. She leads people into a false sense of security, however repeats everything to the Directors. The problem with this is that the Directors have total disregard for her.

A very good example of Rizqah doing nothing is the constant times I have told her that Mark Keohane is doing drugs and nothing has happened, nor have I been offered any explanation or counselling. This is the most sexist and indecent company I have ever had to work for, relating to directions from the Directors saying:

Only hire bar girls with big tits

Not being able to hire a well-qualified staff member as she was fat, with Mark Keohane walking past me when I greeted the interviewee, loudly saying 'no'

Being instructed that under no circumstance could I hire males for the marketing team. It must be pretty females only.

I am scared of taking on the beast of Highbury Safika Media. They are vindictive and it is very obvious they think they are above the law.

They even boast at Christmas parties that they have never lost a CCMA case. They make up lies about staff members and spread malicious rumours to make themselves look good.

I do know now that what is happening there is very wrong. I do know that what has happened to me in the past 2 years let alone the last 5 months is horrific.

I know that I am telling the truth, and whilst I am scared, at this stage I have nothing to lose.

***

HSM obviously ran for cover and settled with the employee. She signed a non-disclosure agreement preventing her from disclosing details of the CCMA proceedings.

South African expat in Zambia, Chris Swart had been following my twitter expose of this HSM mob and he became a good source of information. He had made acquaintance with Gary Lemke, who sang like a canary towards the end of 2012.

Gary stated the following:

Seen (CCMA) dossier. All true ... These okes survivors though, bulletproof. Arrogant. Juveniles, big inflated egos. Got too big for the game. Believe their own publicity, untouchables, connected with drug dealers.

As for the Kings, how many times has HSM gone to PE (Port Elizabeth) and why, if there is no company interest? They want to do the match programmes and even a newspaper. So, with the Kings in S15 (Super Rugby) there's revenue in the form of the programme. How many times did our CEO and Cheeky (Watson) meet and how many times did the two Keohane brothers meet with them in the past year? After making the Lions and Winning Ways a priority they parted ways when Jake (White) started asking questions. I believe he settled for around R1.4m.

Heyneke Meyer has been promised one year of positive publicity (as Bok coach) (so, that he's on side). Hence, the buddy-buddy approach. "If England pump us 53-3 we'll celebrate the 3 points. Wait until 2014 and Heyneke will be spat out and chewed up.

My emails are monitored and my phone records are checked. As you saw from the dossier, the HR manager is the eyes and ears for them. Two editors have recently resigned because of sexual harassment but obviously they get nowhere, as she alluded to in her dossier.

Keohane and HSM had also got their claws into former Bok coach, Jake White but that didn't end too well.

Jake's business goes belly up

A business deal between former Springbok coach Jake White, local publishing business Highbury Safika Media, and rugby writer Mark Keohane has turned sour, ending up in the Western Cape High Court. Keohane, employed by Highbury Safika as the publishing director, said in court papers that the application was in fact a last resort after every □riticiz to resolve the dispute over the joint company, Jake White's Winning Way (PTY) Ltd, of which they are all shareholders. (sport24, 21 September 2010)

Gary confirmed the HSM fall out with Jake White and how they were planning to blackmail him.

Sounds all too familiar!

I was in India in 2010 in Delhi when Jake (White) and Keo (Keohane) fell out. Jake was threatened... that if he went ahead with the court case that was in the newspaper, things would be leaked to the media. HSM had employed a pretty young thing especially to flatter Jake and like any red-blooded guy he was tempted into a boardroom table dalliance (don't think he followed through though). That would be leaked. ,someone saying he's Christian tried to f..k a marketing girl on HSM's boardroom table. The case was quickly settled out of court. As we speak, both Keohanes in air, biz class, to London with Tubby Reddy. Daylight robbery. Sascoc/HSM milking it. – Gary Lemke

Lemke was threatened with dismissal by HSM in January 2013 when they alleged he was leaking company information.

I'm facing a disciplinary meeting in 48 hours, where I'm being charged with Breach of Trust, which is a dismissible offence. It relates to an email/DM from me sent by you to someone in May last year and they have on-passed to HSM. In it I said something like, "everything in the dossier is true, except for the part about me. These guys are arrogant and they won't go down". I have no doubt it will be a kangaroo court and I'll be sent on my way. And I have a family to support. I'm not even sure how to begin.

Lemke knew too much for HSM to get rid of him and was still one of their senior staff writers and part of the 'SASCOC PR' team at the Rio Olympics in 2016. Keohane and Ferguson had a major fallout towards the end of 2016 and according to fellow staff members, the cocaine addiction reared its ugly head again.

But that didn't stop Media24, which had exposed Keohane in 2012 from hiring him as a rugby columnist in 2017.

It's a rugby media 'boys club' in Cape Town!

Keohane has a history of getting 'close' to the newly appointed Springbok coaches by promising them favourable journalism in return for the inside scoop on squad and team selections. His 'keo.co.za' blog and SA Rugby magazine would then appear to be one step ahead of the other rugby publications with breaking stories.

When Rassie Erasmus was going to be the new Springbok coach to succeed Heyneke Meyer in 2016, Keohane had the inside track again and sent a text message to Jake White saying:

I hear Rassie will be appointed interim/caretaker Bok coach and with Gav as his media advisor the 2 could redefine the phrase of a Bok tour being a bit of a grind lol. Rassie to coach Boks in June and Rugby Champs and Allister (Coetzee) to take over end of year tour on a three- year contract to next World Cup. That is his or was agreed by executive. Did you see my col today on Hoskins and Jurie? (sic)

'Gav' refers to Gavin Rich, a rugby journalist/author and one of Keohane's big buddies. The 'grind' refers to the grinding of teeth due to the increase in anxiety levels from cocaine use.

Erasmus was already rumoured to have had a substance abuse problem during his playing days.

Cocaine rumour-mongerer must pay, says Rassie

Axed Springbok rugby star Rassie Erasmus is to launch a private prosecution against the person spreading rumours about him snorting cocaine ... The allegations follow a series of setbacks for the ace flanker, who earlier this season fell out with Laurie Mains, his team coach in the Super 12. At one point Mains dropped Erasmus as captain of the Cats, but later claimed the player was suffering from depression. (IOL, August 2001)

Rumours?

I recall a chance meeting of a girlfriend of Rassie's in a Johannesburg bar on a Monday night after a SuperSport TV show, where the subject matter was discussed. She confirmed how they (Rassie and herself) would do 'heavy nights of cocaine and it was a drug of choice for a number of SA rugby players.'

12 April 2016: Allister Coetzee named as the new Springbok coach

SARU did an about turn on Erasmus being the caretaker coach as there was transformation pressure from various circles including government. Rassie didn't take the snub very well and jetted off to coach Munster in Ireland in July of that year but behind the scenes, SARU had already hatched a plan to get their 'golden boy' back.

Coetzee would be set up to fail and Erasmus would take over the reigns as soon as possible.

I really pity Allister, he was set up to fail. I don't know why, but if I look at what they've given him it cannot work, it's impossible. It seems nobody takes responsibility. The whole circus around how Coetzee was appointed was disastrous from day one. If you look at his support team – who are they? Where do they come from? What kind of experience do they have at international level? Zero. Nothing. – (Former Bok and rugby commentator, Kobus Wiese on Sky Sports)

Coetzee was also unable to select overseas based players and these were part and parcel of what he alluded to as 'acts of sabotage' by SARU.

2 February 2018: Allister Coetzee sacked as coach of the Springboks after winning just 11 of 25 test matches

And guess who was already back in South Africa to take over the reigns? Yes, Erasmus had cut his contract with Munster short to come back for the 'promised job' from his good friend and SARU CEO, Jurie Roux.

1 March 2018: Rassie Erasmus named as new Bok coach on an unprecedented six year deal

Ten questions for the new Bok coach, which I would have loved answers to …

Did you apply for the Bok coaching job or was it just offered to you by SARU?

Were you able to select your own coaching staff?

Mzwandile Stick was sacked as the Bok backline coach in 2017. You've brought him back. What will his role be? Did you consider any other black coaches?

You've got a six year deal which gives you an unprecedented **two** *World Cups – do you have a performance clause in your contract?*

Frikkie Erasmus is your personal lawyer and business partner along with SARU CEO, Jurie Roux. Frikkie Erasmus is also the SARU lawyer and does all the staff contracts. Did he draw up and negotiate your deal?

You have an IT company contract with SARU, you own a share of BokPulse (only supplement supplier to the Boks) with Jurie Roux and Frikkie Erasmus. If this not a conflict of interests?

You are now the Director of SA Rugby, Bok coach and control all IT outsourcing and development for SARU. Is this not too many hats?

It was reported in June 2017 that you'd be leaving Munster and together with your Bok assistant, Jacques Nienaber you came back to SA in December 2017. Did you know last year already that you were going to be the new Bok coach?

You were very upset when Allister Coetzee got given the job in 2016. Would you have come back to SA if you were not going to be Bok coach?

Do the likes of Keohane get inside information in return for favorable journalism?

I was never going to get answers from SARU but had them already from a number of different sources close to the scrum.

SARU's internal policy relating to the appointment of the Springbok coach and management team was previously handled by an appointed selection committee as in the case for the selection of Alistair Coetzee. In the instance of May 2017 – Jurie Roux was "mandated" by the Exco, namely Francois Davids and Mark Alexander to confirm Rassie Erasmus' appointment. So when Jurie Roux met with Rassie Erasmus in Dublin Ireland in May 2017 he confirmed his appointment would be effective following the termination of Alistair Coetzee's coaching assignment. Whether this process was followed in the appointment of Rassie and his management team. Absolutely not – this was Jurie Roux together with his lawyer – Frikkie Erasmus – conspired and colluded to engineer the removal of Coetzee and replace him with their friend & client Rassie Erasmus.

Whether Rassie and his management team actually applied for their respective positions. If not, how and why they were appointed. No. Generally these are advertised and no positions were advertised.

Also, SARU like to give their coaches carte Blanche to appoint their management teams. So already in May 2017 Rassie Erasmus insisted that where he goes – Nienaber goes – so Nienaber also knew of this. The leak came from ……. And the new SARU Coaching Team was formed in Dublin Ireland over a few Guinness's at last years PRO12 final at the AVIVA Stadium. Roux and Erasmus were seen carousing around the bar celebrating this deal. Why the process wasn't opened up to other candidates? Because Jurie Roux wanted to hand pick his own chap – Rassie Erasmus and under the pretense of a legal coaching and Director of Rugby appointment – manufactured by none other than the personal attorney of Jurie Roux & Rassie Erasmus'- the erstwhile Frikkie Erasmus – so the appointment was hatched in February 2017 already without regard to any conflict of interest or bias. The General Council's pre- approved selection criteria for the Springbok coach was waived by Jurie Roux using his Exco foot soldiers Mark Alexander and Francois Davids. (sic)

Stratus and Footprint – both owned by Frikkie and Rassie Erasmus in a company (I know Frikkie called Jake White to ask him to market the software in Australia and Jake declined). They presumably own the IP and patent of this software if they developed it themselves. It is apparently brilliant software so brilliant in fact that the only company that PAYS big money to use it is SARU whose Director of Rugby apparently developed and has a share in the company that owns it. If the Software is so ground breaking that SARU just had to have it above any other world class software then why isn't it selling successfully internationally?

Think there are a few people running around at SARU at the moment. They are blaming Andy Marinos (SARU GM) for the "supplements" leak. All levels of national side use these bok pulse supplements as it is endorsed by SARU. French company financed….first and foremost what you need to understand is EVERYTHING goes through Frikkie Erasmus….he is their firewall. All front companies gets created by him and all the "dirty" money from competitions, software, contracts, sponsorships etc filters into those company accounts and it basically untraceable. For Example, SARU is busy with software to assist coaches. The union invested heavily into this software the last couple of years. Developer is paid by SARU which the developer in turn pays a "front" company for "intellectual property" all corrupt stake holders make money which majority of the funds actually comes from government to advance transformation.Another example. Contract gets negotiated, when a certain agencies players get

Springbok contracts it gets inflated whereby commission is again paid into a "front" company. Started at (Western) Province where avg players where getting R2.5m annual contracts, obviously players contracted to a certain agency. (sic)

Jake White also weighed in on the appointment of the new Bok coach …

Between 2012 and 2016, SA Rugby paid the same director of rugby to spend 100 percent of his time putting systems in place and streamlining pathways for all of the national teams, except the Springboks. Then, during Coetzee's term, SA Rugby □riticiz that they actually needed a director of rugby and they were very pleased to bring back the guy who had left the job 18 months earlier. And now it's okay that the director of rugby only spends 30 percent of his time in that role. Either SA Rugby has been deceitful about the reasons why they originally brought Erasmus back, or they've massively oversold the importance of the director of rugby role. So which one is it? – (Jake White)

There are so many secrets closely guarded within the four walls of the SA Rugby offices in Cape Town but as one SARU EXCO member put it to me:

The fact of the matter is that the appointment of Rassie was handled in a complete undercover manner.

No kidding!

Chapter 3: Unhealthy State of SA Sport

A prominent athletics administrator penned a very disturbing dossier, addressed to the then Minister of Sport, Fikile Mbalula in 2011 regarding the unhealthy state of sport in South Africa.

The dossier included allegations of corruption, maladministration, nepotism and lack of transformation. But instead of acknowledging the problems and consulting with the author, the Minister conveniently turned a blind eye.

I must clarify to everybody that we are a government and we are transparent. We don't work with fly-by-night self-appointed people who are basically cowards and can't face their issues. If you allege that there is any form of corruption there is a presidential helpline and there is an anti-corruption helpline so you can declare yourself openly. We don't work like zekezeke (masked identity) whereby you drop a note in our offices thereafter you leak it to the media that there are big problems we are attending to. There has never been any report about corruption to the ministry except for an anonymous letter with no letterheads. If you want assistance from us, whoever you are, please come to the fore. – Fikile Mbalula (New Age Daily 2011)

The author came to the fore.

I am the author of the dossier but at the time the media was not interested in writing about it. Only New Age managed to write about it after it was toned down. The minister referred to me conveniently as a "coward"at the time but when I subsequently delivered him a copy through his advisor, Mr. Fuzani, he said nothing and did nothing.

Mbalula was appointed Minister of Sport and Recreation on November 1, 2010. He was Deputy Minister of Police before this but 'policing' sport was not one of his priorities for good reason.

His hands were just as dirty!

The dossier highlighted the systemic corruption, maladministration and nepotism in SA sport.

South African sport needs a total overhaul in order to remove the corrupt elements within it and to create a healthy state, where athletes will be the focus of the day and their quest to excel in their God given talents. The current state of sport is riddled with covert corrupt tendencies which are similar to the tendencies taking place in other sectors of our society. The only difference is that people in general are not paying the necessary attention to the details for these evils to be rooted out of sport. A lot of our people depend on the media for them to understand what is happening in sport which has unfortunately proven to be a disadvantage as investigative journalism in sport is not the order of the day. Some influential individuals have used sport as a platform to gain access to the top echelons of our leadership in government vying for recognition and acknowledgment. Others have used sport as a means of amassing wealth taking advantage of the ignorance of the people involved within. There is no existence of corporate governance guidelines or policies and those who cite them are very mischievous and hypocrites. There is no sport federation in existence which can boast of corporate governance in their midst, including SASCOC as the coordinating body.

The dossier also makes mention of the 2008 SASCOC elections and how they were rigged to make sure friends got into the board positions. Gideon Sam became president and at the same time, he was Chairperson of the National Lotteries Distribution Trust Fund (NLDTF). A grave conflict of interests which made it easy to sway the votes of the numerous sporting federations who are dependent on Lottery funding.

In other words, votes for Lottery funding!

The leadership of SASCOC thrives on the votes of the □riticized sports . This is further compounded by the fact that SASCOC is controlling the lottery (the sports distribution agency) which makes it easier for its manipulation of these federations. It should be noted that the majority of the federations in exception of football, cricket and rugby are dependent on the lottery grants, it therefore goes without saying that their loyalty will be with anyone who can alleviate their financial situation. Unfortunately given the low budget allocated to Sport and Recreation South Africa (SRSA) by treasury, many federations do not respect the government as they get pittance from it as compared to the lottery. This is the ticket that Gideon Sam used cleverly to topple Moss Mashishi as the president of SASCOC in the 2008 elections.

It happened again with the SASCOC elections in 2012 and I was privy to a lot of the wheeling and dealing, which is covered extensively in Chapter 6.

The dossier also hammered home the point about equal opportunities and that the athletes were a second thought after the self enriching administrators.

The SASCOC mandate from its inception has been to facilitate access, redress and equitable distribution of sporting opportunities with unequivocal bias to the historically disadvantaged communities yet they have spent more funds on administration than on investing on athletes. If one takes a closer look at SASCOC today vis-à- vis the mandate that was central to its creation, one can clearly see that its agenda has veered off its founding principles. SASCOC does no longer see itself as the custodian of development and transformation. It has developed into an elitist structure that serves the needs of a few at the expense of the majority. The manifestation of the administrators who are in sport for money is clearly visible in this structure.

It will be in the best interest of sport and the country if the Honourable Minister can set up a Commission of Inquiry into these allegations to investigate the way sport is being run and in the process root out the corrupt lot before it is too late. The first step in the process will be to set up a life style audit for those individuals involved with the NLDTF. There is no way we can hope for a healthy state of sport if the whole sport movement and SASCOC in particular are not investigated in line with the Minister's vision to clean South African sport. We believe that a corrupt free SASCOC will lead to a strong sport movement while bringing glory to South Africa in pursuit of reconciliation and social cohesion.

The words of wisdom fell on deaf ears.

Laraine Lane was another very brave athletics administrator who spoke up against the injustices and systemic corruption.

In 2008, the Athletics SA Board appeared before the Parliamentary Portfolio Committee for Sport and Recreation and I addressed the committee on what is termed 'the Cinderella sports' in this dossier. I said that the Olympic organization was formulated to support elite sports such as fencing, archery, eventing, rowing etc. that arose out of English universities. As these 'elite' sporting federations receive little or no sponsorship because they have no mass appeal or participation, they rely on SASCOC for funding. In response, they provide Sascoc's leadership with the votes that keep them in power. I agree that the NSC (National Sports Council) focus on grass-roots and development made it a far more idealistic and ethical organization but after it was absorbed by NOCSA (National Olympic I of South Africa), any sense of accountability and/or ethical values were suppressed under the leadership of Sam Ramsamy. Chris Ball refused to work with him during the Cape Town bid for the Olympic Games due to the kickbacks he organized for himself. I was friendly with an English journalist called Julian Drew, who was a great admirer of Maria Mutola. Julian worked for NOCSA on the Cape Town bid and resigned when he discovered into whose pockets the sponsorship monies were flowing. Julian was a close colleague of Olympic 400 metres hurdler, Martin Gillingham, who lived here at that time and is presently an IAAF Commentator. – Laraine Lane

Cape Town's Olympic bid for 2004 was Africa's first since Egypt's failed attempts for the cancelled 1916 Summer Games and the 1936 Summer Olympics. But South Africa lost out to Athens, Greece who won the bid to host the 2004 Games.

Ackerman: Ramsamy scuttled SA's Olympic bid

Supermarket boss Raymond Ackerman has accused Sam Ramsamy, president of the National Olympic Committee of South Africa (Nocsa), of scuttling South Africa's bid for the 2004 Olympic Games, the Sunday Times reported ... Ackerman claims that Ramsamy wanted control of funds in a war chest that would be used to impress the "the right people" The business boss claims he believed Ramsamy was prepared to do this o"ver and above"the rules of the International Olympic Committee (IOC). (IOL, 27 May 2001)

South Africa: Blood Feud Behind Bid

Former Cape Town Olympic bid boss Raymond Ackerman has stepped up his campaign against Sam Ramsamy by claiming that the South African Olympic chief had told him the only way he could win the race to host the 2004 games was through bribery. (Mail & Guardian, June 2001)

Ramsamy hit back at Ackerman in his autobiography, 'Reflections on a Lifetime in Sport'.

When he should have been trying to build a consensus among all the diverse communities of Cape Town, he issued edicts from his office and appeared astonishingly oblivious to the mood and spirit of the New South Africa where people are no longer prepared to bow down and grovel at the feet of the big, white boss. – Sam Ramsamy

Ramsamy was a strong anti-apartheid campaigner in the 1980s from his base in London. He was chairman of South Africa's non-racial Olympic I (SANROC) during the apartheid years and returned home when the ban on the African National Congress (ANC) was lifted in 1991. Ramsamy became president of the National Olympic Committee (NOCSA) which saw the first non-racial SA Olympic team compete in the 1992 Barcelona Summer Games.

It was a very proud moment in South African sporting history.

This is the first time we can say that South Africa is taking part in the Olympic Games. South Africa has never taken part in the Olympic Games before, although a section of South Africa had. And we are very pleased that we can get a South African team representing South Africa which will have the support of all South Africa at Barcelona. – Sam Ramsamy (New York Times, 7 November 1991)

South Africa was banned from participating in the Olympic Games from 1964 to 1988, as a part of the International sporting boycott against apartheid. Ramsamy was elected to the International Committee (IOC) in 1995 and is a long serving member of the International Swimming Federation (FINA) but he's a very slippery customer.

He's (Ramsamy) been the puppet-master and instigator of all NOCSA/Sascoc □riticiz since his return to SA in 1991. – Former NOCSA official

I got to know Ramsamy on a personal level when the Cape Town Olympic committee invited me back to South Africa as an ambassador for the 2004 bid. We had mutual respect but over time, it became clear to me that he was arrogant, power hungry and had a big chip on his shoulder.

Speaking of big, Ramsamy's 75th birthday bash didn't go unnoticed in my column for sport24 in January 2013.

SASCOC is sicker than sick
30 January 2013

South Africa's IOC executive member, Sam Ramsamy celebrated his 75th birthday at a four-star hotel in Umhlanga at the weekend. A birthday bash attended by the SASCOC big wigs, other high profile people, some Olympic athletes and theSA SCOC PR team.

I applaud some of the work Ramsamy has done for SA sport but who gives SASCOC the right to use public monies to pay for guests, airfares, hotel accommodation and of course the extended stay for some to watch the AFCON game between Bafana Bafana against Morocco in Durban?

My calls to the hotel finance department were not returned but only after the receptionist had told me that the accommodations bill was picked up by Mr Reddy. SASCOC must have got in before me as they would have been alerted that I was snooping around.

It is just sickening how SASCOC continue to spend on themselves and friends whilst the majority of SA sporting codes and athletes are suffering. One hand continues to wash the other and I'm disappointed in Ramsamy, who as an IOC executive member, should be making sure SASCOC runs a clean ship.

Chances of that happening are slim and none and slim just left town.

Ramsamy and SASCOC CEO, Tubby Reddy go back a long way and the former even wrote the letter of support for Reddy when he stood for president of Africa Volleyball (CAVB) in 2011.

Mr Ramsamy wrote:

Tubby Reddy has now become one of the most respectable leaders of Sport in South Africa, the African continent and indeed the world.

I am going to throw up.

*Volleyball has been completely destroyed by the complete lack of ability by our self-proclaimed CEO. From being a premier televised sport 10 years ago with annual world-series events taking place, we can't even get 20 men's teams to compete at a national championships! As a reward for complete and utter incompetency, they now make him CEO of something bigger to F*** that up completely too. We could tell you more stories about our intrepid leader and his useless executive. What I can tell you is that if this idiot was in a real business he would have been collecting UIF many years ago. The form of UIF he is collecting now is just disturbing, what worries me more is that he has absolutely no conscience, he is ultimately a politician, and the manner in which sport is "administrated" in this country does not do anyone of any colour any favours! – SA Volleyball player*

Sounds like a very respectable leader?

Ironically, Reddy only got six out of a possible 47 votes at the CAVB election – the only other candidate, Dr Amr Elwani got 41 votes and was re-elected. Needless to say, a whole SASCOC delegation went over to Sudan for the CAVB elections and no doubt a good time had by all with public monies.

Spike!

"SASCOC's new spokesperson", Shane Keohane tweeted from Durban at the weekend:

Durban you have been an excellent host to honour a legend who has given his all to SA sport. Happy 75th Birthday to Sam Ramsamy

Keohane has seemingly assumed the position of SASCOC's PR spokesperson, taking over from his brother who resigned in disgrace just before the London Olympics.

Happy birthday Sam!

***

Not only was great public expense spared for Ramsamy's 75th birthday celebrations but also strong allegations that SASCOC paid for his book launch and publication back in 2004. I tried in vain to get some numbers on what was spent on both. I sent a couple emails to the SASCOC president, Gideon Sam and CFO, Vinesh Maharaj but got no response. It was the usual taking of the fifth amendment from SASCOC – no response from either the SASCOC president or the CFO.

It became the norm when they couldn't answer the tough questions. I had become a thorn in their side long before this but I kept on probing.

Ramsamy was said to be the driving force behind the Gleneagles Agreement which was unanimously approved by the Commonwealth Nations in 1977.

Following the Soweto uprisings in 1976, Ramsamy petitioned countries to □riticize a boycott of South African sports, which culminated in the Gleneagles Agreement of 1977. Ramsamy, who up to this point was still employed as a teacher at a school in London, left his employment in 1978 and became a consultant to the United Nations (UN). His core responsibility at the UN was to ensure the drafting of an international convention against apartheid sport that would make for punitive measures to be placed against those countries who continued to engage South Africa in sporting activities. The convention was finally drawn up and signed by various countries in 1985. He took over running, managing and providing impetus to the sports boycott from the late 1970s onward. The sports boycott was important in spreading awareness of the evils of apartheid to the rest of the world. (www.thepresidency.gov.za)

Ramsamy was hailed as a hero but not by all.

In 1997 I was awarded the Olympic Order. I was recommended by Ram Ruhee (The IOC member for Mauritius) for my work against Apartheid Sport. Sam Ramsamy was present in the hall but evaded me! I sometimes wonder if Ramsamy had an objective when he approached me in 1973! I am now convinced that Ramsamy was sent to infiltrate Sanroc (South African Non-Racial Olympic Committee) by the Bureau of State Security (BOSS). Sanroc and South African sport would have been better without Sam Ramsamy. – Chris de Broglio.

De Broglio was a champion weightlifter who was dedicated to fighting racism in sport. Together with Dennis Brutus, they were founder members of the South African Non-Racial Olympic Committee. Brutus was a human rights activist and champion of non-racial sport who stuck to his guns.

Dennis (Brutus) did not know how to play the game, Ramsamy style. His refusal to be inducted into the SA Sports Hall of Fame alongside apartheid apologist Gary Player, apartheid police captain Naas Botha and apartheid money bag-man Ali Bacher suggests that he never understood what a complex business is airbrushing history, nor did he get it that those who question the fabrications can come across looking quite mad. – (Solidarity, March 2010)

Ramsamy's style is hypocritical.

He spent most of his adult life fighting for the eradication of the colour bar in sport and creating a fair playing field but is now suspiciously quiet about what is happening in SA sport today with all the corruption, cronyism and racism including quota selections of national teams that are no longer based on merit.

Moreover, Ramsamy is a close ally of IOC president, Thomas Bach and covers up for his SASCOC cronies at the highest level of world sport.

Nothing gets past the goalkeeper. Ramsamy finally had to retire from the IOC and SASCOC at age 80 in 2018 but don't worry, SA's dirty Olympic rings are well covered.

South African film producer Anant Singh has been named as one of the newly elected International Olympic Committee (IOC) members This means SA will' for the first time' have two IOC members. Singh's friend and mentor Sam Ramsamy was re-elected to the IOC.(Business Day, 5 August 2016)

Singh produced the film "Mandela: Long Walk to Freedom" about former South African President Nelson Mandela in 2013. How he got nominated to the IOC is not in any script.

No mystery around Ramsamy's political power and control. Suggestions he ran NOCSA like his own personal business.

When Nocsa was dissolved, (former president) Sam Ramsamy was given a Mercedes-Benz C320, still new, for nothing. There was no brouhaha. – Dan Moyo (Sowetan, 3 March 2010)

There were also allegations of inflated construction prices for the building of the Olympic House in Melrose, Johannesburg for kickbacks under his watch.

Ramsamy bought a R5.2 million house in Pietermaritzburg, KwaZulu-Natal in 2007 and there's talk of a mansion in Houghton, Johannesburg as well.

The questions remain – what's on the house and what's not?

Chapter 4: London 2012

Things began to snowball after my first couple exposes.

Athletes, coaches and administrators started to confide in me as to what was really happening in South African sport. There would be days I would have tears rolling down my face. I could not believe how some of the sportsmen and women were being treated and how deep the corruption was among the greedy sporting officials.

It was my obligation as a sports journalist to expose this corruption and maladministration.

Sport24 had given me an online platform. I was armed and ready!

SASCOC not fit to run SA sport.

20 August 2012

For months now I've been following SASCOC and just waiting for the bubble to burst but it seems as if they've managed to politicize their efforts and sweep things under the carpet time after time.

I just feel for our incredible sportsmen and sportswomen in this country that have no voice and are being failed by weak, greedy administrators.

Where to begin …

SA got six medals in London – SASCOC had predicted 12 and president, Gideon Sam said he would fall on his sword if they didn't get 12. Now all of a sudden, Beijing is a benchmark, where we managed to get just one lonely medal.

No. Mr Sam, we should be using Atlanta, Sydney and Athens as benchmarks where we got a total of 16 medals.

How far have we really progressed as an Olympic nation in the last 16 years?

To say SA finished top of the African medals table in London is very misleading. Kenya and Ethiopia both got more medals than SA in London and it's only because the medals table puts gold above everything that we are "on top of Africa". If a country gets one gold and another 16 silver, the country with one gold will be on top – so, that should conclude any arguments that in London, we were the best in Africa.

Ironically, SASCOC didn't regard Africa qualifying strong enough for some of our sporting codes, meaning they would have to qualify at world events eg. Hockey but now it's okay to brag that we were the best in Africa.

There should be no argument.

With what SA has in the way of facilities, finance, sportsmen and sportswomen, we should be on another level to the rest of the African countries.

So, you have to ask, where is all the money going?

I heard that a (London Olympics) dinner costing 40 000 pounds was held for "officials/mates of Gideon Sam". I cannot say where I heard it from but we were staying out of the village eating pre-packed sandwiches from Sainsbury's, Cups of soup and bread, and Weetbix! That's all we could afford (out of our very own pockets to boot). I am unsure as to the reason for the dinner other than to surmise it was the good old Gravy Train catching a decent meal at the Country's expense! Between Messrs Sam, Reddy, and Ramsamy, I often find myself asking what on earth they firstly know about ANY sport, what their respective CV's look like, and why they are so hell bent on destroying so many young South Africans Olympic Dreams. – SA official

The Sports Minister continues to fool the public with his rhetoric and political motivational speeches. I was embarrassed to hear his speech on the Olympians return last week. He created two new Olympians in SA swimmer, "Cameroon" (Cameron) van der Burgh and Michael "Flaps" (Phelps), who just happens to be the most successful and decorated Olympian of all time. And he shouted at corporate SA to get behind our athletes 'to get them to drive Porsche's etc.

Mr Mbalula, let me tell you corporate SA would get behind all our athletes if they knew where the money was really going.

Sascoc in dog box over SA's Olympics team kit (Mail and Guardian, 5 April 2012)

The South African Sports Confederation and Olympic Committee (SASCOC) was ☐riticized on Thursday because the South African Olympic and Paralympic Games teams kit was not produced by a local manufacturer.

Why did things go so quiet about the Chinese Olympic manufacturer uproar? Was corporate SA given a chance to kit out our own Olympians?

Mr Sam told me on SportsFire that R30 million from the Chinese manufacturers, Erke would come into SASCOC coffers for Olympic sports. SASCOC reportedly spent only R33 million on our athletes for the Olympic and Paralympics in London.

Where is the rest of the money from government, lottery, sponsors etc.?

Mr Sam was at odds to answer a lot of other questions on that same show relating to the PR tender worth at least R12 million that never happened and a horse racing sponsorship that SASCOC has, which he says "costs them nothing".

To have a sponsorship "SASCOC triple crown" cost nothing? What is SASCOC doing in horse racing anyway?

I will give Mr Sam some credit in that he has always been available for interviews, unlike SASCOC CEO Tubby Reddy who refuses radio interviews at every opportunity.

Wonder what there is to hide? Hard to hide a gravy train.

Speaking of which, I wonder how many SASCOC board members, officials, friends and family flew business class to London for the Olympics and spent two and half weeks in a top class hotel? Money that should have been spent on our athletes and not some officials, who believe it's their right to be at the Games.

I've seen it with my own eyes in Atlanta and Sydney. The SASCOC gravy train sitting in the "SA Olympic house" in those countries with meals and plenty of alcohol.

As my memory serves Gert Oosthuizen (Deputy Sports Minister) really enjoyed himself in Beijing....and lunches at the Kensington Hotel in London were proper. – SASCOC sponsor

Let us not forget the SASCOC five-man delegation that "had" to go to Austria to accompany the country's lone participant in the Winter Youth Olympics at the beginning of this year.

Row over five top brass to back one athlete (Times Live, 12 January 2012)

South Africa's top sports body has sent a five-man delegation to Austria – to accompany the country's single participant in the Winter Youth Olympics. While administrators have questioned the wisdom of blowing big bucks on business-class flights and accommodation for the delegation , the SA Sports Confederation and Olympic Committee (Sascoc) says the decision is " nobody's business".

These are just the trips we know about. Mr Reddy must have more frequent flyer miles than Sir Richard Branson.

12 medals from London was always going to be a big ask, but I can assure you some officials have put on 12 kilograms after a great two week holiday!

Apart from the Chinese kit deal, PR non-tender, horse racing sponsorship and the gravy train, it was interesting to note many SA sporting codes were suspended by SASCOC over the last year for poor governance and power struggles.

At least four that I know of: Squash, Equestrian, Powerboating and Karate.

There are a number of interesting links here, especially the one between Mr Sam and Powerboating which was well documented: Mr Sam allegedly trying to score commission on National Lottery money granted to Powerboat SA.

What isn't well documented is the findings of the forensic audit that was supposedly carried out.

Other allegations that a marketing company in which Mr Sam is a shareholder would be paid close to R1 million in commission for facilitating a Lottery grant for Cycling SA.

How easy when Mr Sam sits on the Lottery agency distribution board as well but said he excused himself when the cycling request was tabled.

Conflict of interests, perhaps?

I could go on and on, but the fact of the matter is that our athletes continue to achieve despite the poor cards they are dealt.

Can you imagine what South Africa would be achieving if we had administrators who were passionate about the sport itself instead of lining their own back pockets. We should be calling for a full independent forensic audit of SASCOC.

Should these fat cats be running amateur sport in SA?

You be the judge.

***

Just read your newest report on news24. Enlightening as always and of course you'll get no response from them! At least 5ppl went to china to meet with erke. The reason minister hasn't done an inquiry into Sascoc is cause they all in cahoots. In 2008 the dep minister the one that looks like a bullfrog took his mistress with to Beijing. And it's not a month they away its closer to 2months. And they at the best hotels and every gala event. (sic) – SASCOC contractor

During the Olympics - 3 Gauteng based Inflatable teams left for Norway to compete in the World Championship 2 of the teams with the goal of defending their World Championship Titles which they won in Dec 2010. Let it be know these teams were also part of the team who came second in the Gauteng Sports Awards last year losing to the Blue Bulls. The trip was paid for by the teams with no assistance from sponsors or SASCOC. When they arrived there they were informed by the UIM that they had been instructed by Kobus Marais of SASCOC that although teams may have national racing licences they were only allowed to race with SASCOCS permission. Request were made by the UIM and the teams but their requests were denied, The teams returned without being allowed to put their boats on the water. I think it is a complete disgrace that for an organisation whose purpose is to promote South Africa and South African Sports and sportsmanship that they could not rise above whatever political issues the administrators and governing bodies were experiencing to have South Africa prove that we are the best in the sport. - Gabrielle Brookstein

I have seen so many athletes at age 17 - 20 ranked number 1 in the world and then at the next Olympics you don't see their faces in the group, I asked some of them why this is, the reply was always the same, you cant have a full time job and be a athlete competing at that level. Most athletes don't get financial backing at all, travel economy class only and live in the cheapest hotels where they most often cant afford to be on the right diet and therefore are a few steps behind the rest they are competing against. The SASCOC officials travel and live in the best that money can buy, how does the house Mr SAM lives in compare to that of our javelin silver medalist who have to share a room with her sun as SASCOC only take money from athletes and don't support them most of our athletes suffer the same faith. Some complain that most of our swimmers live in USA, well they get sponsors there, and through competing for clubs they are able to make a living and train as hard and long as they should. Working for a company that have a massive advertising / sponsorship budget, the decision was made that we will not sponsor Cricket or any sport SASCOC is involved with, as they are corrupt and understand sponsors wrongly, the money should go to making the best of the athlete not for your house/car/restaurant payments and nothing for those who work very hard for it. SASCOC should be honorary only and members should not be allowed to do what they are, they should be locked up for corruption! (sic) - Marthunis Britz

I just wanted to email and tell you I am really enjoying your columns on Sport 24. It is so refreshing to see actual journalism and reporting and calling a spade a spade. For far too long it has appeared to me that certain journo's have a little clique and they seem to be patting each other on the back each week. PLEASE take all these men to task and expose as much as you can. Don't ever stop because the more that comes to light the less people can keep their heads buried in the sand. We need to stop the rot in this country, we can be the best but only with people like yourself calling out the bad apples. Thanks again for the superb articles. – Gilbert Howard

South Africa is a sports crazy nation and sport is the one thing that unites the country, more than anything else.

The Springboks winning the 1995 Rugby World Cup and Bafana Bafana winning the African Cup of Nations a year later are two of SA's proudest sporting moments and what it did for country was immeasurable. Tears of joy flowed uncontrollably around South Africa as President Nelson Mandela walked onto the hallowed turf of Ellis Park after the IRB World Cup final, wearing the Springbok rugby jersey.

That was a massive victory in itself and his words will always resonate from the heavens above.

Sport has the power to change the world. It has the power to inspire. It has the power to unite people in a way that little else does. It speaks to youth in a language they understand. Sport can create hope where once there was only despair. It is more powerful than government in breaking down racial barriers. - Nelson Mandela

Bees in my bonnet
24 August 2012

Seconds out, round number 2.

From my first column, "SASCOC not fit to run SA sport", we box on against a heavyweight administration that punches low below its weight.

But they won't go down without a fight.

Kobus Marais, a politician and SASCOC board member commented on my first Olympic expose.

This is a lot of lies and assumptions which is meant to jeopordise (sic) our athletes who all give credit to SASCOC, These allegations are false, and such rumours most certainly cannot be intended to benefit our beloved sporting nations. Mr Joffe has a few bees in his bonnet. Someone at SASCOC must have "deprived" him from benefits to owed to huim (sic). Shame on yoy (sic). – Kobus Marais

Apologies for the spelling errors but that is a direct quote from Mr Marais - perhaps, no spell check on the PC's at SASCOC!

Mr Marais, please could you specify which are the lies, the assumptions and the rumours that have jeopardized our athletes.

Who are you trying to kid by saying "our athletes who all give credit to SASCOC"?

The athletes are between a rock and a hard place and would be committing career suicide by criticizing the sporting body that is "supposed" to look after their best interests. Furthermore, the athletes had to sign a code of conduct before the London Olympics, which forbids them from criticizing or chastising SASCOC for six months after the Games.

Code of conduct was signed before, and a follow-up letter was sent after to remind us of the contractual obligations. Confirmed. As discussed before - who would dare speak out against the regime with these kinds of measures in place? – SA Olympian

The sporting federations also rely on good favour from SASCOC for Lottery funding and therefore, their futures. Any noise will be squashed or the individual will be worked out the system very quickly.

Corporate SA can only do so much.

Without Investec's continued financial support, the SA women's hockey team would not have made it to London 2012. But during the Olympic build up and the Games, the Investec brand could not be associated with the team. SASCOC want corporate SA involved but then chase them away in the most crucial time.

It's almost like US Postal sponsoring Lance Armstrong but not allowed to be associated in the months prior to or in anything associated with the Tour de France. Lance Armstrong may not a good example right now but it kind of changes the dynamic for a corporate sponsor, doesn't it?

The problem with uncovering any of this is that it is all contained in a self-preserving system and SASCOC will always be protected by Department of Sport and Recreation on a government level.

Mr Marais went on to say, "someone at SASCOC must have 'deprived me' from benefits owed to me."

That is a pathetic political deflection, which we have been accustomed to in SA but what we are "deprived" of is an open, honest sporting administration that looks after the best interests of our athletes.

Ironically, it is the same Mr Marais, who is now at the centre of the current controversies raging in Powerboating SA (PSA). Mr Marais is an administrator of PSA (due to the federation's SASCOC "suspension") and he allegedly took it upon himself to deny SA Inflatable teams including the defending champions from racing in the World Championships in Norway recently. He was also part of some "secret" meetings with the International Governing Body of Powerboating (UIM) that saw Powerboat SA lose out on hosting the 85th general assembly of the UIM (400 delegates) and the Formula 1 Nations Cup in Durban. Both events could have been worth some R30 million in foreign investment to SA. The F1 Nations Cup would have been over three years.

Meanwhile, the power struggle continues and Powerboat SA has a couple of legal cases pending against SASCOC, which have been dragging themselves out in court.

SASCOC likes to bully the small federations until they have an iron grip, with one of their "boys club" in control.

The weightlifting and SA Equestrian rider selection controversies for London 2012 were sad to say the least and SASCOC didn't exactly cover itself in glory with either.

With regards the latter, the Court of Arbitration for Sport in Lausanne found that the behaviour of SASCOC and the SA Equestrian Federation was unethical and in breach of the Olympic charter.

They were also handed a hefty costs order. I wonder where that money will come from?

SASCOC is a Section 21 company and they preach good governance and accountability to the sporting federations but do they practice what they preach?

The Public Protector is currently investigating SASCOC's shareholding in horse racing in South Africa and where there is reason to believe that there is a lack of accountability and misuse of public funds.

Gride Investments (Pty) Ltd, a commercial arm of SASCOC holds a 5% shareholding in Phumelela (an inter- dependent business consisting of both an international and South African division which operates at the intersections of a betting and information business and that of a horseracing/destination marketing business) and the president of SASCOC, Mr Gideon Sam is a trustee of the Thoroughbred Horse Racing Trust.

But believe you me, there's no "horsing" around when it comes to the salaries of some SASCOC officials.

CEO Tubby Reddy is earning R148,000 per month.

There can't be too many Section 21 company CEO's who earn around R1.7 million a year.

Still bewildered how the position of SASCOC CEO and CFO (occupied by Vinesh Maharaj) were never advertised and no due process was followed in the appointments. Also, Mr Reddy is the president of Volleyball South Africa (unconstitutionally) and Mr Maharaj is the treasurer of Volleyball South Africa.

And can someone please tell me why the SASCOC big wigs flew business class on Emirates to London for the Olympics, separate to the team.

Would it not be good business acumen or common courtesy to use the airline that is a major sponsor of the SA Olympic team in South African Airways?

To quote the Sports Minister, Fikile Mbalula: "You bring back glory, we treat you as a king. You bring back mediocrity, we'll pretend we don't know you."

Looks like the hockey girls got the short end of the stick, no pun intended.

SASCOC made the SA women's team leave the Olympic village before the hockey competition had finished and they were not allowed to attend the closing ceremony as South African representatives.

Yes, I understand their games were over but if the closing ceremony is not for the athletes – who is it for?

***

No comment
6 September 2012

Are Gideon Sam and Tubby Reddy resigning and is the sports minister leading a full forensic investigation into the affairs of SASCOC?

Dream on.

In fact, Mr Mbalula and Mr Sam were exchanging compliments this week for a job "well done".

Mr Mbalula was praised for what he has done for school sport and Mr Sam praised for Team SA's apparently successful Olympic Games.

I've been watching a great deal of the Paralympics and I am amazed at the achievements of these incredible athletes. But my heart breaks for a number of SA athletes who should have been competing in London only to have their dreams destroyed by SASCOC. Two such athletes were SA table tennis stars, Alet Moll and Pieter du Plooy who qualified for the 2012 Paralympics by winning gold (yes, gold) at the African qualification tournament in Egypt.

More disgusting is the fact that SASCOC never informed them that they weren't going – they found out a week before the entry deadline from the International Table Tennis Federation that SASCOC had not approved their selection. The South African Table Tennis Board (SATTB) had signed a discriminate

Memorandum of Understanding with SASCOC, which not only denied them entry to these Games, but also makes it virtually impossible for these players to qualify for any future Paralympics.

The players had no time for proper legal recourse and after challenging SASCOC on their non-selection, the players and members of SA Para Table Tennis committee (six individuals) were banned from all table tennis activity in South Africa.

SASCOC has written a clause into its 'Athletes Agreements', prohibiting athletes from doing or saying anything which might be seen as critical of SASCOC. Not even our government has this kind of protection from criticism!

SASCOC not only took away my dreams but now have taken away part of my livelihood - Alet Moll

Moll would have become the first South African Table Tennis player to receive a special achievement award at the London 2012 Paralympics for participating in four consecutive Games.

SASCOC's selection policy also states: "We will guarantee a place for any athlete who is a probable medal hope or will return commendable performances" …

By winning gold in Africa, you would think Moll and du Plooy would have returned commendable performances at the least in London? Moll is also a former Commonwealth Games silver medalist.

The South African Para Table Tennis Committee (SAPTTC) appealed the decision and included the Minister of Sport and Recreation to review the dubious SASCOC policy that kept the Para Table Tennis players out of the London Games team.

Over the period of February 2012 – April 2012 the SAPTTC exhausted all their options to have this decision reviewed, unfortunately without success.

SASCOC then terminated all the members in their individual capacity without any Disciplinary Hearing, stating that they have brought SASCOC into disrepute.

I was asked to withdraw from the SA Para Championships held in Pretoria in July 2012, Gauteng North League and even my club. Table Tennis is part of my weekly livelihood and sanity as a disabled person. Werksmans Attorneys, which have been absolutely wonderful and supportive to our cause, indicated that they are ready to take our termination review to court. Unfortunately, the reality is always funding and we are now stuck as it is impossible for me financially contribute to this. – Alet Moll

How can it be that an organisation of a democratic country can have the power to prevent a citizen from pursuing a sporting endeavor or earning a living, without so much as affording that citizen the opportunity to be confronted by her accusers or to present her case?

How can it be in a democracy, that a citizen can be bullied into accepting SASCOC's decisions and to avoiding legal action, through the threat of suspension?

This harps back to the darkest days of apartheid, when labourers had to put up and shut up.

I have no doubt that the suspended SA Para Table tennis players and SAPTTC members will be re-instated after successful legal proceeding but they don't have the resources to go to court because SASCOC has deprived them of the means to earn a living.

How can we allow this to continue?

It is the flagrant disrespect from a sports administration that continues to ride a gravy train and derail the dreams of many SA sportsmen and sportswomen. We may never get answers from SASCOC, just continued deflection but some more to ponder:

SASCOC sent a pre and post games letter to each athlete notifying of a breach of contract if SASCOC was mentioned in a negative light.

Is this not unconstitutional, never mind draconian?

All the countries athletes received a certain number of free tickets from the IOC for stadium events in London. SA were also allocated tickets but did our athletes receive them all?

While I was at the Olympics, I couldn't but be amazed/staggered at how all those you mentioned plus the crowd at Highbury Safika looked after themselves PLUS their partners, in terms of flights, shirts, tickets to events, while the media who were there to cover the events, had to beg for tickets! Don't think you mentioned him, but that Mark Alexander, interesting chap to say the least... last seen demanding tickets for a number of very random "friends". Mark was definitely at the Olympics. I can't say for how long as I arrived a week before then left with a week to go. He popped into the SA media hotel a few times. Weird thing is I had a few chats with Shane Keohane with him saying how shocked he was that these guys were giving away tickets to friends who could easily afford to buy themselves. The owner of Shamwari Game Reserve and his wife popped into the SA media hotel to pick up tickets. But then again Shane Keohane's wife was also in London... No idea who paid for her. – Garrin Lambley, sport24

Tickets were on offer to the athletes before leaving SA but the athletes were made aware of this only a day or so before the offer expired and they had to be paid for in cash, in pounds.

What happened to these pounds?

I have it on extremely good authority LOCOG (London Organising Committee of the Olympic and Paralympic Games) gave every single athlete 2 tickets to every event they were in and they were able to purchase a further two tickets for £140. South African athletes were only given one ticket to events they were in and were able to purchase a further single ticket for £140. – SA sports official

SASCOC athletes were allocated tickets for limited family, which needed to be paid full price for. Nothing free at all! Tickets for other events (not our own) were in theory going to be made available to athletes to purchase, but in reality these were extremely limited (and usually for lower profile events). It appeared that there was always a healthy contingent of SASCOC personnel at all the high profile events while the athletes had no choice but to watch on TV back at the village. If you put two and two together it seems like the allocation of these tickets needs investigating. – SA athlete

Some athletes even had their accreditation for attendance of stadium athletic events cancelled once at the

Games.

Why?

Many of SA's athletes had to leave the Olympic village a day after their event but how many officials stayed for the duration of the Games?

Personal coaches had a nightmare just trying to get into the village, let alone getting accreditation. SASCOC were given a daily allocation of day passes and managed them as they saw fit.

The system is all wrong.

***

SASCOC – you disgust me!
14 September 2012

14-year old table tennis star, Jade Sassman, from a disadvantaged community in Cape Town has been told she is not allowed to participate in the SA national championships, which start at the end of the month.

Jade didn't want to attend the World Cadet championships in Guam without her personal coach, Greg Naik. Naik has been Jade's private coach for the last three years and has also helped to fund her amazing progress through the ranks.

But the South African Table Tennis Federation (SATTB), with their own agenda (as with the Paralympians) labelled it as bringing the sport into disrepute. SATTB also informed the International Table Tennis Federation that Naik held back Jades' passport and another player was sent in her place to the World Cadet champs.

The SATTB did not even bother to enquire as to whether she has a passport or not. She was not even called to a disciplinary hearing of any sort and already she has been informed that she will not be allowed to participate in the National Championships as punishment. To add insult to injury, a member of the Western Province Table Tennis Federation Executive has already declared publicly that Jade was suspended.

This was clearly a matter of jealousy and politics to ensure that Jade and Naik remain isolated from Table Tennis.

How can you treat any athlete this way, never mind a 14 year old?

The fact that Jade won an African bronze medal, the youngest to do so in South African Table Tennis history and was then chosen to represent Africa, could surely be used as an opportunity to 'draw' money from the Sport & Recreation South Africa to attain funding for her and her personal coach?

Naik's club, Boundary Table Tennis, has also produced 21 athletes that have represented South Africa over the past ten years.

Ironically, the vice president of SATTB is Hajera Kajee who just happens to be on the SASCOC executive committee and also sits on the Lottery distribution board.

Hardly surprising that SATTB would rake in millions from the Lottery.

But if you ask SASCOC, there's no conflict of interests there. That's how they get control of SA sport for their own benefit.

It's a common thread, just like Gideon Sam is President of SASCOC who sits on no fewer than three other boards, Athletics SA (ASA), Lottery distribution and that of a big sports marketing company, which just happens to be owed millions of rand by Athletics SA.

Tubby Reddy is less fortunate, he's only President of Volleyball SA but his family still had a great time at the London Olympics.

At who's expense?

The Teddy Bear Clinic, a charity that helps more than 3000 abused children every year, has been allocated only R4-million since 2007, while SA table tennis was given more than R8-million in the same period. - Sunday Times

You would think with all the money, the SATTB is getting from the Lottery, we would at least have some table tennis representation at the Olympic or Paralympic Games?

But we did not have one SA table tennis player in London because of administrators that don't give a damn except for their own back pockets which will kill the drive and desire of a 14 year old girl like Jade Sassman.

SASCOC – you disgust me!

***

Well done Joffee. Keep going. As a former athlete I've been through several Games and I absolutely agree with everything. Athletes and Federations in SA don't have a voice, they're too scared that the little bit of money they get from SASCOC will be cut off and in the absence of any corporate sponsorships their very existence is entirely dependent of SASCOC. I can guarantee that every athlete in this country who read your articles will agree with you. SASCOC is nothing but a VERY exclusive club of fat useless ass kissing cats, a very, very VIP travel agency. (sic) - Cristian Brezeanu

As a swimmer I criticised Swimming SA's handling of the selection of the women's swimming team for the 2004 Athens Olympics - my prize from Gideon Sam was suspension! They cannot stand being told the truth. Graeme - the only way to get them to attend your meeting is to provide a great meal and a bottomless bottle of the finest Johnny Walker available! - Graham du Toit

Graeme, you are the platform that speaks for the poor and scared masses out there against the Huge Monster called SASCOC. They will defend their positions by any means necessary, even going the route of discrediting people who dare be on their wrong side. Gramme, i want you to look at what Mr mubarak is doing in Karate. He is a judge and a jury at the same time. He is supposed to be the chairperson of ethics and transformation committee but he is an administrator for karate. The question that was asked to Tubby and Mr sam was that if Mr Mubark is an administrator and chair of ethics, who are we to complain to about his ethics, there haven't been answers to our questions.Mr Mubarak in Karate is intimidating people who have different opinion to him on how he conducts himself in Karate. He tells people that he will get them fired at their work, he will ask SARS (South African Revenue Service) to investigate them, he suspends at will, any federation that differs with him. They have instituted Forensic Investigations to almost 5 federations since last year, who pays for these investigations, its us taxpayers. A forensic investigation will cost to the tune of R1 million, depending on the size of the organization and the time frames given for investigation. Already since from last year they have spent almost R5 million on investigations. (sic) - Frans Mamabolo

I hope your articles raise public awareness but unfortunately everyone operates in a circle of fear and wears a mask of smiles. Your facts you present are true and the athletes are not allowed to speak out, it is criminal the way they are treated like possessions. This is politics at its best, I'm not sure how its going to change and its very sad. - Kary Sharratt

A few weeks after my article, *SASCOC – you disgust me* was published, SA Table Tennis overturned the unethical and wrongful suspension of Jade Sassman and she was able to play in the SA National championships.

A little vindication.

But coach Naik was prevented from entering the playing hall due to his suspension. He watched her games through a high window to enable him to give some advice from the car park during the changeovers.

Jade won gold in the girls U-17 division.

Go Jade go!

Chapter 5: Oscar Pistorius

On 14 February 2013, South Africa woke up to the shocking and tragic news …

The South African blade runner, Oscar Pistorius has fatally shot his girlfriend, model Reeva Steenkamp, in his Pretoria home. He claimed he had mistaken Steenkamp for an intruder hiding in the bathroom, but he was arrested and charged with murder.

The world was stunned. Oscar had become a household name around the globe for his heroics at the Olympic Games in London.

I knew Oscar as more than just an athlete (or at least I thought I did) and put pen to paper a few days after the tragedy.

Who is the real Oscar?
18 February 2013

I had the great pleasure of meeting Oscar Pistorius on a charity weekend in Kuruman, South Africa nearly ten years ago.

I was taken aback by this smiling, charismatic, charming youngster, who looked set to take the world by storm. Humbled by his story and amazed how positive he was, despite his life changing disability and having just lost his mother.

He was then still the real Oscar Pistorius.

I followed his career with an eagle eye and when the bombshell dropped last week Thursday, I was numb with shock but not totally surprised. My first thoughts were, how will a family cope with this tragic loss of a daughter?

My heart was and still is aching for the family of Reeva Steenkamp.

As I waded through the initial reports, I went back to my tweets from London 2012 when I was critical of the way in which Oscar was being used as a political pawn by SASCOC and the way in which he behaved after losing at the Paralympics.

I had lost a lot of respect for SA's blade runner.

Oscar shouldn't have been at the Olympics in London in the first place – he didn't qualify but pressure from sponsors and politics made sure he was selected.

We will leave the dirty laundry for another day but would be interesting to know who was paid or promised what to make sure Oscar was at the Olympics.

Even when asked about Oscar's Olympic selection last year, Sports Minister Fikile Mbalula was quoted as saying:

It's a political decision.

It was a bad decision and it also made a mockery of SASCOC's selection criteria.

Why weren't the likes of Simon Magakwe (athletics), Greg Shushu (weightlifting) and Natalie du Toit (swimming) at the Olympic Games?

Many other athletes also missed out on the qualification criteria, similarly to Oscar and SASCOC always states they only select medal potential athletes.

Was Oscar really going to win a medal in London?

Regardless of the selection, did SASCOC, his agent or his sponsors prepare the 25 year old athlete for the pressure and stresses of the Olympic stage? They sure knew how to milk the popularity of the situation, to an extent, that it became somewhat nauseating. It seemed as if every day in London, there was an Oscar Pistorius press conference.

It was overdone.

Yes, Oscar was a poster boy of the Olympics, even more so at times than Usain Bolt and everyone was getting their pound of flesh. But was he prepared for the new status, all the media attention and competing in front of 80 000 people?

Never before had South Africa been seen in such a positive light but how it has all backfired.

The trials and tribulations of Oscar Pistorius (boating accident, assaults and threats) have been well documented but each time they would quickly disappear and almost treated as not a big deal.

The youngster needed professional help but while he was making money for those around him, it didn't seem to matter.

How many people in their early 20's have ownership of such arms and ammunition? How many people in their early 20's have million rand race horses and 3.2 million rand cars?

Someone needed to guide him.

When Oscar stormed out of a BBC interview in a rage in 2011, I thought someone close to him would have taken heed but a year later on the biggest international stage, he acted in a very similar fashion.

Very poorly!

Oscar's outburst at the Paralympics after his defeat in the T44 200m smacked of sour grapes and the majority of the SA media in London, spun it to look like he was the victim.

The majority of the headlines were: *SASCOC defends Oscar, Oscar to appeal, In the heat of the moment and Oscar apologizes* but he only apologized a day later for the timing of his comments and not for what he said.

He needed professional help. Was Oscar ever coached on a mind level? Does SASCOC have a full-time psychologist?

Sadly, there was little if none in the way of objective journalism about Oscar's outburst from the SA media. Most defended Oscar to the hilt and some even tried to discredit SA scientist, Dr Ross Tucker, when he suggested Oscar had no argument.

Part of the problem is that SASCOC paid for a number of journalists to go to London and some media are even on the SASCOC payroll, which makes it even more disturbing.

Oscar was made into an untouchable by the SA media.

No-one wanted to dig a little deeper and when I was critical of the "blade runner", I was shouted down and told to stop being unpatriotic.

SA needs a free media and not a manipulated one.

SASCOC needs to be exposed for their corrupt practices that are shattering the dreams of our athletes.

How many more stories does one need to read before action is taken?

Hopefully, not until another deeply traumatizing tragedy unfolds.

South African Olympic sport is being run by the SASCOC mafia and this sickening tragedy could have perhaps been prevented if we didn't have corrupt and greedy administrators, continually serving their own interests.

Oscar was traded like a commodity in London and not that of a troubled sports star.

It also covered up the fact that South Africa had a disappointing Olympic Games and in a bitter twist of irony, Sports Minister Fikile Mbalula was quoted before the Games as saying:

I say to the President (Jacob Zuma), we stick to our guns, we know our preparations - forward ever, backwards never.

"Oscar's guns" have sent us all reeling backwards.

RIP Reeva

***

I thoroughly enjoyed your refreshing insight into the Oscar Pistorius tragedy. Many sporting celebs succumb to the pitfalls of extraordinary wealth and fame far too easily and quickly as they seem to have no guidance along the way. Perhaps we need a Sir Alex Ferguson type of person to help guide our troubled superstars before their descent to ignominy. It's not for me to judge Oscar and my heart goes out to the Steenkamp family. Thanks for your time, Graeme and keep up the great work! – Paul Khan

All I have to say I WOW!!!!!!! It's been a while since I have read an article that really kept my attention. I'm a teacher and I must admit your writing style, your choice of diction and your choice of words really is ravishing. You a truly remarkable writer and got your point across. It wasn't the monotonous usual article of how u felt but a wholesome idea of what's going on. Thumbs up to you!! - Naazneen Mather

I read your article about Oscar Pistorius and how you thought he should've been managed properly. Thought I'd share my opinions with you. Being a sportsman with a disability myself (I'm completely deaf in both ears), I was extremely proud about how far Oscar came in his sport. It showed the rest of us guys with disabilities that if you put your heart into it and work hard for it, anything is possible, and not just on the sport field. He was even an inspiration for the everyday Joe who longed to achieve something great. Although I wouldn't be surprised if SASCOC-meddling was proved in SA Sport, I really believe Oscar would've came far, with or without them (SASCOC). And in a crime-ravaged country like ours, people longed for a pure, heart-warming story and a story like Oscar's would've been big, regardless how his management people steered his career. But I do agree with you, his career was pushed too far without the proper management and care for him at the time. But what shocked me most about Oscar was the way he lived his life post-London 2012 and his personality traits. Although I never met him, it seems like he was headstrong and actually, arrogant. Like you said, the sports car, the home etc. And if you believe the reports on his previous altercations with other people, I just cannot believe it. Because I know that any sportsman (actually anyone) with a disability faces his/her disability every day, you are constantly reminded of it. And if you as a disabled person knows the extra hard work you had to put in to be where you are today... It makes you humble. And keeps you humble. It certainly did with me. And Oscar showed none of it lately, even when his career and personal life was at a high. I just can't comprehend that. I'm very sad for both Oscar and Reeva. This points to more than just Oscar. I hope this is a wake-up call for all high profile people to make sure their life is still in order. South Africa still needs its heroes. Thank you for your article. I'm sure it would make people sit and think for a bit. - Werner Dove

David Walsh used a term for himself, when in the 80s and 90s he realised that he had lost his objectivity in covering the sport, and it became a term he would later use for most other journalists in cycling. He called them fans with typewriters. For the last five or six years, we have had fans with laptops and iPads. I read one article recently where the journalist told of his first meeting with Pistorius, and getting him drunk in a bar for over- 23s. Pistorius was 18 at the time. It's a farce. Those journalists are the ones who refused to give me any credence in the legs debate, who only tried to discredit me and the science, and now they're silent. But alas, our incredible police force, second only to SASCOC for astonishing ineptitude, have created a case so airtight that an elephant could walk out of it. – Ross Tucker

Read your article on Oscar. Man this thing is upsetting me. I'm hoping there's some explanation but who knows. I've been checking thru these "friends" of his twitter accounts. This Kevin Lerena who has now been quick to tell the press how he disarmed a gun in public is as obsessed with guns. He has pics on 19 Jan on his twitter of ak47 at the shooting range - wtf where do u even get guns like that? I just keep trying to think that surely if he felt scared why didn't she get out? Surely she knew he had a gun? Everyone else did? Also sorry but once someone is dead they are always an angel free of sin but what is a 30 year old doing dating a 26 year old and a 24 year old? On Oscars twitter a young girl called her a fishwife and said she had said nasty message to her and her 14 year old friends? So u just wonder...did he have a temper for sure, who doesn't! But premeditated, I can't think it because that would mean he would have known he would be murdering her and ruining her life.

There is a long road ahead for this young man and I feel horrible for him and his family. My heart goes out to the Steenkamp family as no one should bury their child. The media shit storm is only just starting and this will only get worse before it gets better and not that it gets better. Of course they (the media) will now be interested. It has taken a tragedy like this to wake them up and see how corrupt everything is. How they (SASCOC) abuse our sports stars. The Oscars, the Natalies (du Toit), the Hansies (Cronje). And how when things go so terribly wrong how they have no comment and just walk away. They disgust me, and they shot that girl as much as he did. The boy I met in 2008 was cocky but he was 21. The boy that crashed the boat in 2009, grew up very quickly, because suddenly he realised that he almost lost it all. He is a good person when he's around the right crowd. When he started associating with all these other "fame"seekers is when the trouble came. It's like Lance Armstrong said, he didn't feel he was wrong, it was a culture like putting water in your bottle and air in your tyres. Hanging out with these people is part of the culture...footing the bill obviously too, being seen with him a status symbol. (sic)– Adele Koolen

From this column, I was inundated with media interview requests from home and abroad. Perhaps, it was a different angle and most South African sports journalists, who knew Oscar well were not willing to speak out.

You are one of the few people who have seen through the whole hero-fiction and I would like to have a conversation with you about all this to discuss OP (Oscar Pistorius), the whole meltdown at Olympics, whether you think he was showing signs of not handling etc. the whole politicisation of the Olympics and OP. Whether he qualified etc." – (Melinda Ferguson, Author of Oscar: An Accident Waiting to Happen)

Graeme. I shed tears when I read your article. Not only for Oscar and Reeva but for the human tragedy, that ought to have been prevented. The extent of Oscar's violence is disturbing. A tsunami of rage that must have developed over time. Oscar's entire life had become a competitive struggle to prove himself equal to able- bodied men. This, when perceived limitations could have resulted in hypersensitivity and a sense of inadequacy in relationships. Maybe he found that all the money and toys that were thrown at him didn't give him back his legs. Aberrations of nature were common attractions at circuses in the past. I'd hoped we'd evolved from those days, but it seems that parading human beings as freaks still guarantees crowds. As before, ring-masters get off scot free. I'm sure you never planned to be a Delphic oracle, Graeme, but the country owes you a debt of gratitude for your unflinching courage and insight. – Laraine Lane

Laraine Lane is an amazing woman, who gave so much back to the sport of athletics and it's sad that she wasn't repaid for her dedication and service. Instead, she was suspended by SASCOC along with several other ASA officials over the handling of the Caster Semenya gender testing debacle back in 2009.

Gender Test After a Gold-Medal Finish

On the blue track at the Olympic Stadium, all three medalists celebrated after the women's 800 meters at the world track and field championships. But when it came time for the post-race news conference, the gold medalist, Caster Semenya, was nowhere to be seen. She had been replaced on the rostrum by Pierre Weiss, the general secretary of the International Association of Athletics Federations, the sport's governing body. Earlier in the day, I.A.A.F. officials had confirmed that Semenya, a muscular 18-year-

old from South Africa competing in her first senior championship, was undergoing sex-determination testing to confirm her eligibility to race as a woman. (New York Times, 19 August 2009)

Lane, a psychologist was the one person who protected and supported Caster but that didn't matter to the powers that be.

One woman's battle to clear her good name spotlights seething corruption in sport – (Noseweek, October 2011)

I felt as if I was getting the punishment without having committed the crime. I approached a number of journalists to try and tell my story – but they were just not interested in exposing anything to do with Sascoc. Many were only concerned with getting their accreditation – and a trip – to the Olympics and other international events. They didn't want to jeopardise all the favours. Journalists often have to go to international sporting events under Sascoc's jurisdiction. - Larraine Lane (Noseweek, November 2013)

Lane fought a legal battle for over four years against SASCOC to get re-instated. She won round one in the South Gauteng Court as the judge set aside the SASCOC suspension, but the judgment was upheld in the Supreme Court of Appeal in Bloemfontein with costs.

I was gutted for Laraine, who I had gotten to know through her legal battle. A very brave 70 year old woman, who has more to offer the sport than most but was denied justice.

It's so easy for SASCOC to keep on litigating (until they win) when they're using and abusing public funds.

A dream client for any lawyer!

What really happened: Oscar Pistorius?

29 March 2013

It's created one of the biggest media frenzies in South Africa and international press crews are still clamouring for the real story but will anyone ever get it?

The BBC's documentary title, "Oscar Pistorius: What Really Happened" was perhaps a little misleading as the only one who really knows what happened that Valentine's morning is Oscar himself and he obviously wasn't interviewed for the programme.

Still so many unanswered questions, some of which may or not come out in the trial.

There's seldom a day that goes by without someone mentioning the tragic story and just this week, I met someone who was at the table next to Oscar's when the gun went off in the Tasha's restaurant earlier this year.

She said there was a scary silence at the sound of the blast but that no-one really knew what it was.

A small commotion ensued but everything returned to normal in the restaurant fairly quickly without too much fuss.

Chatting to some a little closer to the tragedy, one gets the feeling that Oscar is going to find it very, very hard to convince the court that the death of girlfriend, Reeva Steenkamp was just an accident.

Many legal experts agree and believe his affidavit for the bail hearing was not necessary and that the prosecution now holds all the aces.

Only time will tell.

The question that bothers most is how did Oscar not notice that Reeva wasn't in the bed when he picked up the gun and proceeded to shoot through the bathroom door and after one shot, would she not have said something for him to realize it wasn't an intruder?

I fail to understand how I could be charged with murder, let alone premeditated murder, as I had no intention to kill my girlfriend Reeva Steenkamp. - Oscar

Regardless, he has admitted to shooting and killing Reeva in his affidavit and he has left a family reeling.

I've recently run into some people from Pretoria who know someone, who believes they can shed more light on "what really happened".

The common themes range from: Text messages sent or received, possessiveness, jealousy, untouchable, former girlfriends, a love triangle and other incidents of rage not yet known to the public at large.

What is now known to the public is that Oscar is free to compete again after his bail conditions were relaxed but a spokesperson for the world governing body of athletics (IAAF) said: "All invitations are at the discretion of the meeting organizers, and not the IAAF."

It remains to be seen just how many invites the "Blade Runner" will get and will the sponsors come running back?

I have serious doubts.

The whole story will always be so sad and tragic as Reeva will never be able to compete on the modelling ramps again.

What really happened: Oscar Pistorius?

One thing you can never take away from Oscar is what he has achieved on the track and the inspiration he has been for millions of people around the world. Speaking on SportsFire last week, Samkelo Radebe, who was part of the SA 4 x100m relay team who won gold at the 2012 Paralympic games in London said:

Oscar has always been someone that I've looked up to. He has inspired me by what he has achieved and it was an honour to be part of the same relay team that won gold in London. Oscar is a role model for what he has done for disabled athletes and he has put disability sport on the map in South Africa.

Few can argue with that.

I was working in the USA in June 1994 and I will never forget the day of the OJ Simpson car chase through the streets of Los Angeles. The police chasing the white Ford Bronco is still fresh in my memory. Millions of people were glued to their televisions. The morning headlines of 14 February 2013 will do the same.

The world media have chased the Oscar story since day one but no-one seems to be any closer to finding out what really happened.

Chief prosecutor, Gerrie Nel said there is a possibility the Pistorius trial will begin by the end of the year. The murder trial in which OJ was a defendant lasted for nine months. The jury deliberated for four hours and OJ was found not guilty.

The million dollar question is – will Oscar be found guilty or not guilty?

***

We don't know EXACTLY what happened "behind the scenes", but most of us have the gist of it. Reeva Steenkamp, a beautiful young woman in every sense, was gunned down. She is dead, and will remain so. Pistorius pulled the trigger. He is a killer. He must pay for robbing her of her life. And let me tell you, there was no intruder. When last have you heard of an intruder locking himself/herself in the bathroom? Did you see that the estate security were called out to the house an hour or two BEFORE the shooting because of the shouting that went on in the house? Use your logic. So now there was this huge domestic dispute, and all of a sudden there is an intruder that strangely has locked himself/herself in the bathroom. In a security estate. Please. - Liza Kemp

Perfect! This article describes Pistorius perfectly. He was a ticking time bomb.! He had no control over his anger was far too uptight majority of the time. His behaviour at the Olympics says it all.. Something had to give. In the end it was his girl friend who died because of his anger. Not the first time that he has lost it with one of his partners. Now the beautiful Reeva is dead. How her mother and father must ache to have her back. RIP Reeva. May your family find peace with all the wonderful memories they have of you. - Fran Greening

Without prejudice:

The real Oscar ,is a young man who has never come to terms with the loss of his lower-limbs, despite capitalizing/gaining success as a para-Olympian. No amount of money/fame and success can make up for his deep-rooted feelings of insecurity, in terms of having long-standing relationships with woman!! They probably enjoy the initial share of his fame/fortunes. and as the relationships continue/develop, find it difficult to deal with his disability,in terms of doing normal things that couples do, like strolling on the beach/swimming etc. (not to mention/imagine intimate-issues, which could be hard to accept. At the same time. there are many able-bodied /equally-wealthy sportsman, who may have been a threat to his previous relationships. Oscar would have always been on his guard/ distrustful of his partners in public-places, acting macho in terms of his arms-collection/possible use of anabolic steroids in order to enhance his upper body(the only real appealing physical-feature to show off. A crime of passion, fuelled by the possibility of her wanting to end the relationship. .. an alleged text-message from a previous boyfriend/friend.. could have ensued in a scuffle, in order to see the latter. No amount of money/fame/adoration could replace his deep- rooted feelings of inadequacy. He may have been shunned once to often. He should have received psychological-counselling years ago. These are my opinions. I may be wrong. - Pierre Opperman

Oscar is crying out for help and no-one can see it, or wants to see it. He has been pushed to perform all his life and it has caught up with him. It has also been reported that he has narcissistic personality disorder. If one looks at the signs of NPD in comparison with what has been written about Oscar over the years, then he definitely needs help but no-one has seen this, or maybe no-one wants to see. An NPD sufferer cannot see that there is anything wrong with himself. While he has been making money and others are gaining from it, none of them will see that he desperately needs help. Who should be blamed for what has happened ? Parents, relatives, managers, trainers? Certainly not Oscar alone. - Jean Rebow

On 6 July 2016, Pistorius was sentenced to six years in prison for the murder of his girlfriend Reeva Steenkamp.

There was even talk that he could be out on parole and back on the track for the Tokyo Olympics in 2020.

SASCOC CEO, Tubby Reddy told the UK publication, Daily Mail in July 2016 that the 'Blade Runner' could still represent South Africa at the highest level.

He would have paid his debt to society and will be back in society, living as a normal South African citizen. There is no rule that says he would not be able to participate. Yes, the sentence he has been given has divided opinion – there are those who are happy about it and there are those who are unhappy, and you will always have that. But if he is out on parole, as it seems he will be before then, and qualifies for selection then I don't see how there can be a problem – why not? – Tubby Reddy

Reddy was way off the mark as was Judge Thokozile Masipa who presided over the murder trial.

As a result of the errors of law ... and on a proper appraisal of the facts, he ought to have been convicted not of culpable homicide on that count but of murder. In the interests of justice the conviction and the sentence imposed in respect thereof must be set aside and the conviction substituted with a conviction of the correct offence.

After the long drawn out, live televised trial (a first for South Africa) and an incorrect initial judgement plus all the appeals, Oscar Pistorius was finally sentenced to 13 years in prison for the murder of his girlfriend, Reeva Steenkamp.

In April 2011, I was invited into a horse racing ownership syndicate with Oscar by a mutual friend, Jessica Slack.

I had one bad previous experience with horse racing ownership, having paid R60,000 to a rogue SA owner, Robert Zackey for shares in horses that I would never get to own and money I would never see again.

I applied it to the little I remember from my Economics one course at Rhodes University, that of a 'sunk cost' (money you never see again) and as a good friend told me, it was a cheap lesson in horse racing.

Robert befriended me and took full advantage of my lack of horse racing knowledge.

I got my fellow radio employee and friend, Darren Simpson involved in the syndicate and I should have known there was something amiss when we were hurried for payment. It turns out that Robert needed the money fast to pay off gambling debts and the price of the horses were nowhere near what he paid for them.

Fortunately, I had other friends in the industry who guided me to a website where you could view the racing sales prices.

When I questioned Robert about the ownership and inflated prices, he draw up a document from "Summerline Stud" which turned out to be an appliance store in Durban. It could quite easily have been confused by a racing rookie like myself with Summerhill Stud, which is a legitimate Champion Thoroughbred Stallion Station and Racehorse Stud Farm in KwaZulu-Natal (South Africa).

Robert must have thought I was horse racing stupid!

On principle, I fought to get our money back but it was all in vain. Officials at the top of the horse racing chain had promised to assist me but as it turned out, they weren't really interested in exposing the filth, which would have been a black eye for the sport.

Today, those officials are even higher up in the chain. Thanks for the assistance and sticking to your word Vee Moodley.

Not!

Robert threatened me in Vee's office and said I should stop crying over R60 000 when he had lost R5 million in his divorce. He promised to pay it all back to me by a certain date, which Vee marked on his calendar.

The date came and went. No payment. My calls and emails to Moodley went unreturned.

I was a little gun shy (no pun intended) to get involved in ownership again but the photograph Jessica sent me in her email on 19 April 2011 was a deal breaker.

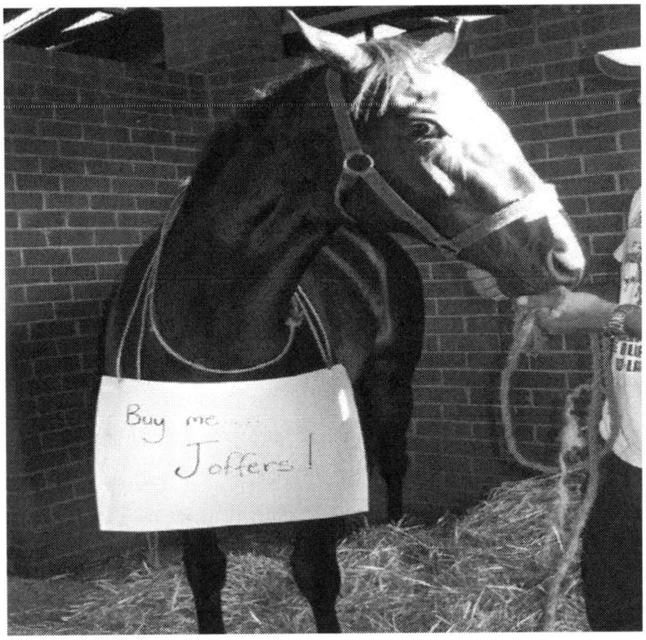

The great thing with the Wilgerbosdrift marketing manager is that he doesn't believe in hard sell!! I couldn't resist, sorry. His name is Tiger Canyon. He is by Tiger Ridge out of a mare called Mischief Maiden. I can't guarantee that he will win the July (although of course I think he will), but I can guarantee that you will have fun. You can take as small a piece as you like. So far it's me and Oscar – there is 25% up for grabs so if you can think of anyone who might be interested, let me know. - Jessica

Jess was a great friend and I couldn't resist.

On the 5th of May 2011, Jessica invited us to the stables to see our new baby, Tiger Canyon who was being looked after by trainer, Mike Azzie, whose sons had gone to Pretoria Boys High School with Oscar.

They had a very close relationship with the blade-runner.

The Azzie's had gotten Oscar into horse racing ownership and they would go onto have great success in their partnership with the R3.6 million buy, Potala Palace. Oscar would later have to sell his share in the horse to pay for his legal costs.

Unfortunately, Tiger Canyon wasn't to be anywhere close to as good a race horse as Potala Palace was.

I met Oscar and Jess at the Azzie stables one morning in Randjesfontein in May 2011 to see our new baby.

It was the first time I had seen in Oscar in a number of years although I had done a few radio interviews with him along the way.

Adam Azzie, Tiger Canyon and Oscar Pistorius

After watching Tiger Canyon gallop for the first time, we had a breakfast at the stables and I chatted to Oscar about his training and next goals. Something about him had changed significantly for me.

Oscar was a little stand offish which I had never encountered before but I couldn't put my finger on it. Jess agreed that he wasn't the same Oscar she had first met.

As a journalist, I had always kept a social distance from the sportsmen and women out of mutual respect.

Perhaps, Tiger Canyon had brought us too close.

> *12 June 2012*
> *Hello,*
> *RUNNER: TIGER CANYON*
> *I'm pleased to inform you that Tiger Canyon is running on Saturday 16 June at Turffontein Standside Track in race 1 over 1160m. Anton Marcus up, 57kg's, drawn 1/14, race goes off at 11:55. He has been working very well at home, shows a lot of speed and we expect him to at least run into the money here!*
> *Kind Regards,*
> *Natalie Faasen*
> *Assistant Trainer (Mike Azzie)*

Unfortunately, Tiger Canyon didn't live up to his billing on debut.

He was very green first time out, not the work that he shows us at home, so we thought we would get him in again quickly to teach him to race. – Natalie Faasen

Tiger Canyon was never going to win us the Dubai millions but we gave him some time including a move to Cape Town before a premature retirement.

Ahead of the London Olympics, I tried to get Oscar on my sports talk show for a telephonic interview. I went through his agent, Peet van Zyl and sent Oscar a courtesy email as well. Weeks went by with no reply.

It was a busy time for the Paralympian.

Apart from final preparations, every media outlet in the world wanted a piece of him after the International Association of Athletics Federations (IAAF) couldn't find a reason to stop him from competing with able bodied athletes in London.

I didn't expect favours but just the courtesy of a reply, which eventually came via a text message from his agent two weeks after the request.

Sorry, Oscar is in Italy and won't be able to do interview.

Why would he decline the interview?

Oscar supposedly had a black book of journalists he would no longer speak to, if they had been critical of him or interviewed someone else who was critical, while he was legally fighting with the IAAF.

I had done an interview on my radio show with a SA Professor of Exercise Physiology, Ross Tucker, who was strongly of the opinion that Oscar's blades gave him an advantage and he should not be allowed to compete against able-bodied athletes in London. He had scientific facts to back it up.

I tried to remain an Oscar fan during the London Olympics as he became a world icon but I had lost a lot of respect for him. And the final straw was his bratty behaviour, calling the race "unfair" when beaten by T44 200m gold medalist, Alan Fonteles Cardoso Oliveira in the Paralympics.

He couldn't handle defeat.

Everything he had fought so gallantly for had been destroyed in my eyes. Fame and fortune had changed him.

Then that fateful night that would change lives forever.

14 February 2013. Oscar Pistorius murders his girlfriend, Reeva Steenkamp.

Jessica and I spoke a few times after the murder - she was devastated. She had become very close to Oscar but had seen changes that she didn't like including a night he came to her house for dinner with some shady looking friends who were armed.

The guns made her scared.

Oscar is the only one who knows what happened that fateful night and he will carry that to his grave one day. There were suggestions of drug use at the murder scene but never confirmed.

Oscar Pistorius will be tested for steroids after the banned drugs were allegedly found in his house after he shot dead his girlfriend Reeva Steenkamp. Police are also reported to have recovered a bloodied bat from the Paralympic champion's bedroom and to have established that model Miss Steenkamp's skull had been 'crushed'. (Mail Online, 18 February 2013)

South African police say they found two boxes of testosterone and syringes in the bedroom of murder suspect Oscar Pistorius which would, if confirmed as true, give impetus for the anti-doping authorities to initiate a formal sports drugs hearing. (The Telegraph, 20 February 2013)

A top SA cyclist called me the same week these drug allegations surfaced and asked if Oscar had a biological passport.

Did he know something?

The passport is an individual, electronic record for professional athletes, in which profiles of biological markers of doping and results of doping tests are collated over a period of time.

The South African Institute for Drug Free Sport (SAIDS) conducted 42 urine test samples on Paralympic athletes in 2012.

Was Oscar Pistorius one of them?

If not, when was the last time Oscar was tested?

On 12 March 2014, I received this response from the CEO of SAIDS, Khalid Galant.

Thank you for your enquiry. Mr Pistorius was one of the athletes that was tested by SAIDS as reported in our stats. He was last tested at the London Olympics. Due to his international ranking he falls under the jurisdiction of the International Paralympic Committee and IAAF. They will authorise out-of-competition on him and have a comprehensive record of his tests.

The IAAF and drug testing?

I guess we don't want to go there with the whole doping scandal, which brought the sport to its knees in 2015.

Russia was condemned to a humiliating exile from world athletics on Friday night after the sport resorted to desperate measures to confront the worst drugs scandal in history. The world's largest country became the first to be banned for doping offences as the International Association of Athletics Federations acted decisively over an independent investigation that found the Russians guilty of a state-sponsored programme which "sabotaged" the London Olympics. (Daily Telegraph, 13 November 2015)

Six months later, the World Anti-Doping Agency (WADA) suspended the accreditation of the drug-testing laboratory in South Africa, the only accredited facility in Africa, until after the Rio Olympics.

The suspension, which takes effect immediately, prohibits the Laboratory from carrying out any anti-doping activities including all analyses of urine and blood samples. During the period of suspension, samples are required to be transported securely to another WADA-accredited laboratory, ensuring that athletes can have full confidence in continued high quality sample analysis and the wider anti-doping system. – WADA

No reasons were given for the suspension.

Many unanswered questions including who influenced the decision for Oscar to be selected for the London Olympic Games?

There was strong speculation that Nike paid a SA official, perhaps someone at SASCOC to make sure he was there to compete.

Nike denied it!

I remember following Oscar's qualification trials and tribulations on twitter until he ran out of time.

He didn't qualify to run the individual 400m.

Giving South Africa another shot at a possible medal was the inclusion of a 4x400m relay squad. Among those names were Paralympic ace Oscar Pistorius who ran an A standard qualifier in the 400m and will now compete at his first Olympic Games. Pistorius will be joined by Willem de Beer, Ofentse Mogawane and Shaun de Jager. The South African 4x400m relay team won silver at the IAAF World Athletics Championships in Daegu, South Korea last year. - SASCOC press release

Oscar didn't run in the final in Daegu but made history in London.

He reached the semi-finals in the 400, which was an amazing achievement and the relay team finished 8th out of 9, some four seconds behind the bronze medalists and seven seconds behind the winners, the Bahamas.

SASCOC stated over and over again, they only send potential medal winners to the Olympic Games.

Was Oscar and the relay team potential medal winners?

Meanwhile, even a year before the Games …

Blade Runner' Oscar Pistorius sits for torso sculpture

Paralympian Oscar Pistorius is being immortalised in bronze to feature in an exhibition of the world's top athletes. A plaster cast of the South African, who is known as the Blade Runner, has been taken in Manchester. Bath-based artist Ben Dearnley is to create a sculpture of the 24-year-old athlete's torso for a display at Salisbury Cathedral during London 2012. (BBC, 24 May 2011)

A bronze sculpture/torso of the Blade Runner in London to market British Telecom's 'Art of Sport' and the Olympics.

The Games needed him.

Nike and numerous other sponsors wanted him there as did British Telecom who supposedly paid for some of Oscar's family members to be in London for the Olympics.

When I asked a source with close ties to the British Embassy for some information, he responded by saying:

If you have the budget to make lunch with two diplomats and get them drunk on a lakelet of white wine, I'll throw 'em to you and extract the juicy tales. But they need to be drunk and you need to think about the repercussions.

I didn't have the budget and didn't make the lunch but wish I would have.

Oscar's agent, Peet and I met up for coffee in August 2014. I thought it may be a little awkward, but it wasn't. We chatted briefly about Oscar. He told me about all the international trips he had planned for Oscar and Reeva and how much he loved her. He also spoke of the errors the investigating team made on the night of the tragedy.

But the main reason for the meeting was more to do with SASCOC.

Peet showed me some of the email correspondence or lack thereof and how his athletes get the run around when it comes to OPEX payments and re-imbursements.

We were in August …

And yes they have yet to be paid for their expenses incurred such as flights, hotel accommodation, meals, land transport etc. since end May already and when the athletes ask when they will be paid the answer we don't know.

It's disgraceful that professional athletes have to worry about where their next rand is coming from and SASCOC refuse to deal with agents. I made a song and dance about it on social media and a few days later, SASCOC sent out a press release saying that the athletes had now been paid and the delay was due to cash flow challenges.

No apology from SASCOC but a message for the media.

We urge our media not to blow issues like these totally out of proportion when we face resolvable problems as this only hinders our athletes' performance. – Tubby Reddy

Really, it's the media's fault now?

I guess we are also to blame for top SA sprinter, Anaso Jobodwana having to spend two nights at the airport in Portugal on his way back to college in the USA after the London Olympics because SASCOC didn't organize a return flight for him.

I watched many hours of the Oscar murder trial and kept expecting SA rugby player, Francois Hougaard to testify. It didn't happen.

Hougaard was a former boyfriend of Reeva's and there were rumours of a love triangle and that he had received a text message from her on the fateful night, saying she was scared. At that point, he and Oscar didn't see eye to eye.

Hougaard seemed to take a lot of mental strain in the months following the murder and missed a number of Bulls games that season through "injury". He also came home early from one of the overseas tours.

Triple injury blow for Bulls

Wynand Olivier, Francois Hougaard and Akona Ndungane will return home early from the Bulls' tour of Australasia after picking up injuries in the Pretoria side's defeat to the Crusaders on Saturday. Olivier, unavailable for four weeks with a knee injury, Hougaard, sidelined for two weeks with an ankle injury, and Ndungane, out for four weeks with a cheekbone injury, would be replaced on tour by

Francois Venter, Ruan Snyman and fit-again Bjorn Basson, the Bulls said in a statement on Sunday. (SAPA, 17 March 2013)

Hougaard was on the bench for this game against the Crusaders and never made it onto the field. How did he pick up an injury in the defeat?

I remember reading a comment from a Bulls fan after the game …

I think Hougaard has some tough personal things he needs to work through in his life at the moment.

He must have read my mind.

Does Hougaard know more about what happened on the night that Reeva was murdered? I think he knows a little more than most.

But only Oscar really knows!

Chapter 6: The Fix is in …

The SASCOC elections rolled around again in 2012 and just like 2008, they were well orchestrated to make sure the inner circle would remain the same.

We've seen it often with corrupt sporting powers around the world e.g. IOC, FIFA etc. Board members get high on greed, golden handshakes, free dinners and trips around the world and will do whatever it takes to hold onto power for as long as possible.

The South African Olympic Committee is no different.

SASCOC CEO, Tubby Reddy was self-appointed and now he was now going to make sure the board was full of his merry-men.

"Yes men" – he didn't want anyone who would ask questions.

Reddy was running the show and there was already talk of a rift between himself and the SASCOC president, Gideon Sam.

My column on 3 March 2013 exposed the election fix.

SASCOC election "fix"
3 March 2013

Dear athletes, sponsors and sports fans:

It is with utter disgust, sadness, anger but no surprise that I share with you what transpired with the recent SASCOC elections.

Firstly, a SASCOC email was sent by Tubby Reddy's personal assistant, Jean Kelly to selected federations, four days before the election on 24th November. It was titled 'SASCOC leadership' and it was 'Gideon Sam's list for the election as discussed with Mubarak' (Mahomed) who was a board member.

Sam was unopposed as president and his 'preferred' list in the email was:

Vice presidents: Hajera Kajee, Les Williams Board members: Mark Alexander, Kobus Marais, Mubarak Mohamed, Keikabile Motlatsi, Themba Hlasho

The federations were also advised to vote for these seven nominees by SASCOC members via secretive canvassing, phone calls and on the day of the election itself.

Some of these seven nominees even had the audacity to pass this email onto federations themselves with broken promises.

No surprise, the voting went as "fixed" by SASCOC.

Voting:

Hajeera Kajee	120	1st Vice President
Les Williams	118	2nd Vice President
Wiempie du Plesis	38	
Colin Webster	13	
Kirsten Nematandani	9	

A landslide win for Kajee and Williams.

Mark Alexander, Jace Naidoo and Kobus Marais withdrew their nominations but don't you worry, it was all well calculated.

Voting: Additional Board Members:

Muburak Mohammed	125
Mark Alexander	112
Kobus Marais	109
Keikabile Motlatsi	94
Temba Hlasho	84

Wiempie du Plessis	52
Ernst van Dyk	24
Nomsa Mahlangu	18
Anthea Harmse	18
Colin Webster	17
James Letuka	16
Tim Noakes	15
Selwyn Nathan	15
Mami Dial	14
Ilhaam Groenewald	10
Elise du Rand	10
Moekie Grobbelaar	9
Goliath Munro	6

Mohammed, Alexander, Marais, Motlatsi and Hlasho voted in as per the email.

Kirsten Nematandani, Jeremiah Segwabe, Merrill King, Kaya Majeke and Jace Naidoo withdrew their nominations.

Boom – co-opted onto SASCOC board: Jace Naidoo, Jeremiah Segwabe and Merill King.

Apart from the ethics of it all, how does Jace Naidoo, the president of Swimming SA, a federation that is broke, doesn't have a main sponsor and is clouded in serious allegations of maladministration, get onto the SASCOC board?

Naidoo will also claim another salary as a SASCOC board member that alone is more than what a junior school teacher gets. Sadly, many of the federations had little or no choice but to vote for these gravy train SASCOC administrators.

Hajeera Kajee was also now chairperson of the National Lottery Distribution Agency.

One hand washes the other and from what I heard, there couldn't have been more false hugs and smiles as Reddy and Kajee thanked the federations who voted the "right" way after the election.

Paddling received an early Xmas present with the announcement from SASCOC that Merrill King has been co-opted as a Board member onto the SASCOC Board? A SASCOC board position in return for Canoeing Vote. Facilitated by Hajera (Kajee). The sports federations don't stand up or won't say anything because they don't want to get on wrong side of SASCOC board / mgt. Otherwise they don't get endorsements and recommendations for funding from government or Lotto. Or SASCOC then comes into the federation guns blazing. – Paddling source

But the federations have a chance to right the wrongs and all stand together to get rid of this SASCOC board, the majority of which are only in it for themselves.

The only thing necessary for the triumph of evil is for good men to do nothing. - Edmund Burke

SASCOC needs to be cleaned out with a full forensic audit.

Professor AM Louw in his 2006 paper, 'why South African sport should say no to a state-sanctioned SASCOC autocracy' …

South African sport cannot afford SASCOC. I would suggest that the response to government by sports federations, players' associations, sponsors and other stakeholders should be the following: No thank you, we do not need this dictatorial creature that is being set up largely against our will, and which we will be forced to support in the furtherance of what remains a shady but painfully clear agenda. Millions of taxpayers' rands and lottery funds can be spent to prop up this creature, but it will always have feet of clay; it will topple spectacularly before long, and we do not want to go down with it.

***

It was confirmed to me by an insider that Merill King was told to withdraw her nomination and in return, her sport of canoeing would receive Lottery funding and she would later be co-opted onto the SASCOC board.

It went according to plan.

The SASCOC hierarchy had a strong hand in the National Lottery Distribution agency for Sport and Recreation.

It was a serious conflict of interest that was highlighted by Fikile Mbalula's predecessor as Sports Minister, Makhenkesi Stofile.

It's just not Lotto, says Stofile

Sports and Recreation Minister Makhenkesi Stofile has called for leaders of the Olympics governing body to step down from the National Lottery Distribution Agency (NLDA). Those he wants removed are

Gideon Sam, president of the South African Sports Confederation and Olympic Committee (Sascoc), president of Triathlon South Africa and the chairperson of the NLDA; Sascoc vice-president Hajera Kajee, who also serves in the NLDA; and Sascoc's chief financial officer and the treasurer of Volleyball South Africa, Vinesh Maharaj. The NLDA pays out substantial amounts of money to Sascoc for the funding of different sporting confederations. Sascoc, as the mother body of these confederations, then sits to decide how much each sport should receive from NLDA funds. The minister has cited a conflict of interest in their dual roles as members of both the NLDA and Sascoc. (Mail & Guardian, March 2009)

I sent an email to a number of the SA sporting federations to see if they had also received the 'SASCOC preferred voting' list, which was sent to SA Squash.

Most of the federations were too scared to reply but the president of the SA Deaf Sports Federation, Julius Maxajwe did:

The list is the same as the one that Kobus Marais lobbied SA Deaf Sports Federation to vote for days leading up to the conference. It is also the same list that was discreetly circulated among delegates by one Themba Hlasho. As the President of the SA Deaf sports Federation, I voted for entirely different people from the list, except for Kobus Marais who has promised to resolve the ongoing dispute that we currently have with SASCOC regarding their continual refusal to recognize Deaflympic Games, once elected. I also voted for Themba Hlasho with the hope that fresh blood will bring changes to SASCOC, although I do not know him. Mind Sport SA President was among the people I voted for the board position.

Marais and Hlasho were rewarded with positions on the board and finance committee.

The SASCOC auditors from Deloitte & Touche, who oversaw the election would not be drawn into the matter when asked if the elections were free and fair and a request for copies of the SASCOC audited financials.

Our South African professional standards restrict us from discussing or communicating any client specific information with the media. You are most welcome to contact SASCOC and request the specific information from them or request copies of their annual reports for the periods.- Bester Greyling, Deloitte & Touche

By then SASCOC already had a "no reply policy" to any questions that came from me. It was a one way street. My questions were never going to be answered. They had too much to hide. But they couldn't hide from the contents of an email that was penned after the SASCOC elections by one of SA's top athletes, Ernst van Dyk and addressed to the president of Cycling South Africa (CSA), William Newman.

In resigning from the board of SA Cycling, van Dyk said:

The glimpse I got into the politics in sport at the recent SASCOC elections also gave me second thoughts on any plans for future involvement in the administration of sport. I had no disillusions about my chances of getting elected and I only went through the process as I wanted to see how these things unfold. Unfortunately what I witnessed during that process with certain last minute withdrawals of candidates to not split the votes on other candidates and then those late withdrawals simply got co-opted on to the board at a later stage was very informative and I now understand it's not a place or a space where I want to be or function.

I had a dilemma whether or not to publish contents of the email as SASCOC were vindictive and athletes were marginalized for speaking out against the system.

Ernst van Dyk's voice needed to be heard

Whenever one person stands up and says, 'Wait a minute, this is wrong,' it helps other people do the same. – Gloria Steinem

But Ernst had a target painted on his back by SASCOC as pathetic as it may seem and Cycling SA became paranoid.

Newman sent a group email to the CSA board stating:

The implications of this means that Ernst could be found in breach of his OPEX contract and have support withdrawn – a scenario we definitely do not want to contemplate. I have sent a letter to Mr. Reddy reiterating that Ernst's email was sent to me in confidence which I passed on to you all when I announced his resignation. I have assured Mr. Reddy that Ernst did not talk to Mr. Joffe and that I therefore considered this matter closed but would brush up on our internal policies and processes to prevent anything like this happening again. So I am going to ask very frank questions:

1. *Did any of us pass on this email to anyone? To the media? To Graeme Joffe?*
2. *Are our emails secure?*

Emails then went back and forth between Newman and the SASCOC CEO, Tubby Reddy, trying to get to the bottom of the leak. Fortunately, Ernst van Dyk had all his ducks in a row, he knew his contractual rights to challenge the bullies if needed and continued to receive his Operation Excellence (OPEX) funding.

It was a moral victory.

Reddy also failed in his backhanded attempt to get business and football mogul, Dr Irvin Khoza in as the new SASCOC president.

It was a well-orchestrated attempt through clandestine meetings during the London Olympics as there was growing tension between Reddy and Sam. Khoza as president, would have given Reddy even more power as the former is heavily occupied as the Premier Soccer League (PSL) chairman and owner of glamour club, Orlando Pirates.

The boys at Highbury Safika Media were always in the know (as spin doctors you have to be) and my mole, Gary Lemke was spot on.

I don't have info but my gut is that both Gideon and Khoza will gauge how the voting is likely to go and one will pull out before the election. Am guessing Khoza... he is also standing for first vice-president. It would be incredibly damaging to his reputation and ego if he wasn't elected as president but got in as first vice. So, if he's not going to win he'll withdraw. (He has history, did the same for the Safa presidency). But ... both he and Kirsten were wined and dined in spectacular fashion at the Copthorne Hotel in London where Tubby and hangers on stayed. And I know that Tubby wants Khoza in "as a figurehead". That gives Tubby more power because Khoza would hardly ever be around to comment.

Tubby's profile would be raised. Gideon is his own man and enjoys talking as well. Will be interesting if the fight for presidency actually takes place. - Gary Lemke

There was no fight this time round.

November 13th, 2012: Dr Irvin Khoza has today announced his withdrawal from the SASCOC Presidential race and all other nominations.

It was a mystery how Khoza even got into the SASCOC presidential race as he was not nominated by his own federation, the SA Football Association (SAFA).

Who was Tubby punting for President, before he realised that it was not going to work: none other than Irvin Khoza. Who are Khoza's men: Raymond Hack and Mubarak Mohamed! SASCOC is going after SAFA (South African Football Association), contrary to what you say. But they have an agenda. Mubarak was involved in SAFA, as was Raymond Hack prior to the coup by Danny Jordaan and Kirsten Nemantandani. They threw out both these gentlemen (Mohamed and Hack) who found refuge at SASCOC. They are now out to wreak revenge. – SASCOC insider

The plot thickened three months later when SAFA submitted a motion of no confidence in the SASCOC CEO.

A few weeks later, SASCOC and SAFA had kissed and made up. Both too powerful for their own good with dirt hanging from the rafters.

But the war erupted again a year later as the two sets of head strong officials got into it over more serious issues including the match fixing allegations from the South Africa (Bafana Bafana) friendlies ahead of the 2010 FIFA World Cup.

Excerpts from an open letter from SAFA to SASCOC
14 June 2014

SAFA is quite disappointed by the manner in which SASCOC continues to disrespect the Association through its continuing disparaging actions through its insistence on dealing with the Association in a very adversarial manner.

It continues to engage SAFA through the media on SAFA matters without first addressing matters of the moment directly with the Association.

We were called by the media asking us to comment on remarks by SASCOC on matters that the Association, FIFA and the South African government had already agreed on the way forward, but which SASCOC now refers to in direct opposition to these agreements.

In April 2013, SAFA, the South African Government and FIFA agreed that all financial matters will be dealt with by SAFA and FIFA and that the match-fixing matter will be dealt with by the South African Government.

SASCOC appears once again to raise the spectre of the match-fixing issue, but, the State President, the Honourable Jacob Zuma, issued an instruction in March 2014 that this matter will no longer be dealt with by the South African Government, instead handing it over to FIFA as it forms part of

FIFA's world-wide investigation into match-fixing.

By instituting an investigation into SAFA's finances, SASCOC is directly defying an agreement made between the South African Government and FIFA on 5 April 2013 that SAFA and FIFA will deal with all financial matters involving SAFA.

This agreement was reported throughout the world as the biggest story of that period. SAFA will seek an urgent meeting with the Honourable Minister of Sport and Recreation to discuss the way forward because SAFA's continued membership of SASCOC has become untenable as SASCOC has chosen to place itself in a clearly adversarial relationship with SAFA and many of its other members instead of working with them to grow elite sport in this country and to be supportive of the very membership who voted the current SASCOC leadership into office.

However, notwithstanding these problems, the Association is still desirous of a dialogue with SASCOC in early August as agreed with them on 2 June 2014 where both sides pledged to work together to improve SASCOC's terrible communication and relationship with its Members, SAFA being one them. It is in nobody's interest that this negative environment prevails between the country's biggest sports organisation (SAFA) and its Olympic body.

However, our patience is wearing very thin with the imperial behaviour of the SASCOC leadership.

***

The match fixing allegations made it a good time for SASCOC (Tubby Reddy, Mubarak Mohammed and Raymond Hack) who were allies of of PSL boss, Irvin Khoza to pick a fight with SAFA under new president, Danny Jordaan.

Jordaan was elected as SAFA president in September 2013.

Khoza wanted the position but was ruled ineligible due to a resolution in the SAFA constitution which prevents a club owner from becoming president of the national body.

Mohammed and Hack, both former SAFA employees also had that old score to settle with Jordaan.

In other words, it was SASCOC/PSL vs SAFA.

And the Khoza/Jordaan heavyweight battle played out for years much to the detriment of SA football.

SA match fixing – when will it be fixed?
18 September 2014

It’s been 21 months since the Bafana Bafana match fixing allegations came to the surface and there is still a mysterious silence.

I was speaking to former SAFA president, Kirsten Nemantandani yesterday and he said he knows no more than we do. Nemantandani just wants to clear his name as he was fingered in the allegations and suspended.

The match-fixing allegations centre round the Bafana Bafana World Cup warm up games in May 2010 against Thailand, Bulgaria, Colombia and Guatemala.

Scores:
SA 4 - 0 Thailand
SA 2 - 1 Colombia
SA 1 - 1 Bulgaria
SA 5 - 0 Guatemala

With that kind of form, we should have won the World Cup.

The game against Guatemala was handled by a referee from Niger and he was also going to do the fifth friendly against Denmark but was changed just before the game as SAFA officials had become suspicious.

The referees for these friendlies were appointed by Football4U, whose head honcho, Wilson Raj Perumal has since been jailed for fixing games in Finland.

In the beginning of 2013, Sports Minister, Fikile Mbalula said a commission of inquiry would be set up to investigate the match fixing allegations.

Pause - a big, long pause.

In November 2013, FIFA says they will take control of the long-awaited investigation.

Mbalula didn't like that.

That Jerome Valcke must get it into his head that FIFA does not run this country. South Africa is a sovereign country and we will never allow ourselves to be usurped by FIFA. – Fikile Mbalula

For the next four months, Mbalula talks another big game about SA doing its own investigation.

Alas, nothing happens.

In March 2014, President Zuma decides there will be no commission of inquiry to investigate the alleged match fixing. The reason given is that FIFA has advised the president there is currently a pending preliminary investigation on the same matter by the football world governing body.

How did we lose our sovereignty so quickly?

Pause again for another five months.

In September 2014, a statement from the then SAFA CEO, Leslie Sedibe asked the Public Protector to investigate the allegations.

There has been much speculation with regard to the match-fixing allegations and the names of many individuals have been drawn into these allegations, including my own name. I was CEO of SAFA at the time. I am determined to maintain and protect my good name and reputation and I am of the opinion that this matter has dragged on for far too long. Justice delayed is justice denied. - Leslie Sedibe

There's no denying that there's something rotten with those friendlies but will we ever get to the bottom of it?

I have my doubts.

It's now been revealed that the Brazilian Football Association gave luxury watches worth a total of $570 000 to FIFA Exco members and officials from the 32 competing national associations at the 2014 World Cup.

Perhaps, FIFA can now 'timeously' look into the Bafana Bafana match fixing allegations.

But first in Zurich today, FIFA are hosting the first World Summit on Ethics in Sport.

The opening address will be made by FIFA president, Sepp Blatter.

That's Football 4U!

***

Almost three years after the corrupt friendlies were exposed, finally we get some real action.

FIFA has confirmed banning former South African Football Association CEO Leslie Sedibe for five years and fine of 20,000 Swiss francs, SAFA confirmed on Monday. This follows a Fifa probe into match-fixing. (Times Live, 14 March 2016)

But Sedibe claimed he was a scapegoat.

In my view, the FIFA investigation remains incomplete and remains unreliable for as long as the documents that I requested from SAFA are not included in the investigation. SAFA has refused to give me access to this information and yet FIFA, in its own infinite wisdom because they think they own the world and they think that they can do whatever they want wherever they go in the world, they say I must give them documents. FIFA has demonstrated little willingness to undertake a full and comprehensive investigation. They seemed very intent on reaching a conclusion and they did, which avoids identifying the true culprits for fear of political reprisal. – Leslie Sedibe

Nine months later and FIFA kicks another top SA football official into touch.

FIFA bans former Safa boss for violating ethics code

World football governing body FIFA has banned former South African Football Association president Kirsten Nemantandani from all football related activities for five years, for violating the organisation's code of ethics. Nemantandani was found guilty of violating article 13 (General Rules of Conduct), article 15 (Loyalty) and article 18 (Duty of Disclosure, Cooperation and Reporting. The ban relates to international matches that were played and fixed in South Africa in 2010, of which FIFA found compelling evidence that revealed that the match fixing was coordinated by Far East betting syndicates. (Anti-Corruption Digest, 9 December 2016)

Nemantandani, like Sedibe, claimed he was a scapegoat and threatened to expose the real culprits.

Why only now after being fingered by FIFA?

So, still we have not gotten to the bottom of the Bafana Bafana friendlies that were fixed in 2010.

Will we ever?

Chapter 7: Press Ombudsman

In March 2013, SASCOC laid a complaint with the Press Ombudsman in respect of four of my exposes on sport24. They moaned like stuffed pigs in a 14-page document, hoping the Ombudsman would make me withdraw my columns and apologize.

The Press Council, the Press Ombudsman and the Appeals Panel are an independent co-regulatory mechanism set up by the print and online media to provide impartial, expeditious and cost-effective adjudication to settle disputes between newspapers, magazines and online publications, on the one hand, and members of the public, on the other, over the editorial content of publications. - (SA Press Council)

What a circus
12 March 2013

The athletic "rebels" backed by SASCOC kind of got their way at the weekend with the overwhelming vote to impeach Athletics South Africa (ASA) President, James Evans.

But many questions need to be asked about the validity of the meeting and the sinister role played by SASCOC, let alone the cheap death threat issued on national radio by the ASA "rebel" leader, Hendrick Ramaala. What was Ramaala thinking during his interview on Radio 702 on Sunday night to say:

Your Athletics South Africa board members want James Evans dead or alive.

As I write this, Ramaala still hasn't had the decency to apologize to Evans and SASCOC have yet to even make a statement.

SASCOC CEO, Tubby Reddy found a reason to threaten action against former SA sprinter, Geraldine Pillay for comments she made on Carte Blanche re: Oscar Pistorius Olympic selection but not a word re: Ramaala's violent attack on Evans.

In a country that has a history of violence, how does SASCOC just let this pass?

Just shows you how the SASCOC mafia takes sides and only make a noise when it suits their needs.

Perhaps Mr Reddy would also like to answer some of these questions with regards the impeachment of Mr Evans.

Why did SASCOC pay for a meeting, which actually has nothing to do with them?

The head of SASCOC's dispute resolution committee attends the meeting and makes rulings, without ever referring to both parties. How does one resolve disputes by speaking only to the one party?

They promise Athletics South Africa support but then withhold it while the person they don't want is the president. No doubt they will flood the money in now.

Is that not how corruption is defined in the Act?

Mr Reddy is never able to answer these tough questions for fear of "impeaching" himself.

SASCOC uses its mediation or disciplinary tribunals to score political points. These tribunals are loaded with Reddy's men who do his bidding.

Watch what happens in the next few weeks with SAFA. Keep an eye on the ball for the hidden agendas.

As for the Cricket South Africa (CSA) appointment of a new CEO, why has SASCOC not shown some balls? It is quite obvious that CSA has buckled to the Board of Control for Cricket in India (BCCI) and are now creating a smokescreen to defend their future position of possibly not appointing Haroon Lorgat as CEO.

A source tells me:

* SASCOC does not want to embarrass CSA
* SASCOC does not want to upset/embarrass our government which has very good relations with India
* SASCOC does not want to embarrass the Minister of Sport who always talks about "our special relationship" with India

CSA President, Chris Nenzani was quoted as saying:

There has been a lot of speculation in the media regarding the appointment with several names being bandied about. There have even been suggestions that the appointment has already been made. The only name that CSA will release will be that of the successful candidate at the completion of the process. We are confident that the process will be completed by the end of April, 2013.

Lorgat was a shoo-in for the CEO position about a month ago, until the BCCI walked to the wicket and a five-man CSA delegation flew first class to India a couple weeks ago to try and mend fences.

It's just not cricket.

SASCOC should be condemning the BCCI's opposition to Lorgat which is about him threatening their hegemony. SASCOC needs to condemn the interference of BCCI in SA sport and also reprimand CSA for its cowardly stance.

Is it not time for South Africa to have an independent sports mediation body that is legislated and outside the partisan interests of SASCOC or Sport and Recreation SA (SRSA)?

Of course it is.

But first, Mr Ramaala should resign from the ASA board with immediate effect and the SASCOC board should be impeaching its President and CEO for bringing all of SA sport into disrepute.

Disrepute, a word Tubby and co know all too well.

***

SASCOC obviously didn't like their reference to a 'circus' and the Press Ombudsman would get a further complaint.

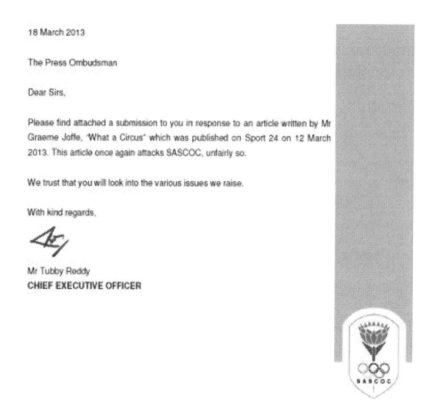

18 March 2013

The Press Ombudsman

Dear Sirs,

Please find attached a submission to you in response to an article written by Mr Graeme Joffe, 'What a Circus' which was published on Sport 24 on 12 March 2013. This article once again attacks SASCOC, unfairly so.

We trust that you will look into the various issues we raise.

With kind regards,

Mr Tubby Reddy
CHIEF EXECUTIVE OFFICER

SASCOC

SASCOC labelled almost all of my ASA and CSA comments as untrue. They wanted the Ombudsman to reprimand me severely and for me to make an apology.

An apology for telling the truth?

Unbelievable. They've blatantly lied to the Ombudsman! Sascoc have been intimately involved with the whole CSA saga. Tubby Reddy was is on the meetings from August 2011, I remember him telling me they need to sort out the wording of the findings ... Sascoc were also brought in by Nicholson, they mediated the whole Norman Arendse thing (probably because he seems to have something on Gideon Sam) & they have been pushing very hard for non-independent directors to form the majority of the board. They are also pressurising CSA to revert to a nine-province system, a la the political boundaries, that gives them all equal representation on the board. So to say they haven't intervened in the affairs of CSA is disingenuous in the extreme! Keep fighting Graeme! - Ken Borland, sports journalist

Norman Arendse sure does have something on Gideon Sam.

'Name your price' bribe offer for R7-billion tender

Top advocate Norman Arendse has alleged that while he was deliberating on a R7-billion state tender in 2008 he was offered an "open chequebook" bribe by an individual claiming to represent Cash Paymaster Services (CPS). Arendse refused to confirm or deny the identity of his would-be corrupter, but the Mail & Guardian has confirmed that Arendse named prominent sports administrator Gideon Sam when he recorded the incident. (Mail & Guardian, 24 February 2012)

Meanwhile, the athletics saga went on for months until SASCOC finally got their way and got rid of Evans to get their corrupt cronies in charge.

But not before Reddy had misled the SA public again.

Open letter to SASCOC CEO
24 June 2013

Dear Mr Reddy

Welcome back from all your June travels. Good to see you still clocking up the frequent flyer miles in business class. I also read with interest where you said the meeting with the International Association of Athletics Federations (IAAF) "went well".

Really?

Do you have minutes from the meeting or was it just another one of your closed-door meetings with the SASCOC slant?

Secondly, did you really believe the IAAF was going to change its tough stance on SASCOC's flagrant disregard for rules and regulations, let alone the nasty arrogance?

The meeting must have gone really well for you to hand back ASA to the suspended board and the SASCOC appointed administrator, Zola Majavu has had to step aside.

Who's going to pay the ASA legal bills that have now run into millions of rand?

But you obviously cannot handle defeat.

SASCOC suspended ASA at its president's council this weekend, which is just unbelievable. It also means no OPEX funding for any of our athletes.

Does this make you happy Mr Reddy?

What part of this letter from the IAAF on 21 June did SASCOC not understand?

Having now met with SASCOC, I can confirm that the IAAF continues today to recognise the ASA Board that was democratically elected in 2012 in accordance with the ASA constitution. As such, that is the body that currently has authority to select and enter teams for the forthcoming IAAF World Championships this summer, starting next month with the World Youth Championships in Donetsk. - Cheikh Thiare, Director of the IAAF President's Executive Office

SA athletes were supposed to compete in the Southern Regions Youth Championships at the beginning of this month in Botswana. The team was announced just five days before the event. The event was cancelled at the last minute and to this date, the athletes have not received their national colours or any other form of recognition.

During last week, athletes received calls from their coaches that they were selected to represent South Africa at the World Youth Championships in Donetsk, Ukraine.

Only one day later they were (again informed) (disappointed again) that this may not be the case, as SASCOC's got a problem with the team which was apparently selected by James Evans, who still just happens to be recognized by the IAAF as the ASA president.

According to the IAAF's website the entries for the World Youth Championships will be closing on 24 June.

If this issue is not resolved before then, our athletes will lose an opportunity that only comes round once in a lifetime - the year during which they turn 17.

On the 6th of June, you made a statement:

The athletes cannot be hamstrung because of this situation. There has been no indication that our athletes would not go to the world championships. We've done special applications to the Lotto and we're doing everything we can to make sure we have the resources to send them, he said. We would still seek every avenue for our athletes to participate.

If participation of senior athletes at the World Championships in Moscow in August is so important to you Mr Reddy why is the participation of our youth athletes in the Ukraine not as important?

Are they being discriminated against because they are young? Why are you hurting them to prove a point to James Evans and the IAAF? Why should the athletes be denied the opportunity due to the arrogance of one man?

South Africa has a number of youth athletes on the world's top-10 lists and you are denying them the opportunity to bring home gold.

With the suspension of ASA, SASCOC has decided that athletes of ASA will not be included in future Team South Africa squads at all youth and senior levels.

Is this what you meant when you said, "the athletes cannot be hamstrung because of this situation?"

Instead, you have put the athletes in the middle of the crossfire.

It also amazes me how quiet SASCOC president, Gideon Sam and the Sports Minister have been on the ASA issue.

You seem to be making all the decisions and in the words of Frank Sinatra, "I'll do it my way".

What also amazes me is how quiet you've been of late on the Safa issue (match fixing allegations) and CSA (bowing to the pressure of the BCCI not to appoint Haroon Lorgat as CEO).

Not as easy to bully Safa and CSA like the small federations, huh?

Oh wait, that's right.

In a SASCOC complaint to the Press Ombudsman, you say "CSA is an organisation independent of SASCOC and SASCOC is not authorised nor obliged to intervene in the affairs of CSA in any way."

Are you saying SASCOC had nothing to do with: The Protea badge saga, the Nicholson inquiry, helping Norman Arendse get back onto the board and pressurising CSA to revert to a nine-province system? To say SASCOC is not authorised to intervene in the affairs of CSA is disingenuous in the extreme! But that's how SASCOC rolls.

Mr Reddy, you were recently quoted as saying, "you are unpopular because you're trying to clean up SA sport."

No sir, you are unpopular because you are doing what's best for you, family and friends and SA sport is just the vehicle.

Finally, I see that Sascoc board member, Hajera Kajee and yourself are standing for election to the Association of National Olympic Committees of Africa (ANOCA).

Is this just to get more frequent flyer miles or to get more fingers in the pie?

I would only encourage it if it means you will resign from your position as SASCOC CEO.

Yours sincerely,
Graeme Joffe

***

He is blatantly punishing the athletes and then asking them to blame ASA. Things were moving in the right direction until they tried to install Hendrick Ramala as ASA president in a very unconstitutional manner. - Cormac Wilcox

Excellent article Graeme. In a recent article, former Springbok captain John Smit said that he had an eye- opening experience at Saracens when on boarding a plane, the players turn left and the administration team turns right (players in Business/First Class, administrators in Economy). Until administrators are appointed on merit and not due to political alignment, our sport will lurch from disaster to disaster. - Lance Rothschild

We are gonna lose great athletes because of these idiots that know nothing about sports. Whats also destroying our sports in this country is all the politics involved in sports. For god's sakes take politics out of sports and put ppl in that know about sports. The way how Mr Reddy and all the other idiots are running SASCOC has destroyed our position with the IAAF. To all our young athletes if you are gonna get messed around like this I hope you will get scholarships overseas and do well in your athletics. Dont let these corrupt idiots come begging in a few years time when they hear your doing great overseas and come begging you to run for your country. Just give them the middle finger and walk away as they are ruining your future here. - Darryl Maze

SA athletics had been stained by maladministration and running battles with SASCOC for years. The dirty tricks campaign against Evans was just history repeating itself.

Athletics South Africa (ASA) administrator Ray Mali expects the federation's suspended board members and employees to face disciplinary hearings within the next two weeks. The South African Sports Confederation and Olympic Committee (Sascoc) suspended ASA president Leonard Chuene, his entire executive, and three employees in November last year. (Mail & Guardian, 4 March 2010)

Evans was obviously not everyone's cup of tea and he was embroiled in another major controversy over the staging of the Soweto Marathon in 2013. The CEO of the Soweto Marathon Trust, Banele Sindani certainly didn't mince his words either in an email sent to certain individuals in the running fraternity.

I must give you a friendly warning, that if the Soweto Marathon Trust does not organise the Race, nobody else will go into Soweto to organise it. James Evans does not know us, he is making a big mistake by thinking that we are the cowards that he is used to. We are not scared of him one bit, we are more than ready to show him who we are. We will make him curse the day he was born, together with the people he will send to organise the Race. They will go into Soweto, but they won't come out. When it comes to athletics, Soweto is the exclusive domain of Soweto athletics clubs, and nobody else's. We are ready to lay down our lives if needs be, to protect our domain. - Banele Sindani

Scary stuff in the battle for money and power! These so-called "Trusts" – one wonders who can you trust?

The 2013 Soweto Marathon was cancelled and two years later, Sindani lost his life in an 'apparent' home robbery.

Sindani's death a hit – nephew

A relative of slain sports administrator Banele Sindani suspects that his killing could be the result of a planned hit. Phelelani Sindani said Banele may have been a marked man. 'We are not ruling out a hit. There were plans for him to go back to Athletics SA and he told me that one of the officials had told him in a meeting that it would happen over his dead body.' (Sowetan, 2 December 2015)

Murdered Sindani was ready to lead ASA

The late Banele Sindani was among the applicants for the vacant Athletics SA (ASA) chief executive job, a position he once held in the early 2000s. This was revealed by ASA president Aleck Skhosana after Sindane (60) was shot and killed in a burglary at his home in Ruimsig, Roodepoort in the early hours of Tuesday morning. (City Press, 6 December 2015)

Had the sport of athletics become a matter of life and death? Someone in SA athletics had to know more about the murder!

Richard Stander, from a corrupt Boland Athletics became the acting ASA CEO in 2016 to work under his 'Boland buddy,' Dr Harold Adams.

The untouchable mafia?

28 August 2014

Harold Adams – ID no: 66 ...
Jacob Herold Adams – ID no: 60 ...

Is this Dr Harold Adams, the vice-president of Athletics South Africa (ASA) with two different ID numbers?

Probably best remembered for his role in the Caster Semenya gender saga back in 2009, Adams was a key figure and reported that he was possibly the "only person who knew when the athlete was tested in South Africa and what happened afterwards."

I was taken aback as I had no idea that Dr Adams had not obtained the athlete's 'Informed Consent' for the tests to be conducted. This is the obligatory responsibility of all Medical Practitioners in terms of The Health Professional Council's Code of Ethical Conduct. It cannot be delegated to a non-medical person as the patient is entitled to ask relevant questions about the procedures and possible outcomes. – Larraine Lane

ASA president, Leonard Chuene and others took the fall for Adams who was protected at the highest level, being a personal doctor for the country's President, Jacob Zuma.

But now the cards are all falling.

Adams is the chairperson of the Board of Onderstepoort Biological Products (OBP). CIPC confirms he is a director, the company itself and their website confirms he is the chairperson. OBP supplies products to the Military Veterinary Institute, which is part of the SA Medical Health Service. Adams is employed by the SA Medical Health Service.

Adams has used two different names and ID number to be registered as a director with CIPC. He was registered as a director of ASA (although since resigned) under a 66 ID number and under the name Harold Adams.

He is also registered with several companies as a director under a 60 ID number and his real name of Jacob Herold Adams. He used the name Harold Adams as part of the court case, which was launched in February to get the court to recognise the 'interim ASA board'.

He signed an affidavit using that name.

So, who is he, what is his name and why does he use two names and two ID numbers?

Adams also serves on the Sport and Recreation Distribution Agency of the National Lottery (NLDTF) and is the president of Boland Athletics.

Boland Athletics, almost without fail, have received lottery funding every year for the last five or more years. This often amounts to more than R1 million per year (provincial bodies are limited to R1 million).

The financial statements for Boland show that it only survives because of Lottery money, otherwise it would be insolvent.

Boland Athletics has been labelled as an "untouchable mafia".

Some of the Boland Athletics board members even reacted angrily to my emails, questioning the Lottery payments.

Do you want me to spoon-feed you? – Richard Stander

Do we really have to entertain this guy's crusade of trying to dig up dirt?? If he wants answers about the lotto let him speak to the Lotto Board. We are not accountable to him. – Michael Fraser

Stellenbosch University filed a complaint against Boland Athletics in 2012 with some very serious allegations of maladministration and are still suing them for money, which is owed.

When asked about the Lottery conflict of interests back in May, Adams responded by saying:

Sorry I am out of town for a few weeks and will forward your questions to the Lotto Chair. The Prof will anyhow be the best person to address these issues.

No reply from the "Prof" and still no-one from the NLDTF is able to confirm which agency adjudicates for the Boland Lottery applications.

There is also a strong allegation that Adams is involved in the R20.8 million Lottery grant to the South African College Principals Organisation (SACPO) for a "sports project" that neither the organisation nor the Lottery can shed any light on.

Adams also sits on the board of the South African Institute of Drug Free Sport (SAIDS) - a board appointed by the Minister of Sport and Recreation. He was reappointed by the Minister despite missing the majority of the SAIDS board meetings the previous year, without apologies.

As for his degree …

8. Dr. Harold J ADAMS APPOINTED FROM 02 DECEMBER 2009 UNTIL 01 DECEMBER 2014	Coloured, Male	Education BSc & BSc (Hon) UWC Aster of Science in Medicine Medical doctor, St Georges, ? Current Employment Management of medical care of athletes ranging in age from youth to senior Management of large teams of officials of all ages Experience Head of Presidential Medical team, CT Principle medical Officer, Internal Medicine, 2 Military Hospital,	Selected taking into account demographics, knowledge, exposure, availability as well as the agency's requirements

Normally one would list a medical degree as MBChB or MD. However, there is a St Georges University that does graduate medical doctors. Also his M asters degree is in Physiology in the Faculty of Medicine at UCT - it was not a Master of Science in Medicine but a Master of Science in Physiology in the UCT Medical Faculty! A little different but easy to spin. -- UCT source

Adams is a close confidante of a number of the top brass at SASCOC and was a "leader" in the attempted coup of ASA, after losing badly in the previous two elections. Now, he's got his reward with the ASA vice- presidency.

Can he wear any more hats?

Yes, one more.

Adams is also a director of the NGO, Brien Holden Vision Institute - the Africa branch which was set up in Durban at the beginning of this year.

When asked for comments via email, Adams did not respond.

In 2005 he was reportedly investigated by the military police in connection with suspected fraud for medicines that he allegedly signed out of the defence force, among other matters. (Mail & Guardian, 18

December 2009)

No charges were brought against him.

Adams is another very slippery customer with friends in high places and when contacted for the first time back in April, he added:

On your crusade on anti-corruption please continue and if I can assist let me know.

Who's he trying to kid?

***

IAAF begins 'fundamental programme of change' to clean up athletics

The IAAF has announced the 21 chairmen and women for commissions and advisory groups it hopes will deliver "a fundamental programme of change" to its administration ... South Africa's Harold Adams heads the medical and anti-doping commission. (Associated Press, 23 March 2016)

If it wasn't in black and white, I would have said, you're joking.

Do these international federations even do proper background checks or is it just a good old fashioned boys club? Was Adams owed a favour from the IAAF?

Meanwhile, SASCOC's complaint to the Press Ombudsman was an Olympic waste of time and public funds.

We have informed SASCOC that the Ombudsman has no jurisdiction over News24 and we won't submit to the processes of the Ombudsman. We have also offered SASCOC a full "right of reply" to the columns we published. We have however decided not to remove the columns as per their request. As mentioned last week, we are waiting on their response, and until such time, we'll refrain from publishing columns on the subject. I expect a response by next week. We'll have more clarity then. It is my view most of what Graeme has written is in the public interest and we'll continue to publish the columns. - Jannie Momberg, Editor-In-Chief news24

The Press Ombudsman sent the following to SASCOC.

When I started to adjudicate Sascoc's complaint against Sport24, I noted that the latter does not see itself as part of our regulatory system and therefore argued that this office does not have the jurisdiction over it. I have also taken note of your argument to the contrary. I then approached Media24 to get clarity on the matter. The fact of the matter is that our system is voluntary, and publications themselves decide if they want to be affiliated to this office or not. If Media24 is satisfied that Sport24 is not part of our system, I have to accept that decision. Therefore, I cannot entertain your complaint. - Johan Retief

No doubt this didn't sit too well with SASCOC and I should have expected what was to come next.

Chapter 8: SASCOC Sues for R21 million

I was at South Africa's premier horse racing event, the Vodacom Durban July on the first weekend of July 2013.

It's a bucket list event for many on the SA sporting and social calendar. I was there with good friends including the former South African cricketer, Richard Snell. We played golf on the Friday at the beautiful Zimbali Country Club and I shot the greenkeeper - in other words, I played very poorly and my form didn't improve with the ponies on the Saturday either.

We were in a small hospitality suite at the races and I kept one eye open for a SASCOC sighting as for years, they've used the Durban July as just another event to wine and dine family, friends and members from the Lottery.

I didn't get a sighting but sure enough, they were there …

Sascoc fat cats live large at the Durban July

Olympic body's bigwigs spend four days at a plush hotel while athletes cry out for funding. South Africa's Olympic bosses spent thousands of rands of the organisation's "limited resources" at the recent Durban July. The SA Sports Confederation and Olympic Committee (Sascoc) claims there are insufficient funds to pay the coaches of top athletes, but the hotel bill alone for their July weekend came to R80 000. The hotel bill shows that Mishen Reddy, son of Sascoc CEO Tubby Reddy, and other guests attended the July at Sascoc's expense. (City Press 21 July 2013)

This was just one of the many stories, which get reported on, then suddenly disappear and get swept under the carpet.

Soon after starting my exposes, I was no longer invited to any sporting events as a journalist and only attended when in my personal capacity.

I was blacklisted!

But I liked it that way.

They owed me nothing and I owed them nothing. It gave me the continued journalistic freedom to expose whoever was doing wrong.

It was a 360 degree turn from being the jovial 'Joffers my boy' character that was on 94.7 Highveld Stereo and Master of Ceremonies at numerous sporting events, many of them at no cost due to their partnerships with the radio station.

MC at the Lions Rugby Union awards dinner in 2011

Joffers,

Just a personal thank you for your efforts and contributions into last night's Player Capping and Awards ceremony for 2011.

We weren't given much time to prepare but without doubt last night's function was one of the highlights in my run with the Lions so far.

You were absolutely brilliant!!!

Thank you for everything Joffers, you created such a wonderful vibe and set the standards for general atmosphere.
Players and guests alike loved every second of having you there last night – THANK YOU THANK YOU THANK YOU.

My gratitude cannot be expressed in more words.

Thank you and kindest regards,

LIONS

Lisa Hack | PA to President Kevin de Klerk / Player Appearances | Tel: 011 402 2960 x182 | Cell: +27827788991
SOUTH OFFICE BLOCK | JOHANNESBURG STADIUM | 124 VAN BEEK ST | NEW DOORNFONTEIN
Fax: 011 402 7913
lisa@glru.co.za
Twitter: Lisa_Hack
www.lionsrugby.co.za

LIONS

Those were the good old days, but the tide was slowly turning and I was swimming against it. Invites to even the Lions rugby and cricket functions dried up. From being top of the guest list for free MC duties, I was now persona non grata.

It hurt but I understood the inner workings of SA sport and how no official or player could be seen to be associating with a whistle-blower.

It would have been career suicide!

On returning to my apartment in Johannesburg on the Sunday afternoon after the Durban July, I noticed a thick paper wad on the table at my entrance. I didn't think much of it at first as no-one apart from my domestic helper had access to my apartment. But before I put my feet up on the couch, I grabbed the large document only to see a big legal stamp on the front.

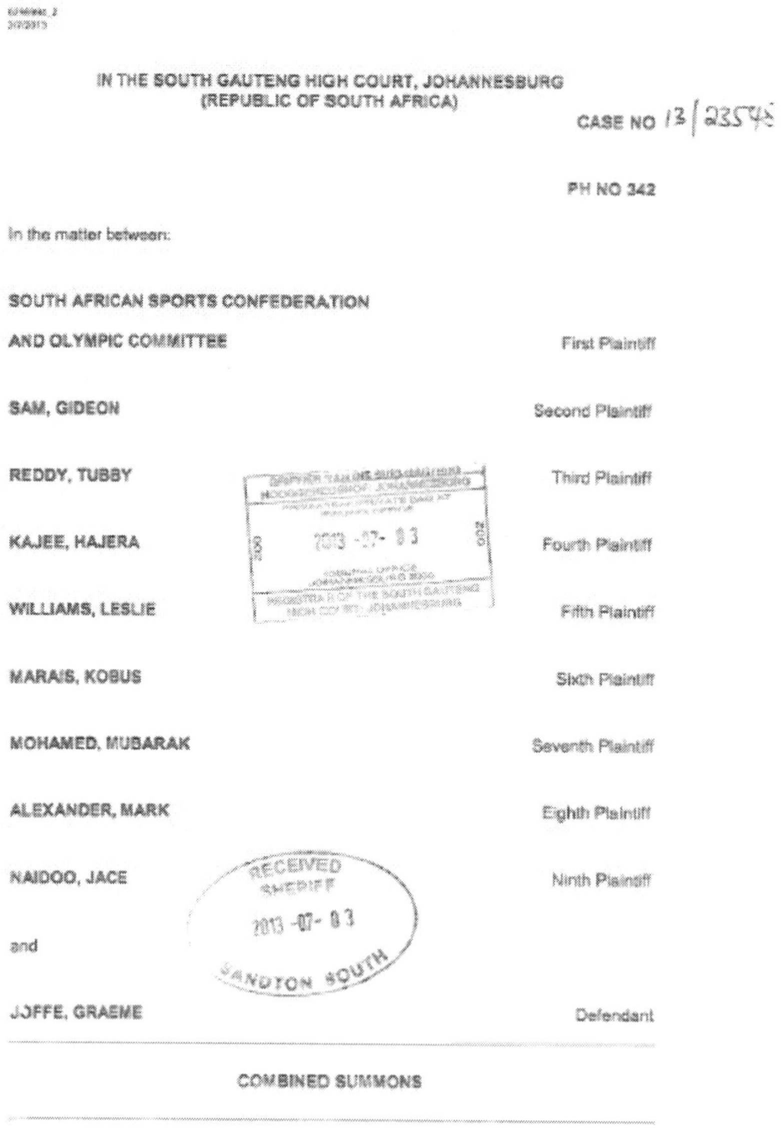

IN THE SOUTH GAUTENG HIGH COURT, JOHANNESBURG
(REPUBLIC OF SOUTH AFRICA)

CASE NO 13/23548

PH NO 342

In the matter between:

SOUTH AFRICAN SPORTS CONFEDERATION AND OLYMPIC COMMITTEE	First Plaintiff
SAM, GIDEON	Second Plaintiff
REDDY, TUBBY	Third Plaintiff
KAJEE, HAJERA	Fourth Plaintiff
WILLIAMS, LESLIE	Fifth Plaintiff
MARAIS, KOBUS	Sixth Plaintiff
MOHAMED, MUBARAK	Seventh Plaintiff
ALEXANDER, MARK	Eighth Plaintiff
NAIDOO, JACE	Ninth Plaintiff

and

JOFFE, GRAEME	Defendant

2013-07-03

RECEIVED
SHERIFF
2013-07-03
SANDTON SOUTH

COMBINED SUMMONS

"Sheriff" was enough to grab my attention.

A combined summons from SASCOC and 8 of their 14 board members suing me for defamation for R21.1 million.

Yes, R21.1 million!

It was a lengthy summons, mapping out each article and attaching a monetary figure next to every statement they deemed to be defamatory, e.g.

In consequence of the aforesaid publication, the plaintiffs have each been injured in their good name, reputation and dignity and have sustained damages in the amount of one hundred thousand rand (R100 000.00) each.

Even one of my tweets made it onto the claim sheet. SASCOC and Tubby's 'good name' had been injured and the tweet made SA legal history.

Litigation: Tweet suit a first for SA
In what is thought to be a first in SA, the SA Sports Confederation and Olympic Committee (Sascoc) and its chief executive Tubby Reddy are suing well-known sports columnist Graeme Joffe for a tweet he made in reference to a sponsorship, writes ***Legalbrief***. They are demanding R500 000 for the tweet as part of a R21.5 defamation claim launched in the South Gauteng High Court. According to ***Rapport***, most of the allegedly defamatory statements at issue were made in Joffe columns published by Sport24 and *The Citizen*, but Joffe is also being sued for this comment made in a tweet. **'Great news re: @Mugg_and_Bean sponsorship of SA men's hockey. Just hope Sascoc don't (get) their 'grubby/tubby' paws on any of the money.'** Paul Jacobson, an attorney spec ialising in litigation and social media, reportedly told the newspaper he was not aware of any prior case where somebody in SA had been sued for a statement made on Twitter.

(Legalbrief LSSA Weekly 76: News for the week of 12 to 19 July 2013)

I was tired from the Durban trip and didn't have the patience to go through all of the claims but what immediately stood out is that only eight of the fourteen SASCOC board members were suing me. Were they suing me in their personal capacity and who would be paying their legal fees?

I knew the answers already.

The six board members not suing were Sam Ramsamy (IOC member), Jerry Segwaba, Motlatsi Keikabile, Emile Smith, Temba Hlasho and Merrill King and as one of them put it.

The reports or articles you write about SASCOC is all true. SASCOC is rotten to its core. They always belief that someone in SASCOC is feeding you information. Always hitting the nail on the head. Tubby Reddy even went to the extreme of putting some SASCOC staff through a lie detector test to see who was leaking the information to me.

The CEO's paranoia was as big as his belly.

I had two big files with all the information and evidence that I had collected over a two year period, hidden under the wash basin in my main bathroom. I quickly went to make sure they were still there as I was concerned that someone else may have had access to my apartment while I was in Durban for the weekend.

The files were there. I breathed a sigh of relief.

I didn't sleep very well that night but maybe I should have known something like this was going to happen. SASCOC never lose, according to Reddy and the Press Ombudsman ruling was a loss.

Now they really wanted to teach me a lesson and silence me.

A number of SASCOC staff members were following all of this closely and I started getting a flow of emails from them, using pseudonyms for fear of retribution.

My name is Candies (pseudonym) and I have been following your article about SASCOC and is true when they say "when credit is due it must be given"well done to all your work that you have done exposing SASCOC for they are really are!!!! A bunch of Greedy-Dictators!!!! Who are there for their own pockets and selfish benefits.

I am one of the SASCOC employees and I pray every day that justice be done to those Greedy Senior managers!!!! I work closely with Tubby and I am more than willing to help you to getting Tubby (that selfish frog) to step down! We recently saw the latest news that Tubby and the rest of his cows wants to sue for defamation!!!! OMG!!! Really? I am sure that they realizing that they found their match! I will provide you with all the information that you require to get justice. Oh-ja by the way, yesterday he travelled to Abujani (sic) (Abidjan) and again as always in a business class with his puppet Mr Gideon Sam to attend the ANOCA meeting. Lord Knows what else they gonna bring. Tubby is a heartless CEO that I've met, doesn't bother to greet people.. what kind of a person are you really? Let me give you a clue of what's really going on @SASCOC. Last year a girl who use to work as a receptionist rescue was fired in order to make way for the new coloured-lady (Monic Tarr) whose has a close relationship with one of the managers (CLIFFORD- COBERS) one of Tubby's best Buddies. They very same women whose supposed to answer phone was designated to attend Road-Shows and a month later sent to attend Wits Management Course along with the other colleges who have been in a waiting list for years and she's only 5months old????? Then the tale goes on, currently SASCOC is experiencing financial crisis and is unable to pay their suppliers and the poor athletes!!!! And guess what?? They were able to fit in the budget of attending the Durban July last week, booking into luxurious hotel from Thursday -Sunday and you can't pay the Poor-Athletes??? Management were told to pay for their own flights if they want to attend the Durban-July Function but wow the Coloured woman was taken along!!! You tell me why????

Let's go to salaries, I've recently realized that the white staff is paid well better off compared to the poor black!!! If we were to review salary figure you will be shocked. SASCOC ship is sinking slowly buy sure, as long as those greedy man are still running that empire. corruption is still going to be our daily food. I work at SASCOC and the staff honestly hate Tubby, he is a heartless, greedy frog who's very racist and clueless about his work.

Every time we see your article, we thank God for all the strength you have to tell the truth. Two months back we were ordered to take a lie-dictator test in order to establish as to whose linking the info to the media. One staff member was suspended (DUMISANE MTWA) because his results came positive. I will be more than happy if you publish my email but keep my identity. Tubby checks our private phone, work phone, emails and everything!!!! Help us from this greedy-selfish man!!!!! (sic) (11 July 2013)

So Graeme, in just June 2013, Mr Tubby Reddy has flown to Russia, New York and Lausanne. What a waste of money. Is he doing any real work? And wait for this, all the office staff were subjected to polygraph tests to check who was leaking information to Joffe! There's a lot of paranoia around."- Sipho Gumede (pseudonym) (18 June 2013)

Sorry for the belated response- Tubby was in HK in June on holiday - but apparently paid for by SASCOC! Hows that. Confirm this. Yes, he did subject all staff to polygraph tests - and suspend one of them Dumisani. Two other polygraphs were suspicious. Staff at SASCOC very unhappy - except a few, such as his Office Manager Jean Kelly who flies with him all over SA and the World. Which CEO of a sports organisation travels with his office manager - not cricket, soccer and rugby. Is there more to it.

Does Jean Kelly have a relationship with Tubby? Someone must request all Tubbys overseas trips, who travelled with him and what it costs - I am sure it runs into millions. Need a forensic audit. He gets a stipend for every trip - how much is that. Does he use the stipend to pay for his meals or his SASCOC credit card. How much has his stipend been for the last few years.

Look at how tubby advances volleyball people in Sascoc - Vinesh Maharaj is the second in charge and Tubby' right hand man and the finance manager (who hides the crap). Another volleyball mate of Tubby is Dr Kevin Subban who gets to go to all the prized games as Chief Medical Officer with none others being considered. He is also groomed to go to Brazil for the Olympics after being CMO at London. He went to the World Games in Colombia as CMO - and took his wife with (not sure who paid). With all the talk of transformation SA has never had a black CMO at the Olympic Games! Tubbys hit men at Board level are Mubarak Mohamed and Sam Ramsamy. Gideon as president is compromised because of his links to corruption. Also what are they paying (Highbury) Safika, and when does the contract come up for renewal (or tender)? Their case against you will go nowhere - but use it to extract maximum information - which i am sure will be damning. Good luck and keep up the good work. They are threatened simply because you reveal the truth. (sic) - Sipho Gumede (29 August 2013)

If it was not for the sake of approaching pension we would have long left this place called SASCOC. We do not look forward to go to work each day. We cannot wait for the Games to start so Mr CEO can go and rest and we do our jobs normally. Just last week we were asked to submit our laptops email password again we are not trusted. This place is in shambles we are happy for the work that you do keep it up. Please check how was Ms.Tarr employed as a Coordinator at our CEO office without qualifications. She was our receptionist for just few months and even there she got the job through some friend of the CEO who is one of our managers. Please hide my identity as I do not want to lose my Job but working for SASCOC is just a nightmare. Please continue to ask those serious questions as to who paid for Vinesh knee operation in Cape Town the Accommodation and Flight. While he was there for a personal matter not SASCOC. We always follow your stories but we remain in fear. " (sic) – Saddened SASCOC employee (21 June 2014)

It took a few days for me to get my head around the summons but this was perhaps my chance to really expose the filth in SA sport.

SASCOC had gotten the big shot media lawyer, Dario Milo to represent them in the case. Milo represents a number of the big media groups including Naspers who own the likes of Sport24, SuperSport and M-Net. Needless to say, it was my exposes published on Sport24 that were getting under SASCOC's skin.

Milo also openly fights for press freedom. Now, he was taking on a member of the media, who SASCOC wanted to silence.

Conflict of interests?

SASCOC sues journo for R21.1m

Johannesburg - The SA Sports Confederation and Olympic Committee (Sascoc) has instituted a defamation claim of R21.1 million against sports journalist Graeme Joffe in the High Court in Johannesburg, Beeld reported on Friday. The court documents, filed on July 3, argued that 23 of Joffe's sports columns, written for, among others, Media24, were defamatory, and that Joffe had accused the organisation of unethical and illegal conduct. (sport24, 12 July 2013)

Sport24 had run for cover.

It falls under the umbrella of Media24, which is the print media arm of the South African media company, Naspers. Naspers is a broad-based multinational internet and media group, offering services in more than 130 countries.

With a market capitalisation of over $66 billion, it is the largest company in Africa and the 7th largest Internet company in the world. - (Wikipedia, December 2015)

SASCOC and their consultant/s were cunning to sue me in my personal capacity. Naspers had deep pockets and that wouldn't have worked.

The lawsuit was to try and cripple me financially as well.

Naspers were never going to get involved in my fight. Through SuperSport, they are in bed with the Sports Ministry and SASCOC and through Multichoice (South Africa's leading video entertainment and internet company) they were bed fellows with the Gupta family of state capture and corruption fame.

It's a very cosy relationship and not difficult to join all the dots courtesy of google and twitter.

Imtiaz Patel had already taken a disliking to me back in 2002 when at the end of a work related meeting that I had requested after being 'blocked' from SuperSport production work, he told me …

You Jews know what to f---ing do.

I left it there but you never forget.

At the same meeting, he also ranted about Dr Ali Bacher, who he felt had previously done him in for a top job at Cricket SA. Amazing, how that relationship all turned around as Bacher got some plum contract work with SuperSport for a series called, "Ali Bacher in conversation with …"

Presenters at SuperSport will also tell you how Patel would often say, 'there are too many f…..g white guys around here'.

Even if said in jest, it's racist and not the kind of person I'd want to associate with either. But Patel had associated himself with some very well connected people including one of the most powerful men in SA sport, Dr Irvin Khoza.

I knew Naspers were going to wipe their hands clean of my legal matter and in a conference call with Jannie Momberg, he said:

We won't be able to assist you in your case against SASCOC as you are not a paid employee of Media24.

I had gotten into an agreement with sport24 whereby I would write weekly columns for them in lieu of a punt for my new radio talk show, SportsFire. I had started something and wanted to keep on exposing the truth.

Sport24 had a big readership but I was no longer going to do it for nothing. Remuneration?

Unfortunately, I have already exhausted my correspondent budget for the current financial year. I really appreciate the time and effort invested in all the columns received. Wishing you all the best with your court case – should it come to that – with SASCOC. - Garrin Lambley, 21 August 2013

It was going to be a long road ahead.

The comments from the general public on news24.com gave me some comfort but I still felt very alone in this fight, very alone.

Do these idiots think that we have forgot them flying first class to the Olympic Games while our disabled athletes had to suffer in cattle class? I hope Mr Joffe drop his evidence in court then it will make interesting reading to see how these gravy trainers try to explain themselves out of the Zuma.- Frans van der Merwe

Good for you Joffers! Great columns and great radio show. We need more journos like you.- Tracy Baard

Sascoc, Sam & Reddy are incompetent administrators who are now on the offensive by laying defamatory charges. - Nathan Govender

At least now the courts will also hear how useless this bunch really are-Joffers, time for counterclaim! - Derrick Pentz

Maybe this is just what is needed for the truth to come out. I am sure Sascoc has sued with the hope that Joffers would apologise and that the truth would then be hidden. Go Joffers, I am sure everyone will back you on this one. - Arnaud Malherbe

Like you, Andre, I hope Graeme will call SASCOC's bluff and that the whole can of worms will be opened in court. I also hope Joffers will get not just public support but financial support from Media24. It costs a helluva lot to defend yourself in a court case like this. - Jeremy Thorpe

Go for it Joffers. Only in SA could the CEO of the major sports association be called 'Tubby'. Overseas they have retired stars like Seb Coe involved in administration, we get Tubby and Sam. Politics. - Freddie Miller

Like useless administrators, they turn to the courts every time they mess and want to always use their bullying tactics to scare off journalist. GJ is my man, expose the culprits. We South African are now really gatvol (fed up) with all the inefficiencies and corruption. You go my man. Joffe for President.- Sagren Pillay

Go Joffers. There is no way you can harm tubby and sam's " reputation." After all the harm they have done, everything you say is actually a compliment. I would love this to go to court and let those parasites explain themselves under oath. But like the zuma/Zapiro farce, they will chicken out. So, publish away and tell the truth while you still can.- Neil Ross

*Graeme, make sure that all your legal applications and so forth, include a *with costs* clause, so you can try and recover a portion of your legal expenses. How unfortunate that telling the truth is going to cost you a fortune in legal expenses. Massive misuse of the court's time and resources.- Sarah Stanton*

I'm surprised Tubby and Sam want all their dirty laundry aired. Under oath. Have fun Mr Joffe. – Chris Whittaker

Not sure what the Minister is waiting for before he removes these whole lot because they are definitely harming our sports, they behave like they are the alpha and omega of sports. Its time they give way for other sports administrators to bring better and refreshed ideas, I mean Sam Ramsamy have been in this all his life. Does he want to stay on until he goes to his grave! Its certainly clear they want to hang on because of the financial benefits that goes with it not because of their love of sports! This is clearly an intimidation from their side so he can stop writing anything about them so I would go ahead and defend your case and stance! We are tired of being fed garbage in this country, they must be exposed and I am hoping in another 6 months they will be deposed as well! - Avhashoni Ramikosi

A R21m claim for defamation is just ridiculous. SA courts do not make such awards and Sascoc's lawyers must know this. It is a clear attempt to intimidate Joffe and litigate him into poverty by forcing him to incur massive legal costs defending a R22m claim. Whose money is Sascoc et al using to litigate? Why was this not simply referred to the press ombud? Sounds like bullying to me. - Kevin Schaafsma

21m it's a lot of money, what's wrong for being told the truth? Even President JZ has dropped all the charges against the journalist. Nobody in the board of sascoc will ever saying against reddy because they getting monthly salaries even though they having their full time jobs elsewere.(sic) - Vincent Tseka

I think Graham is vindicated after the nauseating expenditure at the july was publicised. How can anybody expect that nobody will say something about that We are a sports federation SARL(south african Rugby league) with full international recognition and just returned from the RL student world cup beating Ireland and Scotland Our national team is called the Rhino`s but yet Sascoc will not give us recognition they show such lack of knowledge they want want us to be part of SARU . the sport codes have been seperate for 100 years plus They hide behind all sorts of reasons why we cannot get affiliation, so I say Graham pse do not stop and expose the megalomaniacs who believe they are bigger than the sport. (sic) - Jacey Strauss

Please can we have this court-case televised on the Oscar Pistorius Trial channel so that the whole world can see exactly what SASCOC is all about and why Our athletes are no longer able to compete on the world stage!! - Michelle Vintcent

I would loved nothing more than just to be on that witness stand in court to air all the SASCOC dirty laundry.

SA sport needed it but Tubby and company were never going to allow that to happen.

No-one pushed me into this fight. I had to put on my big boy pants and fight fire with fire. I was now more determined than ever to expose these fat cats but would have to do it using other platforms and social media.

My personal digital platform www.sportsfire.co.za was born.

Chapter 9: By George, More Legal Threats

Through my employment with 94.7 Highveld Stereo (Primedia), I was invited by the CEO of Megapro (Primedia Sport), George Rautenbach to go with them to the 2007 Currie Cup final in Bloemfontein.

The Currie Cup is South Africa's premier domestic rugby competition. Also on the invite list was our breakfast radio show host, Jeremy Mansfield and the Amalgamated Banks of South Africa (ABSA) deputy chief executive at the time, Louis von Zeuner.

ABSA were the title sponsors of the Currie Cup. It was VIP treatment, which included a chartered jet from Johannesburg to Bloemfontein.

Jeremy and myself captured on SuperSport at 2007 Currie Cup final

The Lions led 18-6 with 15 minutes to go, only to lose the game 20-18 with Willem de Waal kicking the winning conversion from the corner.

Heartbreak for us diehard Lions fans.

It was still a great trip and I think we got back to Johannesburg somewhere around 3am on the Sunday. George was certainly the host with the most but hidden was a host of dirty connections and dealings.

Rautenbach, a former rugby player had forged a very close relationship with SA Rugby vice-president and SASCOC board member, Mark Alexander. In August 2014, I was given a big scoop about this relationship and started to dig.

It was explosive information from very good, reliable sources including employees from both SA Rugby and Megapro.

Alexander was getting millions in kickbacks from Megapro/Primedia Sport for the renewal of a SA

Rugby (SARU) commercial contract.

But again, all I got was a brick wall of denials.

I am the current chairman of Sanzar. I don't receive commissions or any other perks from anyone. – Mark Alexander

Primedia Sport was the holding company for five subsidiary brands including Megapro Marketing which was the appointed commercial agent for SA Rugby, provincial rugby, cricket unions and the South African Football Association. Megapro also provides access to sporting audiences as well as sponsorship and advertising.

The Chief executive Officer of Primedia Group Limited was Kuben Pillay and he denied knowing anything about the kickbacks.

You may not be aware that we sold all the Primedia Sport businesses, including Megapro, some time ago to a consortium led by the founding shareholder, George Rautenbach. If your investigation relates to allegations during the period of our partnership with Mr Rautenbach, neither I nor the Primedia Board, including its independent audit committee, were ever made aware of such allegations in any of your audits. As as previous employee of Primedia, and having worked under my tenure as CEO, you would know that I would never have condoned such alleged conduct if brought to my attention in any audit review. - Kuben Pillay

Pillay was in a hurry to squash this story from getting out and copied his financial director in on our email correspondence. He wanted a meeting the next morning. It was going to be very strange to go back into the Primedia building where I had spent seven very good years with 94.7 but I had to expose the truth.

Kuben again denied knowing anything about the kickback or the red flag in the financials audited by Delloite's but said he would get the company CFO to look into it. The meeting was more of a fishing expedition and I wasn't taking the bait.

I didn't get to meet the CFO or receive a call from him.

That same evening, I received several cellphone text messages from Kuben, again denying any knowledge of the kickbacks and making it as though, they were as clean as a whistle.

I knew otherwise and published my expose on 16 September 2014.

SA Rugby on the Ropes
16 September 2014

If SA Rugby (SARU) was a boxer, they would already be KO'd but the dirty rugby administration is somehow managing to avoid the big punches.

However, they may not survive this latest barrage.

In April 2010, SARU renewed a commercial contract with Megapro.

I'm delighted to confirm that our good friends at Megapro have been reappointed as our exclusive commercial agents, said Mr Oregan Hoskins, President of SARU.

Mr Kuben Pillay, Chief Executive Officer, Primedia Group – the majority shareholders of Megapro – said the agency would continue to offer the best quality service to all SARU sponsors while seeking out new sponsors whose strategic marketing objectives align with some of the most powerful sporting properties in South Africa.

One small problem - how did Megapro get the deal done and beat their competitors?

It now emerges that SARU deputy president and Chairman of SANZAR, Mark Alexander was allegedly promised R500,000 per year of the five year contract.

A "kick-back" of R2.5 million?

The first payment of which went through Sedgars, a supplier to a number of SA sporting federations, including the South African Sports Confederation and Olympic Committee (SASCOC).

Alexander is also a well-protected and well connected board member of SASCOC.

Sedgars passed us from their accounts department to the finance manager and finally onto the CEO, Mr Dockrat, who said his uncle was the only one who may know about this payment but he was overseas for the next two and half weeks.

Hoskins was initially interested in the details but when asked by SportsFire if he knew about the alleged kick- back, our correspondence died.

Primedia sold their shares in Megapro back to the consortium in early 2013.

The decision taken by the Primedia Board to dispose of the Sport portfolio is consistent with the strategic positioning over the last few years as Africa's premier advertising, media and entertainment company. - Kuben Pillay

Alexander has not responded to emails from Sunday and Monday.

But when asked back in August if he had ever received a commission or any payment, any benefit or perk from Megapro?

Alexander replied: "Please deal with Andy our media person."

SARU's media person, Andy Colquhoun has since told me I'd be "wasting my time" by emailing him.

Why is SARU so silent?

It's like an unwritten policy of: "You look after me and I'll look after you."

SARU's silence with the Jurie Roux affair is also deafening.

Extending the contract of a CEO, who's under a Hawks investigation for allegedly misappropriating

R34 million while at Stellenbosch University is like winning 34 tight-heads in one game.

It's just not possible. Roux should at the very least be on gardening leave.

But instead he's still shovelling around in an office that should be closed for a good old fashioned house cleaning.

SA Rugby is so full of dirt.

Should the stakeholders really trust SARU with R689 million group revenue, which yielded a profit of just R6.2 million for the year end 31 December 2012?

A full forensic audit of SARU should have happened yesterday.

***

Kuben was obviously not happy with the expose.

Further in my sms to you last night, once your investigation is more conclusive on the alleged Megapro link, we will appreciate the info for our own internal processes. I will not allow Primedia's good name and that of its shareholders to be tainted by any conduct contrary to our core values.

But I had it on good authority that the irregular payments were flagged by the auditors and that Kuben and the Financial Director would have been fully aware of them.

And George Rautenbach wasn't happy to see the published truth either.

You choose to single out Sedgars and SA Rugby in an endeavour to advance your own cause. Your assertions in this regard are defamatory, without foundation, devoid of truth and denied.

Of course, SA Rugby (SARU) wouldn't have anything to say. They had been caught with their pants down again.

Sail were one of the companies that wanted to tender for the commercial contract but didn't get a chance. In a letter addressed to SARU president, Oregan Hoskins, one of the Sail directors, John Newbury stated:

It is with great disappointment that I have learnt that SARU has awarded the contract for the SARU sponsorship and commercialisation activities to Megapro, without (in our opinion) following the correct process. We were informed (by Andy Marinos) that the business would be put out to tender and to our utter dismay this was not the case. It is thus our opinion that the minimum of equity in the process was not followed and that furthermore, the whole aspect of good corporate governance was ignored. I am further alarmed to learn that the contract was awarded just prior to the election process for the new Office Bearers of SARU being appointed. It surprises me that this important matter was not held over for a few days to get the views of the newly elected officials. I cannot understand the motive for rushing the awarding of the contract through before the meeting. As far as I am aware there were no deadlines to meet in this regard? You as a lawyer are well versed as to the demands in South Africa for good corporate governance and total transparency in your dealings. Yet this does not appear to be the way SARU runs its business. (21 May 2010)

SARU and Megapro had a meeting a month prior in which Hoskins had told them they would not get the renewal and it needed to go to tender.

Two of my sources were in that meeting but a couple golden handshakes later …

SARU renew with MegaPro

The South African Rugby Union (SARU) announced on Tuesday the renewal of its contract with South Africa's leading sport marketing agency, MEGAPRO Marketing. MEGAPRO has been reappointed as the official, exclusive commercial agent to SARU for the next five years. (sport24, 13 April 2010)

Though both parties were reluctant to put a figure on the deal, it will no doubt run into millions of rands (Sowetan, 15 April 2010)

Sedgars weren't amused by the SA Rugby expose either and I received a legal threat from them as well.

I had spoken to an acquaintance about my article regarding the Sedgars involvement and I'll never forget his words:

Just be careful, they are very well connected. I am a supplier of theirs and get paid cash by them in shoe boxes…

A few days later, I received a call from Rautenbach saying the Sedgars lawyer was 'over-reacting and they won't be taking any action'.

The legal threat eventually passed but not after a couple meetings with George, which he had requested.

Before my first meeting with George, I thought it would be good to get a comment on the matter from SANZAR (South Africa, New Zealand and Australia Rugby) as Mark Alexander was the chairman of the body.

Greg Peters was the SANZAR Chief Executive Officer.

I have no comment on this.

The good old rugby boys club had obviously closed ranks.

Furthermore, Megapro had also made a 'gift payment' with funds from another company to the then president of SA Football, Kirsten Nemantandani which he wouldn't confirm or deny in writing.

Thank you for your email on the above matter. I will give you a call, are you able to give me a hint on which commercial partner it is perhaps. Does this appear on our audited financial statement?

More questions than answers and my call never shed more light on the matter – just a denial. It was another one of those tough calls as I liked Kirsten as a person and initially thought he was good for SA football.

I had all my ducks in a row ahead of my first face-to-face meeting with George at Tashas Restaurant in

Morningside, Johannesburg. I was a little nervous. George was a former provincial rugby player and had a big presence.

I wasn't sure how this was going to turn out and would someone be waiting for me in the car park?

He started off by telling me, I was isolating myself and that I wasn't going to be able to change anything.

This is how things are done in SA.

He had already spoken to all the "connected" parties as well as Rob Fleming from the exposed Sports Trust who was a mutual acquaintance.

I was making so many enemies and what happened to the old Joffers that everyone used to love?

Then the fishing started …

How much did I know and what evidence did I have?

I kept the cards close to my chest, letting on to just a little and from a position of strength, George was now a lot more circumspect.

So, what was the payment for R500 000 to Sedgars for?

George told me that SuperSport CEO, Imtiaz Patel had told him to give back to SA sport and by giving the funds to Sedgars, they would then look after a development team with kit and equipment.

What happened after the payment and which team was the beneficiary? George didn't have the answers.

He told me to reach out to Imtiaz as he was willing to have a cup of tea.

That meeting was never going to happen (with our history) and I had already been informed by a mutual friend, who told me Imtiaz had called him to tell me that I should fall back into line with mainstream media.

George and I chatted for over an hour and a half (longer than expected) and while we were sitting there, his phone rang.

Guess who?

Imtiaz Patel to obviously find out how the meeting went. There was angst.

As we were leaving Tashas, George asked me about the email I had sent to Greg Peters at SANZAR. They had all spoken. Fortunately, there was no-one waiting for me in the car park or none that I know of.

The following day, I received a text message via a third party, which originated from a former Megapro employee.

George told some Megapro staff that he and I had met. Everything was cleared up and that I left the meeting in tears because I have no job and struggling to make a living.

Some nice big porky pies!

24 September 2014: I received a text message from John van Aardweg (a former Megapro employee) saying*:*

Go you good thing Joffers on the MegaPro skulduggery!!Just be sure to watch your back with Rautenbach. When Kelvin (Watt) and I left MegaPro he had us followed. Especially now that you've got dirt on him.

Kelvin Watt was a mutual friend and I rented office space from him in Johannesburg for a number of years. He had become very close to the sports administrators especially in cricket and rugby and his business partner, Eric Ichikowitz was very well connected to the very top of SA sport.

I knew Eric fairly well.

While investigating the misuse and misappropriation of Lottery funds, I picked up on a payment of R2 million to the Sporting Frontiers Africa account for Netball SA.

62063 Netball SA (a/c NSA Sporting Frontiers Africa) 2 000 000

Only because it was a third-party payment did it raise a red flag.

I remembered that Kelvin had a company called Sporting Frontiers and one of his employees confirmed:

We used to have an arm called 'Sporting Frontiers Africa' in the early days 2003/2004 and Netball SA was a client then but not sure if it got dissolved or what happened to it, once we became Frontiers Group Africa.

Kelvin denied any knowledge of the company and payment.

Our business is Frontiers Sport+Entertainement

Whatever happened then to your business arm, "Sporting Frontiers Africa"?

When we bought out Sporting Frontiers from the UK in 2004 we had to change the name, so that company became Kaelo.

So, the company did actually exist.

The name Richard Glover had been copied into the correspondence as he was now the MD of Frontiers Sport and Entertainment after being the Commercial Manager of Cricket South Africa (CSA).

Glover resigned from his CSA position at the beginning of January 2012.

It was sudden and unexpected after just 18 months in the job.

We have checked with CIPRO and there is no registered company in SA called Sporting Frontiers Africa currently. So, unless there is a shell company operating as Sporting Frontiers Africa, no actual company exists by that name. Very odd. - Kelvin Watt

Very odd indeed!

When Netball SA first received an NLDTF grant, they provided us with a cheque with the name, Netball South Africa – Sporting Frontiers Africa and account number ending in ...934. Our finance department created a beneficiary profile in this name. This is the same account number as the account number given to us by NSA in June 2013 before they received their last payment. The account now goes as Netball South Africa. Our finance department will amend the profile to reflect Netball South Africa. Netball South Africa can independently confirm the account into which their last grant was paid. – Sershan Naidoo, National Lotteries Board

Whilst the emails were going back and forth, I received a call from Kelvin's business partner, Eric Itchikowitz, who was on a business trip up in Africa.

The gist of his call was to ask me to please sit down around a table with Kelvin to sort out these issues as we are all friends.

That meeting didn't happen and I left it there, kind of but I did expose the irregular Lottery payment.

I had no further contact with them until a mutual friend suggested a meeting with Eric towards the end of 2014. We had lunch at an Italian restaurant in Woodmead, Johannesburg and I was on the receiving end of lots of questions.

Who was funding me, who was backing me and who was feeding me all the information?

Eric was more concerned about rugby. He added that I was taking on some dangerous people and would be all on my own if the shit hits the fan. We then spoke about certain individuals in SA Rugby and he showed me a text message from Mark Alexander, requesting an iPad for one of his kids.

Eric even remarked what a "take" Alexander was.

It was a very unproductive meeting.

Eric was fishing and it would be our last communication, despite my email thanking him for the lunch but his name and business interests came up again soon enough.

Ivor Ichikowitz, 48, founder and executive head of the Paramout group, Africa's biggest weapons manufacturer, enjoys close ties with President Jacob Zuma and several other senior African National Congress members. His brother, Eric, 44, confirmed to Beeld that Mayweather was entertained in January at the Molori Safari lodge, situated in the Madikwe Game Reserve, and that the family also paid for his flights. According to Eric, the family did not pay for Mayweather and his entourage's flights to and from the United States. He also denied that Mbalula had used their company Fortune Air's Boeing 727-200 to fly to the United States. - (Netwerk24, 8 May 2015)

Eric had also been very involved with the Guma Groups failed business partnership with the Golden

Lions Rugby Union (GLRU) which ended very acrimoniously in 2011.

In December 2010, GLRU chairman, Robert Gumede, Eric Itchikowitz and Mark Alexander went to the UK to meet with Brian Mujati who was playing in the English Premiership and who the Lions wanted to re-sign.

Obviously, Eric didn't tell me about that little trip at our lunch meeting.

Alexander was their "guest".

There was lots of the blame game as to why the business partnership didn't work but GLRU president, Kevin de Klerk stood his ground.

Fortunately for the Lions, MTN signed a lucrative three-year sponsorship deal with the union at the beginning of 2011, which would save them from bankruptcy.

Kevin seemed like a straight shooter and was in the process of turning the Lions around.

We had a couple meetings, where he shared information with me about the failed partnership and the poor treatment the GLRU was getting from SA Rugby post their relegation from Super Rugby. There was plenty dirt flying around and Alexander was angling for the SARU presidency in 2014.

There was a strong group backing de Klerk for that position and Kevin had a folder with background checks on Alexander.

Mark Alexander had enough company directorships to field two rugby teams with a scrum of voluntary liquidations.

Among his company directorships were: Agecome, Enterprise Bsuiness Technologies, Gulf Petro SA, MJM Financial Services, Tarabowo Trading, Dental Risk Underwriting Managers, SASCOC, Golden Lions Rugby Union, Eastern Province Rugby, Springbok Supporters Club, Ellis Park World of Sports, HunkyDory Investments, Armor Imaging Supplies SA, Labat Business Solutions and Zebra Diamond Corporation.

Kevin de Klerk would call me now and again to see how I was doing and to compliment my work.

Joffers, loved your story this morning.

He would often repeat he wasn't being paid for the job he was doing at the Lions. I didn't think for one minute that he was playing me.

When I broke the Alexander/Megapro "kickback" story, Kevin called to congratulate me, saying it was no surprise how Megapro was wheeling and dealing as he had known George for a long time. In the days after, I received a number of calls from Kevin. He wanted the hard evidence of the Alexander kickbacks from me to give to Hoskins.

We also had a coffee meeting on a Saturday morning in Fourways, Johannesburg and I had a gut feeling that something wasn't right. My immediate intuition was that George knew of my good relationship with Kevin and was using him to see how much evidence I had.

I should have known better.

Megapro Extends Commercial Agency Agreement With Lions Rugby

Megapro is pleased to announce the renewal of their commercial agency agreement with Ellis Park Stadium. This agreement sees Megapro extend its long standing association with the Golden Lions Rugby Union for a further 5 year period. Megapro will oversee sponsorship sales and management for the Lions for both the Absa Currie Cup and Vodacom Super Rugby teams. This also includes stadium advertising and the supply of LED digital adscroll for all competitions. – (Megapro, 18 August 2015)

And as soon as the MTN sponsorship deal was done at the end of 2014, Megapro had brokered the deal for Emirates Airlines to take over.

George and Kevin were tight from their playing days and now through business. I felt stupid to have trusted Kevin who even called me for PR advice before the former Lions coach, John Mitchell was going to release his tell-all book, “Mitch: The Real Story”. There was no love lost between Kevin and John.

I played golf with John during a corporate day at Randpark in Johannesburg after his book was released and was Master of Ceremonies for his fundraiser in Cape Town a couple months later.

With John Mitchell, Birgitte Willers and Gavin Rich (Author of Mitch: The Real Story)

John Mitchell was appointed head coach of the USA Eagles in January 2015 and in a passing shot was quoted as saying:

The Lions situation was orchestrated. I was basically cleared of all 28 allegations and clearly Oregan Hoskins and Kevin de Klerk have still got a vendetta against me here in South Africa. So, my expertise isn't warranted. – John Mitchell

Megapro had infiltrated the SA sports industry (rugby, cricket, soccer and horse racing) and had also signed a five year deal with SASCOC in 2012.

SASCOC inks five-year deal with Megapro Marketing

Under terms of the agreement, financial details of which were not released, Megapro will work alongside SASCOC to further commercialise the South Africa's national governing body for high-performance sport, specifically with regards to the Team SA Olympic platform that the organisation houses. (SportsPro, 13 June 2012)

SASCOC with an annual staff salary of over R15 million had now conveniently outsourced their media, public relations and commercialization for sponsorship.

It's the easy way to get money out with fewer checks and balances.

The Department of Sport and Recreation works on the same irregular system and the Sports Minister was caught out in more lies after he said tax-payers money was not used to fund the visit of American boxing great, Floyd Mayweather.

It was indeed.

Netwerk24 found that R475 950 was paid to Frontier Sport under the disguise of marketing. The same company Eric Itchikowitz and Kelvin Watt were involved in.

When I approached Kelvin on the subject back in January 2014, he denied they received any payment.

Did you guys tender for it?

Tender to whom? Our Group were part of bringing him out here together with a number of other commercial partners who contributed cash and in-kind to the project.

If yes, who were the other companies that tendered? *N/A* Were you paid a fee for the event? *No*

If yes, were you paid by Dept. of Sport and Rec or the Sports Trust? *No*

Where did the proceeds from the dinner go to? *There were no proceeds from the dinner. The costs of the dinner were kindly sponsored by Emperors Palace. The proceeds from the auction at the dinner are being made available to purchase equipment and other refurbishments for the boxing gym in Dube.*

I wonder if the gym in Dube (Soweto), the home of the late SA boxing legend, Jacob 'Baby Jake' Matlala ever saw any of the proceeds?

Money, Secrets and Low Blows As Mayweather Lands In Africa

Floyd Mayweather Jr, the undefeated pugilist from the United States, was treated like a king in South Africa, amid questions over who paid for him and his 16-strong entourage to be here "We did not cough up a cent for the visit of Mayweather. The state can't afford to pay his demands. The trip was sponsored by someone [whose name] I can't disclose in the media," says Mbalula's spokesman, Paena Galane. (Forbes Africa, 1 March 2014)

SA sport is on the ropes due in large to a number of individuals and their companies who are living off corrupt political connections.

17 August 2016 – Oregan Hoskins steps down as SARU president and Mark Alexander takes over as acting president.

In recent months, there had also been a deepening power struggle in SARU's corridors between Hoskins and the CEO Jurie Roux; in early March the latter significantly entrenched his position when he got the unconditional support of his employers, plus a SASCOC nod, despite ongoing publicity surrounding allegations of funds mismanagement during Roux's time in administration at Stellenbosch University. Alexander is not without his own stormy waters in the public eye – he has been accused by former Sport24 columnist and SuperSport and CNN presenter Graeme Joffe of having received kickbacks for the landing of a SARU commercial contract renewal. Joffe also wrote earlier this year, even while Hoskins was still at SARU's helm: "Alexander is close to Mbalula through his SASCOC and Lottery links and was chairman of the Durban 2022 Commonwealth (Games) bid on SARU time ... and is now angling for the SARU presidency." (Sport24, 18 August 2016)

As I predicted …

On 27 October 2016, Mark Alexander was elected as president unopposed. Francois Davids the new deputy president and Jurie Roux remained the CEO.

It was a move well-orchestrated by SARU to keep the dirty hands in power and what's more, Alexander was elected to the World Rugby's Executive Council in November 2018.

Not another boys club!

The Megapro kickback scandal would continue to grow. Alexander and Nemantandani were by no means the only secret beneficiaries.

Rautenbach bought lots of influential people with cash!

Chapter 10: Commonwealth Games

The Commonwealth Games are an international multi-sport event involving athletes from the Commonwealth of Nations. The event was first held in 1930, and has taken place every four years since then. Although there are currently 53 members of the Commonwealth of Nations, 71 teams currently participate in the Commonwealth Games, as a number of dependent territories compete under their own flags. The four Home Nations of the United Kingdom—England, Scotland, Wales, and Northern Ireland also send separate teams. (Wikipedia)

South Africa is one of the 53 members and SASCOC is responsible for the preparation and presentation of TeamSA at the Commonwealth Games.

SA's Commonwealth Games – the real story
3 August 2014

It doesn't matter how much SASCOC's expensive, 'buddy, buddy' public relations company spins it, South Africa has once again under achieved at the 2014 Commonwealth Games in Glasgow.

I'm not for one minute blaming any of the athletes who all gave 120% in an effort to win medals but one needs to look at the facts.

Commonwealth Medals table:	2002	2006	2010	2014
SA medals	46	38	33	40
Winning country	207	224	177	174

Should we be satisfied with 40 medals after getting 46 back in 2002? SASCOC predicted 43 medals for the 2014 Commonwealth Games in Glasgow. 43 was a very cautious estimate, considering they didn't want to expose themselves as they did with the London Olympics, when they predicted 12 medals and we got six.

And I can assure you, SASCOC didn't factor in seven lawn bowls medals in Glasgow in their tally of 43.

What an unbelievable achievement from the SA bowlers, in a sport that survives on scraps when it comes to funding.

So, take away the seven bowls medals and Chad le Clos's remarkable seven swimming medals and what are you left with? It is 26 medals from 118 athletes (excluding the team sports), who SASCOC selected on the criteria that they were ranked top 5 in the Commonwealth and medal potential.

We came here for medals, not to run around in the streets of Glasgow. - SASCOC president, Gideon Sam

Perhaps, that's why we didn't have any marathon runners at the Games.

If the Australian winner of the men's marathon was South African, he wouldn't have gone to the Games on SASCOC's selection criteria. That's how wrong they've got it. SA's Lusapho April, who finished third in the New York City marathon in 2013 wasn't even asked by SASCOC or Athletics SA (ASA) if he was available for the Commonwealth Games.

There was a good, positive feeling in Glasgow that SA track and field was back. SA won nine medals in track and field with gold medals from Khotso Mokoena (Triple Jump), Cornel Fredericks (400m hurdles) and Fanie van der Merwe (100m T37).

But how many more medals could we have got if we had more athletes participating and the Operation Excellence (OPEX) funding from SASCOC was properly administered?

Just as a matter of interest, Fredericks is on OPEX (tier 2) which entitled him to R212 868 from 1 April 2013 - 31 March 2014.

SASCOC always gets involved after an athlete is successful, not before, when they need it most. – Arnaud Malherbe, former SA athlete,

We saw exactly that with Simon Magakwe after he broke the SA 100m record in April this year and suddenly even the Sports Minister, Fikile Mbalula was all over him like a rash.

We are going to take care of him so that he does not have to worry about other things except to run great times. We will put him on the Opex programme. - Fikile Mbalula

Magakwe, who is the defending Africa 100m champion, should have been on the OPEX programme at least two years ago if he was to be given every chance of medalling in Glasgow and in Rio 2016.

Caster Semenya was one of a number of athletes who didn't have their OPEX support extended.

Why was Elroy Gelant not at the Games?

Earlier this year, Gelant finished 7th in the 3000m in the World Indoor championships, beating other international athletes who were in Scotland. The winner of the 5000m gold in Glasgow ran a 13:12:07 - Gelant ran a personal best of 13:15.87 last year.

April and Galant, just two of the many other SA athletes, that should have been in Glasgow.

At 2010 Commonwealth Games, SA swimmers got 15 medals (7 gold). In 2014, SA got 12 medals (3 gold) - why the overall decline?

There could be a couple of factors but most fingers point towards an inept Swimming SA federation (SSA), whose CEO, Shaun Adriaanse was manager of the swim team in Glasgow (against SSA rules) and President, Jace Naidoo who was on pool deck again, using up a precious accreditation, which should be for coaches.

Funding is also a major problem, but you can't blame corporate SA for not taking the "dive" when SSA is plagued by allegations of corruption and maladministration. The success of SA swimmers is by in large no thanks to SSA and the likes of Adriaanse and Naidoo who are protected by SASCOC.

Instead, SASCOC took aim at our female swimmers for their poor performance in Glasgow.

Naidoo is also a SASCOC board member.

The athletes are silenced due to draconian codes of conduct put in place by SASCOC and the federations don't go to bat for the athletes as they are scared of losing their funding and membership to SASCOC.

SASCOC has received more than R600 million in Lottery funding since the National Lottery Board was established.

That’s a lot of money.

So, you have an untouchable SASCOC, controlling the purse strings and making all the decisions including final selections.

SA had seven badminton players at the Commonwealth Games (none ranked top 85 in the world) but no men's road cycling team and no squash players.

Of the seven badminton players, the best result was a last eight qualification in women’s doubles.

The men’s road cycling team would have had a definite chance to medal and there is simply no excuse for squash players, Steve Coppinger (ranked 21 in the world) and Siyoli Waters (ranked 35 in the world) not being selected for the Games.

There are so many other cases of unjust selection but SASCOC simply does as they please without sticking to their own criteria.

Netball wasn’t ranked in the Commonwealth top five at time of selection but it would have been embarrassing for the Sports Minister had Netball not gone to Glasgow considering all the money that has gone into the sport and “his” new domestic league. Netball finished out of the medals in sixth place, after losing to Malawi in the playoff for 5th and 6th.

Funding cannot be used as an excuse for lack of medals - the money is there but where is it going?

SA Table Tennis got over R8.2 million from the Lottery in 2013 and yet, we had no table tennis players in Glasgow or at the London Olympics for that matter.

The alleged misappropriation of Lottery funding will continue to hamper the growth of SA sport and the dreams of our athletes. But there never seems to be a lack of funding for the officials from the Department of Sport and Recreation, SASCOC, Lottery, PA’s, family and friends to attend the Games.

DA parliamentarian and SASCOC board member, Kobus Marais doesn’t miss out on too many “freebies” either and when asked who paid for his trip to Glasgow, what role he was there in and was he on leave?

Marais replied: “You are free to approach the DA Chief Whip. I know the protocol and rules very well, and I'm an experienced MP. Why would I not adhere to these?”

More questions than answers and not a word on what his role was in Glasgow and who paid for his trip. These officials are “living the life of Riley” while so many of our athletes and coaches are sitting at home due to “funding issues”.

The coach of javelin star, Sunette Viljoen's wasn't able to share in her silver medal success as SASCOC wouldn't pay for him to go and we had gymnasts at the Games for the first time with no coach.

For what we have in talent, finance and facilities, SA should be getting at least 80 medals at the Commonwealth Games and not 40.

But 80 is just a pipe dream until we have transparency and real sports people running sport in this country!

***

It was also during these Commonwealth Games that I was a little outspoken on twitter (not me) and must have got under the skin of the Department of Sport and Recreation (ie. Sports Ministry).

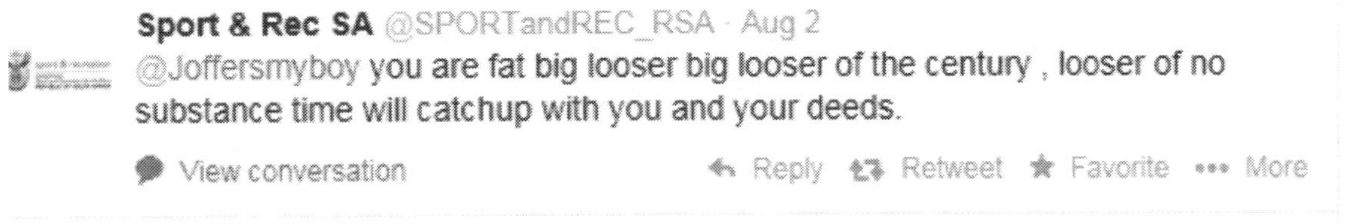

Sport & Rec SA @SPORTandREC_RSA · Aug 2
@Joffersmyboy you are fat big looser big looser of the century , looser of no substance time will catchup with you and your deeds.
View conversation
Reply
Retweet
Favorite
More

I guess I've been called worse.

The series of abusive tweets were later deleted and what must have ignited their 'loose' twitter tongue was a question I asked at the same time about another corruption scandal that had been swept under the carpet i.e. Cathsseta, which is a government body in the Culture, Arts, Tourism, Hospitality, Sports and Education Training Authority sector.

According to the Tourism update in 2014.

The decision (to put Cathsseta into administration) comes after the Department of Education allegedly commissioned a damning internal audit draft report by Grant Thornton. The report allegedly contains accusations of power abuse and nepotism against Cathsseta CEO, Mike Tsotetsi. City Press and South African Labour News reported on the Grant Thornton investigation earlier this year, saying the report contained evidence of unofficial payments for school trips to Italy and university fees for Cathsseta board members' children. An unspecified Africa Cup of Nations project that Cathsseta was involved in also led to the disappearance of R10m, the report claims.

I had obviously touched another corrupt nerve and was blocked by the Department of Sport and Minister of Sport on twitter.

A couple other hangers-on joined the Sports Ministry in their personal, cowardly attack, using pseudonyms and identities of others.

Mdo Michael Zulu @MdoZulu · Aug 10
@MbalulaFikile @Joffersmyboy @MyANC_ we must stop this DA fool joffers th
Jew pro-Israel who undermines us blacks
View conversation

Mdo Michael Zulu @MdoZulu · Aug 10
My comrade @MbalulaFikile u must stop this anti black fool @Joffersmyboy he
writes rubbish for DA stooges. We will March to his house
Expand

Mdo Michael Zulu @MdoZulu · Aug 10
@Joffersmyboy U a fool boy. 947 fired u too because u write rubbish. My ANC
will mobilize to stop u

More threats … I knew I had to be doing something right but just not sure who the real “Mdo Michael Zulu” is?

The elements of his twitter photograph threw up the name Warren J Smith III who on Facebook is from North Carolina and now lives in Dallas, Texas?

Mdo Michael Zulu
@MdoZulu
I'll be on the golf course or in the bunker to be more precise. #Amakhosi4Life
Polokwane
Joined April 2012

(Twitter)

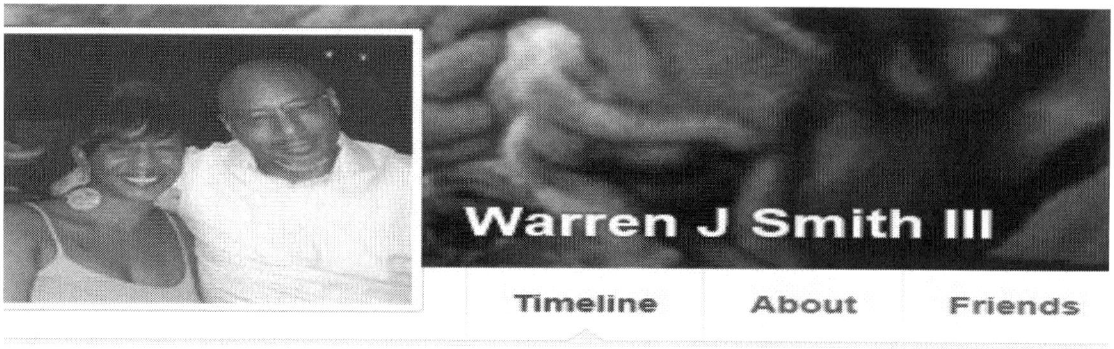

(Facebook)

Another SASCOC Bombshell
14 October 2014

SASCOC CEO, Tubby Reddy is now embroiled in more alleged irregularities including the awarding of a contract to M and M Hiring (with no tender) for the 'Ekhaya' at the Commonwealth Games in Scotland and for having an alleged affair with one of his staff members.

The Ekhaya was managed and run by the Sport and Recreation South Africa on behalf of the South African Government. This is done in partnership with other stakeholders, the main partner being SASCOC. The purpose of this project is to provide for South Africans, Team SA, the sponsors of Team SA, other foreign dignitaries and patrons a home away from home during major sporting events where South African athletes participate.

In other words, it's a "clubhouse" with catering.

M and M Hiring owned by David Naidoo was given the contract with a SASCOC budget of R4.2 million.

But R7.4 million was allegedly paid by SASCOC to Naidoo's company.

Some of our top athletes and coaches weren't selected to go to the Commonwealth Games due to a lack of funding.

SASCOC failed to respond to any emails and Mr Naidoo said he was not prepared to answer questions when reached telephonically. He refused to say how much the budget was and how much he was paid, saying it was confidential and SASCOC must answer. When asked if Mr Reddy's son worked for his company, Mr Naidoo, after a long pause said: "What gives you that idea?"

M and M Hiring has been responsible for a number of government events including the ANC Centenary, Cabinet Lekotla, ANC 53rd congress as well as sporting events with the PSL and Volleyball SA.

Reddy just happens to be long standing President of Volleyball SA (VSA), which is a conflict of interest and he's held the position for longer than the constitution allows.

Why is he untouchable?

The VSA CFO also just happens to be the SASCOC CFO, Vinesh Maharaj.

In 2010, M and M Hiring was accused of racism, irregular payment of staff and illegal hiring practices by former employees and according to an insider, some of M and M's equipment was recently impounded due to non-payment.

Naidoo has been a director of 21 companies since 1994 of which 12 have been de-registered including Geo's Hiring and Event Management which was only de-registered this year. He now trades under the company name of M and M Hiring Marquee.

Reddy earns more than R2 million per annum and travels freely around the world on the SASCOC account.

But it now emerges there's an 'extra' on that account.

Monique Tarr was appointed in January 2013 as a receptionist and two months later, she was recommended to do a Wits Business School course ahead of many other SASCOC employees who have been there for years.

It was an NMP (New Managers Programme) that SuperSport and Wits University put together.

Tarr completed the course and also stayed at a JHB hotel for a week in September during the course, despite having a residence in Johannesburg.

The hotel bill for her five day stay came to R 6993.02 (invoiced to SASCOC).

Reddy was seen at the hotel on more than one occasion during that time.

Not even two months into the course, Tarr was moved into the CEO's office without the job being advertised.

Reddy and Tarr have since been seen together on trips to Cape Town (SA Rugby jersey launch), Hong Kong, Scotland for a recce for the Commonwealth Games and then the Games themselves, where they stayed in the same hotel.

Both travelled business class.

When asked for comment, Reddy and Tarr failed to respond to several emails.

SASCOC receives millions in funding from the National Lottery (NLDTF) and surely it is high time for the likes of their corporate sponsors Nedbank, SASOL and South African Airways to pull the plug until a full forensic audit is done.

I can assure you this is just the tip of the iceberg.

Despite all these dark clouds hovering over South African sports administration, how does the country get to host the 2022 Commonwealth Games?

Well, no-one else wanted it.

South Africa was left as the lone bid after Edmonton withdrew due to economic pressures.

I was trying to ascertain some information regarding the 2022 Commonwealth Bid and its viability and when the Commonwealth Games commission were in Durban for their recce visit, Faizal Dawjee was introduced as the public relations official for South Africa's bid.

Dawjee is a former media director in the Office of the President. Well connected politically!

No surprise that he would have a nice, little cosy job with the SA Commonwealth Games bid team. But when the questions got tough for Dawjee about his company and if they tendered for the work, his response was almost laughable.

I don't do PR work. You should speak to the Commonwealth Bid/Games to find out who does their PR. I am sure they have an HR department.

According to a SASCOC press release on 25 February 2015 …

The City of Durban's Commonwealth Bid Committee will officially launch its bid to the Executive Committee of the Commonwealth Games Federation in London. Media in South African will have an opportunity to interview (via mobile phone) the delegation at the end of the media event in London. South African media that are present in London are invited to the Bid ceremony. To schedule an interview please call: Faizal Dawjee (faizal@africansynergi.com)

I then sent him the SASCOC reference above (quite obvious that he is the PR person) and also asked him why there would be a company listing for a Mahomed Dawjee as well, with the same director titles below:

- Office of President
- Africa Synergi
- Spin Media

Dawjee's response:

I have better things to do than worry about you. And you are making serious allegations and you are threatening me. I will not respond to you in the future.

'Spin Media' - rather ironic and not another person who won't respond to me in the future!

Who is the real Faizal or Mahomed Dawjee?

Can't be good for a Commonwealth Games bid to have a PR person who lacks this kind of transparency.

If hosting the World Cup in 2010 was difficult, this will be impossible! 32 teams of maybe 100 people each, totalling about 3200 people (Including coaches, cooks, physios and such), spread out over the country is not too difficult to accommodate. But 70 countries?! And let's be cautious with estimates here... Let's say 150 athletes per country and each athlete has 1 coach that is 300 people per country. Then we still need to factor in chefs, physios and such, let's cautiously estimate that each country will bring 400 people to the games. that is 28000 people, and all crammed into 1 city! Then add in all the tourists, families and press, where are they all going to stay? What will happen to traffic in Durban around the sporting arenas especially with no public transport system...? This is a disaster waiting to happen! – Mark Young

There is usually an evaluation commission sent out for multi-sport events, including the Commonwealth Games. The IOC president met some green protesters in Rio recently and if there are real concerns cutting across communities in Durban, write to the CEO of the CGF and ask for a meeting if they are going to send an evaluation commission. It is part of the values of the Commonwealth to promote free speech and integrity and those concerned should feel free to make contact to take up the right to free speech and put on the table your concerns about possible corruption, about the need to ensure a "clean Games" as well as to make concrete suggestions - including independent experts to supervise some tender processes, to sit on the Board, to provide risk management and internal audit advice and supervise implementation. Perhaps the office of the Auditor- General (who generally does a good job) should be involved in the bidding and organising process. I would imagine that the Minister of Finance will also be interested in such suggestions and more that you can formulate and present. – Sports administrator

The Public Protector's office under Thuli Madonsela had received numerous corruption reports about SASCOC and the investigation was 'on track' in 2013.

Wonder if the Public Protector's office has had any luck in getting the name of the liquidator who handled the winding up of SASCOC (the non-profit company) when they decided to become an association.

That would open a fresh can of worms.

But five years later, it all went very quiet from the Public Protector's office.

"No financial resources to carry on the investigation." - I don't buy into that!

In August 2015, I wrote to the Commonwealth Games Federation (CGF), highlighting some of the corruption and maladministration in SA sport and the pending investigation by the Public Protector's office.

It took a couple months to get a response from the CGF and it was only forthcoming after Durban had already been awarded the 2022 Games.

Durban confirmed as 2022 Commonwealth Games host

The South African city of Durban was selected as the host for the 2022 Commonwealth Games at the Federation's general assembly in New Zealand on Wednesday. The coastal city was the only bidder for the multi-sports event after the Canadian city of Edmonton withdrew from contention in February, citing falling oil prices. Organisers said the Games would be held from July 18-30, opening on the birth date of the late South African president and anti-apartheid hero Nelson Mandela. (Reuters, 2 September 2015)

In fact, the response I received from the Commonwealth Games Federation was almost two months after the official announcement of the host city.

25 October 2015
Via email

Dear Graeme,

XXII Commonwealth Games

Thank you for your recent communication.

As a means of supporting the continued development of peaceful, prosperous and sustainable communities across the Commonwealth, the Commonwealth Games Federation (CGF) works closely with host cities, nations and other partners to deliver inspiring and impactful Games that directly engage and leave a lasting legacy for Commonwealth citizens.

In working with host cities, the CGF has always advocated the need for transparency, consistent engagement with communities and the need for respectful dialogue in matters pertaining to the bid and the delivery of a successful Games. This is no different to what we have counselled our counterparts in Durban.

Once the Games Organising Committee has been formally constituted, we are confident that the Durban team will establish appropriate opportunities where public engagement and dialogue can take place to enable interested and indeed concerned parties to inform and actively contribute to the delivery of the Games. These pillars of governance and partnership are at the heart of our new Strategic Plan, Transformation 2022.

Already, the Bid Committee has been obliged to provide all necessary and relevant information that would lead to the hosting of a successful Games and this is publicly accessible via our website (http://www.thecgf.com/games/2022/2022_bid.asp) as well as from the website of the Durban Bid Committee (http://www.durban-2022.com/).

Over more than eight decades, many great Commonwealth cities, nations and territories have hosted the Commonwealth Games as a force for good, inspired by the actions and achievements of our Commonwealth athletes, and underpinned by our values of Humanity, Equality and Destiny. Over the next seven years, it is for the key partners and the citizens of Durban, KwaZulu-Natal and South Africa to make the most of this responsibility and opportunity. The CGF will, of course, work closely and enthusiastically to welcome and support the very first Commonwealth Games on African soil, in a spirit of ongoing partnership and through the work of its Coordination Commission.

The CGF would like to express its sincere gratitude for your understanding and participation, and hopes that your views will make a difference to the delivery of an inspiring Games for Durban and South Africa. In the meantime, we have forwarded your letter to the Durban Bid Committee.

CAN Mezzanine | 49 - 51 East Road
London | N1 6AH | UK

Office: [illegible]
Fax: [illegible]
Email: [illegible]

Yours sincerely,

David Grevemberg
CHIEF EXECUTIVE

It was a very poor response and didn't answer most of my questions which included if there was a plan B for another host city?

SASCOC spent over R120 million (that's the funds we know of) on the bid despite being the only horse in the race after Edmonton withdrew in February.

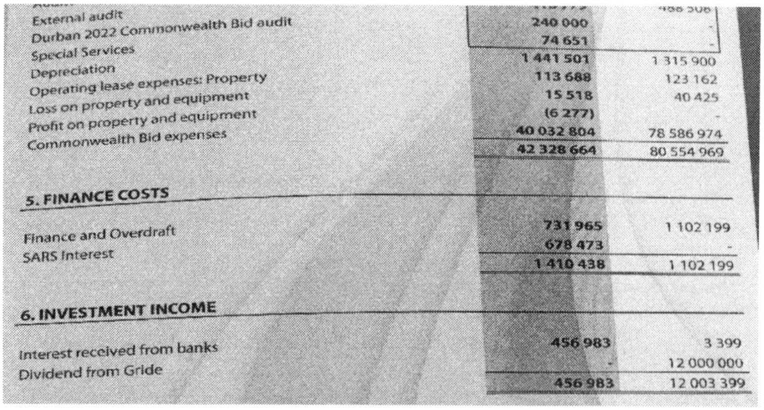

External audit	[illegible]	[illegible]
Durban 2022 Commonwealth Bid audit	240 000	-
Special Services	74 651	-
Depreciation	1 441 501	1 315 900
Operating lease expenses: Property	113 688	123 162
Loss on property and equipment	15 518	40 425
Profit on property and equipment	(6 277)	-
Commonwealth Bid expenses	40 032 804	78 586 974
	42 328 664	80 554 969
5. FINANCE COSTS		
Finance and Overdraft	731 965	1 102 199
SARS Interest	678 473	-
	1 410 438	1 102 199
6. INVESTMENT INCOME		
Interest received from banks	456 983	3 399
Dividend from Gride	-	12 000 000
	456 983	12 003 399

** R78.5 million on the bid in the 2013/2014 financial year and R40 million in 2015/2016*

Durban 2022 would have been just another great opportunity for corrupt officials to enrich themselves as so many did with the 2010 FIFA World Cup.

And it didn't take long for the greedy boys to start fighting.

State fumes as SASCOC steals its ball

Confidential documents leaked to amaBhungane reveal the government's intense anger over the launch of a "legacy project" of the 2022 Commonwealth Games by a little-known company apparently championed by controversial sports administrator Gideon Sam. Also involved in the launch and media briefing was TNA Media, which is owned by the politically connected Gupta family. (Mail & Guardian, 23 October 2015)

Gideon Sam was chairman of the board of this 'little-known' company, Nation of Champ-ions, his daughter was a director and his personal assistant at SASCOC, Kim Schonfeld was made the general manager.

Mark Keohane assisted in putting the legacy project together.

Nation of Champions would have been well positioned to cash in on projects related to the 2022 Commonwealth Games.

TNA media and the Gupta family is another whole ball game and one of the main reasons you have all these untouchables with corrupt links in SA sport.

The Guptas and President Jacob Zuma were one.

It emerged that the Gupta family had 'captured' the state and were responsible for appointing a number of Ministers to suit their own business interests.

Finance Minister, Trevor Manuel placed it on record when he laid into Fikile Mbalula in a letter to the Daily Maverick in June 2017.

It is odd, Fikile, that a mere five years ago you described President Zuma as a "politically bankrupt" leader who married "every week". Odd, because I have a clear memory of an incident that may be at the heart of why you have responded to me in the manner you have. That memory goes back to an ANC NEC meeting in August 2011. There, the Fikile Mbalula we once knew wept as he spoke. He explained he'd been called to Saxonwold by the Guptas in May 2009 and was told that he was being promoted from the position of Deputy Minister of Police to Minister of Sport. A few days later the President confirmed this change. The weeping was about the fact that he, Fikile, was happy that he'd made it into Cabinet but that it was wrong to have learnt this from Atul Gupta. That weeping was then, and this is now. Perhaps there are still a few debts to be called in by Saxonwold. (Trevor Manuel, Daily Maverick, June 2017)

There were financial problems with the Durban 2022 bid from the get-go and in 2016, there were still no government guarantees for the Games, which would cost around R6.3 billion.

I'm sure we will put up the necessary funding. We wouldn't have bid to fail. Sport is business and is a big part of our country's income. It contributes between 6 and 9 percent of our annual GDP. I can't comment on behalf of the government, but I'm sure they would put up the required guarantees. - Mark Alexander, 2022 Commonwealth Games bid committee chairman (IOL, 20 November 2016)

Yes, the same corrupt Mark Alexander who is president of SA Rugby and was now also the bid chairman.

Then 13 March 2017, not totally unexpected.

Commonwealth Games: Durban stripped of right to hold 2022 Games over financial problem

Durban was stripped of the right to stage the 2022 Commonwealth Games on Monday after a trail of missed deadlines and financial problems that highlights the daunting burdens facing host cities for major sporting events. (ABC Australia, 13 March 2017)

How Durban blew its Commonwealth Games bid

Durban made "significant departures" from its original promises, which is why it lost the rights to host the Commonwealth Games in 2022. (EP Herald, 13 March 2017)

Monday March 13, 2017

STATEMENT ON 2022 COMMONWEALTH GAMES

The Commonwealth Games Federation (CGF) has completed its review of the final information submitted by South Africa on 30th November, 2016 to determine whether their proposals for hosting the 2022 Commonwealth Games are consistent with their original bid commitments and the host city contract.

It is with disappointment that the detailed review has concluded that there is a significant departure from the undertakings provided in Durban's bid and as a result a number of key obligations and commitments in areas such as governance, venues, funding and risk management/assurance have not been met under the revised proposition.

Louise Martin CBE, President of the Commonwealth Games Federation said: "In line with the mandate from members at the 2016 General Assembly, the CGF is actively exploring alternative options, including a potential replacement host. The CGF will continue to have an open dialogue with the South African Sports Confederation and Olympic Committee (SASCOC) and the Republic of South Africa and remains committed to realising the shared ambitions of a future Commonwealth Games in Africa. The CGF is fully confident and committed to delivering a successful Commonwealth Games for athletes and fans in 2022."

***

The South African response from the Sports Minister, Fikile Mbalula was long winded and not worth the paper it was written on.

Only the last paragraph made some sense.

As the three spheres of Government and the sports movement, we entered the Bidding process for the City of Durban to host the Commonwealth Games 2022 on behalf of our country and for the first time on the African Continent. However, at this juncture, our country is regrettably not in a position to make huge financial commitments given the current competing socio-economic needs and global economic downturn. In the interests of fiscal discipline and financial prudency, our government has considered all options and remains confident that we have acted in the best interests of South Africa.

It was most certainly in the best interests of South Africa not to host the Games. A blind squirrel could have told them that before the bid but the key players saw big dollar signs for self enrichment until the player pool became too big.

But not before R120 million went down the drain on a failed bid, complimented by the same old drivel and spin from the Sports Minister.

And that's the R120 million we know about!

Chapter 11: Reporting Without Fear or Favour

It was inevitable there would be many strained relationships from my exposes as I was reporting without fear or favour. When I got a lead, I started asking questions. It didn't matter who was involved and I was becoming an arch enemy to many of the sporting federations and individuals with corrupt links.

Taking the high road is usually not the easy one to take or the most popular. The low road seems to offer instant satisfaction. It may seem better for the moment, but if you compromise you principles and your integrity, it will always end up costing you far more in the long run. - Billy Cox

Towards the end of 2013, I was tipped off about a number of financial irregularities with the Sports Trust. Millions and millions from the National Lottery were flowing in and out of the Trust without due process. The Trust was being used as a 'dirty conduit' by the Department of Sport and Recreation (SRSA).

The Sports Trust will increase access to and create opportunities for all South Africans to participate in sport through the provision of equipment and facilities and we will help to create a new sporting tradition for our democratic society. - Sports Trust Mission Statement

But their mission had 'secretly' changed.

Rob Fleming was the chairperson of the Sports Trust at the time.

I knew Rob well as we were both students at Rhodes University in 1989 and his brother-in-law, Paul Barrow is one of my closest friends.

Paul's brother, Roger was coach of the men's lightweight fours, which captured SA's first ever Olympic rowing gold in London in 2012.

It was a remarkable feat for a sport that gets so little in funding.

After the London Olympics, Roger took us through the gold medal race footage from beginning to end.

It was goose bump stuff!

Fleming was also the sports marketing manager for South African Breweries (SAB) for a number of years.

With SAB being a marquee sponsor in SA sport, he was very involved with the SA national teams including players and coaches from Bafana Bafana (soccer), the Proteas (cricket) and Springboks (rugby).

SAB was also a partner of the Sports Trust along with other big corporates, the likes of SuperSport, Nedbank and Sun International.

Rob was SAB's representative on the Trust and was then appointed chairperson.

It was a very odd appointment as he had already left SAB to go and work for Blue Label Telecoms, which was not a partner of the Trust but with SAB's sponsorships in SA sport, he had developed a close working relationship with the Sports Minister, Fikile Mbalula.

I called Rob towards the end of 2013 with some serious questions regarding the Sports Trust and wanted to sit down with him to discuss.

I knew it wasn't going to be easy but as chairperson, he would surely have all the answers and would be forthcoming with the information.

I was horribly wrong.

Rob delayed the meeting for as long as possible until 13 January 2014.

We finally chatted over a cup of coffee, downstairs in my apartment building and up front, he told me he hadn't been sleeping well on the questions I was asking.

That already told me something.

Rob couldn't explain the Sports Trust's alleged financial irregularities and no tenders but promised to get back to me once he had spoken to Anita Mathews who was the Executive Director.

Rob added he was going to get a forensic audit done and asked my advice if he should consult with a lawyer to protect himself.

He knew there was something wrong and when I asked if he was the only signatory on the Sports Trust account, he said:

I'm not sure. Anita puts a whole lot of payments requests in from me and I just sign them off.

You'd think if you were signing off on millions, you'd know how many signatories are on the account?

Rob was very flustered.

By finding out whose bank accounts some of the Trust funds were being paid into, would have helped me to further expose the corrupt in SA sport.

The Department of Sport and Recreation had refused to answer any of my questions.

The Sports Trust had become their secret little nest egg, hatching millions and millions from the National Lottery.

Are the trustees being paid?

No, Anita has a team of approx.7 working for her and trustees don't get paid. Maybe they have certain costs reimbursed but it's not a payment. - Rob Fleming

Again as chairperson, you'd think one should know if the trustees are being reimbursed.

I didn't hear back from Rob for a few days after our meeting and when I called him, he told me he had requested a forensic audit of the Trust and someone high up in the Sports Ministry wasn't happy about it.

He couldn't tell me the name of that official and no other information was forthcoming.

During our meeting, Rob told me he had mentioned my current investigation into the Trust to his brother but wasn't going to mention it to his sisters.

But that all soon changed after I had spent a Sunday lunch with Paul and his wife (Rob's sister) and their family.

On the Monday morning, I received an irate call from Rob questioning how I could take advantage of his sister's hospitality while I'm trying to expose him.

It was a heated conversation and I had to remind him that Paul was my best friend and the Sports Trust was never discussed at the table.

I had kept Paul in the loop confidentially as I didn't want it to affect our relationship going forward.

Rob had other ideas and had now decided to share with his sisters what was going on, twisting the facts and that I was the bad guy trying to expose him.

The same night I received a courtesy call from Paul saying his wife and her sister were very upset, that he was obviously caught in the middle of this and hopefully time would heal the wound.

I couldn't apologize enough but the damage had been done.

Understandably in this situation, blood is thicker than water and my relationship with his family would never be the same.

Paul and I would still chat telephonically and have the odd lunch at Melrose Arch in Johannesburg. He was genuinely concerned for me with the work that I was doing.

He remained the absolute gentleman as he had always been since our great friendship began at Rhodes University, playing on the same cricket and squash teams and living next door to each other in our first year in the Smuts House residence.

Paul was a friend you could go to war with and his kids still Whatsapp me to this day to find out how I'm doing.

I just wish Rob had seen the bigger picture.

The sad state of SA Sport
16 March 2014

Seldom does a week go by without news of more SA sportsmen and women being denied a chance of competing on the International stage because of a lack of funding.

SA did not send a team to the Africa Cross Country championships in Uganda last weekend and the SA Men's hockey side will not be competing in the Champions Challenge in Scotland in April.

The only ones losing out are the athletes.

The problem is the flawed funding model in SA sport and the head strong Department of Sport and Recreation and SASCOC.

The Lottery (which a number of sporting federations survive on) has capped grants to each federation at R2 million.

Some sports used to get between R5 and R10 million.

Now, most of that Lottery money is being channelled directly through the Department of Sport and Recreation (SRSA), with seemingly no cap and a lot of it is allegedly being misappropriated.

From the National Lottery budget allocated to sport: briefing by Department of Trade and Industry & National Lotteries Board on 18 February 2014:

The National Lotteries Board (NLB) reported that Sport received 22% of the Grant Funding budget from Board

NLB said it used the Sport and Recreation Distribution Agency (SRDA) as its implementing wing, where it simply gave SRDA the money and SRDA decided where the money would go to

SRSA spent more than R150 million on the African Nations Football Championship (CHAN) 2014

SRDA funded the World Conference on Doping in Sport (WADA) which had taken place in Johannesburg in 2013

According to SA Institute for Drug-Free Sport (SAIDS):

The conference wasn't ours to organize. We merely had a presence - as the "host"country's National Anti-Doping Organization. It was wholly WADA sponsored in collaboration with SRSA & City of Johannesburg.

Wholly WADA sponsored?

Hmmm …

So, why was more than R10 million paid from the Sports Trust for this conference and why does SRDA not make mention of how much they paid for the same event?

The Sports Trust, SRSA and SRDA have failed to respond to several emails, asking where this money went.

More …

SRDA chairman, Mveleli Ncula in the Lotto briefing report:

SRSA had set-up a Sports Trust as a conduit to apply on its behalf for R200 million for the National Schools Championship. The SRDA had agreed to fund that championship in tranches of R50 million per year over a period of four years in total.

In fact, the Sports Trust was set up in September 1995 by corporates led by Nedbank and from their last set of financials, the Trust received R59 million for the National Schools championship and more than R63 million was spent.

R63 million on a National School's championship in Bloemfontein?

Once again, no reply from SRDA, SRSA or the Trust on the alleged financial irregularities.

Chairman of the Sports Trust, Rob Fleming said back in January, he was going to get a "forensic audit" done – that has now changed to an "independent review".

Why?

The R2.5 million that disappeared for R Kelly to perform at the Nelson Mandela Sports day is a drop in the ocean compared to what is really going on.

According to media reports the Sport and Recreation Minister, Fikile Mbalula and the Arts and Culture Minister, Paul Mashatile paid R2.5 million for an R Kelly concert that never was. - Winston Rabotapi Democatic Alliance (DA) Shadow Minister of Sport and Recreation

It is also noted that there is no mention made in the Lottery briefing about the reported R65 million that was spent on the SA sports awards in December last year.

R65 million for one night in addition to several reports of tender irregularities?

Sports Minister, Fikile Mbalula keeps on telling the public the majority of money for these functions comes from corporate sponsorship, just like the Floyd Mayweather trip.

Instead, the majority of it is coming from the Lottery and public monies that should be going to fund and support South Africa's athletes.

This is what R65 million could have done for SA sport. (Source: DA)

- 86 multi-purpose sports fields at R75,000 each
- 3,250 swimming pools at R20,000 each
- 11 rugby fields at R5.5 million
- 13 soccer fields at R5 million each
- 1,625,000 soccer balls at R40 each
- Support to 541 Mass Participation, Opportunity and Access, Development and Growth (MOD) centres at R120,000 per annum each

Minister Mbalula has made it clear that his main priority in his portfolio is razzmatazz, glitz and glamour and not providing services to those that most need it in South Africa. - Winston Rabotapi

As this maladministration and alleged corruption continues in SA sport, there will be fewer and fewer SA sportsmen and women able to compete on the international stage.

It's a very sad state of affairs.

***

I kept pressure on the Sports Trust for answers, but it took six months before getting a string of weak responses and avoidance of the real issues.

Following a series of enquiries and questions from you which raised, amongst others, allegations of mismanagement of funds by the Sports Trust, the Trustees engaged the internal audit division of the Trust's auditors, KPMG Inc. to undertake a Review of both the allegations and the systems adopted by the Trust in the management of projects and funds. The Sports Trust has always prided itself on its ability to manage projects and to assist in the delivery of facilities and equipment particularly to disadvantaged South Africans and for this reason viewed these allegations seriously. The review has now been completed and considered by the Trustees. Whilst the review identified gaps in the internal control systems that have since been addressed, it did not reveal any misuse or incorrect application of funds.- The Sports Trust

Always easier to mark your own exam papers!

More than three months later …

We do not believe we are required to provide you with further information on the activities of the Trust and that you will use this opportunity to refrain from publishing any further baseless allegations, failing which we will not hesitate to institute necessary legal action. As indicated in our correspondence, there are existing contractual relationships between the Trust and its various sponsors, which include the Department of Sports and Recreation and the National Lotteries Board. Resultant from these contractual relationships, the Trust owes an obligation of confidentiality towards its sponsors. Consequently, the Trust is not in a position to provide you with the actual contractual agreements with its sponsors or divulge any contents thereof. Furthermore, the Trust will not furnish any responses to questions pertaining to the agreements or the specificities of its fulfillment of contractual obligations arising therefrom. - The Sports Trust

In November 2012, the Sports Trust together with SRSA was "supposedly" spending millions on renovating the Sisonke Boxing Club gym in East London.

THE SPORTS TRUST
sport & recreation
Department:
Sport and Recreation South Africa
REPUBLIC OF SOUTH AFRICA
BEFORE
PROPOSED DESIGN
Province: Eastern Cape
Nov 2012 – The Sports Trust together with SRSA is renovating the gym of Sisonke Boxing Club located in Mdantsane Township, East London to a safe and quality gym facility, benefiting 220 general members, 20 amateur boxers, 26 talented boxers, 11 professional boxers, 199 school learners, 17 females and 1 professional female boxer.
Handover – pending completion of project
ENHANCING EDUCATION THROUGH SPORT

As of August 2014, not one bit of ground had been moved. What happened to the renovations and the funding?

No funds have been expended on the actual project itself. The allocated funds remain on deposit with our bankers.- The Sports Trust

I wasn't buying this!

Sisonke Boxing Gym, 15 August 2014

The auditors of the Trust, KPMG didn't want to know about the irregularities and I was stonewalled in similar fashion to Deloitte's when it came to questions regarding SASCOC.

As previously mentioned, both external audit and internal audit has been appointed by the management and board of The Sports Trust, and have separate engagement letters in place, that do not allow us to respond to these type of queries to third parties and specifically not share any documentation, confidentiality clauses. It is my opinion that these queries need to be directed at management and the board of the Sports Trust and it is at their discretion to respond. - Christo Smith, KPMG

SRSA silence
5 February 2014

R63 million was spent on the National Schools championship in Bloemfontein in 2013.

How much did the Department of Sport and Recreation (SRSA) under Minister Fikile Mbalula's watch, spend on the championship in Pretoria last year?

Good question and no answers from either SRSA or the Sports Trust who were used as the conduit in 2013.

Why is it such a secret?

What isn't a secret is how badly the championship is organized and a number of the sporting codes didn't mince their words after last year's event.

At this time of the year (December) teachers are very tired. They are not motivated to bring their teams and would rather withdraw

A number of officials that attended did so purely out of a sense of obligation to the code and didn't have the zest and energy needed to embrace the spirit of such an event

Volunteers were treated as imposters and received nothing – not even food packs

The volunteers felt despondent and unwanted

Accreditation was a total waste of money and time as some people never received it and others got it on the last day

Programmes, names of officials, volunteers, ambassadors, etc. were submitted well in advance but SRSA officials said they didn't receive them despite "read reports" when these emails were opened by the relevant people

Bus drivers did not know the area as they were contracted from the Free State and the local people (Pretoria) were excluded from this opportunity

Transport of players from the residence to the venues were late

No correspondence as to what to expect from the sponsor (Milo). There was no indication that the whole tournament was going to be branded with Milo branding

Milo product was only available to the athletes on a couple of days

ID numbers not available for some of the players and athletes and no age verification

Questioning the ages of certain players resulted in unnecessary confusion, tension and resentment between participating teams

Tournament logistics were left to the last minute

Facilities were poorly managed from day to day

Some codes didn't even attend and accommodation was booked in their athletes names

Payments haven't been made to certain schools for hosting and they will not host again

December is very hot and players ended up with blisters on their feet from the hot surfaces

It seems like the R60 odd million we know about was well spent?

NOT!

The volunteers for me is the saddest part as they give up all their time for no pay and get treated like this.

Why would you get bus drivers from Bloemfontein for a Pretoria event? Two cities separated by 454 kilometres.

But no doubt some of the service providers and friends of SRSA are smiling all the way to the bank from their "winning" tenders.

There are still serious allegations unanswered from the 2013 championships in Bloemfontein re: non tenders and inflated prices from service providers.

But it's much easier to sweep things under the carpet when you use a conduit.

The Director-General of SRSA, Alec Moemi hasn't replied to any of our emails for over a year now and the Sports Trust hasn't made their 2013-2014 financials publically available as they've done in past years.

I wonder why?

Our lives begin to end the day we become silent about things that matter. - Martin Luther King *Jr.*

***

I wasn't going to be silent and emailed Andy Scott who had been COO of the Sports Trust through his employment with Nedbank.

Andy was also a friend and inspirational figure for all his work with the Paralympic athletes and wheelchair basketball.

But his reply was a missed layup.

Joffers, I am out of the loop and strongly suggest that you raise the matter with the Chairman of the Trust. The Sports Trust has always been a partnership between Govt, the Corporate and private sector. Please contact Rob Fleming in this regard. - Andy Scott

The corporate partners of the Sports Trust didn't want to know about the financial irregularities either and eventually they lost patience with me.

I had become a persistent thorn in their side.

SuperSport, had sight of the report as did other Trustees and is comfortable with same. - Brandon Foot, SuperSport

And when asked for a copy of the report?

I am advised that is was done by KPMG and I am unable to forward it to you. It is not in my possession. Please, kindly direct further enquiries to the Trust. - Brandon Foot

South African Breweries (SAB) were just as cagey.

Your interpretation is incorrect as I have not given SAB's view on the nature of the audit process, nor the results. Any view in this regard will be made directly to the Sports Trust and not to the media. I trust that this brings to an end any further communications with SAB on this matter. - Benedict Maaga, SAB

And Nedbank weren't going to spoil the party either.

In our last correspondence in July, I indicated that we had received the report and were expecting the comment from the Sports Trust soon. The Sports Trust published their statement afterwards. We have noted the report findings and statement released by the Sports Trust and are not planning to make a separate statement. - Thulani Sibeko, Nedbank

A real case of don't bite the hand that feeds you.

If big corporates like SuperSport, SAB and Nedbank were content to turn a blind eye to the corrupt practices of the Sports Trust, how was SA sport ever going to be cleaned up?

Government contracts are obviously more important to them.

It felt like I was hitting my head against a brick wall every day and needed to tap into some expert advice.

I made contact with the former CEO of FirstRand Bank, Paul Harris, who was very involved in getting the commission of inquiry into the SA cricket, Gerald Majola and Indian Premier League (IPL) bonus scandal.

Harris confirms CSA's undeclared bonuses

Former Cricket SA (CSA) remuneration committee chairman Paul Harris confirmed on Thursday that Cricket SA (CSA) employees had been paid undeclared bonuses. This happened after South Africa hosted the 2009 Indian Premier League (IPL) tournament, he told a committee of inquiry into the financial affairs of CSA in Pretoria. Harris was ousted by the CSA board when the allegations of underhanded bonus payments first surfaced last year. (IOL, 24 November 2011)

Majola in tears at commission

Cape Town - Cricket SA (CSA) CEO Gerald Majola burst out in tears after appearing in front of a commission of inquiry into the organisation's bonus scandal. (sport24, 6 December 2011)

Majola should have declared a lot more than just the bonusses including his personal relationship with CSA supplier, Sedgars.

This from a SA cricket insider …

Do you not know the Sedgars story? They are the great corruptors in the sports goods industry, well known for offering kick-backs. All started with Khaya Majola when MTN first sponsored development cricket. The scam was almost exposed but Gerald Majola asked UCBSA (United Cricket Board of South Africa) to sweep it under the carpet as his brother, Khaya was dying of cancer and had done so much for cricket development. When Gerald became CEO, things went to the next level. Just about every province has been infected at one stage or another. Still at high levels of CSA (Cricket South Africa) management, people are on the take, directly or indirectly (family). A shopping spree at the Sedgars Vereeniging store, assistance to a family member down on their luck, maybe a cash deposit into some degenerate gambler's bookie account...think creatively.

When I read Andrew Jennings description of FIFA as a mafia, power going down and loyalty coming up, it made sense, it is how CSA works. You can't blow the whistle as people higher up are also on the take. When Gerald was disgraced at CSA, who in their right mind would employ him? Only Sedgars, he was running their Eastern Cape government sports tender's business. Anywhere you see Sedgars/winner/bas vampire you can be sure someone is being greased or pushed from above to place orders with them. Inferior products are delivered at inflated prices. Goods delivered seldom match the sample provided. The Department of Sport and Recreation is also tainted, tenders are rigged to favour people sourcing products from Sedgars. Of course the goods are "just for development so who cares" and we wonder why development fails, it is set up to fail. The sports industry is a microcosm of our country. Sedgars are the Guptas of the sports industry and they are branching into bigger government departments now. No doubt someone from a sports department moved to a provincial department dealing with roads!

The Deputy Director of Gauteng Roads and Transport was SASCOC vice president, Hajera Kajee who has those strong family links to Sedgars.

Wearing her SA table tennis administrator's cap, Kajee turned down a free sponsorship from another company for equipment for her federation, only to purchase the same equipment at an inflated price from Sedgars, who didn't even stock the goods. They had to get it from elsewhere.

It would not surprise me if there were family/friend links. Sedgars get a large amount of business out of Lottery money – I know because I have manufactured and branded many orders to supply them which they in turn supply out. I have often wondered why they always get so many of the orders. – SA sporting goods manufacturer

During the Rio Olympics, I received messages from a number of SA athletes including photographs of the kit they were given for the Games.

It was shocking, especially the tracksuits which were mostly oversized and the SA team were labeled as 'green ninja turtles' at the opening ceremony.

There was another huge public outcry.

SASCOC defends 'ninja turtle' tracksuits

The South African Sports Confederation and Olympic Committee (Sascoc) received a lashing in Parliament on Wednesday as MPs demanded an explanation for the "ninja turtle" tracksuits worn by South Africa's Olympic athletes. (IOL, 13 October 2016)

SASCOC had quietly gone about getting another clothing sponsor from China.

It was Erke in 2012 and now 361° in 2016.

But Sedgars provided the clothing again and just embroidered the 361° logo.

The reason given by SASCOC was that the 361° kit didn't arrive in time.

Really?

SASCOC had four years to prepare for Rio and why would you even put the 361° logo on if they failed to meet their obligations?

Mbalula made as though he wasn't impressed with the kit either but it was his normal hot air and a front.

He was a beneficiary of the Sedgars 'goodwill' in SA sport capture.

Hajeera Kajee's family (Sedgars) also manufactured the dreadful kit worn by our athletes at the Beijing Olympics. Max Fuzani told my husband and myself at our meeting that the government is unable to intervene in SASCOC's actions because the IOC will immediately suspend SASCOC. - Laraine Lane

Team SA will remember 2008 as the year that Korean seamstresses had to be hastily summoned in order to adjust teamwear to fit; when some of the vests started unravelling before they had been worn; when team wear embroiderers renamed it the Beljing Olympics, when performance clothing made from fabric resembling tracksuit material was supplied to athletes who had to perform in excruciating heat; and international tennis players voted the SA tennis team's outfits the ugliest at the Games — and players refused to swop shirts. – Sports Trader (August/September 2008)

SASCOC president, Gideon Sam said they used the Chinese companies because they get R20 million in sponsorship with the clothing deal. It would be interesting to see how that R20 million is spent!

If only every SASCOC 'sponsorship deal' was investigated and they should have to account for every cent of the R70 million they were given from the National Lottery just before the Rio Games.

One insider said the funds were used pay off SASCOC debt and Rio Olympic silver medallist, Sunette Viljoen didn't mince her words.

Her javelin went directly to the root of the problem.

Sedgars was now being cast under the microscope for more than just their 'business relationships' with SASCOC.

Free State Premier Ace Magashule has become embroiled in a dispute over a R9.5m tender for 2010 World Cup soccer-related regalia as a businessman claims his firm was used as a front for an entity allegedly close to Magashule. A Daily Maverick report says Abiel Mokotso, sole director of Bokamoso Media House, has given details of how a meeting with Magashule in February 2010 led to him landing a multimillion-rand contract without exerting much effort. The R9.5m tender was to supply 30 000 soccer T-shirts and 20 000 blankets. The deal has turned sour for Mokotso who is now facing a criminal case and R2.2m fine from SARS. Significantly, states the report, the 2010 deal involved the powerful Dockrat family and their Sedgars group, who have interests in retail, clothing and construction and have long been regarded as close to the Free State premier. (Legalbrief, November 2017)

It seems as if the Free State government may need to answer some tough questions in connection to their relationship with Sedtrade which is part of the Sedgars group.

(Twitter, 26 September 2018)

The meeting with Paul Harris did happen and we chatted at this house in Johannesburg for a couple hours. He wasn't aware of my crusade and lawsuit but told me that I was taking on some very 'dangerous, well connected people' including Tubby Reddy who tried his best to 'sabotage' the cricket commission of inquiry into the IPL bonus scandal.

Paul was very accommodating and suggested I try to create a ground swell via twitter.

Dirt of the Day was born.

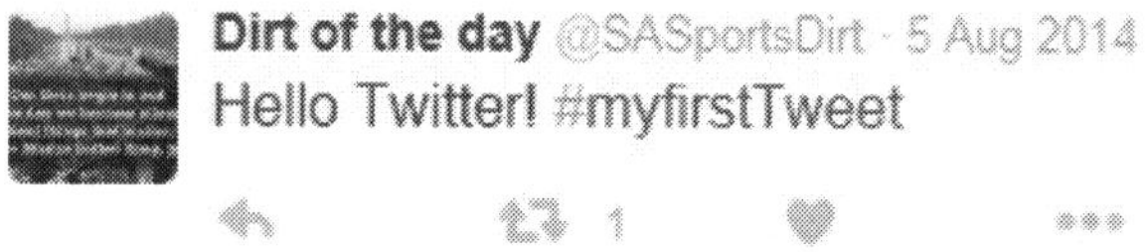

It wasn't difficult to find something to tweet about every day as SA sport had been captured.

It also gave me the opportunity to refresh the sporting public's minds about some of the corruption and maladministration that had been swept under the carpet in recent years.

It was going to be dirty.

Very dirty!

Chapter 12: Dirt of the Day

Dirt of the day @SASportsDirt · 19 Oct 2014
If you want a Lottery grant, "build" a museum ... sportsfiredaily.co.za/article.php?id...

If you want a grant from the National Lottery Board (NLB), just say you building a museum. It's working for quite a few already.

In December last year, a grant of R4.8 million was paid to 'The South African Football Museum'.

Where's the museum 10 months later?

Thank you for your email and continued interest in this exciting project. We advise that the date of the proposed function to announce this project to the media was always subject to the availability of all key stakeholders being able to attend. As the date of 30 September 2014 was not suitable to all stakeholders, we are exploring alternative dates for this media function. As soon as this is confirmed, an invitation to attend will be sent to you. - Pippa Freer, Project Director

On initial investigation back in June, I ran into a pack of contradictions.

The museum is at the FNB Stadium. - NLB manager, Sershan Naidoo

No SA Football Museum at the FNB Stadium and no agreement has been entered into. - FNB stadium management.

The South African Football Association (SAFA) is not aware of this museum and anyone running it is doing so without the blessing of the national association. SAFA actually intends to start its own museum and that project is in the pipeline. - SAFA

Naidoo later tried to correct himself and said:

The fact that the word 'museum' appears in the name of the beneficiary does not mean that the grant was for a museum!

Hmmm …

The Cape Town Minstrel Carnival Association got around R35 million from the National Lottery in the last year and guess what?

The money received was for our 2014 competition and all the other related issues for our minstrel activities like transport, security, stadium costs etc. and to establish a museum. - Kevin Momberg, Cape Minstrels

Where's their museum?

We are still in negotiations with regards to the building which will house the museum, so we will make it public once everything has been finalised as to the location. - Kevin Momberg

That was at the beginning of July.

I shared a 30-page dossier on alleged corruption including these two cases with National Lottery fraud specialists almost three months ago and the latest is:

The matters are still under investigation. I cannot divulge the identity of the individual investigators. – Matodzi Nefale, NLB Fraud Specialist

But it seems as if it's now back into the hands of Sershan Naidoo.

If there are any investigations, there will certainly not be any regular reports shared with you. On completion of an investigation, if there was one, there are processes that will dictate how the information is disseminated. - Sershan Naidoo

If there was one? Really?

The lack of transparency is just unbelievable!

I was told by the SA Football Museum that the museum will be based at FNB Stadium. I relayed that to you. End of story. You can take it up with SA Football Museum. There are processes with the rollout of projects. SA Football Museum reports to us in line with their grant agreement. - Sershan Naidoo

I can't wait to open my own museum. Just got to find a venue.

An invitation to attend will be sent to you all!

Dirt of the day @SASportsDirt · 10 Aug 2014
Swimming SA president. Jace Naidoo uses a limited "coach" accreditation for his own benefit to be on pool deck.

From Swimming SA insider …

Jace Naidoo is currently president of Swimming South Africa. He has served on a number of positions of the national Executive of SSA since 1999. Was first elected to the SASCOC Board in 2007 and was re-elected in 2009.

He is NOT a coach and has not undertaken any coaching duties during these or any other games or any other swimming competitions under the auspices of FINA. He is purely an elected administrative official.

As there only limited accreditations in each category accreditations are usually awarded carefully to ensure that the people most influential in Team South Africa's performance are closest to the athletes.

The SA swimming team coaches announced for London Olympics were as follows:

1. *Graham Hill – head coach and club coach of 4 swimmers on the team including*
2. *Igor Omeltchenko – club coach to 3 swimmers on the team*
3. *Wayne Ridden – club coach to 0 swimmers on the team*
4. *Cedric Finch – open water coach with strong ties to the open water swimmers*

The Personal coaches:

1. *Dirk Lange – coach to Cameron van den Berg Olympic gold medallist*
2. *Pierre de Roubaix – coach to two swimmers on the team*

There were a number of coaches who have swimmers on team who were not afforded any of the accreditation as described above.

At no time was Jace Naidoo announced or mentioned as a member of the coaching staff by SASCOC.

He did not attend the pre-Olympic training camp except for the last couple of days in Monaco to attend Princess Charlene's reception.

Yet Mr Naidoo holds a full swimming team coach accreditation allowing him access to accommodation in the games village, transport food and all the other privileges while an Olympic gold medallist coach and a coach with two swimmers on the team have to struggle for more than an hour to reach the training venue, be delayed in tubes trains and crowds while Mr Naidoo rides the gravy train with Olympic village accommodation and games transport that allows him to access the training venue in 5 minutes.

In fact he denies a swimmer of having his or her coach at the games at all. The comment from a former SSA performance director now working in New Zealand: "If this had happened in NZ it would have been front page news!"

Dirk Lange was delayed during one of the days of competition, which lead him to being late to attend the race preparations.

Fortunately this delay did not occur on the day his gold medal winning charge Cameron Berg was racing. Should Cameron have been without his coach Dirk at the most crucial stage of his bid for Olympic gold it could very well have led to failure?

Dirt of the day @SASportsDirt · 14 Aug 2014
Chairman of SA Basketball league is Albert Mokoena who resigned as Home Affairs DG for misusing dept's resources. zapiro.com/cartoon/947604...

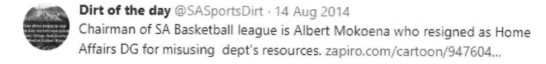

How does SA allow a "Replacement" Basketball Team to play in National colours & represent the country when the original one is sidelined? - Robert Marawa

This is the dictatorship we have been subjected to for years & the minute players stand up for justice, you're thrown out. - Solomzi Ngonelo

Just two of the many tweets last week after the SA basketball team were thrown out of a training camp when they requested amendments to their player contract.

A contract which failed to cover them for medical insurance or detail of what they would be earning from the Four Nations tournament which took place in Johannesburg this past weekend.

Surely, the players have every right to ask for those amendments.

Why should any athlete have to pay out of their own pocket if injured when representing their country?

16 INDEMNITY

16.1 The Player/Team Official agrees that BASKETBALL SOUTH AFRICA shall not be liable to him in any circumstances for death, any injury, loss or damage of any kind whatsoever arising directly or indirectly from any omission (whether negligent or otherwise) by any person whatsoever connected with the Player's/Team Official's membership of the Team, his travel to and from the Four Nations Challenge, his participation at the Four Nations Challenge, or any disciplinary action taken against him by the LOC or BASKETBALL SOUTH AFRICA.

16.2 The Player/Team Official indemnifies BASKETBALL SOUTH AFRICA from and against all claims, legal proceedings and costs whatsoever which may be taken or made against BASKETBALL SOUTH AFICA in conjunction with or arising out of death, any loss, damage or injury referred to in Clause 16.1 above.

But the bully boys of SA basketball administration didn't like to be challenged. They cancelled the training camp and selected a second string side to represent SA at the tournament.

Why? To prove that we can finish 3rd with a second-string side?

SA finished 3rd out of the four nations with their solitary win coming against Kenya.

I can only sympathize with Ngonelo as I've been on the receiving end of this Basketball SA dictatorship run by its president Graham Abrahams, who has become a political pariah, wearing a number of different hats.

Abrahams, the former spokesperson for the Sports Ministry is president of Basketball SA, chairman of the Kwazulu-Natal Cricket Union, an executive board member of the SA Institute for Drug-Free Sport

(SAIDS) and a Trustee of the Sports Trust.

His full-time job is the Director of Legal Affairs and Enterprise at SuperSport.

Despite several emails to find out when Basketball SA had their last elections or AGM, the response is a deadly silence.

In fact, the last response I got from Abrahams was:

Please do not send me emails.

The Deputy President of Basketball SA (BSA) is Albert Mokoena and his track record is not exactly a slam dunk.

Mokoena resigned as Home Affairs director general back in 1999 after a Sunday newspaper revealed that he was misusing the department's resources to run a basketball team. He allegedly used the department's telephone and fax to run his team and illegally registered three Zambians in his team as South African citizens.

Other allegations include an attempt to solicit a R453 000 sponsorship for his team from a computer company, which has a three-year service contract with the department.

A great CV to become deputy president of Basketball SA and chairman of the new SuperSport league that started three years ago.

Millions is being pumped into basketball in SA as promised by the Sports Minister, Fikile Mbalula but it's not making the impact it should be.

Reason number one being the administration, which is of political appointments.

Abrahams is a close confidante of Fikile Mbalula after serving as Sports Ministry spokesperson for a number of years.

Secondly, if you're trying to grow the sport, should it not be on a public/free to air broadcaster like the SABC?

Abrahams is obviously well positioned to look after SuperSports's interests.

Thirdly, it's no use just planting a number of basketball courts around the country if there's no management, maintenance and no coaching systems in place.

Just take a drive through Port Elizabeth and see what most of the basketball courts are used for these days.

Certainly not for basketball!

What about all the missing millions from the BSA coffers?

Sunsport reported as of 31 March 2010, BSA had accumulated losses amounting to R5.7 million and the association's total liabilities exceeded its assets to the tune of the same amount.

SASCOC were left to probe the missing funds.

They're still missing.

And millions more went missing!

Lotto Funding: The great mystery of Basketball SA's missing millions

During 2015, more than R2-million in Lotto money, applied for through Sascoc and reserved for Basketball SA, seemingly grew legs. Nobody knows where the money went, but what we do know is that it definitely didn't go to the NBA as claimed in an expenditure report from Sascoc. - (Daily Maverick, 29 September 2017)

Abrahams and Mokoena both know how to play the political game very well and are always quick to applaud the Sports Minister for his basketball vision.

It's just another boys club, all looking after each other.

The players deserve far better!

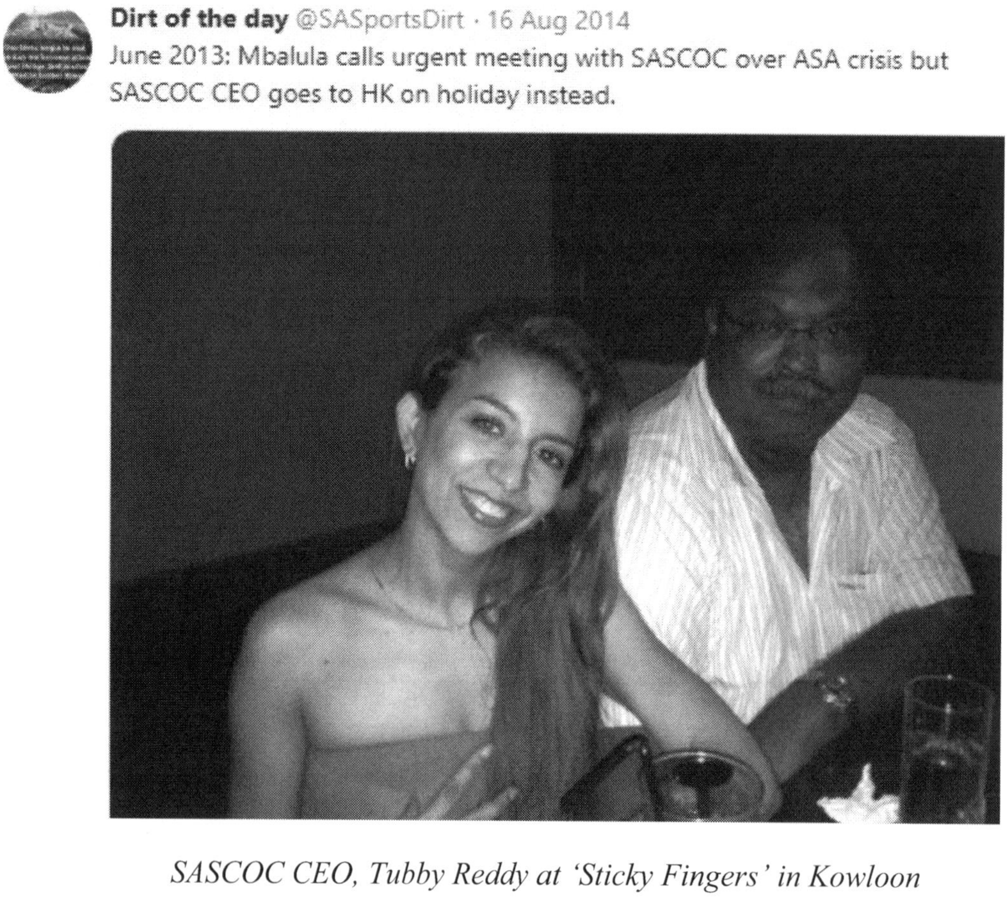

Dirt of the day @SASportsDirt · 16 Aug 2014
June 2013: Mbalula calls urgent meeting with SASCOC over ASA crisis but SASCOC CEO goes to HK on holiday instead.

SASCOC CEO, Tubby Reddy at 'Sticky Fingers' in Kowloon

The CEO of the South African Sports Confederation and Olympic Committee (SASCOC) Tubby Reddy parties up a storm in Hong Kong instead of attending a crucial meeting between the South African Ministry of Sport and Athletics South Africa (ASA). The video clip shows the SA Olympic Sport supremo at a table at one of Kowloon East's more notorious night-spots with a male friend and two regular 'working ladies' around 01:41 on Friday morning 28 June 2013. - Sports-Scoopz

Dirt of the day @SASportsDirt · 17 Aug 2014
Why would Hoskins "cover up" for Roux? Possible answers in a SARU soapbox from last November. sportsfire.co.za/soapbox-maties... - Roux is SARU?

The (KPMG) report confirmed that between 2002 and 2010, the Stellenbosch University (SU) rugby club received around R35-million in funding – this was not part of the official funding allocated by the university, but was "made available" by (Jurie) Roux, using a special piece of software to hide the transactions. The report noted that this mechanism was not supported by SU's financial policies and principles. Roux also made unauthorised payments to the Western Province Rugby Institute. The R35-million that was reallocated was not disclosed to the university council. Roux was assisted in his manipulation of the system by a colleague, Chris de Beer, who was then the deputy director of student fees.(Corruption Watch, 26 February 2016)

22 November 2013

SA Rugby's response to the Stellenbosch University administrative report handed to the South African Police (SAPS), which refers to Jurie Roux, CEO of SARU is a failed drop kick and leaves many questions unanswered.

First, the denial from Roux was just par for the course.

I understand that a report has been filed with the SAPS for investigation, but I have no knowledge of its contents or the accusations against me. I deny any wrongdoing. My main concern now is that this report does not affect the operations of SARU and that the matter is cleared up as soon as possible. With that in mind it would not be helpful in either cause to say anything further at this time.- Jurie Roux

Probably not a bad idea to say anything further in case he incriminates himself, especially as this wouldn't be the first time he's failed to tell the truth.

Just have to go back to the whole Super 15 debacle with the Lions and the Kings.

SARU president, Oregan Hoskins is then quoted as saying:

We are in no position to comment on the detail of the audit as it does not relate to the activities of the South African Rugby Union and pre-dates the appointment of Jurie Roux as CEO of SARU. This is entirely a Stellenbosch University matter and has no bearing on the CEO's role at SARU. All I can say is that Jurie Roux is an outstanding CEO of SARU who, among other things, has been rigorous in ensuring that the highest standards of corporate governance have been applied in our organisation. He continues to enjoy our full confidence and support.

"Has no bearing on the CEO's role at SARU?"

Really?

High standards of corporate governance, like the rogue SARU agents!

It's interesting how SARPA quickly washes their hands off the issue, despite their role to look after the best interests of the players.

SARPA CEO, Piet Heymans said:

According to the SARU Website Chris de Beer is still a registered player agent. Chris is required to submit on a regular basis a list of clients to SARU that he represents. I am not sure when last he has done this. Please enquire from SARU. SARU does have Player Agent Regulations in place and there is a due process to be followed should an agent be expelled or be suspended. Please visit the SARU website and under Regulations view the full detailed SARU Player Agent Regulations. SARPA as such does not have its own rules and regulations pertaining to player agents.

Chris de Beer sold his players to Jason Smith about three weeks ago.

Why? Did he know the South African Police Service (SAPS) was about to take on the case? Many questions but so few answers from SARU, as per usual.

If I was Jurie Roux, I would just resign until my name is cleared. The problem then is - who runs SA Rugby?

Roux has been running the show with Hoskins doing his SuperSport sponsored MBA and SARU deputy president, Mark Alexander has his fingers in a number of different pies including SASCOC and a number of other companies.

May just be a good time for a full forensic audit of SA Rugby.

Dirt of the day @SASportsDirt · 20 Aug 2014
A former and the current CEO of Boxing SA still both suspended on full pay and how did Qithi even get the job? citypress.co.za/sport/boxing-s...

Suspended Boxing SA (BSA) chief executive Moffat Qithi will have pocketed more than R500 000 from taxpayers for doing nothing come the end of this month. Qithi, who earns just more than R100 000 a month, was suspended on full pay in September by his bosses – BSA and the department of sport and recreation – following revelations of previous convictions before he landed the plum job. The South Gauteng High Court was told last year the troubled former Walter Sisulu University chief operating officer had been convicted for possession of stolen property, drunken driving and drinking in public. (City Press, 23 February 2014)

And you can't make this stuff up …

July 2014: Boxing SA CEO suspended, acting CEO then gets suspended and previously suspended CEO comes back, only to be suspended again.

Dirt of the day @SASportsDirt · 21 Aug 2014
Why would SASCOC pay an attorney R 800,000 for working in a "voluntary" capacity on the SASCOC Legal and Arbitration Committee?

From SASCOC insider:

Durban attorney, Siven Samuel served in a voluntary capacity on the SASCOC Legal and Arbitration Committee in 2009

Unbeknown to the Committee, Samuels commenced " working for gain" on behalf of SASCOC (at the behest of its CEO, Tubby Reddy) with Ray Mali, who was appointed Administrator of Athletics SA (ASA)

Fees were paid by the CFO of SASCOC, Vinesh Maharaj, sanctioned by Reddy to Samuels in excess of R 800,000 and when the SASCOC Legal and Arbitration Committee questioned these payments, Samuels did not attend any further meetings and the CEO of SASCOC, "curtailed"the activities of the committee

Subsequently, Reddy then "shifted"the activities of the committee, to another "sub-committee" headed by SASCOC board Member, Mubarak Mohamed

SASCOC was given a "clean audit" for the financial year 2009/2010

Reddy, Maharaj and Samuels are "very long standing"members of Volleyball SA. Reddy is President, Maharaj is Treasurer/CFO and Samuels is a board member. They prepare applications to the National Lottery Distribution Agency ("Lotto") for Sport and Recreation for funding and any attempt to dislodge these persons from Volleyball SA, is met with derision and contempt

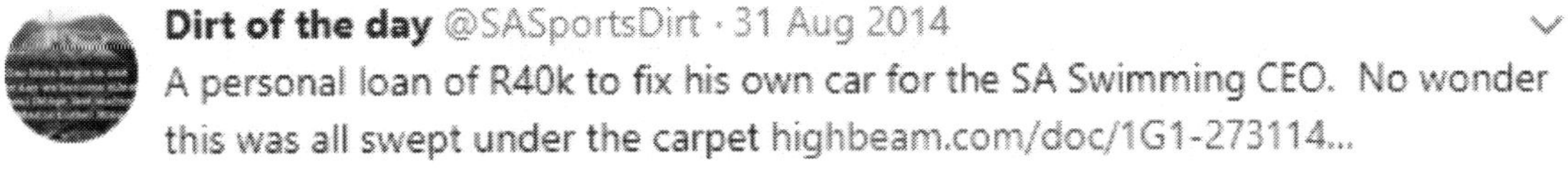
Dirt of the day @SASportsDirt · 31 Aug 2014
A personal loan of R40k to fix his own car for the SA Swimming CEO. No wonder this was all swept under the carpet highbeam.com/doc/1G1-273114...

Swimming SA CEO, Shaun Adriaanse is living the high life while swimmers are still paying their own way. The R40,000 personal loan from Swimming SA account just one of the many accusations levelled against Adriaanse by a former employee.

> Misuse of the withdrawal of cash from the credit card. Financial policies that are never applied by staff, especially you Shaun of flights missed and new bookings being liable for you to pay, the misuse of the company vehicle. Sponsors not getting correct and accurate finance reports, The President spending weekends away with family at the cost of the federation, or certain "friends" of the CEO and President who gets paid in cash for services that was agreed to be sponsored as well as travel expenses that were not paid for others. Believe me it doesn't end here, I have all the facts and documentation – forensic audits need to be conducted immediately as the funding from people like Lotto, Telkom and SRSA is being misused and misallocated – its not going to be possible for you and Samantha to cover all your tracks the bank statements don't lie all the transfers to your and Samantha's account will stand in court – employees might loose CCMA cases but this is no longer the problem the Federation needs to see where the real problem lies. Luckily for the support of the NIA corruption and fraud will not be tolerated.

Adriaanse is another one of those very slippery customers.

When asked about naming himself as team manager for the Commonwealth Games in Glasgow and if there's not a Swimming South Africa (SSA) rule that no employee of the federation can be the manager of a national team?

We would certainly wish to provide you with feedback as context, which is not for quotation or publication. If you are agreeable to this approach we will provide you with detailed feedback. - Shaun Adriaanse

The answer should have been a simple 'yes'.

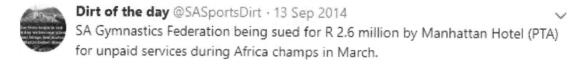

Dirt of the day @SASportsDirt · 13 Sep 2014
SA Gymnastics Federation being sued for R 2.6 million by Manhattan Hotel (PTA) for unpaid services during Africa champs in March.

14 September 2014

The South African Gymnastics Federation (SAGF) is being sued by the Manhattan Hotel in Pretoria for R2.6 million.

The lawsuit stems from unpaid services rendered by the hotel and other suppliers during the 12th African Championships in March this year.

The hotel is the only plaintiff but is also suing SAGF on behalf of other suppliers that form part of the R2.6 million that is outstanding.

According to the hotel, the services included:

- VIP Accommodation and Meals
- Athletes, Coaches, Head of Delegation and Team managers' Accommodation and Meals
- VIP Cocktail Function at Manhattan Hotel
- TV production and SuperSport Broadcasting
- Gautrain Card for all athletes from and to Airport
- VIP Airport Transfers
- Interpreter Fees
- Daily Transfers to and from University of Pretoria's LC de Villiers
- Opening and Closing dancers at event
- Zoo Trip & Lunch packs for Gymnasts
- Printing (Banners etc.) for Event
- VIP Gifts

The championships were hosted by the SAGF and event sponsor, Algrodex under the auspices of the Union Africaine de Gymnastique (UAG).

Before the championships, SAGF CEO, Elizabeth Cameron Smith was quoted as saying:

In partnership with the City of Tshwane and Algrodex the federation looks forward to hosting the 12th African Gymnastics Championships, which will comprise of a fantastic display of entertaining gymnastics, showcasing Africa's top artistic and rhythmic junior and senior Olympic gymnast.

Gymnasts from 12 of the 20 UAG affiliated federations competed in the championships, which catered for some 200 gymnasts, 400 coaches, officials and volunteers.

It is alleged that the SAGF deliberately misled suppliers to save face and continue with event. SportsFire tried to get comment from the SAGF on Friday and got this response on Sunday.

This matter is being dealt with by our lawyers who will reply on Monday morning by 10h00.

The office address for SAGF is listed as 39 Boshof Avenue, Newlands, which also just happens to be a property owned by Cameron-Smith.

Last year, when SportsFire questioned why the SAGF had two offices, the reply was:

The SAGF still has an office supplied by the Johannesburg City Council in Delta Park. This is currently the technical hub of the federation, staffed by 3 full-time staff members. The administrative hub of the federation is currently located in Cape Town, where the CEO and 4 other staff members are based. Having these two offices in the Western Cape and Gauteng has worked for us as these are our 2 largest provinces in the federation.

When asked if 39 Boshof Avenue is also a home address and if any monies from SAGF is paid towards this property for office use?

No reply.

SA has so much gymnastic talent but it's a continual battle due to a lack of funding.

Even at an event like the Commonwealth Games, some SA gymnasts were without coaches and had to move their own apparatus.

The coaches were told they would have to pay their own way if they were to attend.

The federation, unfortunately, does not have any sponsors and relies on various programmes, such as registrations, government grants and events, to remain sustainable. - Cameron-Smith

SASCOC are responsible for the preparation of the SA team for the Commonwealth Games but once again, there were a number of officials, family and friends that were first in line for a 'free trip."

Coaches were expendable.

Dirt of the day @SASportsDirt · 18 Aug 2014
A criminal case has been opened in Paarl re: alleged match fixing in Boland club rugby. Just what SA rugby didn't need right now.

On 14 August 2014 – a case of alleged corruption is opened with the SAPS in Paarl
Complainant: Mr AK Warnick
Suspect: Mr I Pekeur

The description of the complaint:

The complainant received an email stating that there are several referees that have been involved in match fixing. Apparently, suspect threatened them by abusing his position as rugby club president to fix matches otherwise they won't get to referee matches in the future which means they won't receive any match or travelling allowances.

Docket transferred to Wellington SAPS.

Rugby is not so "well" in Wellington and again, SA Rugby (SARU) are ducking and diving.

The former president of the Boland Rugby Union, Francois Davids and the current president, Ivan Pekeur were very close friends up until a couple years ago.

Davids, a former Bok selector, got voted onto the SA Rugby (SARU) executive council in April this year and had to stand down as Boland president.

Pekeur took over as Boland Rugby Union president in June, despite the efforts of Davids to get his new close ally, Bertram Vraagom into the job.

Insiders claim Pekeur is trying to clean up Boland rugby and the match fixing allegations is a "Davids initiated smear campaign" to get him out and Vraagom in at the next Boland elections in February next year.

Boland rugby would seem to be a family affair as Abe Davids was appointed as coach of the senior team last year without the correct qualifications.

It was stated that he was the only coach in the area with an IRB 3 qualification, when in fact he didn't have it and SARU did their best to cover it up, ten months later.

He completed the course, but his coaching diary is waiting to be assessed before he will receive his L3 IRB certificate. - SARU

The Boland academy has raised further suspicions of self gain.

It's alleged that most of the 24 boys in the academy are staying in properties owned by Francois Davids.

Lottery money is being used to fund the SARU academies.

When asked for comment, a touchy SARU GM of Corporate Affairs, Andy Colquhoun replied:

Despite the opinion of colleagues, I have continued to supply you with information and responses to your questions in the belief that, as there is no "smoking gun", you would come to the point where you would have to report that. But you have worn me down and they have been proved correct: I am wasting my time and you'll be wasting your time to email me in the future.

The head of the Boland rugby academy, Barry McDonald failed to respond despite a number of emails and calls.

Davids has bought five properties in the area since the beginning of 2012.

And it doesn't stop there.

There's a company called Wynland Spelersfonds, which so happens to operate out of the Boland rugby offices.

Directors of the company include Francois Davids, Athrop Peterson and former SARU CEO, Riaan Oberholzer.

Is this not a flouting of the SARU Constitution and the Boland Constitution which forbids them from having a vested shareholding in a company doing business with the Boland Rugby Union?

SARU president, Oregan Hoskins emailed me from Argentina last week to say he'll be back on Saturday and will get onto the Boland thing immediately.

Not a word since.

When will SARU and its employees realise they are part of a public organisation and are accountable to the entire rugby community in South Africa?

They have to provide transparency and full disclosure - it is their obligation constitutionally.

SARU has some serious issues to deal with and it doesn't help matters that their CEO, Jurie Roux is under investigation for allegedly misappropriating R35 million while at Stellenbosch University.

Roux's good friend and business partner in a player agency, Chris de Beer was dismissed by the University in 2012 based on his non-compliance to the accepted financial policies and processes of the University.

If Roux was still at the University, sources say he would have also been dismissed with immediate effect.

Instead, he is given a five year contract extension as SARU CEO.

It makes no sense at all.

Hoskins also broke a promise and confidentiality clause by giving Roux a copy of the KPMG forensic report which implicates the CEO in alleged fraud.

So, don't expect much to change in SA rugby - just more smoking guns and mirrors under a cloud of secrecy.

Dirt of the day @SASportsDirt · 14 Sep 2014
SA Rugby lied about the IRB qualifications of Boland coach, Abe Davids to cover for his brother, Francois Davids who sits on SARU exec.

Dirt of the day @SASportsDirt · 27 Nov 2014

Swimmers still having to cough up to represent SA. This is what it's costing for FINA World champs in Doha ...

> This is a partly funded tour for all Team Members. The cost of the tour, for each team member, travelling from South Africa is R15 000.00. Team members travelling from outside of South Africa, must contribute R5000.00 and be responsible for their own flight/travel costs. The full amount must be deposited by 15 October 2014.

Zandberg in deep end with SSA
6 June 2013

Swim SA vs Gerhard Zandberg

The swimmer gets a R50 000 cash fine and a year community service - you'd think we had a criminal on our hands.

Instead, it's just another SA sportsperson feeling the brunt of a bully administration who have little regard for due process.

SA Olympic swimmer, Gerhard Zandberg is a "broken man" after being severely punished for breaking team rules during the FINA world championships in Barcelona.

The story broke that Zandberg had been hauled before a Swim SA (SSA) disciplinary hearing because he had switched hotel rooms to be with his girlfriend.

But according to a couple sources, Zandberg had asked a number of SSA officials six days before his race if he could please move as his "roomie", Cameron van der Burgh had a head cold (which was reported in the media) and he was battling to sleep.

Four days after his request, SSA had not come back to him. So, two days before his race (Thursday) and not being able to sleep, he had little choice but to move to his own room, which he paid for himself.

His girlfriend, Linda joined him in the room.

When SSA management got wind of the move, Zandberg received a WhatsApp message from the team manager at around 10.30pm on the Friday night, asking him to meet with him to discuss some issues. Zandberg didn't respond to the message in time end the meeting was re-scheduled for after lunch on the Saturday after his heat.

Once again, no mention of a disciplinary hearing.

The disciplinary proceedings finished at 4:30pm (30 minutes before he had to leave for the pool to swim the semi-finals).

SSA claimed it was his second breach after criticizing team management on social media earlier in the week.

The combined punishment for the swimmer:

* R 50 000 cash fine (later reduced to R 5000)
* 2 year ban from swimming
* 1 year community service for SwimSA
* Immediate scratching from all World Cup events

Zandberg already does a lot for charity and the community along with his coaching, "Learn to Swim".

How can it be so harsh and were the rights of the swimmer compromised?

For the record, Zandberg, who also didn't receive SA team kit, slipped at the start of his semi and failed to make the final.

He didn't make any excuses for missing out but can you imagine what was weighing on his mind.

I emailed SSA CEO, Shaun Adriaanse asking him for some clarification on the following:

Who did the disciplinary panel consist of, is the punishment in line with the SSA constitution and is the SSA constitution signed?

No response from the CEO.

There has been growing speculation that the SSA constitution is not signed as it does not comply with FINA requirements.

It is also the second time within a week that Adriaanse had failed to respond to an email of mine.

Earlier, I had asked him if SSA had paid for any journalist to attend any championship/event in the last five years.

No response.

It has become a trend for bigger sporting codes to pay for journalists to attend events and I am still of the opinion, it is difficult for some to write objectively and "spill the beans" when they are being wined and dined by officials.

SSA is also forever crying poverty but that didn't stop the CEO from going to Barcelona.

What role did Adriaanse serve when there was already a team manager?

SSA is always looking for handouts but it's time they took a good look at themselves and ask why Telkom withdrew their sponsorship.

Big business leaves SA swimmers to drown

When Chad le Clos edged out Michael Phelps to win the 200m butterfly gold at last year's Olympic Games the future of swimming in South Africa looked bright – but the sport has, since then, seemingly limped from one fiasco to the next. (Mail & Guardian, 26 April 2013)

R2.7 million was given to SSA by the sports ministry for the world champs. Why then did Zandberg have to pay his own way?

Although, SSA have promised to reimburse his flights, Swimmers had to contribute R3000 each for the last World champs in Shanghai and when some questioned why they had to contribute for a fully funded tour, they were told “to be grateful that the rest of the funding was supplied by the federation and not to ask any questions, just be grateful that it wasn't more.”

Meanwhile, the disabled swimmers questioning whether or not, they are getting a fair deal as they head for their championships in Montreal. The able-bodied swimmers spent almost two weeks in Europe to acclimatise whilst the disabled swimmers leave on the 7th of August with a layover in the London for 11 hours then fly to Montreal.

Three days later, some have to swim at the World champs in their main events.

As one high performance coach put it:

There is almost no time difference between SA and Spain, whereas for the disabled swimmers, it’s almost seven hours. One needs at least a day for every hour to acclimatise and SSA knows this. I tell you it is discrimination and they can say what they want.

There has been strong support for Zandberg on twitter:

Former SA swimmer, Kathryn Meaklim tweeted: @ZandbergGerhard it's things like this that make a person glad to have stopped swimming & stay that way. Outrage! Keep ur head high captain.

Media analyst, Lance Rothschild: “Fire SwimSA CEO Shaun Adriaanse. Put the athletes first.”

Don’t hold your breath.

Sadly, SSA is well protected as the president of SSA, Jace Naidoo is also a SASCOC board member.

Dirt of the day @SASportsDirt · 6 Oct 2014
R8.5 million from Sports Trust account paid to "SA Sports awards"? Sports Trust mission is "enhancing education through sport." Really?

Dirt of the day @SASportsDirt · 8 Oct 2014
Octagon suppliers again for Nelson Mandela Sport & Culture day - did they tender? Their response from last Tues?

But the MD of Octagon doesn’t know if they tendered or not?

I wanted to pass it on to Qondisa (Ngwenya) for response as I am not directly involved on the project but we’ve been passing like ships in the night and he is going abroad next week. I will mail him today but please expect a delayed response due to his travel in the coming days. - Mark de Leiburne, Octagon MD

Never heard from Qondisa, who is the Octagon CEO and sits on Fikile Mbalula's transformation committee.

But you can never hide from what is in the public domain. A labour court judgement against the Octagon CEO in October 2013.

[3] The basis for the applicant's claim can be traced to a report prepared by him during March 2013 for presentation to the respondent's board. The report, framed as a draft resolution, summarises nine instances where specific allegations are made against the respondent's chief executive office, Mr Qondisa Ngwenya. These include allegations of financial mismanagement, unauthorised expenditure, breaches of company policy and procedure in relation to the advancement of loans to executive staff and travel, and allegations of misconduct amounting to bribery and fraud. The board meeting was scheduled to consider the report was postponed. Thereafter, in April 2013, the applicant met with the respondent's chairman, Mr Sfiso Buthelezi, when the report was discussed. The chairman undertook to convene a meeting with the applicant and Ngwenya. That meeting did not take place.

Dirt of the day @SASportsDirt · 12 Oct 2014
A powerlifting PR nightmare for SASCOC ...

"Uplifting performances from SA strongmen and women in Argentina" - **SASCOC congratulating power lifters on their home page that are not affiliated to SASCOC and lifters that are currently or previously banned for steroid use? When SASCOC were asked for comment, the story was quickly deleted from the website.**

Dirt of the day @SASportsDirt · 17 Oct 2014
Serious allegations against Shooting SA swept under the carpet in 2012. SASCOC turned another blind eye. Why?

Questions to Shooting SA and SASCOC went unanswered.

After 25 years working as an administrator in the sport of Shooting, I have decided that I can no longer bear what I perceive to be the steady destruction of this sport in the country ... The maladministration, wastage and mismanagement of funds, as well as the disgraceful inability of the Federation to produce medals at the CWG and produce World Class Shooters considering the vast pool of internationally successful juniors in South Africa, or to transform the sport, is not something we wish to negotiate with the very people central to the problem. - Official

President is a guy called Hennie Jacobs and I believe he has a criminal record. Never seen anything so dysfunctional in my life, it is breathtaking. He is violating his own Constitution, the SASCOC arbitration process, everything. He rules by fear. Jacobs goes against every resolution we take to settle the dispute. Jacobs is best friends with Tubby Reddy. - Source

Dirt of the day @SASportsDirt · 6 Nov 2014
How do you develop and grow the sport of Waterpolo when this is what it costs to represent your own country ... ?

Joffers, I saw first-hand last night what you have been talking about with regard to no funding for some of our sporting bodies. I was at St John's last night to watch the SA boys U18 water polo team taking on Zimbabwe in a qualifier for 'Worlds' later this year. On a freezing night at the poolside, our players stood in their speedo's to sing the National Anthem while their Zim opposition were in very smart tracksuits and I'm sure were nice and warm. Our girls and boys teams have NO National kit. Our players also stay with each other during these tournaments as there is no hotel accommodation booked for them. Needless to say, the Zim and Egyptian teams are well looked after. Our water polo coaches managed to find some costume stock (of SA costumes made up for earlier tournaments) at Turbo Sports so at least the whole team has the same costume to play in (despite some sizing issues). This is a disgrace, especially when Zim are very smartly kitted out despite all of their problems and lack of money! These boys and girls also have to fund their own tours to Turkey later this year (like the senior teams going to the Commonwealth Games). By the way, we won the match 18-5 with up and coming star Dayne Jagga in a class of his own (he scored 9 goals!). He really is going to be a superstar and is currently looking at scholarship options at USA varsities for when he leaves school at the end of the year. – via email (14 March 2014)

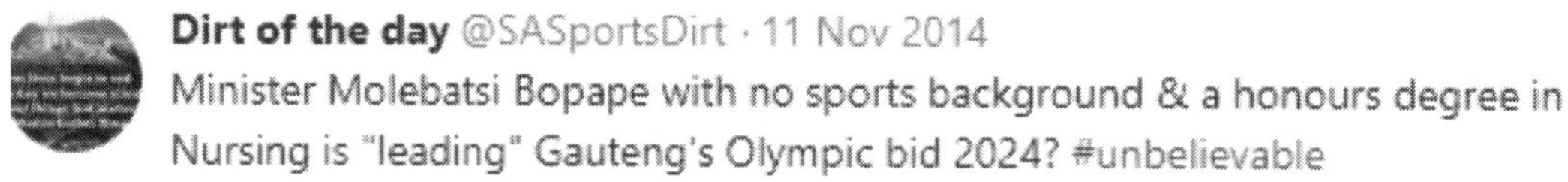
Dirt of the day @SASportsDirt · 11 Nov 2014
Minister Molebatsi Bopape with no sports background & a honours degree in Nursing is "leading" Gauteng's Olympic bid 2024? #unbelievable

Gauteng Olympic Bid
29 April 2015

The Gauteng Province wants to bid for the 2024 Olympic Games.

Yes, the Gauteng Province.

Is this just another "golden" opportunity to loot the state coffers, similar to World Cup 2010, the arms deal etc.?

Gauteng's MEC for Sport, Arts, Culture and Recreation, Molebatsi Bopape made the Province's intentions known during a press briefing at the SportAccord IF Forum in Lausanne last year.

Bopape is the Chairperson of the Health and Social Development Committee and has an honours degree in Nursing.

She has NO sports background.

It would seem that a company, Worldview Sports Management (which I can't find a listing for anywhere) was quickly hired to put a document together before Bopape went to Switzerland.

The proposal was to:

Move some of the indoor sports (or events) in the Summer Games to the Winter Games. This restructuring would most notably increase the number of countries participating in the Winter Games, increasing global interest in the Winter Games.

The Winter Games already have indoor sports -- and these attract attendees who have trouble with the outdoor venues: curling, figure skating, ice hockey, short-track speed skating, and speed skating. The venues for these sports are held in urban venues away from the outdoor venues. Some indoor sports (or events) historically part of the Summer Games could be held in urban venues as part of the Winter Games.

The indoor Summer Games sports (or events) eligible for transfer are: badminton, basketball, boxing, some cycling events, fencing, gymnastics, handball, judo, table tennis, taekwondo, volleyball (not beach volleyball), weightlifting, and wrestling. In addition, some sports or events that may be held outdoors during the Summer Game could easily be held indoors as part of the Winter Games: diving, swimming, synchronized swimming, tennis, water polo, and some track and field events.

Of course, for a variety of reasons, many indoor sports (or events) would not be transferred away from the Summer Games.

For your convenience, I list the following Summer Games outdoor sports: archery, some track and field (marathon, decathlon, pentathlon, cross country), triathlon, canoe and kayaking, rowing, sailing, some cycling, beach volleyball, soccer, field hockey, polo, and shooting.

"Move some of the indoor sports (or events) in the Summer Games to the Winter Games?"

The suggestion of having some sports move from summer to winter games is not new but the decision is made by the IOC and not the host city.

Just who is Worldview Sports Management and how does a person with 30 years of nursing experience become Gauteng's MEC for Sport, Arts, Culture and Recreation?

E-mails to the Sports Ministry, Gauteng Sports, Art and Culture and SASCOC were unanswered.

We may also be putting the cart before the horse with a Gauteng bid as the IOC would still need to change under the Agenda 2020 reform for provinces/regions to host the Games as oppose to just cities.

Six months later …

Sports MEC shuffles off under a cloud

Instead of firing his MEC of sport, arts and culture and recreation, Gauteng Premier David Makhura "demoted" Molebatsi Bopape by making her the MEC for social development, a department with a shoestring budget. His move comes after serious allegations were made implicating her in corruption, maladministration and financial mismanagement … The Mail & Guardian is in possession of a dossier that contains the allegations levelled against Bopape. It reveals how she was implicated in allegedly demanding a bribe, allegedly attempting to manipulate tender processes and allegedly used department funds for expensive trips and to upgrade her home. (Mail & Guardian, 20 November 2015)

Dirt of the day @SASportsDirt · 15 Nov 2014
WADA doping conference in SA in 2013 was "wholly WADA sponsored" - why then was R10 million paid out of Sports Trust account for this event?

Dirt of the day @SASportsDirt · 18 Dec 2014
World Beach Volleyball and UIM Powerboating events in Bloem - something not adding up ... sportsfiredaily.co.za/article.php?id...

“Big in Bloem”
14 December 2014

Two world sporting events in Bloemfontein last weekend as the city played host to the FIVB beach volleyball tour and the UIM F2 Powerboating championship.

An oddity and questions need to be raised about both events and where’s the money coming from.

I actually watched a little of the volleyball on SuperSport and that’s when it immediately struck me – why Bloem?

Surely, an event of that magnitude during the holiday period should have been played in Cape Town, Durban or Port Elizabeth in front of big crowds but the Free State government obviously has some big pull with SASCOC and enough expenditure to go round.

Just who is involved in that relationship and who is really benefitting?

There is allegedly a very beneficial financial relationship between individuals within both camps. Even SA swimming star, Ryk Neethling who hails from Bloem was mystified about the event in his hometown.

He tweeted …

*Ryk Neethling @**RykNeethling** Dec 14 Beach Volleyball World Tour stop in Bloemfontein in Dec must be the oddest location for a world sporting event*

The Powerboating event also raised serious eyebrows.

Which government sporting body gave SA Powerboating (PSA) the permission to go ahead and host a World Championship event when there hasn’t even been a SA National championship since 2010?

SASCOC board member and former PSA administrator, Kobus Marais said:

The F2 World Championship has got no relation to national championships, according to my knowledge. No member of SASCOC can host an international event without the required approval.

But when pushed for answers to the following:

* Even though the F2 World Championships has no relation to Power Boating's National Championships, SASCOC has still given approval for PB to host the event?

* Does PB even do F2, and if so why then have they not held SA National championships for the event?

* How do athletes gain their licences, is it merely a matter of registration and having the money to own a boat, or is there a process of qualification?

* If there is not a process of qualification, is it not an embarrassment for two South Africans to enter when there is no measure of their competence?

* When did SASCOC approve the application and are they not concerned about any of the above questions?

* Also for a code/discipline they do not cater for?

Marais: *I refer you to PSA and SASCOC respectively for these operational questions.*

Nice cop out and no response from SASCOC as usual and the two pilots who competed for SA in Bloem didn't fare too well.

Attie Tromp was 13 out of 15 competitors, two laps behind the winner and Wynand de Jager (the son of the PSA president) did not finish.

Are there more competent pilots just sitting at home and being an international event, did SASCOC rubber stamp these selections with no qualification criteria?

The president of PSA, Christo de Jager told SportsFire that "the event is part sponsored by the Free State Government, hencc the reason for the event to be hosted in Sasolburg in the Free State."

But is it public funds and was there a tender?

I kindly request you to contact the Free State government to find out what money they are using for the event. During the initial phases of the event about 3 years ago numerous cities were considered as host cities but after an inspection by the UIM representatives it was decided that the Vaal River was the most suitable venue for the international event. - Christo de Jager

In other words, no tender and no transparency where the money is coming from.

It would be interesting to see who signed these contracts for the two global events and who is really benefitting from the "sponsorship" money?

Dirt of the day @SASportsDirt · 8 Dec 2014
SASCOC CEO Tubby Reddy would be 7th on this list ...

South African parastatal CEO salaries

CEO	Parastatal	Salary (latest financial year)
Brian Dames	Eskom	R22.8 million
Sipho Maseko	Telkom	R11.7 million
Percy Sechemane	Rand Water	R5.32 million
Siza Mzimela	SAA	R4.96 million
Soane Mohapi	Sentech	R3.14 million
Brian Molefe	Transnet	R2.95 million
Puleng Kwele	Broadband Infraco	R1.84 million
Tian Olivier	SABC	R1.76 million
Chris Hlekane	SA Post Office	R1.56 million

What is the South African 2020 Olympic Bid Company?
14 July 2014

Good question.

The company was registered in 2010 with four directors:

Gideon Sam (SASCOC President)
Sundrasagren "Tubby" Reddy (SASCOC CEO)
Heeralall Dhaniram "Vinesh" Maharaj (SASCOC CFO)
Peter Goldhawk (Director of Gride Investments and board member of the Sports Trust)

The company was registered as a non-profit company but why it was also limited to these four "private" members raises a few eyebrows.

In August 2011, the Ministry of Sports and Recreation and the National Olympic committee (SASCOC) confirmed that there would be no bid for the 2020 Games.

One would have thought that company would have been deregistered.

But three years on, it was still in business with the same four directors.

When SportsFire asked Gideon Sam just before the Commonwealth Games why the 2020 bid company was not dissolved after the bid did not materialise?

His response was:

I draw a blank on this one. 2020 bid of what??

He then called me back 15 minutes later to say the company was dormant but was not deregistered as they were going to use it for the Commonwealth bid. Sam also made it clear to me that he would have to resign as director of the bid company as it would be a conflict of interests as he is vice-president of the Commonwealth Games federation.

Peter Goldhawk contradicted Sam by saying:

The company is dormant and has never operated. It has been deregistered by CIPC. It was formed to protect the name should South Africa have decided to make a bid for the 2020 Olympics.

But as of June 2014, the South African 2020 Olympic Bid company was "in business".

When Goldhawk was made aware of this as well as the fact that that the company had filed annual returns for the last three years, he said:

I am not privy to what has been decided by SASCOC. To my knowledge, the company has been dormant since inception and has not had any activity. Please therefore address any other questions to SASCOC.

Not privy to decisions in a company that you're a director of and what has SASCOC got to do with it as it is a separate legal entity?

Deloitte & Touche (who are also SASCOC's auditors) are listed as the current auditors of the bid company and when approached for comment.

I will need to check the 2020 Bid Company if we have been formally appointed. We have considered the entity as part of the consolidated audit but the company does not reach the threshold for an audit under the Companies Act. - Leonard de Rooij

Deloitte were also not in possession of the founding documents of the SA 2020 Olympic Bid company.

As usual, no reply from Vinesh Maharaj, the CFO at SASCOC.

If two of the four directors don't know what's happening with this company, what is the role of the other two directors, Maharaj and the SASCOC CEO, Tubby Reddy?

Who is actually running SASCOC?

Is Sam just a puppet for the Reddy and Maharaj show?

Dirt of the day @SASportsDirt · 13 Dec 2014
Investigation back on into KZNA athletics where at least R4 million in Lottery money was misappropriated under watch of current ASA boss

Athletics SA ASA) president Aleck Skhosana is not fit to hold any office in athletics and should Skhosana was chairperson of the body between 2009 and 2012. (City Press, 1 November 2015)

Dirt of the day @SASportsDirt · 15 Dec 2014
A number of top SA athletes have still not been reimbursed by SASCOC for their flights to and from the Commonwealth Games #justnotright

Dirt of the day @SASportsDirt · 19 Dec 2014
My wish list for SA sport for 2015 sportsfiredaily.co.za/article.php?id...

None of my wishes came true as the corruption and maladministration in SA sport carries on ad - nauseam.

This would be my last tweet @SASportsDirt as the account didn't create the ground swell desired.

It may have needed more time but twitter is hit or miss as people generally follow hundreds of other handles on this social media platform.

They weren't always going to see your tweet. I was losing hope but couldn't give up the fight.

Never give up on something that you can't go a day without thinking about. - Winston Churchill

I thought about it every hour and had to finish what I started.

Chapter 13: Wanted!

Have you heard of an alleged attempted rape and fraud case in VSA's (Volleyball South Africa's) organisation / members that seem to have been swept under the table? I don't have too much info (wish I had) but know that they are real. Maybe your influence can uncover the truth and expose Mr Reddy and friends on the VSA / SASCOC boards? – Tip off from a South African volleyball player

The alleged rape charges were against a former Olympian.

The victim was a female he coached at the University of Johannesburg, but the charges were supposedly dropped, thanks to VSA's intervention.

It was obviously a very sensitive matter and I attempted to get comment from the coach in question and Tubby Reddy but both failed to respond to several emails.

On 6 August 2014, I received an email from another very good source who had been at a volleyball meeting and at drinks afterwards, he got wind of the potential tapping of my cellphone.

Your name came up and the discussion was how information is leaking to you. (including the financials amongst other) Anyway, as one does, he (Gershon Rorich) went off about you and said that Tubby is going to get you because he has access to people in the NPA (National Prosecution Authority) and can wiretap phones etc.

It came as no surprise to me as even before this alert, I had been asking around how one knows if your cellphone is being tapped.

I got a wide range of answers but nothing to really satisfy the mind.

Often, I could hear a crackling noise on the other end and my phone battery was dying a lot quicker than normal.

Tell-tale signs of phone tapping?

Maybe, this was Tubby Reddy's next move to get me to stop trying to dig up the dirt on this alleged rape case and cover up.

I wasn't going to be deterred and made contact with the University of Johannesburg.

I am concerned about the implications of providing information to you. I contacted our legal advisors and will revert back to you in due course. Mr …….was employed as a temporary staff member at UJ Sport with the portfolio of Volleyball Coach. His employment was terminated in 2012. - Sampat Coetzee, Director UJ Sport

I wanted to find out the reason for the termination of his position as coach before digging deeper.

The legal advisory put a spike in that.

It is our submission that the information you have requested is in fact protected by both the Constitution and the Protection of Personal Information Act. Subsequently, we regret to inform you that we are unable to furnish you with the information requested. You are however entitled to formally request such information through our PAIA system (Promotion of Access to Information Act 2 of 2002) - Eugene Bascerano, UJ Legal Advisory

The PAIA system is tedious and I was a one-man band but I regret not following through with this request.

Did the female victim/s get justice?

A number of current and former SA players have lost faith in the SA volleyball system and as one put it:

The news of Tubby holding two positions, which appears in conflict with regulations, has come out a number of times but seems never to be addressed. It is good that you write about and highlight problems in the hierarchy of sports administration as I believe there is huge room for improvement. However the question remains – who has the power to address these matters and bring about change, and more importantly what will motivate those influential parties to bring about those changes? I fear the general public are relatively powerless in this regard as are athletes…

The athletes have been silenced and SASCOC are doing their utmost to silence them even further with new President's Council resolutions.

> **There will be punitive measures for any person leaving the country without receiving approval from SASCOC*
>
> ** Any member who institutes legal action against SASCOC and NFs (National Federations) without following the internal dispute mechanism, shall have their SASCOC membership terminated*

Is it not illegal to stop people from approaching the Courts as it is a right given to all South Africans in terms of the South African Constitution?

I am an ex-olympic athlete and come from the federation led by the SASCOC CEO Tubby Reddy. All has not been well for years in volleyball and in NOCSA and now SASCOC. I have refocussed my passion and attention to education (could have focussed this on sport coaching in SA but I chose to get out because of the poison in sport and especially in my sport of volleyball that is controlled by the same "cabal" that manages sport in SA). How many good and learned people have left or been squeezed out I wonder? There is also some very interesting things that went down in Athens that most people don't know about. Most important is the detailed report that the sport psychologist at the games, Clinton Gahweiler wrote and submitted around what the true stress of the athletes at the games were. What the main problem was in effect. I give you one guess... the administrators of course.

Clinton never got feedback on his report, no response at all, and was never invited to another national endeavour again. He runs a very successful sport psychology practice and also performs in and writes songs for his local band. He is not willing to fight these guys and really neither was I. But I think now that I have more than 6 years of space from the toxic sport scene, I may be ready to consider a project that seriously reflects on grassroots sport and the possibility of social cohesion through sport, elite sport and these mega events, how individual athletes make it on their own and in fact in spite of their administrators, and where these leading figures in sport come from, and the politics in sport. I think this could be an interesting read for the general public and also to try and expose some of these assholes that keep earning big salaries and under-performing, and even worse holding sport ransom so they can keep milking it.

No question about it, there is a cabal running sport in South Africa.

On 1 October 2014, I had a breakfast meeting with the Democratic Alliance Deputy Shadow Minister for Sports and Recreation, Darren Bergman at JB's Corner in Melrose Arch.

Ten minutes after we sat down at our table to discuss the state of SA sport, two middle aged white men, looking totally misplaced, sat down at the table right next to us.

Immediately, I had a feeling they were planted there for a reason.

I was uncomfortable but made sure I kept an eye on them as they looked aimlessly around the restaurant within earshot of our conversation. I even glared at them to make sure they knew, I knew something was up.

Darren was mostly interested in what has happening in SA Rugby and said he wanted to find financial support for my new digital platform, SportsFire Daily as it was vital that I keep on exposing the truth in SA sport as the mainstream press was doing very little.

As I stood up to leave our meeting, I saw one of the suspicious looking men quickly pull out his cell-phone to make a call.

I exited the restaurant and could see to my right in the near distance, another middle-aged person standing next to his motorbike on the sidewalk and looking at his cell-phone. I stared at him for a couple minutes before making my way to my car, which was parked around the next corner.

There was no question in my mind that I was being followed.

It was an uneasy feeling and I was now looking over my shoulder wherever I went.

A month later, I was a guest for a television series, #LoveChange stories and was interviewed by former Carte Blanche presenter, Ruda Landman.

The interview gave me a chance to share just about everything on the good, bad and ugly in SA sport.

It was very therapeutic talking to Ruda, who had been an investigative reporter/journalist for over 19 years.

Graeme Joffe on the good, bad, and ugly in South African sport

Most South Africans are at least a little bit crazy about sport. We wear our green-and-gold fan-shirts, we yell and cheer and rant at the ref from our couches or the stands, we deliver our impassioned play-

by-play analysis around the watercooler on a Monday morning. But Graeme Joffe is different. He's a whole lot crazy about sport. As a participant, spectator, commentator and reporter for CNN, Highveld 94.7, and now his own sports journal, SportsFire Daily, "Joffers" has been able to turn his love for sport into a multimedia career. At the same time, as one of the few hardcore investigative sports reporters in South Africa, he has lifted the lid on the dark side of our obsession, bringing corruption, wasteful spending, and maladministration to light, and landing himself with a R21-million defamation suit from Olympic body SASCOC in the process. - Ruda Landman

After the interview, I headed for a lunch with a cousin at a restaurant in Illovo.

I was a little early and was going through some emails on my phone as well as the latest news on twitter.

I was now the news – fake news!

An anonymous, highly defamatory website, Facebook page and twitter account, "Joffers-Exposed" had been created to try and discredit me.

The anonymous cowards tweeted the link for the fake website to SA sportsmen and women, sporting federations and the few companies that were advertising on my SportsFire Daily.

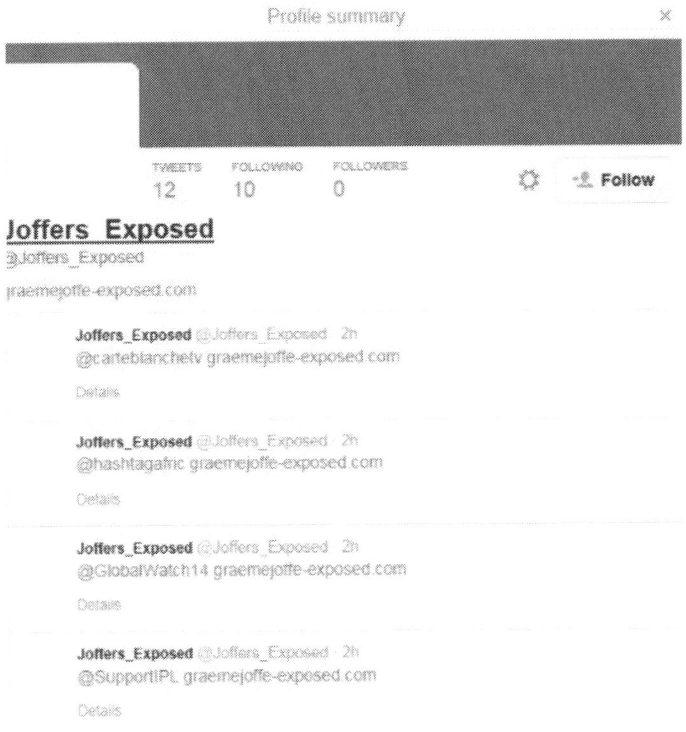

The Facebook page was an impersonation and they were loving their poster of me tagged with "Wanted for Crimes against Journalism".

Oh what fun!

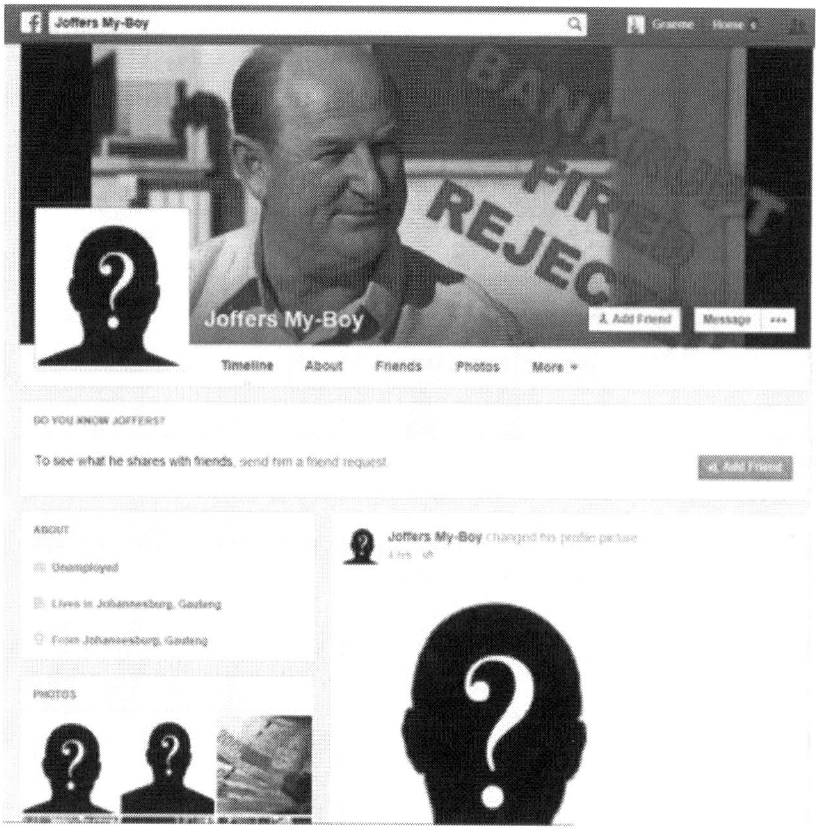

I could barely eat my lunch as I just wanted to get home and start investigating the f…..g (if you'll excuse my French) creeps who had now crossed the line with this sick, anonymous attempt to defame me.

I had a strong inclination who was behind it.

The made up stories were disgusting but there were one or two very personal things including my place of abode, which confirmed my suspicions that my phone was being illegally tapped and my emails were hacked.

My email account, *graeme@butterbean.co.za* had been hacked.

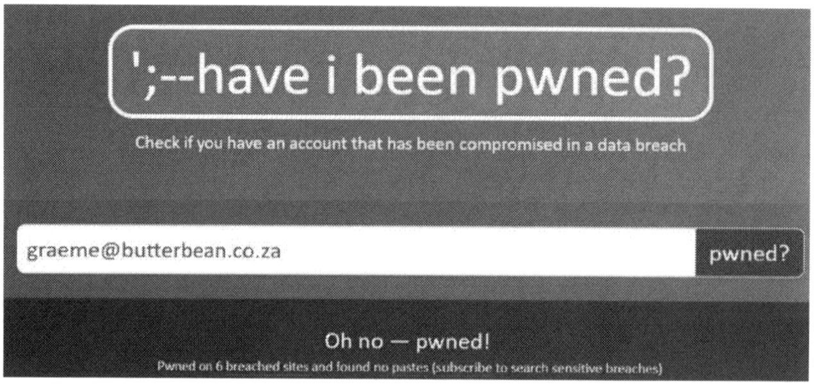

And when you went to Google search "Graeme Joffe", the link to the website was already on the first page.

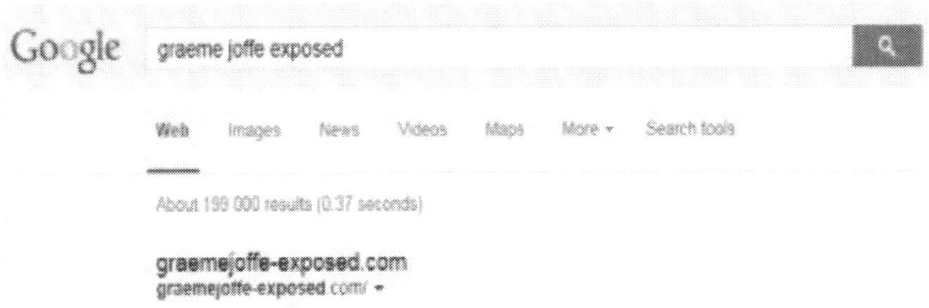

I sent Facebook a report of the fraud, defamation and impersonation.

Within a couple days, the page was removed but the tweets with the link to the website continued relentlessly and every week they posted a new fake story.

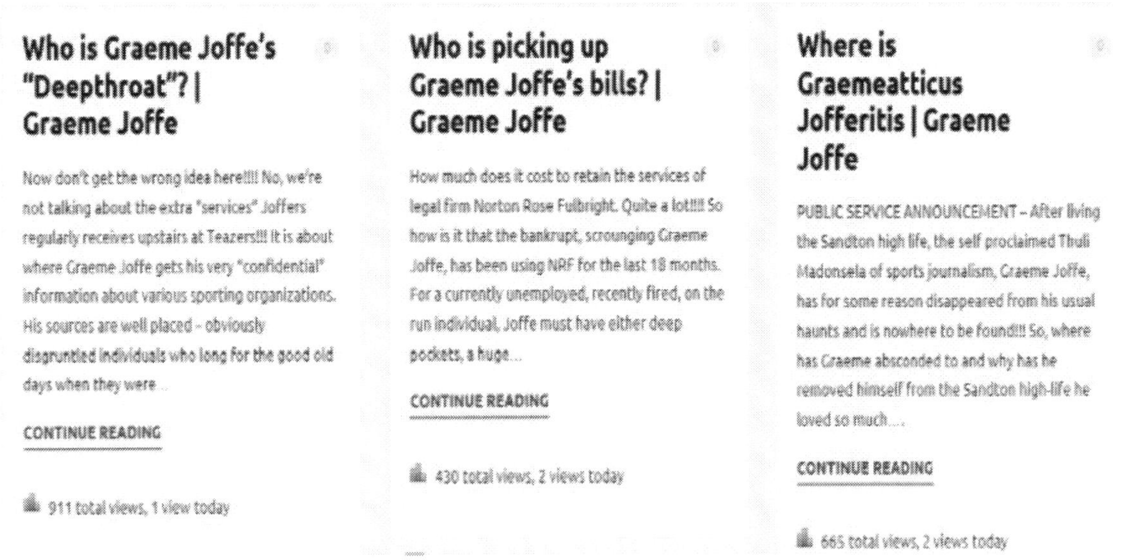

The bloggers were only interested in one thing ….

To discredit and take Graeme Joffe down!

Justice For Reeva @Truth2Come · 24 Nov 2014
@JoffersExposed Here's my issue. WHY are YOU twting ME (& others) about GraemeJoffe to crucify his name (I don't even know Jofffe)?
View conversation

Justice For Reeva @Truth2Come · 24 Nov 2014
@JoffersExposed whatever...however it seems you are on a very determined path to annihilate his name GLOBALLY. Why? What he do to u?
View conversation

Justice For Reeva @Truth2Come · 24 Nov 2014
@JoffersExposed @tyronemaseko @ulrichroux @mariusdutoit @CriminalLawZA @mbaincorporated
This -------> See conversation.
View conversation

Justice For Reeva @Truth2Come · 24 Nov 2014
@JoffersExposed What's your motive? Why are you spamming twitter accounts with YOUR story against Graeme Joffe?
View conversation

Justice For Reeva @Truth2Come · 24 Nov 2014
@JoffersExposed Why a malicious assault on Joffe? Motive? Are u a PISTORIAN (or Carl) getting back forex-ICON #LyingKiller Oscar Pistorius!?
View conversation

They also used different pseudonym twitter handles to get the blogs out and who would be the one guy to re- tweet their link?

DA parliamentarian and SASCOC board member, Kobus Marais @kobusda

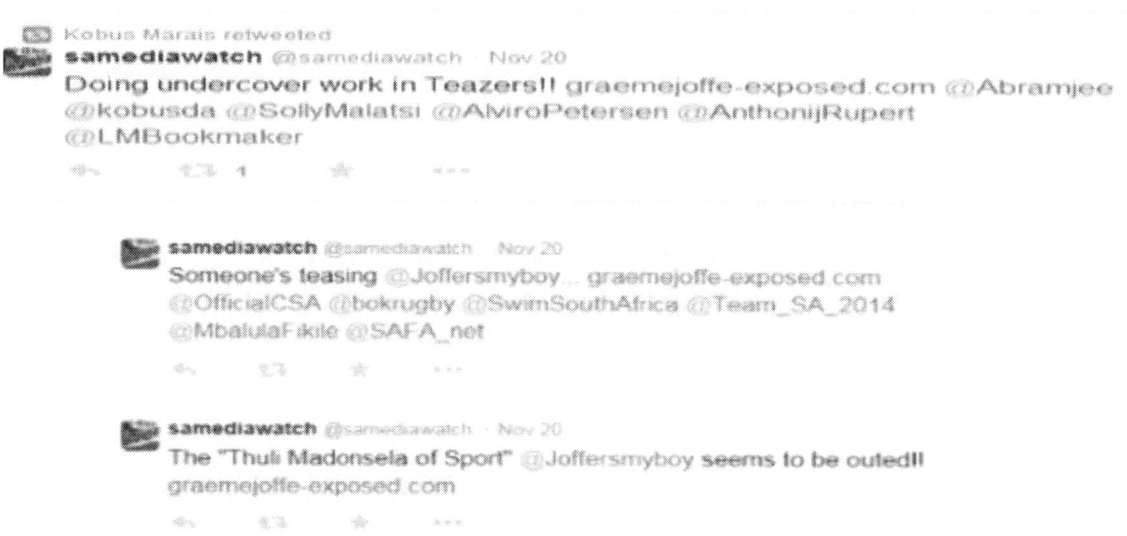
Kobus Marais retweeted
samediawatch @samediawatch · Nov 20
Doing undercover work in Teazers!! graemejoffe-exposed.com @Abramjee @kobusda @SollyMalatsi @AlviroPetersen @AnthonijRupert @LMBookmaker

samediawatch @samediawatch · Nov 20
Someone's teasing @Joffersmyboy... graemejoffe-exposed.com @OfficialCSA @bokrugby @SwimSouthAfrica @Team_SA_2014 @MbalulaFikile @SAFA_net

samediawatch @samediawatch · Nov 20
The "Thuli Madonsela of Sport" @Joffersmyboy seems to be outed!! graemejoffe-exposed.com

I worked tirelessly on finding out the source of the website and what server was hosting it.

Fortunately, these guys were not so clever.

Using my name and a London address, they registered the blog with NAMECHEAP.COM. (ironic for their cheap shots).

Blog: http://graemejoffe-exposed.com/

Domain Name: GRAEMEJOFFE-EXPOSED.COM
Registry Domain ID: 886096184_DOMAIN_COM-VRSN
Registrar WHOIS Server: whois.enom.com
Registrar URL: www.enom.com
Updated Date: 2014-12-06T02:52:13.00Z
CreationDate: 2014-11-19T14:00:00.00Z
Registrar Registration Expiration Date: 2015-11-19T14:00:00.00Z
Registrar: ENOM, INC.
Registrar IANA ID: 48
Reseller: NAMECHEAP.COM
Domain Status: clientTransferProhibited
Registry Registrant ID:
Registrant Name: GRAEME JOFFE
Registrant Organization:
Registrant Street: 100 BOND STREET
Registrant
City:
LONDON
Registrant Phone: +44.2084438765
Updated Date: 25-mar-
Creation Date:
19-nov-2014
Expiration Date:
19-nov-2015

The server for OFFSHORERACKS.COM was in Panama.

It didn't matter how many emails I sent to the registrar or Offshore Racks showing them it was impersonation, fraud and defamation, they weren't interested in helping.

The only way I would be able to get any kind of assistance would be to get a US Court order to try and get them to comply. But after my initial complaints, the registrant's name was changed from Graeme Joffe to Francisco Gonzalez with a local address in Panama.

What some companies will do for money and to protect their sleazy clients?

Registrar Abuse Contact abuse
Email: @enom.com
Registrar Abuse Contact
Phone: +1.4252982646
Reseller:
NAMECHEAP.COM
Domain Status: clientTransferProhibited
Registry Registrant ID:
Registrant Name: FRANCISCO GONZALEZ
Registrant Organization: OR

Registrant Street:
CALIDONIA, 40
ESTE 10000
Registrant Street: E.
BALBOA POINT P7
Registrant City:
PANAMA CITY
Registrant Phone: +507.62488550

I called the +507 number and the person on the other side said he knew nothing about offshore racks but I wasn't the first person that had called him about it.

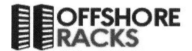

OFFSHORE RACKS

305-647-2581 Call us Now

The office number they listed on their website was also not in use and has since been removed from their website. They really are "high privacy hosting."

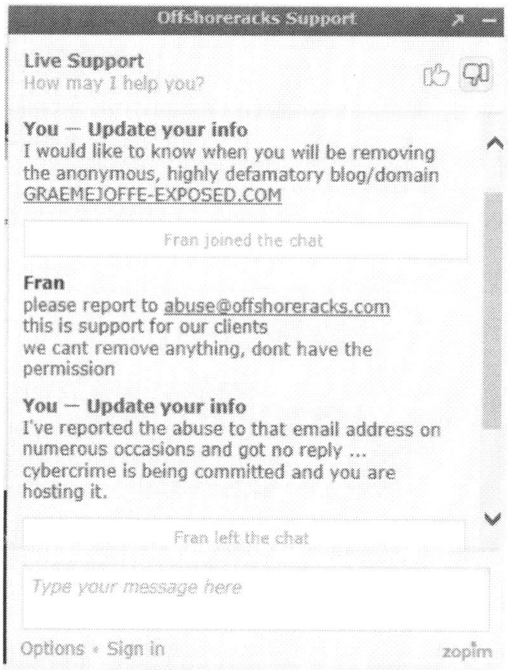

The website disappeared from cyberspace on the domain expiration date, 19 November 2015 but I wasn't going to let them get away with it.

A couple forensic linguists were already working on it for me.

I've spent some time doing some background research and I'm aghast. The Graeme Joffe exposed website is disgraceful in its juvenile vindictiveness and I hope to help bring the perpetrators down. - Colin Michell

Chapter 14: The Missing Police File

Personal threats on twitter, followed at Melrose Arch, cell-phone illegally tapped, emails hacked and now the anonymous, defamatory website.

Who knows what would be next? I felt as if the clock was ticking for something really ugly to happen to me.

I went to the Sandton SAPS (South African Police Service) in Johannesburg on Thursday 4 December 2014 to open up a criminal case.

Officer Ramuru attended to my request but she didn't know under which act the 'unlawful interception of phone calls' fell under and asked for assistance from one of the senior male staff members, whose name I wish I had remembered.

He quickly glanced at some of my evidence including the tweets and told me, "these are no threats" and there's no need to open the case.

The officer was just being loyal to his ANC government/employer as the Sports Ministry and Fikile Mbalula were being mentioned in a bad light.

It didn't take me long to lose my patience and I asked the male officer what gives him the right to decide what is and isn't a threat to which he angrily replied:

We are the first judge.

I wasn't going to win this battle and went upstairs to one of the management offices where a SAPS captain glanced at the evidence, said they were real threats and told the officer to open the case. The next hour was painful to say the least as Ramuru very slowly and unwillingly took down my statement.

I was told to call the next day to get my case number.

I called the next day and there was no trace of my file but was told to call back on Monday.

On the Monday, I called again and still there was no trace of my file.

I made another stop at the Sandton SAPS, went back upstairs and met with a Captain Mabasa. He seemed to recognize my name from somewhere (maybe he was a 94.7 Highveld Stereo listener) and was willing to assist.

He told me to type up the statement and he himself would investigate.

I went back home, typed it up as below and hand delivered it to Captain Mabasa.

Statement: 8 December 2014

I, Graeme Joffe, a sports journalist working for Butterbean Productions/SportsFire Daily, residing at ..... West Road South, Morningside have reason to believe that my cell-phone (083 ....) is being tapped (my calls are being intercepted).

I've been exposing corruption in SA sport for the last three years and have received a number of threats via email and twitter and have been followed to suggesting that some individual/s know my exact whereabouts.

I received a tip off about two months ago saying that the "SASCOC CEO, Mr Tubby Reddy would get me as he has friends in high places and they would tap my phone." There has since been anonymous publication of where I live and some of my personal business.

On Wednesday 1 October 2014, I was followed by two elderly white Afrikaans gentlemen to a meeting at Melrose Arch. They sat at the table next to my meeting at JB Rivers and looked around and stared at me trying to listen in to my conversation. As soon as I got up to leave the meeting, the one gentleman quickly picked up his phone to call someone and there was a gentleman on a motorbike watching me when I left the restaurant. I made sure he was aware that I knew what was going on and I left Melrose Arch and that was the last I saw of them.

During my time of exposing all the corruption in SA sport, I have received a number of threats mainly on the social media platform, twitter.

The threats have come from the Department of Sport and Recreation (@Sport&Rec_RSA) which falls under the Honourable Sports Minister, Mr Fikile Mbalula and from an anonymous source who goes by (@MdoZulu) on twitter.

Hereunder just a couple of the examples of the threats from August 2014:

Sport & Rec SA @SPORTandREC_RSA Aug 2

> *@Joffersmyboy you are fat big looser big looser of the century , looser of no substance time will catchup with you and your deeds.*

MdoZulu<image001.jpg>Mdo Michael Zulu @MdoZulu 1h

> *My comrade @MbalulaFikile u must stop this anti black fool @Joffersmyboy he writes rubbish for DA stooges. We will March to his house*

MdoZulu<image001.jpg>Mdo Michael Zulu @MdoZulu 1h

> *@Joffersmyboy U a fool boy. 947 fired u too because u write rubbish. My ANC will mobilize to stop u*

MdoZulu<image001.jpg>Mdo Michael Zulu @MdoZulu 1h

> *@Joffersmyboy U right rubbish. Cnn fired you? No wonder. You a useless bitter fart*

I opened a case with the SAPS Sandton on Thursday 4 December 2014 but there is no sign of the case or a case no.

The case was opened by officer, Ramuru.

Signed:

Graeme Joffe

Captain Mabasa said not to worry, he'll sort this out but he had no knowledge of twitter and how it works.

I mentioned it would be the important to find out who was the author of the twitter account for the Department of Sport and Recreation and to get MTN (the mobile telecommunications company) to investigate the illegal tapping of my cellphone.

I received a text message from SAPS on 9 December 2014 which stated: CONST. JM MABASO will investigate your case SANDTON ref nr CAS 295/12/2104. Unit contact details: 011-7224200. Do NOT reply to this SMS.

The name of the captain was spelt incorrectly, the case number should have read 2014 and not 2104 but this just was par for the course.

The stakes had been raised by opening up a criminal case and I felt it would be safer for me to move out of my rented apartment in Johannesburg and relocate to Grahamstown in the Eastern Cape, where I had gone to university.

Fortunately, my landlord was very understanding. Thank you, Simon Malone.

I had changed as a person and needed to have some kind of life again, without having to look over my shoulder the whole time.

The daily grind of exposing corruption and the negativity had caught up with me and my fuse had become very short.

I wanted to do as much as I could before leaving Johannesburg and tried repeatedly to get assistance from MTN.

I got a couple automated responses but that's about it and only ten days later, did I get a MTN human.

We apologize for the delayed response. Please be advised that the investigating officer has to call our Fraud department. - Tatum Love, MTN SA

Where was the "love" from MTN after I had been a customer of theirs since returning to South Africa in 1999?

I texted Captain Mabasa the same day to give him the MTN information, their fraud department number and to see if there was an update on my case.

No response.

I packed up my apartment within a few days, put a lot in storage and dropped off bags of clothes for the golf caddies at the Country Club of Johannesburg, where I had been a golf member for 14 years.

Golf had become my only escape and poor old "Snoops", my long-time caddie would often be on the receiving end of my grumpy rumblings after a missed putt and there were a lot of them.

Sorry Snoops!

My golfing buddies had to put up with a lot as well (the happy go lucky Joffers was no longer) but I don't think any of them could really understand what I was going through.

I didn't realize it either.

Boys, I'm sorry!

I was struggling to let my hair down, the little I had left, although I remember letting loose, playing in the same four-ball with SA cricket great, Herschelle Gibbs in a corporate golf day at Houghton shortly before I left Johannesburg.

Golf day at Houghton with Herschelle Gibbs

I could seldom divorce myself from the corruption in SA sport. I was totally consumed by it all but playing with Herschelle was a breath of fresh air.

Just not sure about his colour coded dress sense!

Gibbs doesn't mince his words about much and had a very colourful career.

One just needs to read his autobiography, "To the Point" for confirmation and his father, Herman, a fellow sports journalist had been very supportive of my crusade.

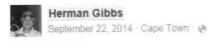

Herman Gibbs
September 22, 2014 · Cape Town ·

Lotto Bombshell
Sometimes, I wish the name Graeme Joffe was a brand name for a soap powder, because if it was, it would be guaranteed to bring out the dirt.
But we have Joffer's Sportsfire Daily, which continues to fire shots across the bows of corrupt SA sport and has lit many fire under officials who masquerade as sports administrators and guardians of the game.
Great balls of fire!
Here's Joffers with fire in his belly:

Herman Gibbs
March 26, 2015 ·

In the world of South African sports journalism, sports enterprise and investigative reporter Graeme Joffe stands alone in the fight against political interference, corruption and maladministration.

We salute you Graeme Joffe !

In his latest 'Soapbox' column in the Sportsfiredaily, Joffe says he learnt that there was indeed been political interference in the selection of the Proteas' semifinal team. ... See More

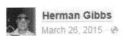

You be the judge: Vern or Kyle

Who could ever forget the Proteas political selection controversy, debacle from the Cricket World Cup in 2015?

It's a sad day for SA cricket
26 March 2015

SportsFire has reliably learned from two sources that there was indeed political interference with the Proteasselection ahead of the World Cup semi-final.

In one of the source's words: *Big political pressure the night before re: Vernon Philander v Kyle Abbott selection!*

Tragic to make players into political pawns and the rest of the team would have known this.

For team spirit, this would have been dire.

Cricket SA (CSA) Chief Executive, Mr. Haroon Lorgat should now be man enough to admit this to the cricket public.

.

There can be no ex excuse for this political interference but no doubt we'll get the same denials and diatribe from the the administrators at the airport press conference.

I did try and get comment from CSA yesterday, granted it was late at around 4pm, to which I got this response from their media spokesperson, Altaaf Kazi.

At this stage we are unable to comment as Chief Executive, Haroon Lorgat is currently on flight from Auckland to Dubai and convenor of selectors Andrew Hudson is asleep (on the other side of the world!!!) and will be travelling back to South Africa tomorrow. I would need to consult with them around your query.

Let's see what comes back from CSA in the next few days but I'm not holding my breath to get a confession from them.

SportsFire was inundated with letters to the editor yesterday in response to my column and this one from John Boulle cut straight to the point.

I couldn't agree with you more. The fact that politics controls sports makes us the laughing stock of the world. I will be just one less viewer of the Proteas and will find something else to watch. This reminds me of my youth when I willed the other teams to beat our national teams because of the exclusion policy. Now I will them to beat us properly as merit selection is out the window and in comes quota selection. The viewing public pay the price. No more support from me.

Here come the denials …
30 March 2015

The Minister of Sport and Recreation South Africa, Minister Fikile Mbalula has noted speculations that he interfered in the selection of team players for the South Africa Cricket World Cup squad. We know who are spreading these speculations and we will not dignify them by mentioning their names. These are acts of desperate colonial apartheid apologist, a very tiny group of a dying breed of political dinosaurs. We shall not be deterred by their mischief. - Statement from the Ministry and Department of Sport and Recreation

There was and is no political interference in our selections. We have a selection panel that includes the coach and independent members, and this panel selected all the teams at the World Cup in the same way that they did before the World Cup. There was a similar query raised yesterday on Phangiso not playing a game and coach, Russell Domingo explained the rationale for him not being selected in the last group match against UAE. - CSA Chief Executive, Haroon Lorgat

But according to an inside source:

It was H Lorgat himself – it lead to great unhappiness in the squad, and he was told "this is going to cost us"

Welcome to the future of all SA Team sport……

Not sure what the Phangiso query has to do with this but the fact is that the Proteas team was changed the night before the World Cup semi-final due to political interference and it caused unhappiness in the squad.

This was confirmed by a third reliable source on Saturday night.

So, we can argue and debate until we are blue in the face but it won't help.

One day in a player's autobiography, we'll read about the cover up: Abbott vs Philander and how CSA did them both a great disservice at the 2015 World Cup.

End of story.

***

Saturday 23 December 2014, I bought a small car trailer (didn't even have a clue how to hitch it - Joffers not really a handy man) and with a heavy heart, I drove out of Johannesburg in my Chevy, in search of a better quality of life.

As they say, change is as good as a holiday.

It broke my heart to say goodbye to my domestic helper, Josephine, who had worked for me for five years and never missed a day.

She had tears in her eyes when I dropped her off at her shack in Diepsloot with household appliances, food and clothes.

I met her husband for the first time and he couldn't have been more grateful.

It brings tears to my eyes just writing this.

I had very special friends and people in my life.

Diepsloot was also where we had put up our first Township TV (social responsibility project) back in 2007.

It brought back so many fond memories.

I was leaving so much behind.

The drive to Grahamstown was long but it gave me the chance to do some real soul searching and I was going to first spend some vacation time on the coast in Port Alfred with very good friends, Warne and Wendy Rippon.

The Eastern Cape had always held a special place in my heart as the three years at Rhodes University gave me so much and friends for life.

The Port Alfred Golf Club is one of those special places. Where else in the world can you get a good steak, egg and chips for R25?

And not to mention, one of my favourite places in the whole world.

Horns Up, Kenton-on-sea

Joffers, 'the knife and fork champion' was back in town.

I had gained numerous pounds and had some minor health issues. It was part and parcel of my life, which had taken a whole new lonely path.

After ten great days in Port Alfred, it was time to set up shop in Grahamstown to continue with my SportsFire Daily publication early in the new year.

I still hadn't received a response from Captain Mabasa to my text from the 23rd of December and he hadn't bothered to make contact with MTN either.

A real top notch investigator moving at speed.

Not!

It didn't take long to settle into Grahamstown life again.

I had a lot of old friends around from my Rhodes University days and everything is five minutes away. A small town with a big soul!

I rented an apartment which backed onto the main St Andrews College Cricket Oval and felt I had made the right decision to relocate.

I was contracted to do some public relations work for the inauguration of the new Vice-Chancellor of Rhodes University, Dr Sizwe Mabizela.

What an honour it was and what a person. If only SA had more leaders, the likes of Dr Sizwe Mabizela.

I had also started to assist some of the journalism students with sports reporting for their beats with the local Grahamstown newspaper, Grocott's Mail.

It felt so good to be giving back to the university that gave me three of the best years of my life.

Senior staff members then asked to apply for the vacant position for head of Rhodes Sports Administration.

I would have relished the challenge of trying to turn Rhodes Sport around, but the position needed to be filled by a person of colour and in hindsight, it worked out for both parties.

Who would have known what was to come?

Grahamstown had changed a lot but the Eastern Cape people were still the same. Caring, fun, very hospitable and thirsty.

Perhaps, my liver wouldn't have lasted!

But even with a little booze under the belt, it wasn't difficult to get a win in our social Monday night tennis school as there were plenty of pigeons around.

No names mentioned, Milo Mills!

I called Captain Mabasa towards the end of January and he told me he had been to see the Director General from the Department of Sport and Recreation (SRSA), Alec Moemi.

Moemi told him they weren't tapping my phone and they didn't have the authority to do so.

Needless to say, the statement I had given the SAPS was about the twitter threats from SRSA and the tapping was most likely SASCOC.

I texted Captain Mabasa again on the 3rd and 9th of February and again on the 11th after I had a call intercepted by someone called "Cedric" at 9.13am.

No reply from Mabasa.

I texted him again on the 23rd of February for any update and only after my text on the16th of March, did he finally respond asking for the address of Tubby Reddy and SASCOC.

Really?

But maybe MTN were finally doing something about it.

I spoke to the Captain they will be sending the subpoena to our office. - Primrose Nhlapho, Senior Fraud Analyst, MTN SA

A month later on the 16th of March, Mabasa texted me to say Reddy would give a statement.

A statement about what?

On 27th of April, I texted Mabasa to tell him that my safety had been threatened and he replied saying he was going to fetch the statement.

No jokes!

Nothing again from Mabasa again until the 7th of May, saying 'come see me urgently'.

My reply was, 'I am out of the country.'

As of end of May, he had still not been to see MTN.

Having had no joy with the SAPS and MTN, I wrote to both the Public Protector's office and the South African National Editor's Forum (Sanef) in March 2015 to see if they would be able to assist me in any capacity.

How else is a freelance journalist supposed to get any protection?

I got no response from the Public Protector's Office and got a reply from Sanef three weeks later.

I tried to reach you to understand what you had in mind in terms of what Sanef should/could do. – Mathatha Tsedu, SANEF Executive Director

How about condemning the threats from the Department of Sport and Recreation and supporting the freedom of expression of an investigative journalist?

Sanef supports freedom of expression and the right of the media to work without fear of reprisal or intimidation. - Sanef

I returned the call to Mathatha the same day and we spoke for about ten minutes. He said they had a big meeting with national editors coming up that weekend and he will revert.

That's the last I heard from Mathatha and Sanef.

Chapter 15: Private Eye

I had been making a new life for myself in Grahamstown but was still naming and shaming the corrupt officials in my digital publication, SportsFire.

On 1 April 2015, I received a very intriguing email from Clem dos Santos. I didn't know Clem but later learned that he was a former Karate South Africa administrator and was now very involved in South African Equestrian. It seemed urgent, but I suggested to him that it would be best to email me the information and I would investigate what was going on.

I already had been inundated with other emails from sources alleging woeful administration and misappropriation of funds in SA Equestrian.

Clem had probably seen more than his fair share from the ongoing battles between Karate SA and SASCOC.

Karate South Africa (KSA) were directed by the (SASCOC) board to grant reinstatement to the individuals who were implicated in the forensic audit report of Karate, given the fact that the public prosecutor declined to prosecute these individuals citing insufficient evidence. The board has set-up a three-person committee to call in the Karate leadership and investigate the reasons for the non-compliance. The committee is to be chaired by Kobus Marais accompanied by Jerry Segwaba and Merrill King. (14 July 2015)

The Karate SA forensic audit report was the second such investigation within a few years. Both of them alleged mass fraud and misappropriation of funds.

Why are these people being protected?

The good old story of looking after friends.

SASCOC and then Minister of Sport, Ngconde Balfour also did nothing after the first forensic audit. Par for the course.

SASCOC's Mubarak Mohamed was appointed as an administrator to oversee the restructuring of Karate in SA, the provinces and regions back in 2011.

But four years later, the sport was still in a mess.

According to an insider:

It is really tragic to see how karate in South Africa has deteriorated to the point where every karate practitioner is caught between being patriotic and doing the right thing. We cannot blame people for being totally petrified by the numerous threats made by SASCOC, Karate South Africa and members serving on the current KSA National Executive Committee. We are nevertheless pleased that there is acknowledgement for the fact that the South African Constitution permits its citizens the freedom of association and that a recent legal opinion confirms that the Constitutions of the above mentioned organizations does not permit them imposing sanctions on any person without prescribed process. Karate activities are not illegal activities and managed by disciplined and professional persons. It is not surprising that SASCOC has now targeted certain individuals giving the impression that they are anti-establishment, when in fact they all have the advancement of karate at heart and to make sure that our athletes are not deprived of the opportunity to compete at the highest level. It is disturbing that SASCOC now also plays the role of SARS in reporting citizens who they suspect of tax evasion. No professional and disciplined karate-ka should accept these numerous threats lightly and be brave enough to do the right thing at the right time. We condemn, with the strongest terms, that karate officials are communicating with the employers of volunteers in order to discredit them. These individuals will have to account for their actions. The intention of SASCOC to unify karate in South Africa has dismally failed and has resulted in more fragmentation than prior to the commencement of the process.

WORLD KARATE FEDERATION

Recognized by the International Olympic Committee (IOC)
Member of SportAccord and of
the International World Games Association (IWGA)

Madrid, 14th August 2015

To: Mr. Tubby Reddy
Chief Executive Officer, SASCOC

Mr. Reddy,
We refer to your letter of August 12th to Karate South Africa (KSA), who is the WKF NF member in the country, where you inform KSA on its deregistration from SASCOC, as well as to KSAs answer of August 12th.

Karate, a sport recognized by the IOC through the World Karate Federation (WKF), has many styles and schools of technique, but remains one sport unified under the WKF with one set of rules for all participants. That said, various styles of karate from time to time hold their own internal friendship tournaments where they may use modified rules peculiar to their group. However, all official championships, being international or national, have to deploy the rules of the WKF, an organization open to, and including, all styles of karate.
The position of SASCOC is not easily understandable. Following the Olympic Charter SASCOC has to recognize KSA, if any, as the Karate body in South Africa. However, in your letter you are mentioning "how now you will constitute Karate in South Africa"; you seem to forget that as long as KSA is the WKF member you are not entitled to do so. So far, KSA has been a loyal WKF member, resisting your unacceptable pressure to accept other dissident Karate groups in the country, something that would have been violating the WKF Statutes and would have jeopardized KSA membership to the WKF, as it already happened a few years ago. Fortunately KSA has rejected this pressure. Their choice has been the right one. You have for several years attempted to impose measures on South African Karate that can only be understood from a total lack of understanding on what Karate is and how the sport is structured.

The doors of the WKF, and therefore of KSA, remain open to any outsider group with the only requirement to follow our Statutes and Regulations; this is the way that SASCOC has to support, and not to create division through dealing with parallel dissident bodies.

We expect KSA to take the appropriate legal measures to protect Karate in South Africa as endorsed by the WKF, and be informed on the continuity of KSA as the WKF member in South Africa.

This dispute went to arbitration and a victory for Karate SA with more legal costs for SASCOC.

SASCOC had failed to adhere to their own constitution and had to pay KSA's lawyers R250 000, more than some OperationExcellence (OPEX) athletes get in a year for Olympic funding.

SASCOC got another karate chop in 2016 with the clear example of a corrupt board member, supported by the president and the board, breaking all of SASCOCs constitution's dispute resolution procedures and rules of engagement to destroy a national sports organisation for personal gain.

This is an extract of a letter from the president of the Union of African Karate Federations (UFAK) to Sam Ramsamy on 27 February 2016.

On December 2015 KSA settled its arbitration matter against SASCOC which was obliged to rehabilitate them as from Aug 2015.

Mr. Mubarak very strangely via a number of regular telephone calls begged us to terminate KSA's membership of UFAK. I found this strange as we in UFAK could not understand how a senior board member of SASCOC, the governing body for sport in your country, could persist in encouraging us UFAK to terminate the membership of one of your bona fide affiliates viz KSA. Nevertheless we did terminate KSA's membership of UFAK given Mr. Mubarak's insistence together with reasons mentioned in point No. 5.

Mr. Mubarak expressed his delight upon receiving the news of KSA's termination and informed my personal assistant Mr. Arab Yacine that Mr. Ramsamy, Mr. Sam Gideon and Mr Tubby Reddy are congratulating UFAK for this decision.

With the strong willing once again of Mubarak, a new group is formed and called SAKF led by Mr. Peter Brandon pending new elections. Mr. Mubarak wanted strongly to be a leading senior member of this group, this was denied by my assistant Mr. Arab Yacine and Mr. Peter Brandon since Mubarak was under an interdict by the high court.

On the manner in which Mr. Mubarak Mohamed handled matters during this very challenging time, it clearly showed UFAK he was working in his own interest and certainly not in the interest of karate. He further through one of his regular phone calls promised to my assistant Yacine Arab an unexpected reprisal, with a strong shocking statement that "SASCOC will not recognize SAKF (new group) and will continue to recognize KSA". I was shocked by Mr. Mubarak's change of heart given that it was he who coerced us into terminating KSA membership and then suddenly he is the first to engineer the demise of SAKF an organ that he proposed and fully supported. Moreover he strongly indicated to both Peter Brandon and my assistant that he wished to serve on the board of SAKF as a senior member!

SASCOC were working behind the scenes to get one of their cronies, Imtiaz Abdulla to lead a new umbrella body of Karate South Africa.

Imtiaz Abdulla @ikkokarate · May 15
Great News UWKFSA at forefront in unifying South African Karate meeting with SASCOC towards this goal.

(Twitter)

Abdulla had also been very involved in SA Karate administration back in the 1990s.

In 2002, PricewaterhouseCoopers were called in to carry out a forensic investigation into alleged and possible irregularities regarding utilization of grants received by the Karate Association of South Africa.

Imtiaz Abdulla had a lot to answer for.

G <u>CONCLUSION</u>

14. POSSIBLE CRIMINAL CHARGES

14.1 Unauthorised expenses charged to KASA for his or related parties personal benefit, payments and/or transfers to institutions, where he has definite interest could form the basis for criminal charges. As mentioned we could not obtain proper supporting documentation and/or explanations for such expenditure. It is clear that financial regulations were not adhered to and that this in itself created an environment for financial abuse and skulduggery.

14.2 In order to conclude on the institution of criminal charges, Mr Imtiaz Abdulla, should once again be afforded the opportunity to comment on allegations against him. Should he waive this right the SA Sport Commission should consider proceeding with the laying of criminal charges.

The Mail & Guardian Investigative Unit, Amabhungane seemed interested in this story when I started to expose a little bit of it on twitter in May 2016.

We must talk about this. Imtiaz Abdullah a big player. – Stefaans Brummer, Mail & Guardian

But I never heard from Brummer again.

In the meantime, I had picked up on some stories related to Abdullah.

He was a director of the electrical company, Ukubona which lists high profile contracts among its projects, including the stadia for the 2010 FIFA World Cup, Gautrain, various Eskom projects and the upgrade of the airports.

And the same company made IOL headlines in 2009.

BEE blacks used as front

An electrical company is being investigated on allegations that it appointed two staff members as BE directors so it could get fat contracts at OR Tambo International Airport, but used the pair as a front and syphoned off the money ... Ukubona operated for years under a previous name and was restructured in 2007 when Ukubona Holding was set up with four directors: founder Alfred Faber, son Michael, and directors Subash Dowlath and Imtiaz Abdulla. (IOL, 30 March 2009)

Abdulla is a big player with strong political connections.

Back to the equestrian allegations and Clem said they would fly from Johannesburg to Grahamstown on a private jet to come and see me that afternoon, April 1st.

I had nothing to lose from their extravagant visit as I had been fighting this lone crusade of exposing corruption and maladministration for three years now and maybe this was going to be the big breakthrough.

At 3.30pm, I went up to the Grahamstown air field which was five minutes from my apartment in anticipation of their 4pm arrival.

The Grahamstown air field is as simple as it gets. An unmanned, small military runway and a few hangers on either side of the strip. I stood at the end of the runway with not a single other person in sight, looking numerous times up into the sky to catch a glimpse of the private jet coming into land.

What movie was this?

The 4pm came and went but I got a text message from Clem to say they had to re-fuel in Bloemfontein and would be arriving a little late.

It was at that point that I thought, Graeme you're an "April Fool".

Look at the date, 1 April.

Really, why would complete strangers spend all this kind of money to fly on a private jet to come and see me for a couple hours?

Me being the lone crusader with a small daily digital sports publication, SportsFire.

I was wrong.

At around 4.15pm, I heard the noise of an engine up above and from the clouds emerged this spectacular looking white jet.

The Eagle had landed: Grahamstown airstrip

I was relieved that I wasn't the butt of an 'April Fools' joke but there was still a sense of make belief and just maybe I was still being set up.

Five people got out of the plane, Clem, Bob O'Neill, Tim Marsland and the two pilots. Warm, friendly guys, a good first impression.

Guys I could trust?

Trust had become the most important thing for me as I was consistently having to sift through endless fake sources who were hoping for me to publish their own hidden agendas.

Bob and Tim also had strong links to Equestrian.

I packed the five guests in my car (one pilot in the boot/trunk). I'm sure he'll never forget that but it was only a short five minute drive to the Highlander Pub and Grill, my new local in Grahamstown which was run by friends, Dale and Ros Paul.

We ordered pizzas, the pilots went outside while Clem, Bob, Tim and I sat around a table to discuss equestrian matters.

They proceeded to fill me in on the tragic plight of the SA Equestrian Federation (SAEF), individuals using the sport to fund their own lavish lifestyles and now SASCOC was trying to get their hands on the riches by putting one of their cronies in as acting president.

I wasn't at all surprised as a number of other sporting codes had gone through the same aches and pains.

After an hour of talking equestrian woes, Tim told me to close my laptop in which I was making notes as they now wanted to share some explosive information with me.

I wasn't quite prepared for what I was about to hear as it involved an SAEF member and his alleged links to Rhino poaching in Mozambique.

Tim had hired a private investigator to track his unlawful trade.

The meeting ended but not before Tim had kindly offered the services of the same Private Investigator to assist me.

I had mentioned to them that I still strongly believed my phone was being illegally tapped and emails hacked.

The SAPS had let me down but this visit gave me some hope.

People who were prepared to put their money with their mouths are to help me in the crusade of exposing the rot in SA sport.

They needed to take off for Johannesburg while there was still light and it was back to the airfield with the pilot once again in the boot of the car.

The jet started up and within minutes had disappeared into the Grahamstown sky.

I was standing next to the runway still trying to make sense of what had just happened.

It was surreal!

That night in the Albany club pub, some of the locals were talking about a jet over Grahamstown that afternoon.

That's how small the town is.

The next day, I went back through the numerous previous emails I had received on SA Equestrian from riders and officials and started to dig further.

It was fairly complex in that equestrian is made up of so many different disciplines but I was on my horse, if you'll excuse the pun.

On the 5th of April around 6pm, I received a call from 'Theo' who was a Private Investigator.

Tim had kept his word.

Theo told me my cell-phone had three diversions. In other words, all my calls were being monitored by three sources.

I had the suspicion for more than five months that my phone was being illegally wired but to hear it first hand was a reality check.

What an invasion of privacy and who gives anyone that right?

I was angry and nervous but relieved that I finally had some help.

Theo said he had now derailed their illegal process and would put a block on my device but I needed to switchoff the phone for a couple hours and take the battery out.

He would call me back in a couple hours and I must give them the code that appeared on my screen when I switched the phone back on.

I did as requested and he later explained the process of tapping and if I should get a call from a private number, I must try and keep them on the line for as long as possible and that would give him more time to track their location. Would they try to re-tap my phone?

It didn't take long as the very next day, I received this security message on my cell-phone.

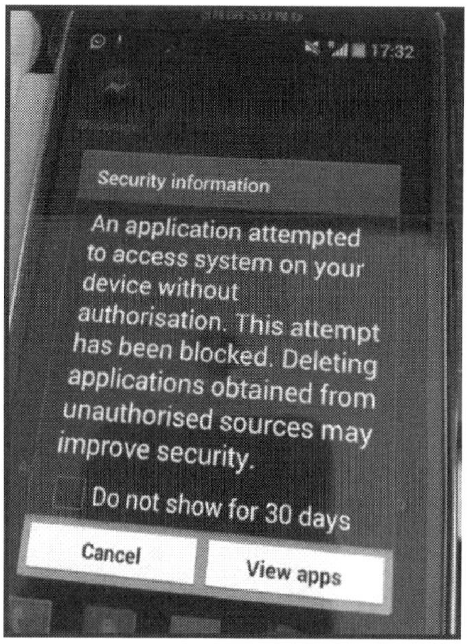

After days of research, I felt I had more than enough evidence to write the equestrian expose. I had done at least fifty hard-hitting exposes over a three year period but this one really seemed to strike a nerve.

Sports Fire Daiiy April 2015

SA Equestrian is in dire straits and the SAEF annual AGM this weekend is putting the cart before the horse. There are serious issues that need to be addressed and it seems as if the current administration has its own personal agenda, which is playing nicely into the hands of SASCOC.

The SAEF under acting president, Johan Koorts put this memo out last month:

On the 28th February 2015, SASCOC wrote to the Acting President, Ms Dineo Molomo, to inform her that as the SAEF has not indicated its willingness to comply with the Transformation Charter and that SASCOC had been inundated with many disputes which were without resolve, that the SAEF had 30 days to resolve all its challenges to SASCOC's satisfaction, failing which SASCOC would terminate SAEF's membership.

The Transformation Charter intrinsically requires the sport to adhere to the structures prescribed by the Government.

At a Special General Meeting held today, 11th March 2015, a motion of no confidence in Ms Dineo Molomo as elected SAEF Vice President and Acting SAEF President was tabled and carried unanimously.

As per the constitution of the SAEF, the acting SAEF Vice President, Mr Johann Koorts, will fill the role of Acting SAEF President.

In addition, a number of important motions that promise to remedy some of the challenging issues were also tabled and carried unanimously.

The SAEF Council has requested that SASCOC appoint an Administrator with immediate effect in order to assist the SAEF Council in fulfilling all the requirements of SASCOC, the SRSA Act and the SAEF Constitution.

The SAEF Council is confident that this positive development offers the opportunity to restore equestrian sport for all going forward.

The SAEF Council assures the equestrian community that it is committed to this process and is counting on your support during these difficult times.

The most obvious question is why there was suddenly a motion of no confidence in Dineo Molomo, who previously had the support of all 14 disciplines in SA Equestrian?

Is it because she is transparent, neutral, has business savvy and would ask all the right questions?

The timing of the "no confidence" also seems to be rather ironic, just six weeks before the AGM and elections.

Also, there is strong evidence to suggest that some Provinces didn't even have a mandate to vote her out.

Who is hiding behind the stable door?

SASCOC had already put their big dirty hoof in last July by telling all 14 disciplines/legal entities that they no longer exist and they would all have to conform under one body, the SAEF with a new adopted constitution.

It's like telling squash, table tennis and tennis that they must all fall under one administrative body.

Under the new SAEF constitution, there is a compulsory affiliation fee for all individual members and the disciplines can apply for associate membership to SAEF.

Makes no sense whatsoever.

The World Governing Body of Equestrian (FEI) for seven of the 14 disciplines, three of them being Olympic sports and Polo has its own world body.

Molomo replaced Dewald Viljoen as SAEF president at the end of last year and saw the need for disciplines to remain autonomous.

She also wanted to implement the FEI registration system (which is freely available to all FEI National Federations) from top to bottom.

A system which makes proper business sense.

Surely, if it's good enough for the world governing body, it's good enough for SAEF.

But alas, certain individuals must have seen this as a potential loss to their own little personal nest egg.

SANESA the school league of Equestrian sport run by Marlene du Plessis, where every school kid pays an entry fee to SANESA to compete on an entry platform owned Quadrat Plan CC – a company which is owned 100% by Du Plessis.

With over 20 000 entries per year, that's a tidy sum and it's alleged that Quadrat Plan CC gets paid a fee per entry.

On 11 March, the SAEF under new leadership agrees to implement Du Plessis's registration system. In the meantime, 16 applicants are issuing a court summons against Du Plessis's company Quadrat for alleged data theft.

The new SAEF constitution also states that its council must be 40% women but SASCOC have conveniently turned a blind eye.

At the end of last month, Koorts was ousted as the acting president of the Limpopo Equestrian Federation, a position he allegedly held without any election.

It comes as no surprise that the election for a new SAEF president this weekend has been taken off the agenda, given that the acting president and acting vice-president must be from among the provincial presidents, which Koorts no longer is.

Is someone protecting Koorts? Not all of the 14 disciplines enjoy the same fruits and the SAEF is sitting on around R2 million in Lotteryfunding owed to some of the disciplines.

SA has a bright Paralympic prospect in dressage, Tamsin Mbatsha Bouwer who needs some of that funding to qualify for Rio.

When will SA athletes be put first ahead of the selfish administrators who are in it more for themselves?

There could be more than just horse play this weekend at the AGM.

Within a couple days of publishing the expose, I received numerous calls, text messages and emails from people claiming to be involved in SA Equestrian.

There was growing division in the ranks. It was getting heated. Some had an axe to grind and some had too much to lose.

One disgruntled member even decided to post a Facebook link to the defamatory Joffers-exposed website to try and get even.

Pathetic if you ask me!

Marlene du Plessis's personal assistant called me for a meeting on the same day my expose was published.

I asked for a comment in writing.

I never heard from them again.

Rider and trainer, Rogan Asken then penned this open letter to fellow riders and members of the SA Equestrian community as well as to Tubby Reddy.

It has been difficult in the recent past to comprehend the prescribed changes in our sport, including the motivation for the changes and the execution thereof.

Here is what seems (in my opinion) to have transpired.

All SA sports fall under the control of SASCOC-if they want to participate in International Competition.

Several years ago, SANEF was ordered to disband. It was instructed to form clubs and unite with ALL Equestrian sport and form the SAEF. This would comprise all other horse related sports such as Polo, Endurance, Polo-crosse, Tent-pegging, Western riding and of course, all the former SANEF disciplines (jumping, dressage, eventing, equitation, showing, driving, vaulting).

It excluded horse-racing.

There was to be freedom of association (a good principal). Like minded and interest-sharing members could form clubs.

The disciplines were ordered to separate into club discipline structures, each to look after its own form of the sport. When the disciplines structures were in place and functioning SASCOC introduced a new constitution, where the disciplines where no longer members of SAEF.

The clubs now elect representatives to regional and provincial committees (even if these did not represent the disciplines).

THEN Mr Johann Koorts(from Limpopo, his daughter has a small riding school in Bela Bela) leads an unlawful SGM of the SAEF where they removes Dineo Molomo (first black female president of Equestrian sport) as President of SAEF and after the SGM he emerges as Acting President of SAEF. Mr Koorts had been previously unanimously rejected by all disciplines in Limpopo. His only possible claim to office in Equestrian sport may have been via an alliance with SANESA.

Why would SASCOC order a restructure and shortly thereafter another one? It appears that SASCOC interferes in a sport code, creates confusion and destroys-or tries to-the leadership, and then imposes/deploys one of its "lieutenants"as the President onto the sport in question. Mr Koorts is a SASCOC insider (8 years as treasurer of SA tennis). There is nothing remotely democratic about the way Mr Koorts became President of SAEF.

SASCOC is widely alleged as corrupt, and has been responsible for the demise or collapse of many smaller sports.

There are, of course, alliances.

Mrs Marlene du Plessis has for many years been President or Chair of SANESA. She also owns the IT system that processes all SANESA entries-charging a fee for every single entry. Mrs du Plessis is looking to expand her network into adult competition (i.e.-the FNB league).She has her sights set on her system being used for the entire SAEF-which will expand her income massively. She also intends to contest the legitimacy of the ownership of KP. Assets such as KP are of significant interest to people such as Mrs du Plessis!

SANESA is a wonderful thing. It provides the opportunity for many young riders to compete in and gain recognition for Equestrian sport under the banner of their schools.

Where it currently fails-

1. *National and International rules are ignored or changed.*

2. *Shows are not properly supervised leading to abuse of horses, and many dangerous practices.*

3. *The shows are run for the profit of a private individual who gives nothing back for the sustaining of the sport.*

4. *The shows give provincial and national recognition for low levels, and riders earn school colours and recognition that is not legitimate. This is fraudulent.*

5. *The shows and competitions sometimes take place at venues that are not ratified by official bodies. Facilities are inadequate to dangerous.*

There seems to be an alliance or conspiracy between Mrs du Plessis, Mr Koorts, SASCOC and members of the Equestrian community who are still under a shadow from former fraudulent occurrences, during the SANEF era.

These include Mr Tony Lewis who was SANEF chairman and the former temporary secretary-general Mrs Angie Meredith.

This latter team un-officially tried to visit the president of FEI Princess Haya a few years ago, trying to have our own SANEF declared illegitimate and create a new one of their own.

There is a lot of money that moves in Equestrian sport. When lotto funds are added, the stakes become high. It is clear that a hostile take-over SAEF, SANESA and the above-named individuals must be resisted at all costs. There is an "us and them"situation.

If we let the high-jackers win, our sport will be lost to us for a long time, and much valuable ground and time lost. Please stand together and resist this at all costs!

Rogan Asken.

PS: A massive and heart-felt thank you to those warriors fighting our fight for us-
There is much that skulduggery that can be easily verified and revealed publicly. Our opponents would be wise not to draw any unnecessary attention to themselves!

***

Johan Koorts was voted out as SAEF president in August 2015 but that wasn't the end of the drama as six months later, the new president, Andre Truter resigned under a cloud.

25 April 2016, a statement from the SAEF:

Mr ANDRE BRAHM TRUTER is exonerated from any allegations of misleading anybody or being dishonest in any way within the auspices of the SAEF and/or SASCOC to date hereof.

A couple weeks later, the SAEF suspended some 20 members without due process.

SASCOC's interference in the SAEF is one of the chief reasons for the mess the sport now finds itself in.

But they would never admit to that.

Then came the written threat from Tubby Reddy on 17 May 2016 of "get your house in order or the SAEF will no longer exist as a national federation in this country."

And who does SASCOC send in to be the mediator?

Mubarak Mahomed.

Who's not telling the truth?
21 January 2014

Two months down the road and still no clarity on who is telling the truth on how the SA jockeys managed to get national colours for the Jockey's international in November last year.

According to the Racing Association and ProSport International sports agent, Mike Makaab, a recently formed National Jockey Association had become a member of the South African Sports Confederation and Olympic Committee (SASCOC), which allowed national colours to be awarded for the three-day international against a select International team of jockeys.

But SASCOC CEO, Tubby Reddy begged to differ and was quoted as saying:

Please note that the Jockey's Association of South Africa has not been accepted as a member of SASCOC, and as to how this information was conveyed to you I have no idea.

Perhaps Mr. Reddy was just trying to backtrack on a document sent from the SASCOC offices to the RA, which gave them permission to award the colours.

Membership can only be conferred on a member in terms of SASCOC's Constitution and its previous memorandum and articles, and then can only be approved by the general membership at an annual general meeting or a special general meeting convened for a specific purpose. At this stage this has not been done and therefore the information conveyed by you is unfortunately incorrect and an article written by Mr. Joffe, wherein his imagination again seems to have run away with him. - Tubby Reddy

I guess I should take that as a compliment!

It took Reddy a week to reply to top racing journalist, Robyn Louw after I had sent questions to SASCOC president, Gideon Sam, SASCOC CFO, Vinesh Maharaj, Racing Association CEO, Larry Wainstein and Makaab.

* When did the National Jockey Association become a member of SASCOC?
* At which AGM was their membership tabled?
* Do you have minutes from this AGM?
* Protea colours were awarded to the jockeys for the recent International – who at SASCOC rubber stamped this and do you have minutes from this meeting?
* Is this not misuse of the Protea emblem, which is a state asset?

I didn't expect a reply from anyone at SASCOC but Wainstein sent me a couple emails.

Please let me know who wants this information and what is this about? - Larry Wainstein, The Racing Association (RA) CEO

And that was followed up by another Wainstein email.

The R.A assisted the Jockeys Association to we did not apply the R.A HAS NOTHING to do with this association. We just run the jockey's International event. I am busy trying to sort out Summer Cup issues today and have given the people to speak to Prosport International or Sascoc what is this issue with the R.A. Has the R.A transgressed any Rules have we all did was host an event that had been sanctioned by Sasoc. (sic)

Not easy to make or head or tail of what he was trying to say.

I don't begrudge the jockeys getting national colours as they are top sportsmen and women in their own right but it's the irregular and unconstitutional way in which SASCOC has done it.

There are also sports like rugby league that are hitting a brick wall when it comes to getting SASCOC membership and out of nowhere, a jockey association gets "membership" and national colours.

Makaab is still sticking to his word and tweeted earlier this month:

@Joffersmyboy Graeme, the Jockey Association of South Africa followed the proper process in their application to become members of SASCOC and did what was requested of us. If you have any further questions, please direct this to SASCOC.

The next tweet from Makaab a little more personal, no doubt in an attempt to deflect …

@Joffersmyboy Hey Graeme, my brother- in-law says you were a good oke (guy) at school - what happened?

It might also be worth noting that two SASCOC officials, Gideon Sam and Vinesh Maharaj sit on the

Horse Racing Trust board.

SASCOC owns 100% of Gride Investments (Pty) Ltd, which sole asset is 3880887 shares in the horse racing group, Phumelela Gaming and Leisure.

The directors of Gride:
Mr G N Sam (appointed 19 October 2009)
Mr M M Mbebe (appointed 2 July 2000)
Mrs H Kajee (appointed 10 August 2006) – a SASCOC vice president
Mr P O Goldhawk (appointed 19 October 2009)

Secretary of the company is listed as Goldhawk Corporate Advisory.

The board members of Gride are not listed in the latest financials and when asked for the names, Goldhawk and the auditor, Bester Greyling (Deloitte & Touche) referred me to SASCOC.

No reply from SASCOC again.

Greyling is also the SASCOC auditor and when asked if SASCOC and Gride had got clean audits over the last few years, his reply:

Our South African professional standards restrict us from discussing or communicating any client specific information with the media. You are most welcome to contact SASCOC and request the specific information from them or request copies of their annual reports for the periods.

At the end of the day, surely any horse racing or jockey association should fall under the SA Equestrian Federation, who in turn would have membership of SASCOC.

Why the separate membership?

***

Sad day for our 'Springbok' jockeys

The National Horseracing Authority has investigated allegations that the organisers of the Jockeys International Challenge acted fraudulently and have brought racing into disrepute ... SASCOC's Chief Executive Officer has confirmed that no Jockeys' Association in South Africa has been registered as a member of the South African Equestrian Federation nor as an affiliate member of SASCOC. The awarding of the "unauthorised" Protea colours was done on the strength of an email which was sent to the organisers (Mr Larry Wainstein) by the Chief Financial Officer of SASCOC (Vinesh Maharaj). (Sporting Post, 27 July 2014)

Another prime example of the good old 'boys club' just doing their own thing to suit their own needs.

Chapter 16: "They're coming to get you."

Friday 17 April 2015, the day my life changed forever.

I was in my apartment in Grahamstown after having a dinner with a good friend, Lindy.

My cell-phone was on silent but I could quietly hear the ringing vibrations on my bedside table at around 10.15pm.

I thought it was one of the boys wanting to go out for some drinks, but I was tired and not in the mood.

I wasn't going to take the call.

But there were three missed calls in quick succession and something told me I better just answer it.

Just as well I did. It was Tim Marsland.

Graeme, our guy (Theo, the PI) has intercepted a threat to your safety. They're coming to get you, get to a place of safety, don't go to any bars or public places, get out of your apartment. Call me if you need any help.

The call was short and hurried. I remember it like it was yesterday.

My heart started pounding.

How much time did I have to get out?

I packed an overnight bag and drove through the pouring rain, following Lindy to her house in Port Alfred, which was about 45 minutes away.

I didn't want to involve Lindy in this mess, but she was adamant that I stay the night at her house.

She was very brave.

I took the sim card and battery out of my cell-phone and when we got to the road stop at the Pig and Whistle in Bathurst (which felt like an eternity), I told Lindy we needed to leave my car at a remote location in case they were tracking my vehicle.

My mind and heart were now racing.

We left my vehicle in the car park at the MyPond Hotel in Port Alfred and went to Lindy's house.
I immediately called my sister in Cincinnati from the house phone.

I told her my life was under threat and I may need to come to the USA but that I'd call her tomorrow once I knew more.

Lindy had two beautiful, big old dogs and needed to keep the front door of her house open during the night to allow them to get out. You can imagine how little sleep I got.

In fact, I don't remember sleeping at all as every car light or noise that came down the road, I remember thinking the worst.

As soon as the sun came up on Saturday morning, I took a quick shower and Lindy took me back to my car at the hotel.

I drove back to Grahamstown and dropped off my car at Kenrich Motors, owned by good friend, Dean Kent.

It was close to my apartment and I called another good friend, Alje Bouwer to pick me up and take me to my apartment.

On the way, we stopped back at his house to pick up his gun, just in case.

Before entering my apartment, I spoke to the security guard at the complex to see if there were any problems the night before and remember looking up to see my patio sliding door was open.

Did I not close it in my mad rush the night before or had someone gained entry overnight?

I had forgotten that my domestic helper, Monica came early on a Saturday morning and she was already there.

Phew, a big sigh of relief. But that was my state of mind.

We went upstairs, Alje stood by my front door with the gun cocked while I ran inside to pack a suitcase and grab my passport.

I didn't know where I was going. I just knew I had to get out of town.

Alje dropped me back at Kenrich Motors and Dean got one of his drivers to take me to the airport in Port Elizabeth, about an hour and a half drive from Grahamstown.

I asked the driver if he knew where I could get a new sim card without having to register it with personal details (RICA), which was South African law.

I now needed to be discreet with everything.

I got the sim card in a Grahamstown township and on the way to the airport and called Tim who suggested I fly to Johannesburg. He would pick me up and we would evaluate the threat before making any rash decisions.

I agreed although I was contemplating a flight out to the USA.

I also called the Private Investigator, Theo to find out where the threat was coming from and he asked me if I had written anything more on Lottery corruption in recent days.

I had!

SportsFire Daily: 13 April 2015
Lottery Lies ….

The lies they just keep on coming.

National Lottery Payment: December 2013

59103 The South African Football Museum **4 875 630**

24 June 2014: Email from Sershan Naidoo (National Lotteries Board: Beneficiary & Player Relations; and Media Liaison)

As stated on the payments list, the applicant is the SA Football Museum. The museum is at the FNB Stadium. You would have to check with the beneficiary if they have the 'blessing of SAFA'. The beneficiary met with our requirements and were considered for a grant.

Sports Minister, Fikile Mbalula told parliament last month:

The South African Football Museum is a private initiative, and it is not a museum but an exhibition. It will therefore not be opened officially like a museum would. However, it runs exhibitions from time to time, when funds permit they say. The organization reports that it does not have adequate funds to open and operate a museum. The Department has not contributed any funding to this project.

How can R4.8 million be given to the SA Football Museum from the National Lottery in December 2013 as the first tranche and 16 months later, we are here?

We advise that the exhibition is currently in the infrastructure 'build' phase. More details will be released to the media imminently which will include the date of opening. – Pippa Freer, SA Sports Museum Director

SportsFire also asked if the SA Football Museum had received a second tranche payment of the grant.

Freer replied:

In terms of any other information regarding the grant, please can you engage directly with the NLB (National Lottery Board).

When SportsFire told Naidoo that the football museum didn't exist and was not at the FNB stadium.

He responded by saying:

What made you think that the funding was for a museum? Did you speak to the beneficiary organisation? The fact that the word 'museum' appears in the name of the beneficiary does not mean that the grant was for a museum!

Oops, he must have forgotten he told us it was at the FNB stadium.

The beneficiary's PR company added their spin last June:

The South African Football Museum has recently evolved to encompass a number of sporting codes, not just football, and these developments involve a number of stakeholders, including the National Lotteries Board. A project of this size and scope takes a significant amount of planning, as I'm sure you will understand, and as we are still in the initial stages we are not yet in a position to communicate the finer details or conduct any site visits.

A site visit would have been really interesting.

Next thing we'll be told it was a statue and it's been taken down.

We were approached by the South African Sports Arts and Culture Hall of Fame ("SASAHOF") in 2009 with a proposal to establish the hall of fame within the FNB Stadium, on or about 6 January 2010 SASAHOF presented to the COJ Community Development Department as well as COJ Arts and Culture department, an agreement was entered into on 7 June 2011, however, the agreement were terminated in its entirety on 20 September 2013 by SASAHOF due to a lack of funding. - Jacques Grobbelaar, CEO Stadium Management SA (Pty) Ltd.

The Executive Director for COJ Community Development was Dudu Maseka.

Thanks for your query in this regard. The City of Johannesburg wishes to clarify the following: The City did not receive money from the Lottery for a Football Museum. The City is not responsible or even involved in the Football Museum. To our knowledge there is no football museum at the moment. The questions you raise should be directed to those who received the money. The City, as it stands now, does not have a standing agreement with anyone on the football museum project. According to our understanding, a football museum can only be sanctioned and commissioned by SAFA as custodians of football. - Nthatisi Modingoane, City of Joburg

It was never sanctioned and commissioned by SAFA.

So, have they paid back the R4.8 million?

Of course not!

National Lottery payment: March 2014

75079 South African College Principals Organisation 20 896 666.00

Naidoo is also ducking and diving when it comes to the R20.8 million that was paid to SACPO, which is a voluntary association of FET College principals for a so-called "sports project."

A year later and still no-one from the National Lottery or SACPO can tell SportsFire what or where the project is.

As mentioned in my initial email, SACPO is a voluntary association of FET College principals and the organisation has no statutory status with the Department of Higher Education and Training (DHET). As such we have no jurisdiction over them or formal relationship with them. We do however meet with them as a 'stakeholder' grouping from time to time. Since we have no jurisdiction over the organisation we are not in a position to request details of their financial transactions – if we did, they could refuse and we would have no legal recourse to enforce such disclosure. - Keith Loynes, DHET Project Manager

Thank you Mr Loynes, as the new President/Chairperson of SACPO I can acknowledge that we did received the funding from Lottery which was applied by the old office bearers. I am not sure if it is of any media interest to mention amounts but should the department want to know we will gladly forward the agreement. I am not aware of any commission to be paid and that is also unacceptable according to the contract.As far as the usage of the money that is operational functions of the organisation and we will ensure that process if finance public management are followed. (sic) – Hellen Ntlatleng, SACPO Chairperson

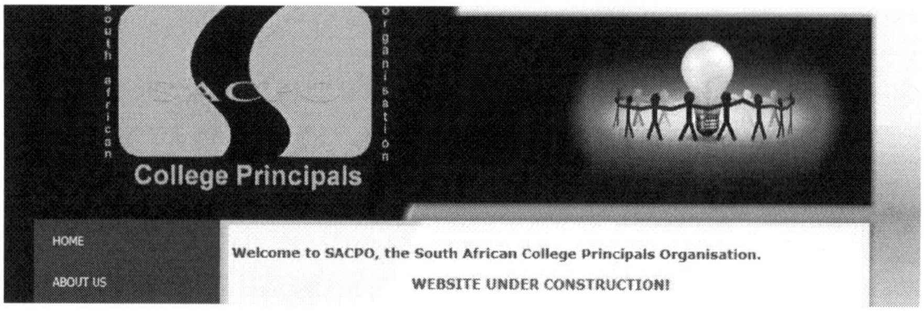

The SACPO website for the last three years ... under construction!

It was confirmed to SportsFire that the former LoveLife CEO, John O'Connor did the Lottery application for SACPO as a third party after meeting with his good friend, Dr Harold Adams who just happens to be the deputy chairperson of the Lottery Distribution Agency for Sport and Recreation.

Adams and O'Connor have not responded to a number of emails from SportsFire.

They are "loving life", if you'll excuse the pun.

The former president and secretary general of Karate SA, Leon Beech is one of the directors of SACPO and also a good friend of Adams but no comment from him either. Beech left Karate SA under a cloud after more allegations surfaced of fraud and misappropriation of funds back in 2011 and this was the second time he had been fingered in a forensic audit.

Adams wears a number of hats.

Apart from his role with the Lottery, he is vice president of Athletics SA, president of Boland Athletics and sits on the board of the South African Institute of Drug Free Sport (SAIDS) – a board appointed by the Minister of Sport and Recreation.

Boland Athletics and SAIDS are regular beneficiaries of National Lottery grants.

William Lloyd Primary School in the Boland area has received R720 000 from the National Lottery Distribution Trust Fund in the past year.

That is more than ASA and most of its provincial members have received in the same period.

Pieter Lourens is the headmaster of the school. He is also the vice president of Boland Athletics.

Neither Adams nor Lourens would comment on the Lottery grants to the school.

Again, we have told you on numerous occasions that where there is a conflict of interest, the application is adjudicated by another distributing agency. Please accept that. The "Headmaster" of William Lloyd Primary is not a distributing agency member. There is therefore no conflict of interest. - Sershan Naidoo, National Lotteries Board

Email from a concerned reader when SportsFire first exposed these allegations of corruption.

My heart breaks when I read these stories. There are so many NPOs and NGOs that annually rely on funding to continue valuable work for Early Childhood Development-preschools in disadvantaged areas, HIV testing and medicating, Hospice, FAMSA and after school care programmes, and real skills development for out of work youth etc, that fail to receive any funding at all even though they toe the line, run audited financials and report on all money spent in a responsible, open and transparent manner, as per the agreed Lotto application. Those that do receive funding on occasion are limited to R2M per entity, which when, in once case servicing 37 preschools, educating and training 120 teachers and over 2000 children in a rural area is a challenge, yet delivered on by a group of 6 individuals. Where are the checks and balances? Where is the governance? Where's the accountability? Where's the transparency? Why's the abuse allowed to continue? Where's the museum?

Good questions.

I've been trying to get answers for months, but Lottery lies, lies and more lies.

***

Theo seemed agitated during our phone call and said he would take these corrupt people down.

I told him I was going to Johannesburg and we would talk again from there.

He was based in Bloemfontein.

I got to the airport in Port Elizabeth and paid cash for an afternoon flight to Johannesburg. I wanted as little trace as possible of my plans and whereabouts.

On arrival in Johannesburg, I was met by Tim who was armed. We walked briskly to his vehicle which was parked in one of the underground bays at O.R. Tambo International.

I had only met Tim once and he even said to me while driving – "how do you know I'm not one of the bad guys?"

Good question and the timing couldn't have been worse!

I had to go with my gut feel and he was doing a favour for someone he didn't know too well either.

On the way to his house in the South of Johannesburg, we stopped at a Woolworths store where every car with tinted windows gave me a nervous reaction.

Tim bought food for dinner and flowers for his wife. I felt kind of re-assured that he was a good guy that I could trust.

Tim told me that Theo had diverted my cell-phone location to Rustenburg and that I needn't worry about anyone tracking me down.

One thing for sure is we weren't anywhere close to Rustenburg.

I had lived in Johannesburg for over 30 years but had never been to the suburb where Tim resided. It looked like a number of mini farms in a very secure estate.

A real country feel.

Tim's own property was also lined with an electric fence and his big dogs came running to greet us. Tim's wife, Trudy made me feel very welcome.

We had dinner and spoke a lot. I was mentally exhausted.

I asked Tim to do some security checks on my laptop as it had become very slow and every time when shutting down, I would get the same message with a number of updates.

If my phone was being tapped, why wouldn't they be hacking into my emails?

I wasn't wrong.

Tim picked up numerous intrusions on my laptop including the use of my camera. Whoever probably had full control of my laptop?

More anger, damn them!

I was angry for not having done something sooner as I had been suspicious for months.

Tim was very helpful with cleaning up my laptop, adding some spyware and putting tape over the camera.

I had a restless first night in Johannesburg. I was over-tired from a lack of sleep the night before and my mind was still racing.

All of Sunday was spent at Tim's house.

We talked and tried to come up with a plan of action. He showed me around his property which boasts a number of stables, some beautiful horses and an indoor equestrian arena, specifically built by an expert from Holland.

I watched his wife do some dressage training with a couple of the baby horses during the afternoon. It gave my mind a break.

Tim was a keen and competitive rider himself.

On Sunday night, we went to Bob and Jenny O'Neill's house for dinner, which was in the same estate. Bob and Jenny were also incredibly hospitable despite me almost being a complete stranger to them. Over dinner, I gave them the full run down on the corrupt state of SA sport and the lone battle I had been fighting.

I spent the night at their house on Tim's advice to move around. There was armed security and Bob had the big boys on speed dial if need be.

Even then, I still slept poorly. My mind was all over the place.

Early the next morning, I went with Bob to his workplace to be able to publish my Monday edition of SportsFire Daily.

It was a massive office space that had stables and an indoor jumping arena over-looking the work cafeteria.

These were real horse people with a real passion for the sport.

I also met one of the groomsmen who had been with them for over twenty years and had travelled overseas with their son to compete.

A great story on its own.

I needed to continue publishing my SportsFire Daily.

A threat to my safety wasn't going to stop me but I wasn't mentally ready to write about what had transpired in the last three days.

For now, the less said the better.

Only a few people knew.

I was too scared to go anywhere on my own and we all agreed I'd be better off getting out of the country for a while to let things settle down.

It was as if I was a prisoner in my own country.

Tim had been in daily contact with Theo and he also agreed it would be a good idea to get out of the heat.

On Tuesday morning, I emailed my sister in the US to ask her to book me a ticket from Johannesburg to Cincinnati for the following night. I didn't want to put it on my credit card and raise an alert.

But while going through the passport in my possession, I realized it was my new passport which didn't have my ten-year USA tourist visa in it.

It's the last thing I needed.

My old passport with the visa was in my apartment in Grahamstown or at least, I thought it was.
Trying to get a new US visa could have taken days and time wasn't on my side.

Tim had an early morning flight to Botswana on Wednesday and I went with him to the airport.

I paid cash again for a return ticket Johannesburg to Port Elizabeth and had asked a very good friend, Andrew McLean who worked for Eastern Province Cricket to organize a private security person to meet me on the other side.

On arrival in Port Elizabeth, I was met by a local security boss who escorted me to the airport parking lot, where we jumped into his fully armed Hummer and headed for Grahamstown.

He drove, so I wouldn't have to rent a car but I still found myself looking in the passenger side review mirror the entire time to see if we were being followed.

It was an eerie feeling when we got to my apartment.

I opened the drawer where my personal belongings were, only to find that the passport with my visa was not there.

No!

It could only be in one other place and that was in storage on the Warne and Wendy's farm, which was about 15 minutes away.

I had left some personal belongings there, which I wasn't needing yet in Grahamstown.

I began to panic as I wasn't sure if I was going to make it back to Port Elizabeth in time to make my return flight to Johannesburg to be there in time for my Delta flight to Atlanta, connecting to Cincinnati.

A quick dash to the farm and fortunately, my passport was there.

Thankfully, we made it back to Port Elizabeth in time for my Johannesburg flight with a little extra speed from the Hummer.

I was still a little concerned that I could have a problem with the USA visa in an expired passport, knowing how stringent the immigration regulations had become since 9/11.

I had a green card (permanent residency) while working for CNN but had to relinquish it when I went back to South Africa as I was no longer spending six months of the year in the US and didn't own property.

Larry King and I didn't exactly earn the same whilst at CNN.

There were no problems at the Delta check-in counter with the visa and now I just had to get through SA customs and onto the plane.

I had a very uneasy feeling as the customs official scanned my passport. Was there a red alert out for Graeme Joffe?

He stamped the departure date (a huge sense of relief) and I was on my way to a very uncertain future.

The flight to Atlanta was long as usual. I don't fly well at the best of times and I was now caught up with everything that had just happened in the last few days.

I choked back some tears at various times during the flight.

We landed in the early morning in Atlanta, giving me enough time to make the connection to Cincinnati.

No problems at customs.

It was too early to have buffalo chicken wings with blue cheese dressing (my food addiction).
A McDonald's sausage egg biscuit with a hash brown would have to suffice.

It was an hour and half flight to Cincinnati, where I arrived to the welcoming arms of my sister.

She was just as relieved.

It had been a long few days for both of us.

All I had with me was a suitcase with two pairs of jeans, some shirts, couple pairs of shorts, shoes, flip-flops and my laptop.

Just as well, it was almost summer in the United States.

Chapter 17: WhatsApp

I had been to Cincinnati on a couple previous occasions to visit family but this time it was under very different circumstances.

My brother-in-law and sister had again opened their house to me and I have to be honest, I got a real scare when the door-bell rang within a few hours of me being there.

My first thought was how did they find me so quickly?

Fortunately, it was just the neighbour coming to say hello and to find out about my well-being.

My nephews were at college and I took over Adam's bedroom, which became jokingly known as the "Michael Jordan suite".

"The Michael Jordan suite"

Not quite how I planned my life.

At 46 years old, forced to flee South Africa, living with my sister and brother-in-law and sleeping in my nephew's room with a Michael Jordan poster above my single bed.

Slightly ironic in that the time I had spent with my sister and brother-in-law in Chicago in 1992, I became a big Michael Jordan and Bulls fan.

It was a sporting experience like no other to go to the old Chicago stadium and see MJ in full flight. The guy was a genius. Now he was my roommate, well kind of.

The first few months in Cincinnati were extremely tough. I was homesick but in the back of my mind, I knew I could not go back.

I had been displaced.

I had no grasp or understanding of the mental strain and no medical insurance to get any psychological assistance.

There were times I was on my knees, praying for answers from South Africa.

But I wasn't getting any. I spoke to the private investigator, Theo twice in the first couple months of being in the US.

The last call was a heated one on the 21 June 2015 when he berated me, accusing me of interfering in the investigation as I had sent a text message to Captain Mabasa asking him for an update. Theo added that he and his family (wife and child) were being threatened and that Mabasa wants to walk away from the case.

But tomorrow (June 22), 'he is leaving early morning for Johannesburg to arrest four people and then he's wiping his hands clean of the case.'

The four people going to be arrested: Tubby Reddy (CEO of the SA Olympic Committee), Raymond Hack (SA lawyer who sits on SASCOC, FIFA and IOC commissions), Johan Koorts (then president of SAEF) and Marlene du Plessis (SANESA president)

From what I can gather, the arrests didn't happen and I had no further communication with Theo.

After my arrival in Cincinnati, Tim Marsland and I remained in regular contact for the first four months, mainly on "WhatsApp" and it was a real roller-coaster ride.

4/25/15, 9:36:48 AM: Graeme Joffe: Any good news?

4/25/15, 1:19:20 PM: Tim Marsland: Something happened this morning - I'm waiting for confirmation as to exactly what.

4/26/15, 8:25:29 AM: Tim Marsland: Hi all ok there?

4/26/15, 10:00:01 AM: Graeme Joffe: All ok Tim, thanks. Any news? Wanted to try and email Theo to see if he had any leads on threat and phone tapping and if he had spoken to investigator in my case, Capt Mabasa who has done nothing in 4 months except have coffee with sascoc and dept of sport and rec.

4/26/15, 10:21:36 AM: Tim Marsland: He (Koorts) was taken in for questioning yesterday and spent the night in chukkie (jail). Just waiting to hear if he will be charged. Theo wanted to check that message was from you. Will let him know it was. Please don't mention the other guy just yet.

4/26/15, 10:30:10 AM: Graeme Joffe: Good news - hope they throw the book at him and more. Yip message was from me. Thanks Tim

5/7/15, 9:03:13 AM: Graeme Joffe: Just got sms from Capt. Mabasa at Sandton SAPS to come see him urgently. Have sent you email. Theo mentioned that he does know him.

5/11/15, 2:20:36 AM: Graeme Joffe: Hi Tim, sorry missed your call. Is it urgent?

5/11/15, 2:20:37 AM: Tim Marsland: Hi Graeme. Theo needs you to phone Mabasa before 11 this morning and tell Mabasa that Theo Bronkhorst is assisting you

5/11/15, 2:21:46 AM: Tim Marsland: They want to seize du plessis computer because the evidence is on it

5/11/15, 2:22:38 AM: Graeme Joffe: Will do

5/11/15, 2:24:12 AM: Tim Marsland: Cool. Nearly there :)

5/11/15, 2:24:32 AM: Graeme Joffe: Thanks Tim

5/11/15, 2:27:34 AM: Tim Marsland: Sorry to wake you!

5/11/15, 2:28:27 AM: Graeme Joffe: No problem at all. Will send Mabasa a sms now

5/12/15, 6:57:38 AM: Graeme Joffe: Any news Tim?

5/12/15, 7:09:00 AM: Tim Marsland: There is, but I don't yet have the details. Apparently sandton cops now taking your case seriously. They have linked du plessis to Reddy as I understand it. But I am waiting for Theo to get the full story

5/12/15, 7:14:08 AM: Graeme Joffe: Thanks very much Tim

5/12/15, 3:12:50 PM: Tim Marsland: Ok, your case has become a big thing. A colonel will call you tomorrow around 8am our time from sandton police station. Theo will also be there. It seems they need you back here urgently - they need you to expand on your statement. Seems they have proof that du plessis was behind your issues and acting under instruction. It explains why the SAEF article attracted so much hostility.

5/12/15, 3:20:19 PM: Graeme Joffe: Interesting thanks very much Tim but I won't consider coming back to SA until there are arrests and people charged. I'm happy to give them as much as they want in writing. I don't trust the SAPS as they have done nothing after 6 months and only Theo's intervention has got them to do something.

5/12/15, 3:32:48 PM: Tim Marsland: Ok well discuss with the cop. Sounds like he is taking it seriously.

5/12/15, 3:52:03 PM: Graeme Joffe: Thanks Tim

5/13/15, 2:52:02 AM: Tim Marsland: Hi Graeme. Ok I've spoken to the guys. I explained you are not keen to return yet. Want they need from you urgently is for you to rewrite your statement in much more detail. For example, the motor cycle that followed you (number plate, colour etc - anything you can add). They also want the articles you wrote that caused the problems. Also the stuff you sent to SARS (my suggestion). If you email to me I will go hand it over for you.

5/15/15, 10:16:07 AM: Graeme Joffe: Just checking if you received extended statement for Theo

5/15/15, 11:20:58 AM: Tim Marsland: I did thank you. I sent it to him. Your material is dynamite!

5/28/15, 12:34:25 PM: Graeme Joffe: Hi Tim. Hope you're well. Is there any news? I see Raymond Hack commenting that SA has nothing to worry about with World Cup bribe. I want to throw up!

5/28/15, 1:10:20 PM: Tim Marsland: Please keep this confidential. The police are at Koorts right now. I'm not 100% certain if he is being arrested or searched. I will be able to confirm later. They are going next to du plessis. They have 100% proof that she harassed you.

5/28/15, 1:17:00 PM: Tim Marsland: They are going to use du plessis as bait for hack and Reddy.

5/28/15, 1:22:31 PM: Graeme Joffe: Great, thanks Tim. Please keep me posted

5/28/15, 1:45:29 PM: Tim Marsland: I will do. You are being vindicated.

5/28/15, 1:45:58 PM: Graeme Joffe: I can only hope

5/29/15, 9:05:32 AM: Graeme Joffe: Any news?

5/29/15, 9:18:48 AM: Tim Marsland: Du plessis arrived at sandton police station this morning with hack, Copeland and Bolhuis (private investigator) and proceeded to scream like a banshee to get one particular computer back. She was not successful. Koorts meanwhile called the cops and has requested a meeting to propose a deal. The cops are with him now.

5/29/15, 9:19:40 AM: Tim Marsland: Also, with all the extra heat they have decided you must remain put because they are trying again to locate you. Why I am not sure.

5/29/15, 9:20:17 AM: Tim Marsland: So ,at the moment the police have seized evidence but not actually laid charges, which I guess is the next step.

5/29/15, 9:34:54 AM: Graeme Joffe: Thanks Tim. I see they have been trying to re-tap my phone. Some info I haven't been able to verify is that Tubby has a brother or family member working for Ernst and young who did 2010 World Cup audit and that's why he is being well protected.

5/29/15, 9:48:18 AM: Tim Marsland: That's very interesting!!!!

5/30/15, 2:23:55 AM: Tim Marsland: Hi Graeme. Did you SMS Mobasa? He doesn't want you to do that. Please understand we are close to getting it done and quite a few people are real risk. The other side have made a number of direct threats. It's ok to call Theo though or me. Hope this makes sense

5/30/15, 4:58:58 AM: Graeme Joffe: Makes sense, thanks Tim

6/2/15, 2:07:11 PM: Tim Marsland: Hi Graeme. Theo and Mabasa have an appointment tomorrow at 10 with the senior state prosecutor to apply for warrants to arrest Koorts and du plessis. Police legal signed it off yesterday. The charges stem from sascoc/lottery irregularities. I will update you tomorrow.

6/2/15, 2:09:19 PM: Graeme Joffe: Great news, thanks Tim

6/2/15, 2:38:36 PM: Tim Marsland: Lets hope that we are finally there!

6/2/15, 2:39:22 PM: Graeme Joffe: Holding thumbs and that Reddy and Hack are next.

6/2/15, 3:45:33 PM: Tim Marsland: They should be. The expectation is that du plessis will rat on them

6/3/15, 5:49:57 AM: Tim Marsland: Hi Theo will contact you shortly. The prosecutor needs some technical amendments to your statement to include that you authorized Theo to investigate and that you didn't authorize anyone to harass you!!! SA law is astounding!

6/3/15, 8:10:23 AM: Graeme Joffe: I give up Tim - makes no sense to me anymore.

6/3/15, 8:50:25 AM: Graeme Joffe: Why harassed now when I was threatened?

6/3/15, 9:21:02 AM: Tim Marsland: It's a technical thing they want added to your initial statement. It's to show that you were not, for example, getting them to harass you for the sake of a better story. I know it sounds stupid but SA law is stupid these days.

6/3/15, 9:37:32 AM: Graeme Joffe: It is a joke. Okay I await Theo's call. Thanks

6/3/15, 5:03:35 PM: Graeme Joffe: Have sent email

6/4/15, 5:49:09 AM: Tim Marsland: Hi Graeme. The prosecutor is happy. He has instructed that they draw up the suspects' police records which will form part of the bail process. My estimate is that they won't make the arrests until next week because it will take a day to draw up the warrants of arrest

6/4/15, 5:54:52 AM: Graeme Joffe: Great news, thanks Tim

6/4/15, 7:03:28 AM: Tim Marsland: The prosecutor has hack and Reddy firmly in his sites. Of course my interest is in the other two but it has ended up dovetailing quite well

6/4/15, 7:05:34 AM: Graeme Joffe: All 4 would be the best result. But any arrest will do. I had kind of lost faith in the system. Thanks for all your efforts.

6/4/15, 7:07:36 AM: Graeme Joffe: My article today kind of sums up my frustrations and how crooked they are.

6/4/15, 8:33:09 AM: Tim Marsland: I haven't seen it yet. I must say I'm astounded at how bureaucratic the legal system is. Almost impossible to have someone arrested. But we are very nearly there. Theo has been like a dog with a bone and refuses to give up.

6/4/15, 8:39:20 AM: Graeme Joffe: Good stuff

6/5/15, 2:45:21 PM: Graeme Joffe: Nothing happen today?

6/5/15, 3:45:25 PM: Tim Marsland: They were downloading police background reports today. The prosecutor has told your cop that this is a priority case relating to hack and Grubby Reddy. I think my two will be arrested next week and the other two thereafter. The FIFA thing has actually helped with those two.

6/5/15, 3:50:22 PM: Graeme Joffe:Good stuff

6/9/15, 7:35:09 AM: Graeme Joffe: All still on track?

6/9/15, 7:58:18 AM: Tim Marsland: Yes.

6/9/15, 8:46:23 AM: Tim Marsland: Hawks may pick up hack this afternoon. Will confirm when I know for
sure.

6/9/15, 8:48:16 AM: Graeme Joffe: Thanks Tim

6/11/15, 7:48:56 AM: Graeme Joffe: Any news Tim?

6/11/15, 8:56:47 AM: Tim Marsland: Hi yes. Tue Hawks had taken over Hack but the NPA and the chief magistrate of randburg overuled as they say this is the best chance they have had of nailing hack. So the arrest has been handed back to sandton. They are drawing up the warrant for Koorts, as well additional seizure warrants. The arrests for all four (koort, du plessis, hack, and Reddy) are diarized for Wednesday, although I think koorts might be earlier.

6/11/15, 9:06:46 AM: Graeme Joffe: Thanks Tim

6/17/15, 5:23:18 AM: Graeme Joffe: Arrests still happening today?

6/17/15, 2:30:28 PM: Tim Marsland: Hi no. It's become messy again. Now it's apparently on Friday.

6/17/15, 2:36:17 PM: Graeme Joffe: Sadly it will never happen. But I have a contact at the FBI here and sent them a lot of information.

6/18/15, 5:20:21 AM: Tim Marsland: Ok that was a good idea. I can put you in touch with the FBI guy who was the head of Africa until recently.

6/18/15, 8:41:03 AM: Graeme Joffe: Not to worry, thanks Tim. What does Theo say about latest mess?

6/18/15, 9:17:02 AM: Tim Marsland: Well he says Koorts will be arrested tomorrow but I have heard that so many times that it becomes difficult to believe

6/18/15, 9:23:00 AM: Graeme Joffe: I'm afraid I've lost all faith.

6/18/15, 9:25:23 AM: Graeme Joffe: But would still like to know from Theo exactly who was behind the threat and where it came from.

6/19/15, 4:44:41 AM: Tim Marsland: It was Marlene and it came under instruction from sascoc. They are trying to set up the arrest for tomorrow. If not then Monday.

6/19/15, 4:45:12 AM: Tim Marsland: I must admit there is a huge amount of paperwork that has to be produced relating to evidence.

6/19/15, 6:54:37 AM: Graeme Joffe: Thanks Tim

6/19/15, 11:09:34 AM: Tim Marsland: Hi. Norman says you called him and he was worried you were taping the call to go public. I've assured them you won't do that. But I also said they are wrong not to keep you updated. I only know parts of what is happening so I can't update you properly. Anyway Theo is driving through tonight. He says the one arrest is tomorrow but until it's done it isn't done!

6/19/15, 11:13:49 AM: Graeme Joffe: Hi Tim, no idea who Norman is?

6/19/15, 11:29:23 AM: Tim Marsland: Oh the Sandton cop. Mobasa

6/19/15, 11:33:40 AM: Graeme Joffe: Haven't spoken to him for months

6/19/15, 11:55:16 AM: Tim Marsland: Someone just impersonated you. Norman said nothing fortunately

6/19/15, 11:57:05 AM: Graeme Joffe: Crazy stuff - he should have my number on his phone from all my text messages.

6/19/15, 11:59:20 AM: Tim Marsland: True. But I understand he received hundreds of calls so he won't keep any one number. And he might assume your number has changed

6/19/15, 12:01:58 PM: Graeme Joffe: It's like a never ending movie (lol) ...

6/19/15, 12:07:37 PM: Tim Marsland: Yeah as you say it's crazy! These are really bad people!

6/19/15, 12:10:12 PM: Graeme Joffe: Yes they are. Seen too much for last three years. Thanks for all your help

6/19/15, 12:11:39 PM: Graeme Joffe: I only know him as captain John Mabasa - hence the confusion.

6/19/15, 12:43:42 PM: Tim Marsland: Ah ok! They ate tracking the number that was used. It was from somewhere in fourways

6/19/15, 12:49:49 PM: Graeme Joffe: Please let me know. Interesting

6/19/15, 2:50:50 PM: Tim Marsland: Will do! Marlene lives in fourways

6/20/15, 9:50:19 AM: Graeme Joffe: Anything happen today?

6/20/15, 3:01:30 PM: Tim Marsland: They went to pick up Koorts today. I know that by 4pm they couldn't find him. Since then I have not had an update. There is a lot of intimidation and phone hacking on the go

6/21/15, 4:33:02 AM: Tim Marsland: Hi Graeme. I saw the email. That's unfortunately the truth about our police these days. Without a Theo you get nowhere. In any event, they could not find koorts yesterday so they are going back tomorrow. Theo needs to speak to you - can you please call him at 12 today your time (6pm our time)?

6/21/15, 4:33:25 AM: Tim Marsland: This whole business has been an eye opener for me!

6/21/15, 8:05:33 AM: Graeme Joffe: Will do Tim

6/21/15, 12:44:13 PM: Graeme Joffe: Shew, Theo is very angry with me. Do you know why?

6/21/15, 2:22:03 PM: Tim Marsland: No idea. I know he is very tense because his life has been threatened. His wife and child are in protective care. They broke into his house and took a lot of stuff but basically they were after his filling cabinet.

6/21/15, 2:22:45 PM: Tim Marsland: I told him it was not you who contacted the captain. His name is Norman by the way, I checked.

6/21/15, 3:10:00 PM: Graeme Joffe: Ok, thanks Tim, it's scary stuff. Hope they're safe. I thought they had traced the call to Fourways - so they knew it wasn't me. I'm not sure what I've done wrong except ask for an update on the case.

6/21/15, 4:15:12 PM: Tim Marsland: I'm sure nothing. I just think theo is understandably tense. I thought he needed info from you. I'll chat to him tomorrow.

6/21/15, 4:18:12 PM: Graeme Joffe: No problem, he didn't ask for any info but said he's leaving for JHB at 4am tomorrow to make arrests.

6/22/15, 3:44:26 PM: Graeme Joffe: Was there any news today? You don't perhaps remember the name of the Athletics project that Hack laundered Lottery money for? Theo mentioned it to me but can't remember the name.

6/23/15, 3:55:03 AM: Tim Marsland: Hi Graeme. This is critical. Please don't write anything this week. I received a full briefing and we are right in the middle of it. It's critical nothing leaks or gets said. Having spent R600,000 on this I don't want to go to jail as a result!!!!!!

6/23/15, 4:01:16 AM: Graeme Joffe: Sorry Tim, phone was on silent. Won't write anything this week. When you say we're right in the middle of it? Are they still going to arrest them?

6/23/15, 4:06:48 AM: Tim Marsland: Yes. It's a big thing this.

6/23/15, 4:09:10 AM: Graeme Joffe: Ok, thanks. Are Theo and family ok?

6/23/15, 4:21:57 AM: Tim Marsland: Yes they are thanks. He is at the coal face as you know!

6/23/15, 8:25:26 AM: Graeme Joffe: When do they expect to make the arrests?

6/23/15, 9:42:04 AM: Tim Marsland: It's under discussion by the NPA at the moment. Will know their thinking later

6/23/15, 9:43:19 AM: Graeme Joffe: Ok, thanks

6/23/15, 1:19:32 PM: Tim Marsland: Trust me, it's all happening

6/23/15, 1:31:53 PM: Graeme Joffe: Thanks Tim

6/26/15, 8:44:31 AM: Graeme Joffe: Any news Tim?

6/26/15, 10:59:36 AM: Tim Marsland: Hi, yes we are still right in the middle of it. I don't want to disclose over this line

6/26/15, 11:20:12 AM: Graeme Joffe: Ok, no problem

6/28/15, 2:28:18 PM: Tim Marsland: We need to be ready for media exposure this week, maybe as early as tomorrow. How should we handle that?

6/28/15, 2:31:41 PM: Graeme Joffe: Hi Tim, depending on what happens. If there are arrests, then media picks up an alert from SAPS within minutes I would think. If not, I have all the big media editor contact details ...

6/28/15, 2:33:11 PM: Graeme Joffe: Whatever you need me to handle, be happy to do so.

6/28/15, 2:50:44 PM: Tim Marsland: Do you want to break it?

6/28/15, 2:58:53 PM: Graeme Joffe: Think it will be much better if the mainstream press breaks it - like a primedia and got the contact details for bbc and sky.

6/28/15, 3:00:19 PM: Tim Marsland: I was gagged. Koorts was arrested at 4am on Tuesday. He said he would cooperate in taking down hack but he has double Crossed the prosecutor. Hack has been laundering cash via Marlene (provable) via property deals.

6/28/15, 3:01:40 PM: Tim Marsland: So a lot will happen this week. I'm not letting hack walk Scott free and blame the ANC guys. He set up the entire thing.

6/28/15, 3:06:15 PM: Graeme Joffe: Surprised media didn't pick up on Koorts arrest. But please keep me posted.

6/28/15, 3:10:46 PM: Tim Marsland: They can only report when he appears in court

6/28/15, 3:15:29 PM: Graeme Joffe: Makes sense. Hope something happens this week.

6/28/15, 4:14:52 PM: Tim Marsland: Bear in mind no one knows who Koorts is

6/28/15, 4:33:52 PM: Graeme Joffe: Sports media should remember him from tennis days but maybe not.

6/30/15, 7:15:06 AM: Tim Marsland: At this point Koorts will appear in court on Thursday.

6/30/15, 7:15:21 AM: Tim Marsland: So I am thinking the Sunday times is the way to go

6/30/15, 7:34:58 AM: Graeme Joffe: I can send you the contact details for the Times. Is it just Koorts?

6/30/15, 11:13:11 AM: Tim Marsland: Not sure yet. I do know Ivan has been added to the list.

7/3/15, 10:01:46 AM: Tim Marsland: Hi Graeme. I will call you tonight from a Botswana number. Lots has happened.

7/3/15, 3:45:35 PM: Graeme Joffe: Ok, thanks Tim

7/4/15, 2:21:41 PM: Tim Marsland: Hi Graeme will call you tomorrow. I took the weekend off to go to Dullstroom. I can assure you that the big guns are now involved and they are targeting the guys of interest

7/4/15, 2:37:47 PM: Graeme Joffe: Thanks Tim

7/5/15, 2:54:58 PM: Tim Marsland: Hi Graeme. There is a major meeting tomorrow morning which is what I have been waiting for.

7/5/15, 2:58:27 PM: Graeme Joffe: Cool, thanks

7/6/15, 5:16:45 AM: Tim Marsland: Hi Graeme. Please let me know what time I can call you.

7/6/15, 8:39:16 AM: Graeme Joffe: Hi Tim, available any time now. Probably best on my SA number as I'm battling to hear the international calls on my US number.

7/6/15, 12:28:36 PM: Tim Marsland: Tried to call but it went to voicemail

7/6/15, 1:38:40 PM: Graeme Joffe: Sorry Tim. Available now - can you talk

7/10/15, 2:30:48 PM: Tim Marsland: Please call me asap on the +267 number

7/10/15, 2:33:50 PM: Graeme Joffe: Available now – sorry

7/17/15, 5:27:52 AM: Tim Marsland: Don't blame you for going public. Having been in the center of this I have totally lost faith in the legal system.

7/17/15, 7:21:22 AM: Graeme Joffe: Response has been overwhelming - now for media circus which is not what I wanted.

7/17/15, 7:49:31 AM: Tim Marsland: Well at least the publicity might do some good. Because nothing else has worked.

7/17/15, 8:12:20 AM: Graeme Joffe: True - will keep you posted.

7/19/15, 5:40:49 AM: Tim Marsland: Hi. What is the true story about you and CNN?

7/19/15, 5:46:58 AM: Graeme Joffe: True story? As in the defamatory blog? Laughable - never been fired from a job in my life. We're getting close to finding the anonymous bloggers - getting a U.S. Court order to obtain the personal information from domain and registration.

7/19/15, 5:53:06 AM: Tim Marsland: Well done! Can you give me anything about the CNN thing? The cops here (please don't use this info) have brought that up.

7/19/15, 5:59:47 AM: Graeme Joffe: Tim, all they need to do is call Yusuf Abramjee or Terry Volkwyn at 94.7 to find out the truth. The blog also says I was fired by 94.7. My contract was up at CNN and I decided not to renew. But the cops gave hard evidence of the crimes? I've passed on all the info to Carte Blanche. What is Mabasa saying now?

7/19/15, 6:14:19 AM: Tim Marsland: Seems that article has woken them up and they are trying to cover their arses

7/19/15, 6:18:24 AM: Graeme Joffe: Ok - fortunately the FBI have taken an interest in my story due to the FIFA scandal - so will see where it all goes.

7/19/15, 6:19:35 AM: Tim Marsland: I think that is the way to go. Hack is seriously protected here.

7/19/15, 6:21:28 AM: Graeme Joffe: Thanks Tim

7/19/15, 6:50:39 AM: Tim Marsland: From what I have seen, hack is the brains behind the FIFA thing. There is more bribery than they saw plus theft. It looks like hack set up the theft mechanisms, and then laundered the funds into dollars via Marlene and I assume others. That is where the FBI should be interested - because they used dollars it falls under FBI jurisdiction.

7/19/15, 6:51:07 AM: Tim Marsland: We have details of bank accounts and some transactions. Not sure how much you want to get involved though.

7/19/15, 6:52:37 AM: Tim Marsland: It is clear to me that the Sa police will not take this further. Also there are a lot of lies told, which I am not sure who is the lie telller. I know the sometimes embellishes and sometimes guesses in enthusiasm, but overall he is on the level.

7/19/15, 6:55:41 AM: Tim Marsland: The FBI will be very interested to see the phone calls between Koorts and Suleman.

7/19/15, 6:58:37 AM: Graeme Joffe: Thanks very much Tim. Who is Suleman?

7/19/15, 7:20:13 AM: Tim Marsland: Google him. Bashir Suleman. One of the fbi's most wanted men. Blacklisted by the us treasury. He is the biggest drug trader in the world. Based in Mozambique. He buys rhino horn and trades it for heroin.

7/19/15, 7:31:40 AM: Graeme Joffe: Scary stuff. Who is protecting Koorts?

7/19/15, 7:33:44 AM: Tim Marsland: Hack. Because he also knows stuff about hacks laundering. I never spoke to my mate at the FBI because I thought our cops would actually arrest Koorts. The FBI were likely to do a deal though with Koorts to nail suleman. But since our obviously wont touch him the FBI may as well have the info.

7/19/15, 7:34:30 AM: Tim Marsland: It seems Koorts at tennis put in place the base scheme they use to pinch funds. Hack calls Koorts a low life, interestingly enough.

7/19/15, 7:36:37 AM: Graeme Joffe: It's unbelievable. Thanks Tim

7/19/15, 8:08:23 AM: Tim Marsland: I think mobasa is innocent but I am reasonably certain that the npa has been stringing Theo along.

7/19/15, 8:33:56 AM: Tim Marsland: If you are not comfortable passing on the Koorts info then I will pass it on to the FBI guy I know who was head of Africa. We should just make sure that the FBI know there are two approaches.

7/19/15, 8:34:07 AM: Tim Marsland: I'm also tired of it.

7/19/15, 8:41:36 AM: Graeme Joffe: Will let you know

7/20/15, 1:27:16 AM: Tim Marsland: Hi. We are going the FBI route. We've got lots of documentary proof some of which relates to the sports side as well. It's probably good that the FBI have two separate approaches.

7/20/15, 9:26:50 AM: Tim Marsland: You've gone silent? There is a meeting tomorrow with the npa. My view is to tell them thanks, but no thanks, we prefer to hand all the info to the fbi.

7/20/15, 9:40:32 AM: Graeme Joffe: Tim, NPA should be doing their job and prosecuting the lot of them. I've given my story and FIFA info to FBI and don't want to abuse their privilege.

7/20/15, 9:49:03 AM: Tim Marsland: Yes I think we will approach my guy at the fbi. I don't believe the npa will touch hack and anyone he instructs them to leave alone. To be honest, I have been extremely naive as to just how corrupt Sa has become. I was warned in the beginning not to touch sascoc because zuma is linked to it.

7/20/15, 9:55:16 AM: Graeme Joffe: It's tragic Tim but that's SA and when you have conflicted media - it makes it even worse.

7/20/15, 10:41:59 AM: Tim Marsland: Typical. The anc made deliberate moves to control the media. They have orchestrated the firing of all of the top investigative journos.

7/20/15, 11:10:29 AM: Graeme Joffe: What I will never understand is the last time I spoke to Theo - he was going to job next day to help Mabasa arrest Reddy, Hack, Koorts and Marlene - who stopped the arrests?

7/20/15, 11:21:15 AM: Tim Marsland: The prosecutor. They keep sending him off to get more "evidence". I think they were deliberately wasting our time in the hope that the funding would run out. What annoys me is the evidence they wanted was on the lottery not Koorts. So I was prepared to assist thinking they were serious. Now I'm sure they were wasting our time.

7/20/15, 11:22:12 AM: Graeme Joffe: Do you have the prosecutor's name?

7/20/15, 1:10:47 PM: Tim Marsland: Will find out

7/20/15, 1:32:16 PM: Graeme Joffe: Thanks

7/20/15, 1:52:31 PM: Tim Marsland: My assumption is that it is this Balla guy and someone called Hiemstra. Just not sure of spelling.

7/20/15, 2:17:52 PM: Graeme Joffe: If you can confirm with Theo - would be good. Thanks

7/21/15, 5:01:36 AM: Tim Marsland: The meeting never took place. I am meeting Theo later to get an exact update. As I understand it the cops are scurrying around relating to you. My own assumption is there will be some token arrests. Hack I believe remains untouchable. The hawks have taken over Koorts specifically to do with the poaching. He may well end up being a token arrest.

7/21/15, 5:02:25 AM: Tim Marsland: I've asked Theo to show me the actual evidence before handing over to fbi. I want to make sure it is what I understand it is.

7/21/15, 5:02:32 AM: Tim Marsland: Hang in there.

7/21/15, 6:31:08 AM: Graeme Joffe: Thanks Tim

7/25/15, 12:18:34 PM: Tim Marsland: Hi. There is a tremendous about of police activity at the moment. I will make sense of it during the week. We won at sascoc yesterday. The das are back in charge. Please hold off mentioning it.

7/25/15, 1:11:19 PM: Graeme Joffe: So is Koorts gone?

7/25/15, 4:34:48 PM: Tim Marsland: In the process of .....

7/29/15, 11:11:55 AM: Graeme Joffe: Any news Tim? Got a fright when I saw a Theo Bronkhorst linked to Lion story in Zim. But I take it no relation?

7/29/15, 2:19:43 PM: Tim Marsland: Yeah wrong Theo

7/29/15, 2:20:16 PM: Tim Marsland: I spoke to VP in Zim today to make sure they properly punish those hunters. I am assured they will.

7/29/15, 2:21:46 PM: Tim Marsland: Please don't let this be known but your cop has been suspended and the case moved to I think krugersdorp. Apparently, a lot of your fans called sandton police station to complain about your treatment.

7/29/15, 2:22:46 PM: Tim Marsland: Does this however mean anything will actually happen? Personally, I still think a token arrest or too but the real thieves won't be touched. Hope I'm wrong.

7/29/15, 2:31:43 PM: Tim Marsland: I don't think the cop is entirely to blame. Sounded to me that the NPA are the ones that stone -walled the investigation. They kept asking for more and more evidence. I was on the receiving end as I was the one paying. I think they were wasting our time hoping the funding would dry up.

7/29/15, 2:33:27 PM: Graeme Joffe: Thanks Tim

7/29/15, 2:34:21 PM: Tim Marsland: I think they should become aware that you are going to write a book

7/29/15, 2:35:48 PM: Graeme Joffe: I'm done - time for me to move on and live again

7/29/15, 2:38:35 PM: Tim Marsland: Fair point. So no book?

7/29/15, 2:39:20 PM: Graeme Joffe: Maybe one day but for now just going to travel a bit

7/29/15, 2:40:03 PM: Tim Marsland: I can understand that. But will you be able to leave the job unfinished?

7/29/15, 2:41:22 PM: Graeme Joffe: Probably not knowing me ...

7/29/15, 2:44:40 PM: Tim Marsland: That's what I thought. You have a lot of fans who believe in you

7/29/15, 3:15:32 PM: Graeme Joffe: Thanks Tim. Hope you guys are well.

8/9/15, 7:11:19 AM: Tim Marsland: The situation has become interesting. Sascoc publicly said it is going to investigate Marlene and sanesa. Koorts has been kicked out.

8/9/15, 7:12:57 AM: Tim Marsland: On your business, it seems we may finally be at a point where something is going to happen. There are definite signs that sascoc is distancing itself from lotto issues. The police have seized a bunch of records so sascoc know what is coming. Hack is no longer protected.

8/9/15, 7:15:34 AM: Graeme Joffe: Very interesting Tim. Thanks for update.

8/9/15, 7:18:32 AM: Tim Marsland: Apparently the amount missing far exceeds the r200m we know about. And there is also something to do with equestrian. I suspect they got lotto funds using saef's name but saef didn't know about it.

8/9/15, 7:58:39 AM: Tim Marsland: Yup. Any idea who Johan Oosthuisen is? I assume he is at sascoc. He is suspect number 5.

8/9/15, 8:57:18 AM: Graeme Joffe: I know of Wessel Oosthuizen who is the sascoc photographer and Gert Oosthuizen who is the deputy sports minister ...

8/9/15, 9:13:30 AM: Graeme Joffe: I see there's a Johan Oosthuizen who is president of Ringball SA – never heard of that sport.

8/9/15, 10:42:24 AM: Tim Marsland: Maybe its him.

8/16/15, 3:44:27 AM: Tim Marsland: Hi Graeme. Korrts was finally arrested and is out on 5000 bail. As to sascox, well there is an internal war going on. Looks like mm is trying to kick out fatboy. They have both tried to get our guy to hand over his evidence. Yet another cop, and brigadier, has tried to get involved. And more physical threats - this time by fatboy's thug. We traced the callbox he used and it was in a shopping centre. Trying to get camera footage. His usage of language is similar to that used against you. So we might get lucky.

8/16/15, 3:44:35 AM: Tim Marsland: How are things over there?

8/16/15, 8:26:08 AM: Graeme Joffe: Great news Tim, just hope the mainstream media pick up on the arrest. Things are ok over here - just taking it day by day. Starting to live a little - didn't realize how much the corruption exposes actually consumed my life for three years. How u guys?

8/16/15, 8:27:04 AM: Tim Marsland: Yeah good. I've realised having been involved in this just how far SA has sunken. There is basically no rule of law.

8/16/15, 8:29:47 AM: Graeme Joffe: That's what I keep telling people. It's tragic. There was an interview with advocate Paul Hoffman which sums up the whole legal situation - I can send it to you

8/16/15, 8:31:26 AM: Tim Marsland: Ok thanks. The cops and the prosecutors are either inexperienced, overworked, or corrupt, or a combination thereof.

8/16/15, 8:31:47 AM: Tim Marsland: And I don't see any light at the end of the tunnel

8/16/15, 8:33:12 AM: Graeme Joffe: Sadly I don't see any light either - so maybe hard to justify ever coming back to SA.

8/16/15, 8:35:25 AM: Tim Marsland: I think if you have other options you should take them. It is very hard to be part of a system where for example, rhino are going extinct in front of your eyes.

8/16/15, 8:36:03 AM: Tim Marsland: I mean, they spend R100m a year protecting rhino and the poaching numbers go up every year. Its obvious the top guys protecting the rhinos are actually involved.

8/16/15, 8:36:28 AM: Tim Marsland: Even I could irradicate the problem with R50m.

8/16/15, 8:36:40 AM: Tim Marsland: Cry the beloved country, I guess

8/16/15, 8:37:20 AM: Graeme Joffe: So true. Always an inside job where there's millions involved.

8/16/15, 9:18:06 AM: Tim Marsland: Try very hard to get hold of a movie called 204 Getting Away With Murder. Its a documentary about the Kebble murder. Its exactly what I have experienced with korrts and your issues.

8/16/15, 9:37:34 AM: Graeme Joffe: Will have a look for it

8/17/15, 1:30:15 PM: Tim Marsland: Mm called our guy today and said sascox has laid criminal charges against Marlne and korrts.

8/17/15, 2:12:57 PM: Graeme Joffe: Good to hear - and that should make the media unless they're token charges

8/17/15, 2:16:01 PM: Tim Marsland: Lets wait and see

It was a real rollercoaster ride on WhatsApp but I still wanted some form of conclusion and vindication.

I started to do some of my own investigations to see where my case was, why nothing had happened and why nobody from the lead investigating teams had even bothered to make contact with me.

I had also requested for the SAPS officer who initially responded to my emails to look into the cybercrime and criminal defamation that had been committed with the graemejoffe-exposed website.

It took weeks to get responses but finally, I got something - again, not the answers I was looking for.

SAP 21

SUID-AFRIKAANSE POLISIEDIENS **SOUTH AFRICAN POLICE SERVICE**

Privaatsak/Private Bag

Verwysing Reference	Sandton cas: 295/10/2014
Navrae Enquiries	Col modise Lt Col M J Mokoena
Telefoon Telephone	(011) 951 1914
Faksnommer Fax number	GP:prov. Detective piu

OFFICE OF THE PROVINCIAL COMMANDER
PROVINCIAL INVESTIGATION UNIT
DETECTIVE SERVICES
SOUTH AFRICAN POLICE SERVICES
GAUTENG
2017

2015-09-09

OFFICE OF THE PROVINCIAL COMMANDER
DETECTIVE SERVICES
SOUTH AFRICAN POLICE SERVICES
GAUTENG
2017

FEEDBACK ON SANDTON CAS: 295/10/2014 TO MR Graeme Joffe

1. The correct case number is sandton cas: 295/10/2014.
2. The case docket was taken to randburg magistrate court for decision as an investigation was completed.
3. Advocate Sikhosana of the above magistrate court decided to send the matter to DPP.
4. The matter presently is at DPP for decision.
5. Feedback will be given as soon as the docket is received back from DPP.

_original signed _______________LT COLONEL
PROVINCIAL INVESTIGATION UNIT COMMANDER:
MJ MOKOENA

Received on 21 October 2015

The investigation was completely done on your case. It was then taken for decision at court. The court withdrawn the case, no successful prosecution in this matter. Further inquries can be directed to Justice Department. - Lieutenant Colonel: MJ Mokoena, Provincial Investigation Unit Commander, SAPS Krugersdorp

Received on 26 October 2015

The case was dealt by Randburg Magistrate Court and the issue was booked to SPP Sikhosana. The docket came back from court on 2015-10-12 and docket came back as decline to prosecute. The office does not have the contact of Randburg magistrate court. The private Investigating officer was informed about the outcome. - Lieutenant Colonel: MJ Mokoena

I forwarded the SAPS response to Tim via email.

11/1/15, 10:15:08 AM: Tim Marsland: Hi. I've take a while to reflect on the email. I had heard that the police had withdrawn, but that says the prosecutors have drip

11/1/15, 10:16:20 AM: Tim Marsland: Declined to prosecute, which is interesting. It is remarkable that according to the prosecutors not one of the allegations you made were worthy of pursuit, which is statistically highly improbable.

11/1/15, 10:16:58 AM: Tim Marsland: I am of the view that you are safer where you are. Our guy did say you have serious enemies, for what that is worth.

11/1/15, 10:17:52 AM: Tim Marsland: I still think you did the right thing. On the one hand it was a high price to pay, on the other perhaps it has created a better future for you.

11/1/15, 10:18:33 AM: Tim Marsland: I am very negative on SA's future - I see nothing the ANC is doing that will turn SA around - it will simply sink further.

11/1/15, 10:18:45 AM: Tim Marsland: Anyway, let's keep in touch.

11/1/15, 10:42:26 AM: Graeme: Will do, thanks Tim

My case was obviously a hot potato as it bounced around from Sandton SAPS to Randburg SAPS to Krugersdorp SAPS, to the Provincial Investigative Unit to the NPA.

The untouchables were untouchable!

Theo Bronkhorst, the private investigator and I never met face to face. He was based in Bloemfontein and we had only spoken telephonically.

So, when the tragic story broke about the beloved Zimbabwean lion, Cecil who was killed by an American trophy hunter in July 2015 and the name of the guide was Theo Bronkhorst, I did a double take.

I obviously wasn't the only one.

The Afrikaans headline loosely translated as: "Theo Bronkhorst from Bloemfontein is getting threatening phone calls because he has the same name as the hunter from Zimbabwe who accompanied Dr. Walter Palmer."

Beeld
Beeld.com
August 4, 2015
Theo Bronkhorst van Bloemfontein kry dreigoproepe omdat hy dieselfde naam het as die jagter van Zimbabwe wat dr. Walter Palmer van Amerika, vergesel het.
See Translation
Verkeerde Theo Bronkhorst gedreig oor jag op Cecil die leeu
'n Private speurder van Bloemfontein word nou 'n "leeu-moordenaar" genoem omdat hy verwar word met 'n professionele jagter.
NETWERK24.COM | BY NETWERK24

It was the first time I had seen a photograph of Theo as there was very little on him in a google search until this article was published in August 2015.

Always helpful to put a face to a voice.

But was I still being hunted?

Chapter 18: SA Sports Awards

The South African Sport Awards is a Winning Nation programme, initiated in 2004 in partnership with South African Sport Confederation and Olympic Committee (SASCOC) and South African Broadcasting Corporation (SABC) and a host of other generous stakeholders and sponsors. Guided by the core values of an athlete-centered and excellence-driven sports system, the Department aims to incentivize and applaud individual athletes, teams and administrators who continue to make our nation proud by displaying exceptional performance and attaining remarkable results. - Department of Sport and Recreation South Africa

8 November 2012
SA "gravy train" Sports Awards

Dear Sports Ministry and SASCOC (all protocol observed)

Fortunately, I was not invited to the SA Sports awards but managed to sit through an hour of it on television.

With a budget of R30 odd million - was that really the best they could do?

I'm still looking for more adjectives to describe the boring, embarrassing, cringe worthy, amateur, uninspiring, political production that was a complete waste of money.

Granted Mr Mbalula, I tuned in late (just a little dig at the Minister who is late for every sports function). So, I may have missed the best parts of the awards but my first point of reference was yourself and your speech centered round how we must reward those that were not rewarded during apartheid.

Why do we keep having to try and correct the wrongs of the past?

Can we not just move on and celebrate all the incredible athletes of all race and creed that South Africa has today?

Moving on …

MC: "On stage now to hand out the next award, Miss South Africa, Melinda Bum" (Melinda Bam) - I guess you also have to have a good "backside" to be Miss SA.

Onto the nominees for federation of the year, "Swimming SA" - are you kidding me?

A federation that lost its main sponsor, a federation that doesn't have enough money to pay for the swimmers to go to World short course champs and a federation that is widely accused of mismanagement and misappropriation of funds.

The swimmers achieved at the London Olympics despite the federation and I see that Swimming SA

President, Jace Naidoo is standing for SASCOC election.

OMG!

I'm surprised Swimming SA didn't win the award but that went to the right winner in Rowing SA.

What this code has achieved with limited funds is truly amazing and hats off to Wimpie du Plessis, Roger Barrow and the rest of that team.

We are in "oar" of you!

So many of the nominations left me totally perplexed.

How does someone like Suzanne Ferreira, who had no few than nine medallists at the Paralympic Games not even get nominated for coach of the year in an Olympic year?

And was winning the Open Golf Championship not enough for Ernie Els to maybe get a nomination for either Sportsman or Sports Star of the year?

Come on, who does the nominations and who really does the voting?

Would love to have seen the criteria and the judge's score cards.

Other bits that caught my attention: SASCOC officials who can barely open an envelope and how good they are at building up a climax before announcing the winner. "Guess who" – must be taught in their team building sessions at Toastmasters. (An overseas Toastmasters, a package that includes business class air tickets and bring a friend)

If there was an audio glitch or sharp camera movement, SuperSport messaging: "Pictures courtesy of SABC" - no love lost there.

Every politician seemed to be there except President Zuma and "First Lady" Helen Zille but they had other pressing issues eg. "Nkandla-gate" (sorry, not allowed to call it that) – but maybe they were there and I missed them in the hour that I was watching.

Tokyo Sexwale calling Chad le Clos "Chad le Claude" and saying "Natalie du Toit was the best Paralympian at the Olympics."

There was plenty of gravy on the red carpet but no invite for rugby legend, Joost van der Westhuizen who got a Lifetime Award.

Not sure if his invite is in the mail or if there just wasn't enough in the R30 million odd budget for one more guest.

You would expect the award winners to be invited. Yip, a R35 million budget for the awards and a golf day - a sports ministry 'tender' won by 'guess who" (thanks Toastmasters)?

Drum roll please …

The winner: C-Squared with a CEO, Ben Moseme who just happens to be a good friend of the Sports Minister, Fikile Mbalula.

Is this perhaps why Mbalula is so soft with SASCOC and allows them to use public funds as if it is their own bank account and change the rules willy-nilly to suspend federations?

We need new blood in SASCOC, we need people with a real passion for sport and not a passion for travelling around the world.

The sporting codes have a chance to make that change at the SASCOC elections on 24 November but I fear, not much will change as the sporting bodies have been sucked in by this SASCOC vacuum.

Sports Ministry and SASCOC (all protocol observed) – hope there will be vast improvement in the 2013 awards - our athletes deserve better!

Yours sincerely,

Graeme Joffe

PS: Tubby, you looked great in that suit – is it an Erke suit? (Just a little dig at the SASCOC self-appointed CEO who did the Olympic clothing "deal" with the Chinese Manufacturer)

***

I read your article that you wrote about the sports awards and I just had to write a response to you; to say thank you and tell you how spot on you are. There are a few points that you focused on that absolutely amazed me after watching the awards. Especially about Swim SA being announced as federation of the year. I have been a South African waterpolo player and competing in the national team for the last 9 years. That means dealing with Swimming South Africa for 9 years now. I cannot tell you how incompetent and corrupt it has been. There have been so many inconsistencies and incidents that have happened that have driven players out of the sport.

At last year's World Championships in Shanghai, it was supposed to be a completely funded tour paid for by Swimming SA. We got an email saying that R3000 had to be paid to Swim SA towards the tour. R3000 is not a lot of money in the greater scheme of things but I wanted to know what it was for? When I or anyone asked what the money was going towards, we got into so much trouble from management and got told to be grateful that the rest of the funding was supplied by the federation and not to ask any questions, just be grateful that it wasn't more. This all happened and then while we were in China, it came out that the federation was in trouble with corruption and fraud. This is just one incident. I am in love with South Africa, my brother, Paul Harris has represented South Africa in cricket. I have always been so proud to be a South African and to sing the national anthem for my country. Things have got so bad in the sport of waterpolo and things are so corrupt in Swim SA that it has driven me out of the country. I am one of the most experienced players in the SA polo team and have been in the set up since

I was 16. I have led the team at many tournaments but the federation is so out of control that I have been asked by the Australian waterpolo coach to come and live there and join their set up. They got bronze at these last olympics. It is so sad that one federation can ruin a sport and then when there is a success, they pat themselves on the back, like they were the reason for the success. When in fact, the success came in spite of them and the federation. - Sarah Harris

And the sentiments of Sarah Harris had a loud echo.

For context, consider that for our Olympic athletes, most media were able to discover that about R80 million was spent on London preparations. In other words, we spent R80 million over 4 years on sending a team to represent SA, and we spend R35 million on a single evening to congratulate anyone who happens to be in favour, politically. We could be so much better than this. R35 million would fund 35 athletes for 2 years, giving them the opportunity to dedicate themselves to professional training and support services. But alas, in SA sports, the wants of "the few"take precedence over the needs of "the many. Thanks Graeme for writing the story, though of course the impact it will make will be minuscule and the only result is that you'll be labelled unpatriotic and anti-South African. – Ross Tucker

It was a toss-up of either watching the SA Sports Awards or watching true life drama in the Jerry Springer show. Thnaks Graeme, for your feedback on the Awards. Plese let me know if you want to hear what happened on the episode of Jerry Springer that you missed, or did you record it on your PVR. Mabula was singing the praises of the Awaards ceremony on the radio the following Monday moring, typical of an ANC clown.. - Lionel Schultz

Graeme, you took the words right out of my mouth! I thought Joost just could not make it... not getting an invite...?? Another question I had was if the SA Amputee Relay Team, who won gold and broke the world record at the Paralympics, did not at least deserve a nomination for team of the year? The only thing they did get right was to name RowingSA the Federation of the Year! If you look at the presidential candidates for the upcoming SASCOC Board elections, the possibility of things getting better is very slim. - Petronel Wit

Well-constructed and factual account of another occasion where tax money is needlessly squandered, just to provide another "dinner"where the fat cats can enjoy themselves. There is just no logic to be found anywhere in any of the Government Departments. I even fear for the future of our Sport - all the disciplines - if this continues! No wonder "athletes"who excel in their sport, rather leave South Africa to represent other countries! This is a joke indeed, if it were not so terribly sad. - Zondra Hoffmann

Sports Awards a big bore

An unseemly spat over money and behind-the-scenes chaos at the South African Sports Awards led to the event being slammed as "disastrous". - (City Press, 10 November 2012)

19 June 2013
The moral decay of SA sport

South African sport is in massive trouble as millions of rands continue to get wasted by selfish, gravy train administrators.

The rot starts right at the top.

In trying to justify a spend of R65 million on the SA sports awards this year, Sports minister, Fikile Mbalula said that 30 million people watched the awards on television last year. But a Rapport investigation report under the headline, "Sport se Oscars was bekonkel' (concocted) showed those viewership figures were not even a tenth of that.

The irregularities with the tender process are also well documented. The public is continually being misled by our own administrators.

Cricket South Africa (CSA) is still trying to cover up their CEO appointment or lack thereof. I have it on good authority that CSA has told the Board of Control for Cricket in India (BCCI) that they won't appoint Haroon Lorgat as CEO. Lorgat was about to be appointed in April until the BCCI interfered and threatened to cut the amount of games India play against the Proteas.

CSA then sent a five-man delegation, first class to India to mend fences and on return, appointed an independent company to find a CEO (easy cop out).

They also asked some officials to apply after the deadline, knowing full well Lorgat was the right man for the job.

Talk about a waste of time and money.

Speaking of money, why is it that nothing more has been said of SA Rugby officials paying themselves a bonus increase of 107% after the SARU tax profits plunged 87%?

On top of that, SARU are spending a ludicrous amount on a 'Springbok Experience' rugby museum, in the V&A Waterfront in Cape Town.

A R45 million experience, a rental of R150 000 per month and only due to open in September, with the design and production awarded to a company in London.

Proudly South African?

Sounds more and more like SASCOC's deal with the Chinese clothing manufacturer, Erke and should be fully investigated.

SASCOC, meanwhile are still trying to fool everyone what a great job they're doing in cleaning up SA sport.

It couldn't be further from the truth. If athletes, coaches and others were allowed to speak out without victimisation, the stories would make your hair stand up.

SASCOC CEO, Tubby Reddy and company spend more time with hastily arranged press conferences and meetings behind closed doors than anything else.

They are facing legal action on so many fronts and have the arrogance to ignore the instructions of bodies like the IAAF.

The bubble has to burst.

I heard a SASCOC official on 702 this week trying to justify all their business class travel and accommodation in five-star hotels and then try to justify why SA's number one ranked fencer, Sello Maduma, is currently not getting a cent from the OPEX programme.

Maduma went to the Olympics in Beijing, just missed out on qualification for London and could so easily qualify for Rio if given the chance.

It is good to see how well our swimmers are still doing on the international stage despite an inept federation. Swimming South Africa (SSA) has so many dark secrets and should have been placed under administration a long time ago. But the SSA president and CEO are "SASCOC buddies" and can do no wrong.

How does SASCOC turn a blind eye to SSA president, Jace Naidoo using a limited "coach accreditation" at the London Olympics?

Naidoo took full advantage to abuse his position, which allowed him access to accommodation in the Games village, transport, food and all the other privileges while a SA swimmer is denied having his or her coach at the games at all.

Is this the way the leader of a federation should act in his personal interest at the cost of the South African national interest?

And just when you think things are going "swimmingly" well in SA cycling ...

Cycling SA (CSA) changes its constitution to write out the Pedal Power Association (PPA) which has been promoting the well being of cyclists in SA for over 30 years.

PPA has filed an application in this regard with the High Court.

CSA also wants to introduce a membership fee for all cyclists, even for a fun ride.

Wait until The South African National Roads Agency (SANRAL) hears about this - cyclists could need an E- Toll tag as well!

It should be an honour and privilege to be a SA sports administrator but for many, it's just an opportunity to enrich themselves.

Mbalula now says cabinet will have to budget at least R10 billion towards the fulfillment of the objectives of the NSRP (national sport and recreation plan).

Milk it while you can "Mbaks"!

SA sport cannot survive the moral decay.

***

Well said Graham, unfortunately it will never change. These leaders neither have the moral fortitude nor the will to even attempt running the sport business transparently. Why bother when their political masters show the crooked ways and prove time and time there is no accountability because the rot slivers from the top right down to grassroots level. It is simply because the people of SA are more interested in their own gain than making a decent contribution to society! - Andre Burger

Where have you been, Joffers my boy? The lone voice of reason not afraid to speak out. Good to read one of your columns again. Keep hammering away. Eventually the rock must break! Would like to have your opinion on what we as John Q Public can do to increase the pressure on these corrupt fat cats. - Arno Louw

It is a tribute to South African athletes and sportspeople that they can compete on the international stage with distinction despite the disgusting, self-serving and sometimes criminal behaviour of their administrators. Keep up the good work shining a light on the dark cesspool of South African sports administration Mr. Joffe. - Christian Koegelenberg

Makes you wonder – if a specific sporting code does not dance to Reddy and Co's pipes it also might mean an improper over haul which will be detrimental to that sport. SASCOC has now become an unnecessary evil. - Clint Leeh

Climb aboard the gravy train awards
16 November 2014

Some of the headlines last year around the SA Sports Awards and sadly not one investigation or audit.

> *SA Sports Awards: a shady - and shameful - waste of taxpayers' money – Daily Maverick*
>
> *Tender questions dog SA Sports Awards – City Press*
>
> *Sport se Oscars was bekonkel (concocted) – Rapport*

Around R60 million was spent on the awards last year (most of which is Lottery money which comes from different entities including the Sports Trust) but the Sports Minister, Fikile Mbalula still likes to tell everyone, it's corporate spend.

The nominees for the 2014 South African Sports Awards were announced yesterday and some of the nominations are an insult to our sportsmen and women.

None more so than Swimming nominated again for Federation of the year.

Ironically, I received an email yesterday shortly before the nominations came out.

I am a sports administrator who has seen the best & worst of our sports system over the years. Firstly, just to say thanks for the work that you are doing. There are some of us administrators who try to do the job entrusted to us properly, and we are grateful for your resistance! I have been wondering how Swim SA is paying its bills and staff just discovered (rather belatedly I think?) that Swim SA is now billing its provinces – collecting money from them to keep afloat! I was suitably horrified! I hear the big provinces are paying around R200k each into the coffers of this disgraceful administration, keeping the CEO, Shaun Adriaanse in a job.

The e-mailer's name will remain anonymous as anyone who speaks out against the system is marginalized.

Just ask Roland Schoeman who has now had his OPEX funding totally withdrawn by SASCOC.

Schoeman, a medal hope for the Rio Games and who could become SA's first five time Olympian, is now left without funding and there are so many similar cases of top athletes who get not a rand from SASCOC but instead we will spend R60 million on one night for Mbalula and company to have a party and for friends to benefit from "tenders".
Are we surprised that we only get six medals at the Olympic Games?

Also, what more do the likes of Ryan Sandes (trail runner), Hank McGregor (canoeing) and Jordy Smith (surfing) need to achieve to get nominated for Sportsman or Sports Star of the year?

Shakes Mashaba has been in charge of Bafana Bafana for just over two months and he's nominated for coach of year?

Don't get me wrong, I'm loving what Shakes is doing with Bafana Bafana but far more appropriate nominations would have been the Proteas coaching staff of Russell Domingo and Adi Birrell as well as Roger Barrow who has been nominated for coach of the year by World Rowing.

So, a coach that is good enough for international recognition but not good enough for a domestic nomination?

Please.

Just who are the judges?

Also no disrespect to Graham Hill but I'm sure he'd be one of the first to say, his swimmers didn't have the best of years, especially if you take a holistic approach and include the women.

In fact, he did take the blame for the poor performances of the female swimmers.

But to slide in Swimming as Federation of the year, I guess they had to endorse the head coach as well.
The transparency of the nominations just makes a complete mockery of the awards.

This year's winners will be announced at a gala dinner at the Sandton Convention Centre in Johannesburg on 30 November.

Can't wait – sorry, forgot I'm blacklisted.

Tender questions dog SA Sports Awards

The department of sport and recreation (SRSA) awarded an R18 million tender for the management of this year's SA Sports Awards to a company with no "traceable" business premises or website. Sabela Uyabizwa Media, which belongs to former Generations actress and television host Sulungeka Dazana, also seems not to have the necessary tax credentials to be in contention for such a massive government contract. (City Press, 1 September 2013)

Another scandal that just disappeared.

How do these tenders get awarded?

I haven't gotten answers to any of my questions from the Sports Ministry since I started the exposes back in 2012.

***

What is the fetish with multiple national and provincial sports awards every year?

Is it really to reward the athletes or is it more about 'staging' a business opportunity and getting money in and out?

The gsport Trust in partnership with SRSA have their annual awards to recognize SA women in sport.

A non-profit organization in partnership with a government body for more awards?

Many of the recipients are also recognized at the SA sports awards.

Kass Naidoo, a sports journalist, is a founder of the gsport Trust and would often publicly pamper the ego of Mbalula and his department without ever questioning their ethics and integrity.

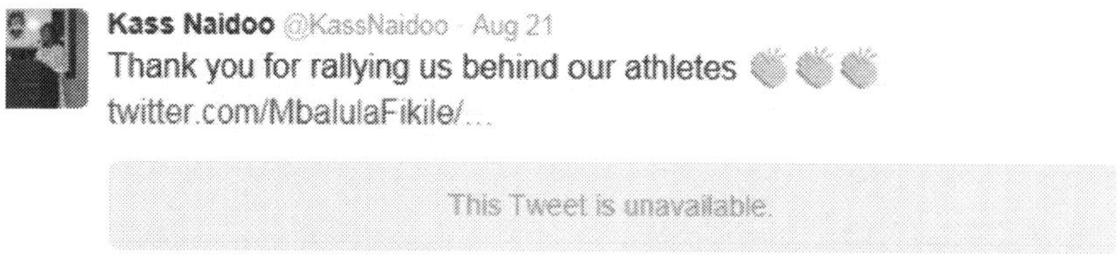

Naidoo was the Cricket SA brand and communications manager when CEO, Gerald Majola was caught with his hands in the cookie jar and she defended him to the hilt, before resigning from the position.

The gsport Trust in partnership with SRSA raised a red flag.

Was this just another dirty conduit for Mbalula and company?

The reply came from Kass's husband, Ryk Meiring who is a lawyer and one of the trustees.

The gsport Trust is in partnership with SRSA and is not in a position to issue unilateral statements regarding the relationship. Please pursue your questions with gsport's liaison at SRSA, Ms Kenetswe Mosenogi. - Ryk Mering, The gsport Trust

As I began to dig a little further, it got personal.

Another one of the gsport trustees, Anele Mdoda (94.7 Highveld Stereo radio presenter and SABC show host) decided to jump in on the action with a group email.

Guys, Graeme is a mad man and no one listens to him. He does not even live in the country anymore and everyone knows he has a few screws loose. I like the stance you are taking with him but please do not lose sleep if he does do something. I know him well and no one listens to him. NO ONE! - Anele Mdoda

Personal slander is often the best form of attack when you're on the back foot.

Anele, just hope one day you take your blinkers off to see what is really happening in SA sport or maybe the honeypot from the gsport Trust/SRSA partnership is just too good for you to ever reveal the truth?

Not too long after Anele's little personal attack, she was in the headlines for not being transparent about a payment to a minister/guest on her talk show.

Twitter reacts to Real Talk's 'R500K' interview with Bathabile Dlamini

Popular SABC reality show, Real Talk with Anele Mdoda came under fire by social media users after reports emerged that the public broadcaster received a R500K payment for controversial Social Development Minister Bathabile Dlamini to appear on the show. (Times Live, 18 January 2018)

It wouldn't surprise me if Sports Minister, Fikile Mbalula was also paid to be a guest on Real Talk with Anele.

That show was back in November 2016.

Mbalula ignoring protocol in Monaco ahead of the London Olympic Games is typical of his self-inflated arrogance and ego.

Charlene Wittstock is a former SA Olympic swimmer and the wife of Prince Albert II.

Princess Charlene has never forgotten her roots and had invited the SA swim team to train in Monaco to prepare for the London Olympics.

It was an incredible gesture, knowing full well how limited the swimming funds are but there would be a gatecrasher.

"Mbaks" (Mbalula) wanted to ignore protocol and cash in on the good French champagne at the Principality.

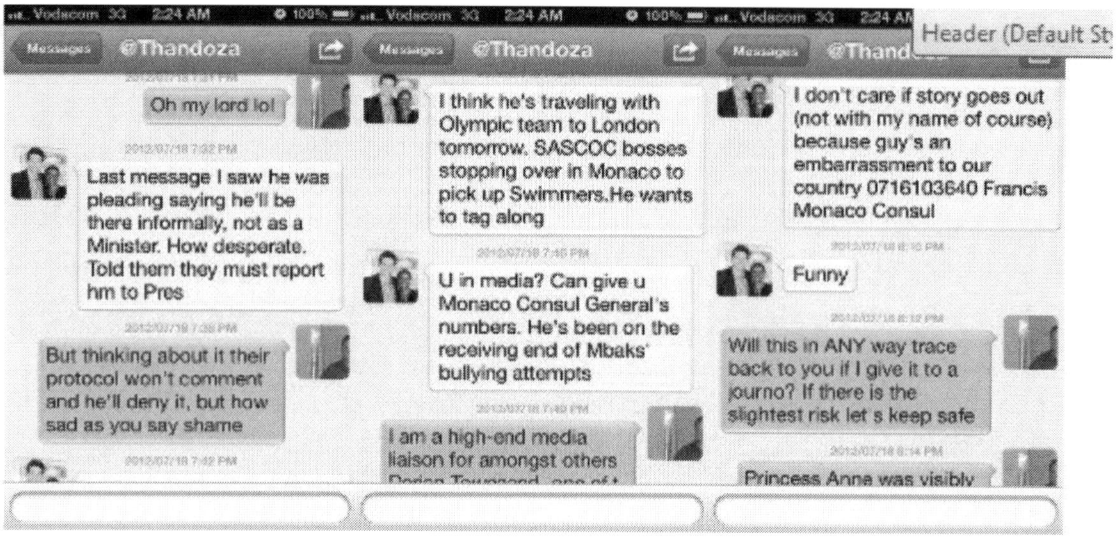

Not that Mbalula has much shame. Many of his comments and tweets over the years lack any kind of diplomacy.

Mbalula, when questioned on the issue why some national teams remain stubbornly white:

You can't transform sports without targets. But at the same time, South Africa wouldn't be like Kenya and send athletes to the Olympics to drown in the pool.

Mbalula referring to the Bafana Bafana players after losing 3-1 to Nigeria in 2014 African Nations championship:

What I saw was not a problem of coaching, it was a bunch of losers.

Mbalula in response to FIFA 2010 World Cup bribery scandal:

I am going to see Floyd Mayweather soon in the US, the FBI can question me then if they want.

Mayweather takes a selfie with a well-known middle-aged woman from South Africa.

RSA Min of Sport Follow
@MbalulaFikile

I understand, ubuhle bethu as yellowbones is not liked. One thing is for sure, I'm not about to Bruce Jenner Mzantsi

11:07 AM - 5 May 2015

RSA Min of Sport Follow
@MbalulaFikile

Pres Obama: who you callin ?

Pres Zuma: The Springboks, telling them to chow your Eagles -

#BOKSvsUSA

1:47 PM - 7 Oct 2015

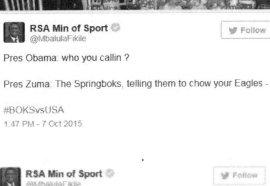

RSA Min of Sport Follow
@MbalulaFikile

today we play USA - they will know Africa is a continent and South Africa is a country within it - they will learn

1:57 AM - 7 Oct 2015

326 175

Sports coffers being milked
1 December 2014

Around R80 million left SA sports coffers over the last few days with SA Sports Awards at the Sandton

Convention Centre on Sunday night and SASCOC's lavish dinner at Emperors Palace last night to celebrate their 10th birthday.

I hear the dinner party was for 800 people.

It would have been most of the same guests that attended the awards the night before - so, you don't think they could have just had a cake for SASCOC's 10th birthday at the awards and saved millions for our athletes.

No, that's not how they think when it's public money!

How can the Department of Sport and Recreation (SRSA) and SASCOC even begin to justify this kind of spend while the OPEX funding for our Olympic athletes has just been cut again and SA sportsmen and women still have to keep fork out large amounts to represent the country?

The swimmers have each had to pay R15,000 to represent SA at FINA World championships in Doha from 3-7 December and the SA angling team had to fund their entire trip (R13,000 each) to compete against Namibia in Walvis Bay.

Where are the priorities?

Do these administrators even care?

If one just did a forensic audit on both these heavyweight functions, one would pick up so many financial irregularities (with services) but there's no-one to deliver that knockout punch.

It makes one sick to the stomach.

As for the awards, I'm glad I missed them (not that I was invited) but couldn't even bare to watch the farce on television. And from the comments of other journalists on twitter, it looks like I didn't miss much.

Antoinette Muller: SA Sports Awards is the definition of insanity. Same embarrassing thing every year, expecting different results. #PayBackTheMoney

Karien Jonckheere: You'd think they could get the SA flag the right way round on the screens at the SA Sports Awards... #SASA14

Sbu Huck Mjikeliso: Switched on to watch 5 minutes of the SA Sports Awards. I might need to read the bible for an hour to cleanse my eyes off this gluttony

David Moseley: Audience at SA Sports Awards has been darted with elephant tranquilisers. Or they're watching Bok highlights on Drifta.

Kevin McCallum: Athletes are not happy with these awards. They see the millions poured into them, but dare not speak up against them.

The whole nomination system for the SA Sports awards is also a joke and some winners are as far-fetched as they come.

This comment on Facebook pretty much sums it up.

SA Bowls win 7 medals at Commonwealth Games - 5 of which are GOLD and still cannot win Team of the Year at SA Sports Awards - SASCOC your voting council is a disgrace along with some of the Ministers Awards!

Team of the Year went to the SA U-19 cricket side that won the World Cup.

Yes, a great achievement but it doesn't compare to what the lawn bowlers achieved in Glasgow and how many more nations compete in their discipline.

It's actually an insult to our bowlers.

Just glad the "drowning" Swimming SA didn't win federation of the year again but not quite sure what Triathlon has done over the last year to get the award.

Back at the ranch, it appears that SASCOC NPC (non-profit company) was not 'dissolved' in March 2014 and is still registered with CIPC as an active company, contrary to what was in the latest SASCOC financials.

The Companies Act does not provide for a company to 'convert' into a voluntary association and it would appear that SASCOC NPC has in fact not done so, as it is still registered as an active company. CIPC does not register or regulate voluntary associations.

The likes of SRSA and SASCOC have become a law unto themselves, untouchable and with zero accountability.

SA sport is in serious trouble but the awards, dinners and parties will never stop.

It's the easiest way of getting money out to feed their corrupt need

They've got the cake and eating it!

***

Joffers, just a heads up, end of November. I have been tasked with buying media space in newspapers ... I have been to the M&G, Citizen, New Age, Independent Group etc and got quotes. a suggestion ... when the adverts appear, make a call or two to the newspapers and ask them how much an advert costs ... it's to celebrate a birthday. The quotes range from around R200k to R900k ... complete waste of money. But, I'll be in touch nearer the time ... just thought you might want to raise it at a later stage (obviously after the advert has appeared) and once I've seen the signed invoice with the amounts. – Gary Lemke

A simple way to buy favourable journalism but SASCOC pulled the ads at the last possible moment.

It was during these 10th anniversary celebrations that I got a text from good source and SASCOC photographer, Wessel Oosthuizen.

He had bumped into Mark Alexander and asked him about my expose of the Megapro/SA rugby kickback scandal in which he benefitted from millions.

Alexander's reply:

Don't worry, our government will take care of him (Joffe).

I guess they did take care of me!

Chapter 19: Meeting with the FBI

The first few months in Cincinnati after fleeing South Africa were very tough. I harboured a great deal of anger and bitterness.

How could I be chased from the country that I was born in, loved and was giving so much back to in trying to make a difference?

I was still very concerned for my safety and that of my sister's family.

A sports journalist, with links to SASCOC had tried to befriend my sister on Facebook. What was his agenda?

They would stop at nothing.

I continued to poke the bear back in SA and there were daily attempts to illegally re-access my SA cell-phone.

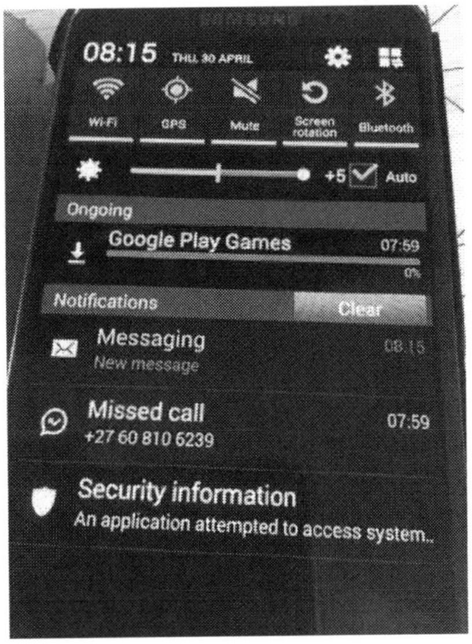

Breaking News: 27 May 2015: Seven* FIFA *officials were arrested at Hotel Baur au Lac in Zürich

The timing of this FIFA news was good for me as South Africa were implicated in the scandal for bribery in 'winning' the bid to host the 2010 World Cup.

The FIFA angle and all the dirt I had on SA football was perhaps my chance to get in front of the FBI, although I knew it would be a long shot.

One of my brother-'s brothers had served as an assistant United States Attorney in the Southern District of Florida for over eleven years and he made an introduction for me.

It was an FBI Special Agent in New York, who was working on the FIFA scandal.

A couple weeks later, I received a call from the FBI in Cincinnati.

Mr Joffe, we are here to help you, come and see us anytime today.

How refreshing and different to the South African Police service that didn't give a damn about protecting one of their own citizens.

I went to see the FBI the same afternoon and going through the security process at the entrance to their building in Montgomery Road, Cincinnati was daunting.

The agent and his assistant met me on the other side of the entrance and escorted me into the FBI building itself. We sat in one of the enclosed meeting rooms downstairs.

I shared my information on the South African football contacts/links to the FIFA scandal and gave them some of the background and personal threats, which forced me to flee the country.

The Special Agent then made a call to a staff member upstairs for verification on a few of the names that I mentioned.

He nodded.

I spent about an hour with the FBI and left them with a folder of notes as well as a memory stick with two phone recordings.

The first recording was a telephone conversation I had on 3 June 2015 with a driver who worked for Megapro/ Primedia Sport.

He told me about the "cash payments" he had to drop off for the likes of Danny Jordaan related to the 2010 World Cup hospitality rights and to Dr Ali Bacher for the Indian Premier League (IPL), which was hosted in South Africa in 2009.

Jordaan was the Chief Executive Officer of the 2010 FIFA World Cup South Africa at the time.

Bacher was the former CEO of the United Cricket Board of South Africa and still had strong links with India.

The second recording was the telephonic conversation I had with the Private Investigator, Theo Bronkhorst on 21 June 2015, where he spoke of the four arrests in my case that were going to happen tomorrow.

Then he was going to walk away from the case as his family was now being threatened.

The FBI agent said he would forward the football information to the FBI team in New York and would contact me if they had any further questions.

It was a big weight off my shoulders.

I didn't have any further communication with the FBI until I saw an article quoting South Africa's FIFA presidential candidate, Tokyo Sexwale who had appeared before the US Grand Jury in December 2015.

SA is clean, we had a clean 2010 World Cup. - Tokyo Sexwale

SA was not clean and the spin doctoring had become nauseating especially after all the denials from Sports Minister, Fikile Mbalula.

We have no obligation to explain ourselves to the FBI. The onus is on them. We never bribed. - Fikile Mbalula

South Africa were awarded the 2010 World Cup bid on 15 May 2004 and a couple weeks later, the big role players were lining up.

2010: Big names to get involved

Government and business people are likely to form the top structures of the local organising committee (LOC) that will take over when the 2010 bid committee folds in January next year. The four-man preparation committee formed by SAFA last week will be a frontrunner to the LOC. The committee comprises chairperson, Irvin Khoza, Danny Jordaan, South African Investment Limited (Sail) Chief Executive, Selwyn Nathan and Tokyo Sexwale, Chief Executive of Mvelaphanda Holdings. (News24, 31 May 2004)

The preparation committee were no doubt preparing themselves to cash in on the World Cup.

Who is Irvin Khoza?

Despite a controversial past, Irvin Khoza was recently named as the chairman of South Africa's 2010 World Cup Local Organising Committee. But the powerful political connections of football's 'Iron Duke' mask a criminal past which includes insurance fraud, tax evasion and charges of drug dealing. Khoza has since used his football profile to continue amassing a private fortune, which tax assessors value at more than US$10m. (BBC Sport, 10 December 2004)

Sexwale opened himself up for scrutiny by throwing his name in the hat to replace Sepp Blatter as FIFA president in the emergency election of February 2016.

Why Tokyo Sexwale is wrong for Fifa

Announcing he was running for the Fifa presidency on Tuesday, Tokyo Sexwale said he would bring "good financial management ... transparency and accountability" to the scandal-plagued football governing body. The politician-businessperson's past, however, is littered with controversies involving secretive business deals and problematic partners. Equally problematic for Sexwale may be his close relationship with the Caribbean football boss, Jack Warner, before and after the 2004 Fifa executive vote that landed South Africa the 2010 event. (Mail & Guardian, 30 October 2015)

Sexwale withdrew from the race with little to no voting support and Gianni Infantino became the new FIFA president.

It was all a bit awkward.

There were many people back at home who did not even want me to leave the blocks. - Tokyo Sexwale

The sole African in the race also failed to receive the support of African football's ruling body the Confederation of African Football, which asked its members to vote for Sheikh Salman. (BBC, 29 February 2016)

Sexwale, Khoza, Jordaan and Nathan were involved in the set up and vital decision-making committees for the 2010 World Cup.

They had to have known about the alleged bribe, the $10 million "diaspora" payment, to get Warner and Chuck Blazer to vote for South Africa.

There was even a paper trail.

SAFA had found a great FIFA ally in Jerome Valcke who was reportedly granted South African citizenship in 2012 for his 'contribution towards South Africa hosting the 2010 Soccer World Cup and the development of football in the country'.

Fifa's secretary general Jérôme Valcke under new pressure over $10m 'bribe'

The position of Fifa's powerful secretary general, Jerome Valcke, is likely to come under intense pressure after new evidence emerged that showed he was aware of a $10m payment from South African officials to Jack Warner described by US investigators as a bribe ... Just an hour after Fifa had released a statement denying that Valcke authorized the transfer of $10m to a Bank of America account linked to Warner, a letter from the South African Football Association was obtained by the Press Association that was addressed to the longstanding Fifa secretary general. It showed he was aware of it and contained detailed instructions for payment. (The Guardian, 2 June 2015)

The signatory of the letter was Molefi Oliphant who was President of the SA Football Association at the time.

SOUTH AFRICAN FOOTBALL ASSOCIATION

First National Bank Stadium
NASREC
PO Box 910
Johannesburg 2000
South Africa
Telephone: (011) 494-3522
Fax: (011) 494-3447

www.safa.net

4 March 2008

Mr Jerome Valcke
General Secretary
Federation Internationale de Football Association
FIFA-Strasse 20
PO Box 8044
Zurich
Switzerland

Dear Mr Valcke

US$ 10 MILLION PROMISED BY THE SOUTH AFRICAN GOVERNMENT FOR THE DIASPORA LEGACY PROGRAMME

In view of the decision by the South African Government that an amount of US$ 10 million be paid to the 2010 FIFA World Cup Organising Committee South Africa, the South African Football Association requests that FIFA withholds an amount of US$ 10 million from the Organising Committee's future operational budget funding and thereafter advances the amount withheld to the Diaspora Legacy Programme.

In addition, SAFA requests that the Diaspora Legacy Programme be administered and implemented directly by the President of CONCACAF who shall act as a fiduciary of the Fund.

SAFA therefore confirms that:

1. FIFA shall withhold US$ 10 million from the Organising Committee's future operational budget funding in order to finance the Diaspora Legacy Programme, thereby reducing the Organising Committee's overall budget from US$ 423 million to US$ 413 million.
2. The Diaspora Legacy Programme shall be administered and implemented directly by the President of CONCACAF who shall act as the fiduciary of the Diaspora Legacy Programme Fund of US$ 10 million.

Yours faithfully

Then on 25 November 2015, the bomb is dropped on SA's dirty World Cup bid.

DSS:EMN/AH/DAL/SPN/MKM/PT/KDE/TH/BDM
F.#2015R00747

FILED
CLERK

2015 NOV 25 PM 3:25

U.S. DISTRICT COURT
EASTERN DISTRICT
OF NEW YORK

UNITED STATES DISTRICT COURT
EASTERN DISTRICT OF NEW YORK
\- -X

UNITED STATES OF AMERICA

S U P E R S E D I N G
I N D I C T M E N T

H. 2010 FIFA World Cup Vote Scheme

216. In or about 2004, the FIFA executive committee considered bids from Morocco, South Africa and Egypt, as

well as other nations that withdrew before the vote, to host the 2010World Cup.

217. Previously, the defendant JACK WARNER and his family had cultivated ties with South African soccer officials in connection with and subsequent to a failed bid by South Africa to host the 2006 World Cup. In the early 2000s, Daryan Warner, a member of WARNER's family, had used WARNER's contacts in South Africa to organize friendly matches for CONCACAF teams to play in South Africa. At one point, WARNER also directed Daryan Warner to fly to Paris, France and accept a briefcase containing bundles of U.S. currency in $10,000 stacks in a hotel room from Co-Conspirator #13, a high-ranking South African bid committee official. Hours after arriving in Paris, Daryan Warner boarded a return flight and carried the briefcase back to Trinidad and Tobago, where Daryan Warner provided it to WARNER.

218. In the months before the selection of the host nation for the 2010 World Cup, which was scheduled to take place in May 2004, the defendant JACK WARNER and Charles Blazer traveled to Morocco as they had done in 1992, in advance of the voting for the 1998 World Cup host. While in Morocco during the 2004 trip, a representative of the Moroccan bid committee offered to pay $1 million to WARNER in exchange for his agreement to cast his secret ballot on the FIFA executive committee for Morocco to host the 2010 World Cup.

219. Subsequently, Charles Blazer learned from the defendant JACK WARNER that high-ranking officials of FIFA, including Co-Conspirator #14, the South African bid committee, including Co-Conspirator #15, and the South African government were prepared to arrange for the government of South Africa to pay $10 million to CFU to "support the African diaspora." Blazer understood the of fer to be in exchange for the agreement of WARNER, Blazer, and Co-Conspirator #16 to all vote for South Africa, rather than Morocco, to host the 2010 World Cup. At the time, Co-Conspirator #16, like WARNER and Blazer, was a FIFA executive committee member. WARNER indicated that he had accepted the offer and told Blazer that he would give a $1million portion of the $10 million payment to Blazer

.

220. In FIFA'S executive committee vote held on May15, 2004, South Africa was selected over Morocco and Egypt to host the 2010 World Cup. The defendant JACK WARNER, Charles Blazer, and Co-Conspirator #16 indicated that they voted for South Africa.

221. In the months and years after the vote, Charles Blazer periodically asked WARNER about the status of the $10 million payment.

222. At one point, Charles Blazer learned that the South Africans were unable to arrange for the payment to be made directly from government funds. Arrangements were thereafter made with FIFA officials to instead have the $10 million sent from FIFA - using funds that would otherwise have gone from FIFAto South Africa to support the World Cup - to CFU.

223. In fact, on January 2, 2008, January 31, 2008 and March 7, 2008, a high-ranking FIFA official, Co-Conspirator #17, caused payments of $616,000, $1,600,000, and $7,784,000 - Switzerland to a Bank of America correspondent account in New York, New

York, for credit to accounts held in the names of CFU and CONCACAF, but controlled by the defendant JACK WARNER, at Republic Bank in Trinidad andTobago.

224. Soon after receiving these wire transfers, the defendant JACK WARNER caused a substantial portion of the funds to be diverted for his personal use. For example, on January 9, 2008, WARNER directed Republic Bank officials to apply $200,000 of the $616,000 that had been transferred into a CFU account from FIFA one week earlier toward a personal loan account held in his name.

225. The defendant JACK WARNER also diverted a portion of the funds into his personal accounts by laundering the funds through intermediaries. For example, in or about and between February 13, 2008 and October 3, 2008, WARNER caused over $4million of the funds received from FIFA to be transferred toIndividual #1, a Trinidadian businessman whose identity is known to the Grand Jury, Trinidadian Company A, a large supermarket chain in Trinidad and Tobago controlled by Individual #1, and Trinidadian Company B, a real estate and investment company also controlled by Individual #1. During approximately the same period, funds equating to at least $1 million were transferred from these same accounts into a bank account held in the name of WARNER and a family member at First Citizens Bank in Trinidad and Tobago. The identities of Trinidadian Company A andTrinidadian Company B are known to the Grand Jury.

226. During the three years following WARNER's receipt of the $10 million from FIFA, WARNER made three payments to Charles Blazer, totaling over $750,000, in partial payment of the $1 million that WARNER had earlier promised Blazer as part of the bribe scheme.

227. The first payment, in the amount of $298,500, was made by wire transfer sent on or about December 19, 2008 from an account held in the name of CFU at Republic Bank in Trinidad and Tobago, to a Bank of America correspondent account in New York, New York, for credit to an account controlled by Charles Blazerat a bank in the Cayman Islands.

228. The second payment, in the amount of $205,000, was made by check drawn on an account held in the name of CFU at Republic Bank in Trinidad and Tobago. On or about September 27, 2010, Charles Blazer caused the check to be deposited into his Merrill Lynch brokerage account in New York, New York. Approximately one month earlier, on or about August 23, 2010, Warner sent an email to Blazer to advise him that the payment was forthcoming.

229. The third payment, in the amount of $250,000, was made by check drawn on an account held in the name of CFU at Republic Bank in Trinidad and Tobago. The check was delivered to Charles Blazer by another individual who traveled by airplane from Trinidad and Tobago to JFK International Airport in Queens, New York, and then to CONCACAF's headquarters in New York, New York, where he delivered the check to Blazer. A representative of FirstCaribbean International Bank in the Bahamas, where Blazer held another account, subsequently traveled by airplane to New York, landing at Kennedy Airport. After arriving, the bank representative traveled to New York, New York, where he took custody of the check. He subsequently traveled to the Bahamas and, on or about May 3, 2011, deposited the check into Blazer's account. Approximately two

months earlier, on or about March 13, 2011, WARNER sent an email to Blazer to advise him that the payment was forthcoming.

230. Charles Blazer never received the balance of the promised $1 million payment.

***

The 2010 World Cup scandal had opened up the Pandora's Box and it didn't take long for new allegations to emerge.

Sent: 17 June 2015 05:21 AM
To: graeme@butterbean.co.za
Subject: Co-conspirators 15 & 16

Graeme, hi

I have been confidentially informed by a person who was bidding to become involved in the 2010 Bid that he was primed for a kick-back on the services he would render.

Khoza & Jordaan were the two crooks involved who stood to make R5 million each. He walked away from the request.

Wonder of this might be of interest to you?

The same source sent the following information the same day in response to my questions with regards the circumstances and what the work entailed.

Just the circumstances and how the "bribes/kickbacks" were asked for and where ... and then how the work was declined or he withdrew. Where: At a breakfast meeting at a prominent Johannesburg Hotel. How: Verbally, (blatantly). Declined: Shocked, indicated their request would not be entertained, and left. When directly to contract adviser at eminent legal firm and advised of the request and his response. The work was subsequently handed to a compliant individual.

Also, what kind of work was it going to be? Fundraising to support the bid. He was told by 15 & 16 that his commission needed be 20% of the required USD100 million which would be split 50/50, R10 million to Danny & Irvin. He'd achieved great success in a preceding bid for SA to host a major international sports event where his commission was 8.5%, an acceptable and standard rate.

Who was this compliant individual?

Morning Graeme

I chatted to my connection last night who reminded me of who it was: Selwyn Nathan.

My connection imparted a thought: That he should discuss with the British High Commissioner (with whom he has good association) an introduction to the FBI to impart what he know. I encouraged him to do so.

Have a good day,

19 June 2015 …

Ironically, I had already sent an email to Selwyn Nathan earlier in June after I had received an anonymous phone message on my SA cell-phone, saying that he was the alleged paymaster in the Paris hotel.

You must be kidding me Joffs, it's a prank. Who would I have been able to bribe. I didn't know anyone and why would I do that anyway for what purpose. Not my style sorry. - Selwyn Nathan

Selwyn's reply didn't leave me with a feeling of comfort, as just like Sexwale, he was very involved with the bid and going forward.

Nathan must have known plenty, wearing all these hats:

* Member of the 2010 Soccer World Cup Bid Committee, serving on the Finance, Procurement, Audit and Marketing sub-committees.
* Member of the 4 person "SA Bid Preparation" Committee of the 2010 Soccer World Cup.
* Member of the 2010 Soccer World Cup Bid Committee, serving on the Finance, Procurement, Audit and Marketing sub-committees.
* Non-Executive Director of FIFA SA 2010 World Cup Local Organizing Committee (LOC).
* Founded Vodacom Sport and Entertainment, the sponsorship arm of Vodacom in 1996. In 2001 VS&E was bought by JSE listed Southern Africa Investment Limited (SAIL), Selwyn became CEO. The company was estimated to have controlled 80% of sport and TV Sponsorship spend in the SA Market.

Packages for the 2010 Soccer World Cup will go on sale in South Africa in June, sales agent Match Hospitality announced on Wednesday ... The exclusive sales agents for South African and sub-Saharan Africa are Circa Hospitality, a SAIL group company, and Warwick Hospitality and Events, a Primedia Sport company ... (Mail & Guardian, 5 March 2008)

The SAIL Group CEO at the time was Brand de Villiers who worked very closely with Nathan.

In June 2013, de Villiers was appointed as the CEO of the Premier Soccer League (PSL) by Khoza but in November 2015, out of the blue, he resigned to take up a job offer from Multichoice in Dubai.

Very interesting moves.

There's a very strong connection between Khoza, Patel, Nathan and de Villiers.

Moreover, a grave conflict of interests between the PSL and SuperSport highlighted by the 'offsides' TV deal, discussed later in the book.

Back to the corrupt World Cup bid and irregular payments.

A good source who worked on the SuperSport '2010 World Cup Bid Diaries' TV series told me, it was overheard on numerous of their travels, Danny Jordaan saying:

How crucial it was to make sure South Africa got the votes of Jack Warner and Chuck Blazer.

Then a week before Jordaan is expected to go to Zurich to vote in the May 2015 FIFA elections as the SAFA President, the ANC appoints him from left field as the Mayor of Nelson Mandela Bay in the Eastern Cape.

And he uses his new job as the reason for not going to Zurich.

Needless to say, he only made the decision not to go, a day after nine FIFA officials were arrested on` charges of corruption.

Danny boy must have been a little too nervous to travel.

Khoza cast the vote on behalf of SAFA at the FIFA congress on 22 May 2015 under the dark skies of the biggest football scandal.

South Africa had played its part and Jordaan failed to travel to Zurich again, this time for the February emergency election in 2016.

Danny Jordaan defends his no-show in Zurich

Safa president Danny Jordaan has rubbished the DA's claims that his absence at the Fifa congress on Friday implied he was running away from the FBI in the US ... Last year, the DA opened a case with the police to investigate the alleged $10 million (R161 million at the current exchange rate) paid to the Confederation of North, Central American and Caribbean Association Football in 2008 after the country won a bid to host the 2010 World Cup. The US justice department last year claimed a South African bid official paid a bribe to host the 2010 soccer spectacle. (City Press, 28 February 2016)

Jordaan then completed a hat-trick of FBI near misses when he was absent from his third FIFA congress in a row.

It was the 66th FIFA congress in Mexico City in May.

Jordaan did not pick up his phone when called for comment, nor did he respond to the SMS sent to him. Safa spokesperson, Dominic Chimhavi said he was also struggling to locate his president. (City Press, 15 May 2016)

How much was the kickback for the hospitality rights for the 2010 World Cup?

During our telephonic conversation on 3 June 2015, the Megapro driver told me he had to drop off a briefcase of cash for Jordaan.

Megapro and Sail were both very involved in the 2010 World Cup.

They obviously had the inside track.

SAIL were then further involved with the operation of the Cape Town stadium – a 30 year lease?

The lease, still to be signed, gives the SAIL/Stade de France operating company exclusive rights to the expensive public asset for the next 10 to 30 years, in exchange for 30% of the after-tax profits. Well, not actually 30% as the stadium rates will be deducted from the City's share. In the not-so-unlikely event that no profits are forthcoming, the operator will pay its landlord just R1 year (and the rates due). But, in credit or in debt, the city will remain responsible for the expensive business of maintaining the high-tech structure, including its extremely elaborate glass, steel and PVC roof. And stadium maintenance, as any former World Cup or Olympic host will tell you, is a bottomless pit. So bad, in fact, that some have elected to demolish rather than maintain them, clearing the way for more sensible development. (Noseweek, 3 June 2009)

The "deal" ended soon after the World Cup and the City of Cape Town took over the operation of the stadium on 1 January 2011.

South Africa is not an orphan when it comes to corruption with global sporting events but they desperately needed some parental guidance with their longwinded, embarrassing denials.

31 May 2015

We remain concerned at the ongoing media speculation which only plays into the hands of those whose objective is to tarnish the good name and integrity of our country. We reject these falsehoods with the contempt they deserve. As a government and people of South Africa we are enjoined to combat such propaganda against our country.

Accordingly, we appeal to all our people, media included to desist from speculating on names of individuals who may or not be implicated in the allegations. Equally, we call on all those involved in the bidding and hosting of the 2010 FIFA World Cup to avoid expressing comments that can only play into the hands of those who seek to perpetuate negative stereotypes against South Africa in particular and Africa in general.

Whatever the motive of those involved, nothing can detract from the fact that the hosting by South Africa of the 2010 FIFA World Cup, the first on the African continent, remains one of the most beautiful spectacle and successful tournament the world has ever witnessed in FIFA's history.

We frown upon any insinuations made in the indictment by the US authorities that suggest that the government of South Africa or any of its citizens have been involved in any wrongdoing without substantiating the allegations, let alone naming the alleged co-conspirators. We refuse to allow the reputation of our republic to be tarnished unduly without affording the republic and its citizens an opportunity to respond to any allegations made. We view this as an attack on our sovereignty.

We wish to reiterate our earlier communicated position that the government of the Republic of South Africa and the Local Organising Committee have not expended any public funds in the amount of $10 million towards bribery of anyone to secure the rights to host the 2010 FIFA World Cup. Any inferences drawn from the statements attributed to Dr. Danny Jordaan which seeks to insinuate that our position is contradictory is therefore not only misleading but mischievous at best. We reaffirm our position that no public funds have been utilised to pay any bribe or to commit any unlawful acts.

Statement Issued by: the Minister of Sport and Recreation South Africa, Fikile Mbalula.

Any unlawful acts?

Danny Jordaan 'asked Guptas for $10 million to fill Fifa bribe hole'

Safa president Danny Jordaan allegedly turned to the Gupta family to cover up a $10 million (R138 million) hole in the organisation's books – the result of an illegal payment paid to an official of *international football governing body Fifa to secure South Africa the 2010 World Cup. This extraordinary allegation is contained in an affidavit by the football association's former chief executive officer (CEO), Leslie Sedibe. (City Press, 14 January 2019)*

There were plenty other unlawful acts and still the unsolved mystery of ANC senior official, Jimmy Mohlala who was murdered by hitmen outside his home in 2009.

Mohlala was a whistleblower on the financial irregularities around the construction of the 2010 World Cup, Mbombela Stadium.

Jimmy Mohlala was murdered after he had uncovered forged contracts for the £80million Mbombela stadium, which staged just four games. He was going to give evidence in court the day before he was gunned down outside his home by masked hit men. (Daily Mail, 13 June 2015)

Needless to say, there was collusion by construction companies involved with the 2010 World Cup stadia, who ended up having to share the cost of a R1.5 billion fine.

Using legislation enacted to tackle criminal enterprises such as the Mafia for its investigation, the FBI is alleging that rampant corruption became "endemic" to international football association Fifa. The recent claims of corruption related to South Africa's hosting of the 2010 World Cup are not the first. Members of a construction cartel, found by competition authorities to have rigged bids and ramped up prices by several billion when building the stadiums that hosted the matches, have already paid R1.5-billion in fines as penance for their collusion. (Mail & Guardian, 12 June 2015)

My husband (Jimmy) would still be alive today if it hadn't been for FIFA World Cup corruption. My husband wanted to report the cheating that went on over that soccer stadium and now where is he? He is dead. (Bonny Mohlala, Daily Mail)

Thanks for standing up for the truth Jimmy!

RIP!

Chapter 20: "Tata ma chance"

"Tata Ma Chance, Tata Ma Millions" is an advertising slogan for the South African lottery. Loosely translated would be something like take a chance, (buy a Lotto ticket) and take home millions.

More cynical …

Civil servants and people connected to those in positions of political power are taking home millions without even buying a ticket through the corrupt practice of fake applications, kickbacks and misappropriation of funds.

In other words, blatant theft!

The National Lottery is regulated by the government's Department of Trade and Industry.

The National Lotteries Board (NLB) regulated and distributed all the lotteries and their proceeds in the country, through the National Lotteries Distribution Trust Fund (NLDTF). The distribution agencies (DAs) were appointed by the Minister of Trade and Industry. The NLB was phasing out the use of temporary DAs for the different sectors as a result of the new Act, which sought to use those agencies on a full-time basis. That would also make them accountable to the NLB board, instead of the Minister alone. Moreover adjudications could be adjudicated expeditiously at the request of the board going forward. Before the amendment to the Lotteries Act, sport federations and organisations such as the South African Sport Council and Olympic Committee (SASCOC) could nominate four to five members into the DA where the very members then would be conflicted, affecting adjudication. The DTI was currently dealing with the matter of individuals with vested interests forming part of the distribution agencies.(Parliamentary Committee for Sport, 29 July 2014)

Beneficiary applications fall under the categories of Sports and Recreation, Arts and Culture, Charities and Miscellaneous.

Grants from the National Lottery Commission (NLC) have been paid out to beneficiaries since 2002.

By 2017, it had distributed more than R24-billion to good causes: R10.7-billion of that has gone to charities, R6.3-billion to arts, culture and national heritage, R6.1-billion to sport and recreation, and R686-million to organisations that fall under the "miscellaneous" category. The biggest beneficiary of the NLC, ever, is the South African Sports Confederation & Olympic Committee (Sascoc), which has been allocated a little more than R779-million since 2006. (GroundUp, 19 February 2018)

SASCOC, the 2010 FIFA World Cup Organising Committee, the Sports Trust, Athletics South Africa and Swimming South Africa all featured in the top 15 of the beneficiary list, according to this graphic illustration from "Open Up" in February 2018.

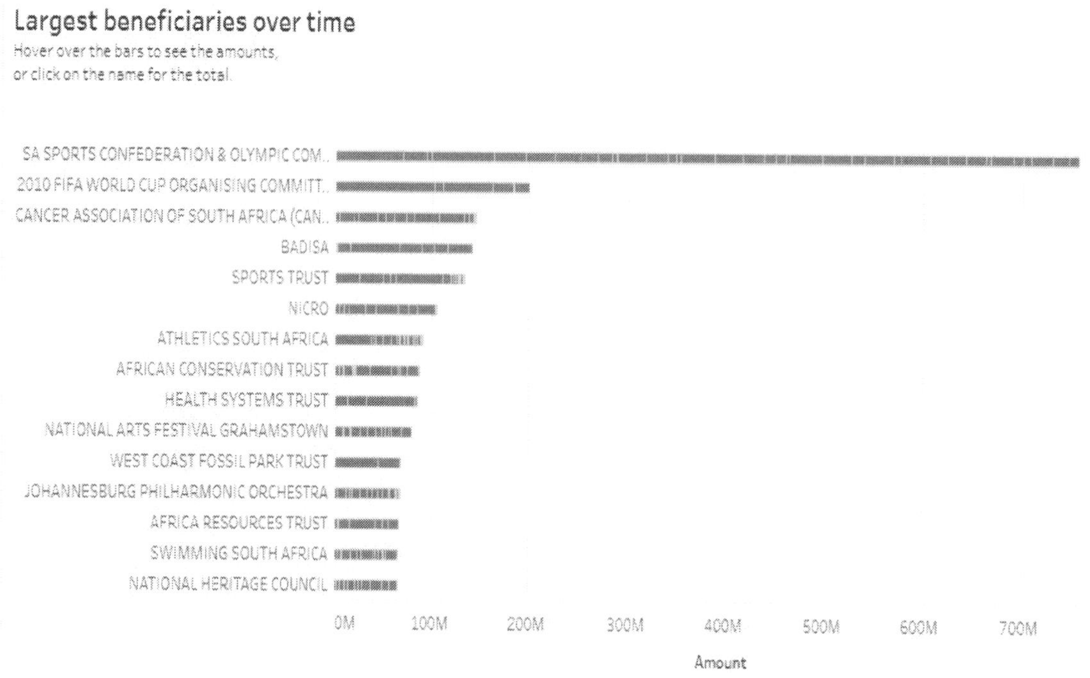

Great investigative work from the OpenUp journalists but not without its dangers.

Shoot the messenger instead of trying to find the criminals who have made off with the millions in unaccounted Lottery funding?

Sanef 'alarmed' that lottery commission has set state spies on journalists

The South African National Editors'Forum (Sanef) expressed alarm on Wednesday at a statement by the chairperson of the board of the National Lotteries Commission (NLC), Professor Alfred Nevhutanda, that the NLC had asked the State Security Agency (SSA) to investigate journalists. In a statement, Sanef said Nevhutanda had appeared before parliament's trade and industry portfolio committee last week to claim that the NLC had "recently learnt" that the NLC's computers were hacked and "information about projects since 2001 was in the US, with a backup in the Western Cape". (The Citizen, 5 December 2018)

The National Lottery was very much on my radar from 2013 but the SASCOC defamation lawsuit had scared off the sports editors and publications.

Young editors said I had been discredited.

SASCOC's game plan to suppress the truth was working as planned.

But in April 2014, I started writing a weekly column for Finweek, another Media24/Naspers publication.

I had to assume the editor, Marc Ashton who offered me the Finweek column didn't know of my history with the Naspers group or the R21.1 million defamation suit.

Or maybe, he was just a credible journalist, seeking the truth.

The Finweek space gave me an audience again to expose the corruption in SA sport.

Tata Ma Chance
2 April 2014

It is scary and sickening what is happening in SA sport with all the allegations of corruption, cronyism, maladministration and misappropriation of funds.

It just doesn't stop and one of the biggest scandals is unfolding right in front of our eyes with the distribution of National Lottery funds.

In a presentation to the Department of Sport and Recreation earlier this year, these were listed as the top ten beneficiaries of Lottery grants for 2013.

South African Institute For Drug-Free Sport	18 800 000.00
Sascoc (CHAN)	17 700 000.00
The Sports Trust (Sports Awards)	6 000 000.00
Chess South Africa	3 998 100.00
South African Sports Aerobics & Fitness Federation	3 852 893.00
Squash South Africa	3 753 840.00
S.A Deaf Sports Federation	3 642 050.00
WP Tug-Of-War Association	2 092 417.67
South African Rugby Union	2 000 300.00

Source: http://www.thedti.gov.za/parliament/Sport_Recreation.pdf

Some of the Lottery beneficiaries NOT listed in the top 10 include:

* Payment of R8.2 million to the SA Table Tennis board in June 2013
* Payments to SASCOC of R4 million, R28 million and R35 million in July 2013
* Payment of R5.5 million to the Free State Sports Confederation in July 2013
* Payment of R2.8 million to SA Hockey in September 2013

The National Lotteries Board (NLB) made a big thing about it in May last year re: the lottery funds "needed to be spread as far as possible".

In response, the distributing agency for sport and recreation capped the amounts that the various structures could apply for:

Municipalities - R1 million

Universities - R1.2 million

National federations - R2 million

How did SA Table Tennis manage to get R8.2 million?

SASCOC vice president, Hajera Kajee is also vice president of SA Table Tennis and a former Chairperson of the National Lotto Distribution Agency.

It's more dual roles that smack of cronyism and a flagrant disregard for the constitution.

Why was SASCOC given R67 million in July and another R17 million for the African Nations Championship Football Tournament (CHAN 2014)?

What role did SASCOC play in CHAN 2014?

I am not sure what you meant by playing a role and as well as spend. If you mean did SASCOC sponsor or make any financial contribution to CHAN 2014, the answer is no, but the application for Lotto funding was facilitated through SASCOC. - CHAN local organizing committee

Please can someone explain what SASCOC did with the R17 million Lottery grant for CHAN 2014?

They refuse to answer.

NLB chairperson, Professor Nevhutanda was quoted as saying, "demand exceeds available resources".

Why then did the South African Rugby Union (SARU) get R2 million, a group whose revenue rose in 2013 to R795 million?

How many charities would have been so grateful for a slice of that R2 million but instead the greed and misappropriation of funds continues.

Also, under scrutiny, a R2 million Lotto payment to Netball SA in July 2013 paid through Sporting Frontiers Africa.

62063 Netball SA (a/c NSA Sporting Frontiers Africa) R2 000 000

President of Netball SA, Mimi Mthethwa: "We have no clue of who Sporting Frontiers Africa is."

The other Lottery payments under Sport and Recreation in 2013 that caught my eye:

Mother Areas Soccer Board (PE) - R4 million (May 2013)
SA Football Association (SAFA) – R2.9 million (June 2013) University
Sport SA – R7 million (June 2013)
Struisbaai Primary School – R2.8 million (June 2013)

No other primary school gets anything close to R 2.8 million. The NLB needs serious introspection and investigation.

But who's going to cut off the hand that feeds you?

***

The "conflicted" Lotto
15 May 2014

Each and every week we read about another SA sportsperson or team having to pay their own way to represent South Africa.

Why is this when millions of rand is paid out by the Lottery monthly to benefit our athletes for this exact cause?

It's the dark space of the Lottery distribution agency for Sport and Recreation.

The chairperson of the Agency for Sport and Recreation is former SASCOC consultant and SA Rugby official Mveleli Ncula.

The Deputy Chairperson is Dr. Harold Adams, a full-time government employee, president of Boland Athletics and a board member of the South African Institute for Drug-Free Sport (SAIDS).

Ncula and Adams meet regularly and are both still close allies of SASCOC.

Ray Mali is also a member of the agency and is still a paid SASCOC consultant.

As a matter of interest, what happens when the SASCOC, SAIDS and Boland Athletics Lottery applications need to be adjudicated?

It (lotto) doesn't adjudicate on any application where there is a conflicted member in the committee on the day of the adjudication. I wanted to help you but the truth of the matter is that they keep such information in files in the office and can make it available whenever it is required. - Mveleli Ncula

As we have informed you many times already, where there is a conflict of interest, that particular application is adjudicated by one of the other Distributing Agencies. That is all we are willing to share with you in this regard. - Sershan Naidoo, Manager of the National Lotteries Board

The reply from Adams after several emails:

Sorry I am out of town for a few weeks and will forward your questions to the Lotto Chair. The Prof (Nevhutanda) will anyhow be the best person to address these issues.

No response from Professor Nevhutanda and no-one can tell me which agency adjudicates when it comes to the SASCOC, Boland Athletics, SAIDS applications and others, where there is a conflict of interests.

No reply from Mali either while other members of the agency referred me to Naidoo.

Boland Athletics has received more than R2.6 million from the Lotto in the last 18 months, yet the SA Athletics Association (ASA) didn't even receive a grant in 2013.

You would think that ASA would be a Lottery beneficiary before Boland Athletics?

But the conflict of interests is nothing new.

Volleyball SA received more than R8 million in 2009/2010 and just over R3.2 million in 2010/2011.

Self-appointed SASCOC CEO, Tubby Reddy is the long serving president of Volleyball SA (VSA) and Vinesh Maharaj is the treasurer of VSA and CFO of SASCOC.

SASCOC president, Gideon Sam was president of SA Triathlon, which received R5.2 million from the Lottery in 2011-2012.

Sam was also a director of Accelerate Sport, a company, which received commission on a R26 million Lottery grant to Cycling SA back in 2011.

Gideon left the building early last year (2013), I acquired his shares and I have all the resignation paperwork was conducted which we have on file so it's annoying that it's showing up on the system? The only two Directors that should be relevant and showing should be myself and Songezo Nayo. - Gary Grant, Accelerate Sport

The Lottery has a KPMG fraud line to report any suspicious activity but even that seems to be conflicted.

I sent an email to the fraud line on the 24th of April, suggesting that there are serious irregularities with the Lottery Sports and Recreation agency payments along with a conflict of interests.

The automated response on the same day:

Thank you for contacting us. We will get back to you as soon as possible.

Guess who pops up at the end of the fraud line?

Your email to our fraud hotline has been received. The people responsible for that will follow their procedures in investigating the matter and be in touch, if necessary. - Sershan Naidoo

If necessary?

Why does Naidoo have access to the fraud line and how would investigators know where to even start if they don't make contact with the whistle-blower?

I heard from some of the smaller sporting federations that the Lottery did carry out audits on spend but when asked about an audit on SASCOC, Naidoo said:

We do not 'audit' our beneficiaries. We receive reports from all our beneficiaries, including SASCOC. If we see the need (based on risk) for any visit or investigation, we then do so. Again, if you have any information of fraud or misuse of lottery funds, we urge you to send us such information for investigation.

It's more of the same old "unaccountable and untouchable" in SA sport and the Lottery millions paid out to SASCOC is more than staggering.

Where is it all going?

***

By now, I (GJ) knew I wasn't going to get any straight answers from Sershan Naidoo (SN) and the contradictions were alarming.

GJ: SA Rugby got a grant of R15 million in April 2012 – March 2013. Why would a company whose revenue rose in 2013 to R795 million get a grant and what was the grant application for?

SN: SA Rugby Union is a "voluntary association not for gain" and can therefore apply for a NLDTF grant, which is open to all non-profit organisations. The grant was for the high performance programme.

Notes: According to SA Rugby (SARU), the grant was for the academies in Boland, EP, Border and SWD. SARU got another R2.4 million grant for "high performance" in 2013.

GJ: The SASCOC grant of R17.7 million for CHAN 2013. Why to SASCOC who had no involvement in the tournament?

SN: An application for funding for CHAN 2013 was submitted and an allocation of R17.7 million was made for host city beautification, advertising, marketing, travel and accommodation, logistics and pre-tournament costs. The grant was paid through SASCOC, who applied on behalf of the Local Organising Committee (LOC).

Notes: A spokesperson for the CHAN 2013 LOC said SASCOC made no financial contribution to the tournament. Where has the R17.7 million gone? There was also no need for SASCOC to apply for the grant as the local organizing committee and host cities could have done it themselves.

GJ: If grants to sporting federations were capped at R 2 million – how did Chess SA manage to get R4 million and SA Table Tennis R8.2 million in June and July 2013?

SN: Chess SA: the grant was allocated over two years (R2m per annum) to assist with transformation and high performance programmes.

Notes: Chess SA confirmed they didn't get the full amount of R4 million and there was speculation that President Zuma was the patron of Chess SA but that denied by the federation.

SN: SA Table Tennis: The grant was not exclusively for the national federation. It included funding for the provinces to participate in junior and senior national competitions up to the 2014 championships in Free State; transformation, development and high performance programmes to promote the sport nationally and internationally; to encourage sportsmen with disabilities to participate in the sport; to assist affiliates to develop and enhance the sport in the provinces; and to host an international event in SA to encourage sports tourism to SA.

Notes: This is a tall story as the Table Tennis provinces apply for their own grants (eg. Boland Table Tennis got R491 000 in September 2013) and the Paralympic Table Tennis players hardly see any of that Lottery money. An R8.2 million grant when the cap is at R2 million is unexplainable and SportsFire got no reply from the SA Table Tennis President, Yusuf Carrim or Vice President, Hajera Kajee despite several emails.

GJ: A lotto payment to Struisbaai Primary School: R2.8m (June 2013) – why did this school receive significantly more than any other school?

SN: This grant is for the continuation of a previous project (sports facility) that will be based at the school but benefit the Boland community and promote community participation in sport.

Notes: According to the school, they actually received R4.8 million in total for a new indoor sports centre with a multi-purpose court that can be used for netball, tennis, volleyball basketball etc. The school is responsible for maintenance of the centre and received no funding for this. So, the community has to pay when they use the facilities. How does that really benefit the community if they have to pay to use it?

GJ: Payment 38571 Athletics SA 2 469 268 – Athletics SA (ASA) have confirmed they never received this payment as listed between April 2012 - March 2013? Whose account was this put into?

SN: We can confirm that we have paid this grant into their registered account.

Notes: ASA financials for 2012 and 2013 don't reflect any Lottery payment. The last Lottery payment reflected in the ASA financials is 2011 for a similar amount. Begs the questions: Where is this money and why did ASA not receive a grant in 2013 when the sport was on its knees financially? Was there a third force trying to keep the federation poor?

GJ: What is the status of an investigation into a payment made to South African Sports Aerobics & Fitness Federation for R3.8m?

SN: The allocation to SASAFF was conditional. The announcement in Parliament was therefore premature. We are attending to the matters that the Distributing Agency wanted clarification on.

Notes: The Lottery was now backtracking due to a current investigation into the affairs of SASAFF, which SASCOC have seemingly turned a blind eye to. SASAFF said they only received the one amount of R280 209.75 on 24 July 2013 as the second payment of Project 46810. How did the Lottery come up with R3.8 if they only paid out R280 000?

GJ: What happens in the case of conflicted applications e.g., if a Lottery distribution agency member is also a board member of the company/association that is applying for the grant?

SN: Where there is a conflict of interest, where a Distributing Agency member may serve on an applicant body, the application is adjudicated by another Distributing Agency.

Notes: SASCOC officials, Gideon Sam, Vinesh Maharaj, Ray Mali and Hajera Kajee were all members of the Lottery distribution agency. Now only Mr Mali remains and according to an insider:

They recused themselves from Lotto meetings, when SASCOC funding applications were being discussed, by standing outside the meeting room door but implored remaining Lotto members to adjudicate wisely.

Another distributing agency doesn't adjudicate?

I was wasting my time with Sershan Naidoo and made contact with Matodzi Nefale, a Fraud Specialist with the National Lotteries Board Risk Department.

On Thursday 24 July 2014, I met with Mr Nefale and a senior member of his department, Vuyisa Gwam at the Mugg and Bean in Sandton City, Johannesburg.

The lunch meeting lasted a couple hours and I shared a dossier with them, showing some sixteen different cases of financial irregularities with the Lottery Distribution Agency payments for Sport and Recreation.

They made as though they were horrified by the information and promised to investigate fully for the betterment of SA sport.

The hamburgers were good but not sure why I had to pay the bill. I thought I was doing them a favour.

Maybe the Lottery had run dry!

I stayed on this case as I felt this was going to be the best shot of getting something meaningful done about corruption in SA sport.

The Lottery funding had become a "private bank account" for many administrators and officials.

Matodzi Nefale responded to me on 18 August 2014.

I apologize for the delayed response, I was out of the office the whole of last week. So far we have compiled the documents and we are in the process of referring the matters to the forensic consultants. The process takes an average of two weeks because we first request for quotes and then allocate matters with value for money as the prime consideration. We will update you of the progress in due course. - Matodzi Nefale

Six weeks later …

We have been attending an indaba at Birchwood Conference Centre. A lot of issues were raised there and the Minister sent a very strong message about fighting fraud in beneficiary organizations, since then we are receicving a lot of hotline reports. With regard to the matters that you reported we have just allocated them to Forensic Service Providers and we anticipate to get feedback in two weeks time. - Matodzi Nefale

Three weeks later …

I apologize for the delayed respone. I am in out of the office and sometimes I don't have access to my emails. The matters are still under investigation. I cannot divulge the identity of the individual investigators. If you need further information you can contact Gladys Petje. She is the Marketing and Communications Manager. I am not authorized to communicate anything that will go to the media. - Matodzi Nefale

Petje was contacted and I was told to communicate with Sershan Naidoo.

Another dead-end! These guys are good!

The National Lotteries Board (NLB) is established in terms of the Lotteries Act, 1997 (Act No. 57 of 1997), as amended, to regulate the national lottery and other lotteries, including society lotteries to raise funds and promotional competitions. The NLB advises the Minister of Trade and Industry on policy matters relating to the national lottery and other lotteries. The NLB does not adjudicate applications for funding or make allocations to organisations. Adjudication for applications for funding and allocations to organisation is done through committees known as Distributing Agencies that are appointed by the Minister of Trade and Industry in conjunction with the Minister of Sports and Arts and Culture. The NLB provides administrative support to the Distributing Agencies. - (www.thedti.gov.za/agencies/nlb.jsp)

I was going to leave no stone unturned in attempt to get some action.

The Minister of Trade and Industry, Rob Davies was my next port of call and I got this reply from his office on 4 March 2015.

Your email to the Minister is hereby acknowledged. Your query has been forwarded to our team working on Lottery matters for consideration and a response to you, which I trust you will receive in due course. - Marlene Ernest, Office of Minister Davies

Just as well I didn't hold my breath for that response.

There wasn't one!

Towards the end of 2014, I got a call from Johan Kloppers, who introduced himself as being from a company that had a contract to do Lottery investigations.

We met a few days later at my apartment complex. Kloppers was accompanied by three other gentlemen and they explained to me how the Lottery fraudsters were operating.

More importantly, they knew about some of the cases that I had mentioned.

Arrests were imminent.

Where had I heard that before?

On 17 February 2015, I emailed Mr. Kloppers to see if there was an update on the 'imminent arrests.'

Three weeks later, I got this response …

Please take note that we are not in a position to provide any third party with feedback, our engagement is bound by confidentiality. Please direct all your queries directly to the NLB. - Johan Kloppers

The merry-go-round was exhausting but I was still like a kid in the candy store when the beneficiary payments were listed on the National Lottery website every month.

Lottery grant paid out after ten years?
31 March 2015

I couldn't help but notice the National Lottery Distribution Trust Fund (NLDTF) payments for last month.

What really caught my eye was:

R3.2 million paid to Volleyball South Africa (VSA) and the R2.5 million paid to the United Cricket Board of SA. Why?

Firstly, the Lottery grants for a federation have been capped at R2 million for the last three years. So, why would VSA get R3.2 million?

Could it be because the VSA president, Tubby Reddy and VSA treasurer, Vinesh Maharaj have friends within the Lottery?

Sershan Naidoo from the NLDTF said:

Volleyball SA (#38852) is a 2009 application, half of which was paid in 2010. This is the second tranche. There were no caps on grants in the 2009 call.

Reddy and Maharaj failed to respond to our SportsFire emails.

Speaking of which - Reddy, Maharaj and Davanathan Moodliar are directors of Devinred Holdings. Moodliar just happens to be a board member of VSA as well and also runs "Apollo Sports" which is allegedly a supplier to VSA and other sporting federations.

A google search on Apollo Sports gives you a couple Durban phone numbers that are out of service.

The R2.5 million paid to the United Cricket Board of SA is also concerning in that the federation changed to Cricket SA (CSA) in 2009.

CSA confirmed that: "The UCB does not exist as the name change came into effect in 2009.

However, the money received from Lotto was in respect to an application made in 2005 which was done under the auspices of the UCB."

A Lottery grant paid out ten years later?

That could be a first.

Cricket SA (#38857) is also a 2009 application. Here too, the first tranche was paid in 2010. Cricket SA uses the same bank account as its predecessor UCB. On our finance database, we haven't changed UCB to Cricket SA. The database names are used on our payments list. - Sershan Naidoo

One says 2005 and the other 2009?

When asked for clarification – Naidoo said: "Please use the response we have given you. There will be no further correspondence entered into."

Looks like CSA has a few tough days ahead of not only answering to this questionable payment but also the political interference in Proteas selection and new quota system for provincial cricket.

Every month, the National Lottery payments are made public and we should all have eyes on who and what is being paid.

Maybe, one day we'll make these agency members and beneficiaries of irregular payments accountable.

The Auditor-General was in Grahamstown a couple weeks ago and even struggled to answer questions about agency payments and where the National Lottery fits in on the scale of under-performance.

He called the questions "difficult"!

***

Howzat!
21 May 2015

Ithuba Holdings is scheduled to take over as the new National Lottery operator next month and if I was an SA athlete, I would be holding thumbs desperately for a clean operation.

The Lottery is where the major problem lies in SA sport funding as individuals/officials have been using it like it's their own bank account.

What's wrong with this?

Cricket South Africa (CSA) declare a profit of almost R200 million for the 2013-14 season.
In 2014/2015, cricket receives the following payments from the National Lottery distribution agency (NLDTF).

November 2014: Border cricket – R17.3 million
February 2015: United Cricket Board of South Africa – R2.5 million
March 2015: Cricket South Africa – R5 million

CSA is still unable to answer the questionable Lottery payment to UCB ten years after the application although Sershan Naidoo from the NLB contradicted CSA by saying it was a 2009 application. I thought an independent director on the board of CSA, Louis von Zeuner would want to get to the bottom of it all.

I was wrong again.

Graeme, I would suggest that you give Altaaf Kazi a call. My understanding is that he did engage with you and did provide information but somehow, something went wrong in the process and communication broke down between the two of you. - Louis von Zeuner

Something was very wrong with the Lottery payment process and it must be some kind of record for a grant to be paid out six to ten years (depending on who you believe) after the application.

The UCB does not exist as the name change came into effect in 2009.

So, Naidoo went for the safest cover up.

Howzat!

Lottery Distribution agency members have got their fingers in the pie and are getting kickbacks when many of the smaller sporting codes are starving and athletes have to pay their own way to represent their country.

SASCOC is one of the biggest abusers of Lottery money but because they have friends within, it's covered up.

According to the Annual Final Statements as at 31 March 2014, SASCOC did not receive an administration grant from the Department of Sport and Recreation (SRSA) or from the National Lottery.

However, salaries were paid in excess of R13 million even though no funds had been received for administration. Thus, such salaries (including Mr. Reddy's) must have been paid by some creative accounting whereby the grants from SRSA and Lottery were in fact utilised.

Sports Minister, Fikile Mbalula is now mooting a levy on match tickets again and says his department, which got "a clean audit" from the AG does not have "an iota of corruption or irregular expenditure" in it.

What he keeps forgetting to mention is the Sports Trust which gets hundreds of millions from the Lottery and other companies which his department uses as dirty conduits.

Wonder if the AG has ever done an audit on the Trusts in partnership with SRSA?

***

Border cricket got another R25 million from the National Lottery in 2015/2016 but my emails to their president, Thando Booi got the silent treatment.

I was curious to know what the excessive grants were for and if Ray Mali or any third party had been involved in the application process.

Mali has been a long serving member of the Lottery Distribution agency for Sport and Recreation. He has strong ties to cricket and the Border region.

He didn't reply to my emails either.

In February 2013, the president of the Border Cricket Board, Chris Nenzani was elected as the new president of Cricket South Africa.

And in the next two years, Border Cricket receives an unprecedented R42.3 million from the Lottery?

The Lottery beneficiary payments were posted on the NLC website the month after they had been granted but something had changed for June, July and August 2015.

None of the grants had been published by September 2015.

Then in October 2015, the National Lotteries Commission posted this on their website.

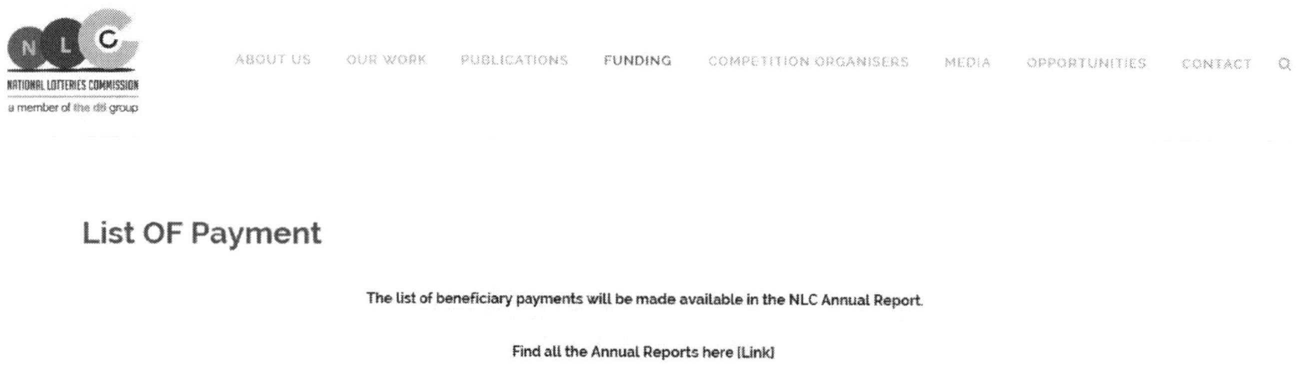

The monthly payments were no longer available for immediate scrutiny.

I guess I can take some credit for that. I was a monthly thorn in their side and the lies were getting bigger and bigger.

I was scraping too close to the bone.

Hundreds of millions were being misappropriated every month and now the beneficiaries were no longer listed monthly for scrutiny.

How convenient!

Since the National Lottery Commission (NLC) first started allocating grants in 2002, sport has received R6 billion compared to the R2.8 billion given to 5,768, mostly public schools during the same period, When it comes to the NLC's funding priorities, education lags far behind sport, despite the deplorable state of education in the country. Of the R6 billion for sport the lion's share of R2.3 billion went to Sascoc) and its affiliates. And, of that, Sascoc, which represents South Africa's Olympic and Commonwealth Games athletes and is also responsible for high-performance sports at home, received R779 million. Other Sascoc associate sports bodies have also received multi-million grants, including athletics, R204 million, swimming, R97 million, and hockey, R94 million. Table tennis got R57 million.- (GroundUp, 19 February 2018)

With the kind of numbers finding their way into back pockets, the South African Revenue Service (SARS) must have had an eye on some of these dodgy sports officials for not paying tax on their ill-gotten millions.

Alas not.

SASCOC photographer, Wessel Oosthuizen got me a meeting with SARS through his daughter's work connections.

On 27 November 2014, nervously, for fear of being followed again, I met with Lufuno Ramasunzi and

Isabel Fourie-Goosen from the SARS Compliance Unit at their offices in Johannesburg.

They too were horrified by the information I shared and promised a thorough investigation and profiling.

Two days later, I got a call from Wessel to say SARS had done a couple quick tests on the leads I had given them (the one being Alexander) and it was big.

Red lights were flashing. The corruption in SA sport was going to explode in the media in the New Year.

I had a follow up meeting on 29 January 2015 as Lufuno's manager, Mandisa Masiba wanted to be briefed as well. Things were on track. We remained in contact via email as there were new stories every week, some involving the same corrupt officials.

Thanks a lot for the new information. I will follow-up on the information. - Isabel Fourie-Goosen

But as time went on, things went very quiet and my correspondence with SARS died after an email I sent to Isabel on 23 July 2015, asking for an update on the SARS investigations as I would like to forward the information to the Public Protector.

Silence!

Wessel and I met regularly for a cup of coffee.

He was close to SASCOC president, Gideon Sam and wanted to help me to get the truth out but after a while, I had a feeling he was playing both sides.

On more than one occasion, the day after meeting with Wessel, new information about my personal life and movements appeared on the anonymous, defamatory website, Joffers-exposed. As the main SASCOC photographer, Wessel worked closely with the good old boys from Highbury Safika Media.

I called him on 'playing both sides' and he denied any involvement in the website, adding that SASCOC had taken him off a couple trips as they believed he was feeding information to me.

Later on, he told me that SASCOC compensated him for the trips he missed after he had threatened them with legal action. Unlike, SASCOC to be bullied!

Our communication slowly faded until Wessel made contact again towards the end of 2015, telling me the big bomb was about to drop with SASCOC.

I was about to be vindicated.

But by February 2016, still nothing and I asked Wessel if there was any news from SARS or was it all covered up.

Apparently you wouldn't give them anything – I haven't contacted them.- Wessel Oosthuizen

"Apparently, you wouldn't give them anything" couldn't have been any further from the truth.
I sensed another cover up. The corrupt were bucking the system and getting away with it at the highest level.

Big four accounting firm KPMG has played an enabling role in the Zuma-Gupta state capture strategy played out across state-owned entities. Its senior employees were so intertwined with the Gupta family that a number were invited to a 2013 Gupta wedding at Sun City – an extravagant do at which the close ties between politicians and the business family spilled out into the open. KPMG helped the Guptas siphon money out of state coffers and dodge tax. KPMG helped fabricate a report that was instrumental in ousting anti-corruption busters at the South African Revenue Service. (BizNews, 22 March 2018)

And remember, KPMG 'administered' the fraud hot-line for the National Lottery which is regulated by the Department of Trade and Industry.

Minister Rob Davies, are you there?

Wessel and I made contact again after his working trip to the Rio Olympic Games in 2016 and during our skype conversation, he mentioned that 'our' SARS connection told him she had sent a profile of the corruption for her boss to expedite the case and that the Public Protector investigation into SASCOC was still ongoing.

The Public Protector/government watchdog investigation into SASCOC was set aside due to "resource constraints".

Not surprising.

Too many have too much to lose!

Chapter 21: Conflicted Media

There needs to be a fairer road for future athletes, one in which their dreams are encouraged, not crushed.

Where their hard work and their undoubted talent is rewarded.

With all the political power of the Sports Ministry and SASCOC, the influence and the largesse they are able to distribute amongst their acolytes, they still have no foil to counter the truth. I always tried to imagine them running around with their knickers in a knot, drawing on their many resources and discussing various strategies.

Why is it that we don't have a hard-hitting, investigative television show in South Africa to expose the corrupt sports administration?

A 60 Minutes type programme?

Is it because too many media organizations are in bed with these sports federations or are we fans before journalists? It's both.

Whilst I acknowledge the importance of uplifting, positive stories, it does not detract from the fact that a job of a journalist is to report and not to ignore those stories which make us uncomfortable.

South Africa has little to no culture of investigative sports journalism.

SASCOC pay millions to their outside PR company, Highbury Safika Media (HSM) to cover and report on the SA teams at the Olympics, Paralympics and Regional Games. So, you only get the good stories. It's a PR machine. But SASCOC still spends more on some hand selected mainstream journalists when our athletes are subject to the strictest of budgets.

The only reason could be to try and buy favourable journalism.

The subject of 'buying favourable journalism' didn't sit too well with some fellow sports journalists, who took exception to a column that I wrote in September 2012, even though I didn't mention any of their names.

I've just read your column and was wondering what you meant by this: "How does a mainstream journalist, whose trip to the Paralympics was funded by SASCOC, then expose some of their actions? And what does it say about journalistic integrity when journalists accept this kind of largesse?"Are you suggesting that myself, Sarel van der Walt from Beeld and Jenny Bernstein from Sapa have no or little integrity because our flights and accommodation were paid for by Sascoc on behalf of the sponsors of the South African Paralympic team? Are you suggesting that they did this to muzzle me? To make me write about them more favourably? Are you implying that I have no ethics and integrity? I'd like to keep our friendship (even though you have unfollowed me on Twitter). - Kevin McCallum

I was unaware that a Twitter follow was a requirement for a friendship!

There was no need to get in a slanging match with Kevin and I didn't reply but my response today would be as follows …

Dear Kevin

Thank you for your email.

I unfollowed you on twitter as I got a little tired of seeing your unashamed punts of cycling merchandise and stores. Hope you managed to get all your cycling accessories free of charge?

You were always too close to Oscar Pistorius and were never critical, even when he acted like a sore loser at the London Paralympics.

Please don't shoot the messenger.

Graeme, I am enjoying your articles with regards to SASCOC. I'm wondering why you don't name the journalist in question in the article? I have a massive problem with Kevin Mccallum. When New Zealand beat us in the last (cricket) world cup, he was one of the main journalists at the tournament. He refused to admit that we choked and went hard at anyone on Twitter who dared to say that we choked. A few months later he was attending Graeme Smiths (SA cricket captain) wedding. I have always seen him as more of a fan than a journalist. And now even Mike Horn says that we choked.- Johann Doms

Too many beers with the great athletes can cloud our objective vision and too many SA sports journalists are more concerned about their free trips and dinners.

I see after the Rio Olympics, you were very outspoken about the SASCOC draconian codes of conduct, which I was happy to see even though, it was something I had exposed four years ago. So, I found it a little nauseating that you would pat yourself on the back because strangers were saying well done to you, keep on the SASCOC case.

Have you ever dug into the real issue at hand, which is destroying the dreams of SA athletes, namely corruption?

Have you ever taken the SASCOC financials and given them a second look over? Have you ever investigated the Lottery payments and who are the real beneficiaries?

You work for a big media group, you have resources.

You can access PAIA (Promotion of Access to Information Act) .

There shouldn't be any excuse to expose the truth.

After the Rio Olympics, I also noted a twitter exchange between yourself and former SA triathlete, Conrad Stoltz.

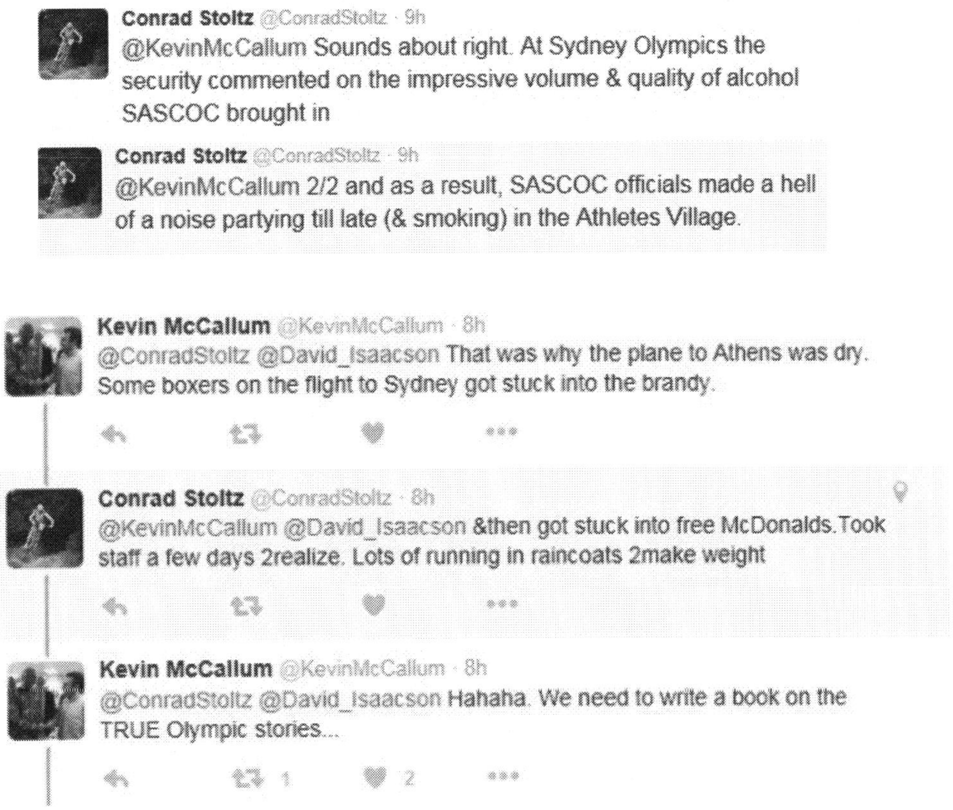
Conrad Stoltz @ConradStoltz · 9h
@KevinMcCallum Sounds about right. At Sydney Olympics the security commented on the impressive volume & quality of alcohol SASCOC brought in

Conrad Stoltz @ConradStoltz · 9h
@KevinMcCallum 2/2 and as a result, SASCOC officials made a hell of a noise partying till late (& smoking) in the Athletes Village.

Kevin McCallum @KevinMcCallum · 8h
@ConradStoltz @David_Isaacson That was why the plane to Athens was dry. Some boxers on the flight to Sydney got stuck into the brandy.

Conrad Stoltz @ConradStoltz · 8h
@KevinMcCallum @David_Isaacson &then got stuck into free McDonalds.Took staff a few days 2realize. Lots of running in raincoats 2make weight

Kevin McCallum @KevinMcCallum · 8h
@ConradStoltz @David_Isaacson Hahaha. We need to write a book on the TRUE Olympic stories...

1 2

Perhaps, you should have written these 'TRUE Olympic stories' then.

Sydney 2000 would have been a good time to expose the SASCOC cretins and maybe SA sport wouldn't be in the same dark space eighteen years later and just maybe we would have had some sober boxers in Rio!

As you well know, Rio was the first time in 100 years that South Africa had no boxers at the Olympic Games.

But had you told these 'true Olympic stories' then, I doubt you would have been invited on any more SASCOC junkets. #justsaying

Cheers Joffers!

***

Kevin wasn't the only offended journalist.

My longtime critic, Wesley Botton also chimed in and got his editor from the SA Press Association (SAPA) to sign off on an email to me, saying:

For the record, Sapa, along with some other mainstream sports newsrooms, did accept an open and transparent offer from Sascoc of a plane ticket and very modest accommodation in London so that we could have a reporter on site to boost our direct coverage of the events. I can speak only for Sapa, but in our case there was absolutely nothing underhand or conditional about our accepting the offer, which was based purely on the editorial news merits of Team SA's participation ... If Mr Joffe wishes to continue to present himself as a journalist and leading commentator he would be well advised to revisit his cadet 101 lessons on balance and fairness, and making sure to hear the other side, let alone the principles of defamation and libel. The latter two are sure to rise up sooner or later and smack him on the nose -- hard and embarrassingly -- like a rake left lying around would be stepped on by a sloppy gardener. - Mark van der Velden

Cadet 101? That got a laugh out of me!

Sapa closed its doors in 2015 due to financial problems but Botton had already jumped ship to the Citizen newspaper and continued his little personal tirade on twitter.

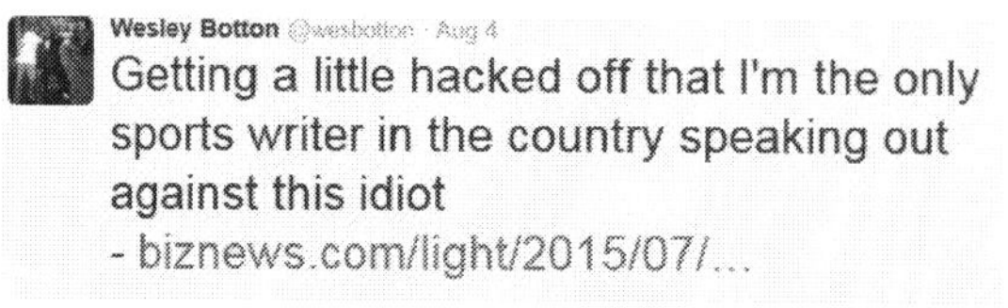

I continued my SportsFire digital publication from Cincinnati for a couple months after fleeing SA but got tired of all the legal threats including an urgent interdict from Highbury Safika Media after exposing them further.

It was mostly information that was already in the public domain, which led to Mark Keohane's sudden resignation as SASCOC spokesperson.

So, how could they get an urgent interdict with jurisdiction in Cape Town and how was I to defend it on a whim from the USA?

Enough was enough!

My co-partners in SportsFire Daily, Ince, were the publishing and sales arm based in Johannesburg, but they wanted nothing to do with the legal battle and turned their back on me.

I wonder if it had anything to do with their business partnership with Caxton (owners of the Citizen Newspaper by the way) who were in the process of doing a business deal with HSM?

Paul Jenkins (Caxton) had sent an email to Alban Atkinson (Ince) saying:

I have reflected on this a bit more. I will also call you if I get more info on Graham. But I think the complexity of this matter dictates you should see a lawyer who understands defamation, even this weekend if necessary, as time may be of the essence. I want to avoid even the perception of a conflict of interest, although please be assured of my unequivocal support.

Who was Paul Jenkins to advise on our business, "get more info on Graham" and then wants to avoid even the perception of a conflict of interest?

Where are the ethics and integrity?

The Citizen is a morning daily newspaper and my free SportsFire Daily was reaching thousands of readers electronically first thing in the morning with domestic and international sports news including the exposes.

Was I becoming competition to them?

Alban saw the lawyer and said it wouldn't be necessary for me to furnish him with all the evidence that I had.

He had already made up his mind, which way he was going to go.

There was already an existing relationship between Caxton and HSM and it was all about looking after each other not to derail the Compleat Golfer deal.

Highbury Safika Media (HSM), one of the largest independent media houses in South Africa, will publish the popular Compleat Golfer monthly magazine after adding it to its impressive stable of multi-platform titles. The development is through a partnership with Caxton.(Highbury Media, 8 October 2015)

Highbury Safika Media (HSM) will publish Compleat Golfer magazine in future through a partnership with Caxton. The final edition to be published by Ramsay Media (owned by Caxton) will be a combined December 2015/January 2016 edition. The first Compleat Golfer under HSM's direction, will be available on shelves in early 2016. (Compleat Golfer, 9 October 2015)

No doubt, Caxton and HSM were in a hurry to get the bad publicity (the truth) out of the public domain and Ince obliged.

I had a call from Paul Jenkins of Caxtons advising me to take down the story as they had heard that this guy (Kevin) Ferguson was taking legal action and they are concerned that they will com after both Ince and Caxtons. - Alban Atkinson

"Concerned HSM will come after Caxtons", their soon to be business partners?

What a joke!

And at this point, Caxtons were also probably in discussions with HSM about buying Ramsay Media, which happened in 2017.

Effective October 2, 2017, Highbury Media will take over Ramsay Media including Getaway, Leisure Wheels, Popular Mechanics and CAR magazines ... Details of the takeover deal are not being disclosed. (Highbury Media, 26 September 2017)

I was also unaware that the HSM story had even been taken down from SportsFire until I was alerted to the fact by a couple readers.

Ince had kept me in the dark.

I was left to fight another legal battle on my own within 48 hours (Urgent High Court order) - this time from the US.

HSM named four defendants, including Ince in their court papers. But they were only after one person – me!

No-one likes the truth to be exposed, especially when you're as dirty as they are.

I should have just left the case alone but wasn't sure of the legal ramifications if I was ever to go back to South Africa.

Johannesburg attorney, David Swartz whom I had met before (he was representing a client who was taking on the Sports Minister in a boxing case) agreed to represent me pro bono.

But Swartz sent my urgent response to the 'wrong' email address of the opposition attorney and didn't send representation to the High Court in the Western Cape on the day of the matter, despite promising to do so.

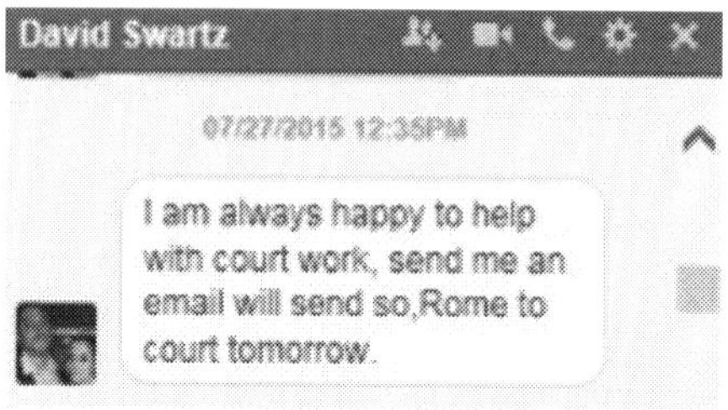

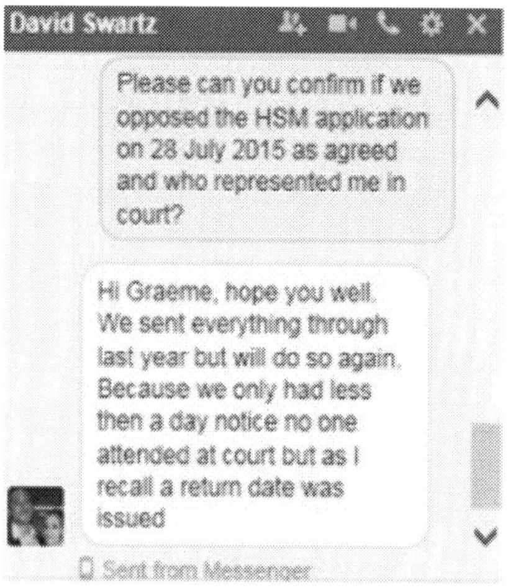

The result …

A judgement against the first respondent (myself).

The judge in the case was the Honourable Jeanette Traverso, who presided over the controversial trial of murder accused, Shrien Dewani. Swartz had dropped the ball.

Cape Town based lawyer, Brendan Commins then agreed to represent me along with former Athletics SA president, James Evans as my advocate.

No problem Graeme, I have actually acted against Highbury Safika before on behalf of Jake White. Lovely boys, those!! - Brendan Commins

Lovely boys indeed!

Initially, Brendan's advice was to leave it alone as I had no assets in SA but later on, he said "*we could have some fun with it.*"

Fun with a legal case?

He had also told me in a skype conversation that he had personally taken down the former employee's CCMA statement regarding HSM's disgraceful business acumen.

He knew first hand it was the truth.

In an email to me on 17 August 2015, James Evans wrote:

This is an urgent interdict to prevent you writing defamatory articles about them. That is going way outside what a court should do. It means you can't publish an article that they are stealing, even if you have solid evidence that they are. That is way too much and a court shouldn't grant that. I also see some dangers in just letting this go – do you really have no assets in SA? And are you really not intending to come back to SA at any time in the next 20 years (the prescription period for judgment)? I doubt it. You get invited back to a Rhodes reunion, they find out, you set foot back in the country and the sheriff attaches your computer and cellphone.

There is always the risk that if they order is granted in the current form and you write about them from the US they may approach a US court on the back of the SA judgement. I still don't know how the Cape court has jurisdiction over you. You were never domiciled here. Personally, I don't think you should leave this one. It will confirm to everyone that you have been making up stories you have been writing, which is what HSM and SASCOC want them to believe.

I had to be guided by them.

I sent as much evidence as possible and we filed an affidavit in time for the court date on 9 September 2015.

I had told James that despite the time difference here in the USA (6/7 hours behind), my phone would be on at all times, if we need to make any legal decisions.

The Honourable Justice Donen was now presiding …

IN THE HIGH COURT OF SOUTH AFRICA

(WESTERN CAPE DIVISION, CAPE TOWN)

CAPE TOWN: WEDNESDAY, the 9th day of SEPTEMBER 2015

THIRD DIVISION: COURT NO. 16 at 10H00 am

BEFORE THE HONOURABLE MR ACTING JUSTICE DONEN

RULES NISI (BEVELE NISI)

1 Berry & Donaldson (Pty) Ltd vs End South Africa Importers & Exporters

(Pty) Ltd – Liquidation (Likwidasie) 5998/15

2 Highbury Safika Media (Pty) Ltd vs G Joffe & 3 others – Interdict (Interdik) 13955/15

James and I attended court today and the matter was initially stood down so that we could talk to the other side re the future conduct of the matter. We then had lengthy and (we think) productive discussions with the HSM legal team. The matter was very unlikely to have been concluded today as the judge would probably have granted HSM a postponement to reply to your affidavit. Their Counsel (an excellent silk) quickly appreciated the difficulty they had with the breadth of the interim order. Accordingly, we have agreed that the matter be postponed to 5 November 2015 for argument on the semi-urgent roll. I attach a copy of the much watered down Court Order which will operate as a temporary interdict until that date. As you can see it pertains only to the allegedly defamatory publication and not to other allegedly defamatory material which you might publish in the future. Both James and I are of the view that Senior Counsel for HSM is not that enamoured of his client's case and that an approach to settle the matter might come in the near future. The attorney and the junior were quite aggressive, but the silk's views prevailed. This is a good result for you in the short term as it seems to make clear to them that a permanent interdict of the type they were seeking would be difficult to obtain. - Brendan Commins

It wasn't easy to know exactly what was going on, thousands of miles away from all the proceedings. To cut a long story short, heads of argument were filed, and we were back in court on 5 November 2015. James was of the opinion, they had a very weak case and jurisdiction was a big problem for them. Brendan led me to believe we had nothing to worry about.

Their reply seems so poor that it may be to our advantage to not try exclude it. On a superficial reading of it, they didn't really tackle the allegations you made in the answering affidavit. Eg they don't really deny that SASCOC had to put the contact out to tender. All my research is 100% in our favour, so I am interested to see how they are going to argue this one. Nothing unexpected. They've got a good silk who is doing the best he can with a bad case. On paper we have a strong case.- Brendan Commins

What changed before the judgement?

I am afraid we got biffed by Traverso DJP. Effectively the second interim order was made final, with costs (not attorney and client costs). My view of it was that she was most concerned with the per se defamatory nature of the remarks about the HSM/SASCOC contract and did not believe that you had put forward any facts in support of the "cronyism and alleged kick-backs" averment. She did not believe that you could show any ground of justification for that allegation, grounded in fact. She regarded your "inferential reasoning" as flawed. She didn't address the Keohane part in as much detail, but she would have been hard to convince on that, as well.

She gave no reasons for her judgment in court, but undertook to provide written reasons and asked for us to act quickly if we do want them. (She is retiring in April). The only reason to do that would be if you wish to appeal this.

Frankly, my advice is to leave this well alone and concentrate on your other targets. You are welcome to use me as a sounding board before writing anything which might run foul of the law.- Brendan Commins

I wanted to see written reasons.

This was ludicrous as the HSM/SASCOC contract/no tender and lies had already been well documented in the press and this wasn't even the main content in my blog.

The public had a right to know and I was really annoyed with this unwritten judgement. Something wasn't adding up!

I requested Brendan to please get the written reasons for me, should I wish to appeal.

Both he and James then responded to my questions with major differences - yet, they were on the same team?

Has a written judgement/reasoning been requested from Traverso DJP?

Brendan Commins (BC): Not yet. I have been awaiting your instructions. However, I will withdraw before putting my name to such a request. Both James and I heard her reasons rather forcefully expressed during the hearing.

James Evans (JE): No, Brendon would need a specific instruction to do so. I know he is of the view that it should be left, but I am not sure. There is no real cost for asking for reasons, so it may be worthwhile. Let me get back to you on this one.

How did the DJP justify the Cape Town jurisdiction?

BC: See my email of 6 November 2015. (The "offending article" was published in Cape Town and therefore she had jurisdiction)

JE: The way defamation works is that it "publication" means where it is read or heard by a third party. I argued quite strongly that they didn't make out a case for that regarding the one website, but most importantly that the court did not have effective jurisdiction because it can't enforce an order against you. She didn't seem interested in that argument. However, the issue has not been clarified, and I'm not sure the Appeal Court will agree with her – how can they enforce an order against you in the US? If you write something there, and it is published in the USA, the SA Court has no jurisdiction. The problem comes if you post it on the internet and it is read here. Even still, I have no idea how they will get the USA to enforce a South African order relating to the infringement of freedom of expression.

How long was the court hearing and did she go through the heads of argument?

BC: It lasted most of the morning. Of course, she did. She had clearly read the papers quite thoroughly before the hearing.

JE: We were in court the whole morning, and yes she had. She had just formed a prima facie view that what you wrote was defamatory and she didn't like it. Unfortunately, the one weakness is our case is what she latched onto. It was fair to say the contract was without a tender and irregular. But there was little tangible evidence that it was awarded due to kickbacks. Inviting people to concerts isn't really kickbacks, and there was nothing to show they awarded the contract because they got the concert invites. To sustain an argument that the contract was awarded due to kickbacks you would have needed to show that officials within SASCOC were promised some kind of reward for which they would award the contract to HSM. Inviting them to concerts after the time was thin evidence of kickbacks – businesses often invite clients to entertainment and sporting events. Unfortunately, she thought it was too thin justify the statement about kickbacks.

Why was no evidence led?

BC: Oral evidence is not usual in applications in which the evidence is set out in affidavits by the parties. Who should have given evidence, anyway? You are in the USA.
JE: That's the way applications work – the court works off the affidavit before it.

Did the DJP refer to the City Press article and its content?

BC: Yes and her answer to that query was that she could not control what HSM did. They fact that they had decided not to go after City Press was irrelevant to whether they were defamed by you.

JE: Yes, I took her through that. I do think this is the weakness in her reasoning. She didn't understand that it was out there in the open already.

Why was the case stood down on 9 Sept and who was the judge?

BC: It was postponed to the semi-urgent roll (normal procedure) so that HSM could file a replying affidavit. The judge was the duty judge for the day, Michael Donen AJ.

JE: Donen AJ was the Judge then. He was not going to hear the case without their replying affidavit. It was originally stood down because it was called in the motion court where there was 20 or 30 other cases waiting to be heard (most or all unopposed). It's the practice to stand down to the end of the roll to argue opposed matters or decide on their future conduct.

Was Kevin Ferguson (HSM CEO) present and/or part of the consultation with legal teams on Sept 9 after case was stood down?

BC: He was present at Counsel's Chambers but not in the room during negotiations. What is the relevance of this question?

JE: No.

Any reason why I wasn't consulted re: standing down and during consultation with their legal team? I did mention that my phone would be on the entire time.

BC: No reason really. The negotiations were about procedure and the watering down of the over broad interim interdict.

JE: On September 9 the issues were procedural, especially after we got them to agree that they could not get a general interdict that you should not defame them. That was a major victory, as if that had been granted you could not have pursued your case against Keohane.

Was the meeting with their legal team on 9 Sept recorded?

BC: No and as part of negotiations for a potential settlement, the conversation is privileged. I have never heard of negotiations being recorded in such a situation. In fact, I have never been in a meeting between legal teams which was recorded

JE: No. It is not practice to record such meetings, and probably would have ended the meeting is someone had tried.

I wasn't satisfied with their conflicting answers from "my" legal team and something was bothering me about all of this.

Brendan withdrew after I had asked him again to request the written reasons including jurisdiction from Madame Traverso DJP.

Needless to say, I had to write to the court myself to get the actual judgement.

HSM put in a legal request on the same day to try and stop me from getting the written reasons, claiming it was past the deadline.

Why did they have to be informed by the court that I had requested the written reasons and there was no delay?

I had already asked Brendan to do so in an email on 11 November.

James had also resigned from the Cape Bar in 2008 and I wanted to make sure that everything was above board.

Your email below refers. There are no records on the DOJ&CD system for a James Evans. Please note that the DOJ&CD publishes and maintains a database of details of admitted advocates for whom we have received documentation that reflects an admission/suspension/striking off. There are several instances in which persons are admitted advocates but whose documentation has not been provided to me for uploading onto the database. I suggest that James Evans be requested to provide proof of his admission as an advocate. - Reesha Ramnarain, State Law Advisor

I asked James if he could please provide me with proof.

Wrong question obviously.

This is the same line of accusations which Richard Stander and Tubby Reddy have tried. You have now placed yourself alongside them. I have no respect for them and you have joined them. I did you a massive favour by agreeing to represent you on the basis I did. I did nothing unprofessional or unethical and withstood withering criticism from the Judge because of the reckless allegations you had made with no factual foundation. My opponent never questioned that I am an advocate, because he represented me when I was admitted. The Judge never questioned me because I have appeared in front her before, often. But you, Stander and Reddy all believe differently. Ordinarily, you would have faced a bill of over R50 000 for my work alone. Instead you repaid Brendon and myself with wild allegations which again are without any factual foundation. You simply will not learn. Please go to hell. The same one Stander and Reddy are heading for. Just don't ever communicate with me again. - James Evans

I must have rattled another cage.

Three months after the judgment, I finally managed to get the written reasons.

The reasons for judgment opened some old wounds and I was angry at being legally misrepresented.

To this day, I have still been unable to get the reasons for jurisdiction from the DJP who has supposedly now retired.

How did HSM even get an urgent interdict?

It was information that was already in the public domain. The only new information I published was HSM getting sponsorship for their SA Rugby magazine by promising favourable journalism to a client in April 2015.

Have concluded a deal with Cooper Tyres for 4 issues, the MD insisted that we do article on his son, Ayron Schramm, I looked into the player and I see he could go into Future star on Club Star. I have not confirmed which issue for client, just let me know when you can put it in. - Ryan Nicolle, HSM Group Sales Director

Schramm did not make the cut for the expanded 40-man SA U20 squad this year, so there are 40 players at U20 level who are more deserving than him, not to mention a number of schoolboys currently playing 1st XV rugby (SACS fly-half Jordan Chait will be the Future Star in the June issue). It is an indisputable fact that we would not be considering Schramm for Future Star if his father had not insisted on it as a condition for advertising in the magazine. – Simon Borchardt, HSM rugby writer

I rest my case but I had been let down by legal professionals, who I thought had my best interests at heart and that of SA sport.

And let down by the legal system!

I was also curious as to why the court roll for that day and judgement wasn't published on the Southern African Legal Information Institute (SAFLII) website as is the common practice.

The reply from SAFLII.

Thank you for getting in touch with us. Although SAFLII makes every effort to obtain judgments from the High Courts across the country, there are occasions when judgments are not sent to us, for a variety of reasons. If you would like us to source the judgment and publish it online, we will gladly try to do so. If you have further details about the judgment, particularly the case number and the name of the presiding judge, please do send these details to us, as this will make the search easier.

I received a copy of the order but was hoping to see a copy of the actual argument and proceedings as well as the reasons for jurisdiction.

I assume there will be a recording of this or maybe not?

Evans was a fighter and was quick to expose journalists who had taken sides with SASCOC during his running battle in trying to hold onto the Athletics SA presidency.

Wesley Botton and David Isaacson (Sunday Times) were two of his main targets and he sent out this group email in June 2013 to a number of media houses in the heat of the battle.

I am answering everyone on this, as this person, who is passing himself of as a journalist, will write another fictitious story as if it is the truth. He, with his publication's consent, is renowned for not verifying his sources prior to pursuing or publishing a story. It is not sufficient for a journalist merely to repeat an allegation without verifying the source. Asking for comment and then repeating the allegation does not rectify the default. A false and defamatory allegation remains that regardless as to whether the person affected is asked for comment.

It has also become clear that this person, with the consent of his publication, is running in vindictive campaign against me and has become the PR arm of a campaign to promote one of the failed candidates from last year's ASA elections. His 'scoops' all come from that source and he is loyal in repeating them.

While most of the media have seen through the attempt to try me in the media, Isaacson and Time Media are persisting with the campaign. We can only ask why and what their motivation is. In a constitutional democracy, I assumed that a person had a right to defend themselves in an independent tribunal. It appears that it is fair game to accuse me in the media but not in an independent tribunal. The biggest threat to that constitutional democracy is the media who allow themselves to be used.

Below is an exchange between me and Isaacson:
6/27/2013 4:22 PM: James Evans: Please comment on the allegations that sascoc promised you payments and free trips to publish stories favourable to them.
6/27/2013 4:24 PM: David: Of course - Times Media can't afford to send their journalists on trips.
Isaacson has also made racist comments about me.

It is becoming clear that Isaacson, with the backing of Times Media, is hell bent on defaming me, with that deliberate intention, and will stop at nothing.

I will answer his allegations, but provide the answers to all the media so that they can assess Isaacson and Times Media when they run the story in the Sunday Times. You will see that Isaacson and Times Media ask the questions as a statement of fact. They are being used as puppets in a political battle, and are not questioning what is being fed to them or verifying their sources.

When a media tribunal is introduced in South Africa, it is this conduct which will have given rise to it.

In April 2012, I emailed Sunday Times journalist, Werner Swart regarding the irregular SASCOC/HSM media connection, the scandal around the Olympic kit and the rugby circus with the EP Kings.

He called me shortly after receiving the email, asking me to please not run with the story as they were very close to breaking it wide open.

They just needed two more bits of information re: a big SASCOC/volleyball trip into Africa and a clothing factory in Vereeniging.

Sedgars just happens to have a clothing factory in Vereeniging.

He also made mention that Mark Keohane had called him earlier to say he was being too hard on SASCOC.

Wish I could have heard that conversation.

Despite several more emails, that's the last I heard on the "big breaking story" from Werner Swart and there was no related SASCOC story from the Sunday Times?

When I found out that the SASCOC elections were 'rigged' at the end of 2012, I emailed and called the Sunday Times office and left messages for the then editor, Ray Hartley but got no reply.

Then from the Commonwealth Games in Glasgow (July 2014), I received an email from Isaacson re: Tubby Reddy's alleged affair.

> A story I'm trying to work, but am struggling with:
>
> Tubby is allegedly having an affair with his "PA". I've heard this from a few people, but I've seen their body language, and it doesn't seem to be straight-forward CEO-PA relationship. They're very touchy, touchy, etc.
>
> I don't normally worry about sexual relationships, etc, but I'm hearing that the PA is getting preferential treatment, such as getting a bigger per diem than she should on her job grade. She's also apparently staying at the Hilton; Gideon's PA is not even staying at the Hilton.
>
> Do you have a source who could help firm this up?
>
> Like I mentioned earlier, please keep this quiet for the moment. I will dig here if I get a chance.

Of course, I shared some of my information but there was never a follow up from Isaacson.

Was he just fishing?

Fast forward to the end of 2014 and Isaacson sends an email to two fellow sports journalists with a link to the anonymous, defamatory website?

> **From:** David Isaacson [mailto:IsaacsonD@thetimes.co.za]
> **Sent:** 04 December 2014 10:38 AM
> **To:** trevor@jacarandafm.com; ken@kenborland.com
> **Subject:** Joffe slander
>
> http://graemejoffe-exposed.com/?p=87

Then out comes another one of those pseudonym twitter accounts to discredit me and the **one** follower of @ExposedSA_Sport account just happens to be Isaacson's wife, Juliette Saunders.

Co-incidence?

There were numerous occasions that I would get calls and emails from journalists wanting more information on a story that I had broken.

But more often than not, their hands were tied by their media organisation or association's conflict of interests.

I had this email exchange with Mervyn Naidoo, a journalist from the Independent Media Group after asking him if he had used my information and run with the story on SASCOC and the Lottery.

Not yet. Some "hurdles"on my side. I won't say what. - Mervyn Naidoo

Sadly, it seems like the majority of the mainstream media have "hurdles" in exposing SASCOC and other sporting federations for what they really are …

You on the mark with that. Look forward to hearing from you. The sense I get is that if I'm able to raise something big as it breaks, it would be too compelling to ignore. - Mervyn Naidoo

Independent newspapers, owned by the ANC benefactor and beneficiary, Iqbal Surve are not so "independent" after all.

The SASCOC CEO has plenty of friends in the media.

On 21 October 2014, Keshni Ramsamy, a journalist with the East Coast Mail required some information.

I'm a reporter at a local publication in Tongaat also the former hometown of Mr Reddy. Graeme is it possible for you to send me his and/or Miss Tarr's contact details and possibly info on the person that has come out with these claims by latest 8:00 this morning (Tuesday) as I need to meet deadline by 9:30. Sorry I've given you such short notice my colleague did not inform me he dropped the article (citing Tubby as a close friend), [as he is the sports reporter of our newspaper] until an hour ago and now my editor told me to follow up the story. Would appreciate it immensly. (sic) - Keshni Ramsamy

The story died.

I sat for hours with City Press (Naspers) deputy sports editor, Daniel Mothowagae and good friend, Dan Retief (who was freelancing for the same paper).

Daniel was shocked at all the information I had accumulated and suggested we do a joint weekly column on the corruption in SA sport.

It never happened.

I sent evidence of blatant Lottery corruption to the Mail and Guardian (amaBhungane Investigative Unit) and corresponded with them for weeks.

They didn't run with it.

Mail & Guardian journalist, Luke Alfred called me in October 2014 to get an update on my SASCOC defamation case to pitch it as a story to the editor.

I suggested he get a comment as well from the SASCOC lawyer, Dario Milo. Milo was also a legal advisor for the Mail & Guardian.

A few weeks later, Luke told me the story was a no-go but had another pitch.

Graeme – Just wanted to keep you in the loop. Charles Leonard at the M&G hasn't responded to my Sascoc pitch. He's busy, I know. Hopefully, this isn't going to die a slow death. Will keep you posted because I'd like to do the story and you need the support. This is probably old news to you but I mentioned to a contact that Sascoc pay Highbury Safika Media (HSM) R6m per year for precious little. Highbury run their website but thats's basically Mark Etheridge] and do a little p.r. work on the side through Shane Keohane when events like the Commonwealth Games going round. Is all this worth R6m? I think not. - Luke Alfred

Again, there was no SASCOC story and no appetite to expose the R6m HSM deal.

Cricket journalists, Telford Vice and his wife, Firdose Moonda got a taste of being blacklisted in 2013.

They were stumped by Cricket South Africa (CSA) for stepping out of the crease with some hard hitting, factual stories.

CSA whipped away some of their journalistic privileges including, taking them off the email notification list for press conferences and player interviews. Just amateurish behavior from a so-called professional organization.

Cricket writers in this country are pretty much happy to toe the line. Utmost, you will get neutrality out of them, in terms of how they might cover a contentious story. But neutrality, objectivity, and fairness, are different concepts. You won't see too much of objectivity, or fairness. You will however, see neutrality, sometimes. And sometimes, even that goes out of the window, and it's just "Right CSA, what do you want us to say?" And that's what happens. - Telford Vice

"Toe the line" is why most of the big stories regarding corruption in SA sport, if any are broken by international media.

The Hansie Cronje scandal, the 2010 World Cup "diaspora" and another SA cricket match fixing saga are examples where SA media is failing in its obligations.

Thami Tsolekile named in South African cricket match-fixing investigation

- Former Test wicketkeeper alleged to have been paid in Ram Slam T20 scandal
- Highveld Lions captain has played three Tests for South Africa

The Guardian in London broke this story on 19 January 2016 when the doves had already been circling in SA from November the previous year.

When I heard that another Lions/Protea player was involved with Gulam Bodi (intermediary in the scandal) but had gone underground, I started to do some digging.

First, a quick look at the Lions website to see who their national players are that weren't involved in the current test series with England.

There were only four.

It dawned on me that Tsolekile hadn't played for a few weeks and all I could find was a story from 16 December 2015 saying he had a minor injury but should be fit within a week.

His twitter account had no activity since November.

Thami Tsolekile @TTsolekile10 · 3 Nov 2015
Unconditional love!

It was all a red flag.

Why hadn't the cricket journalists, especially those that cover the Lions beat not chased this story?

It should be in the blood of a journalist to expose the truth.

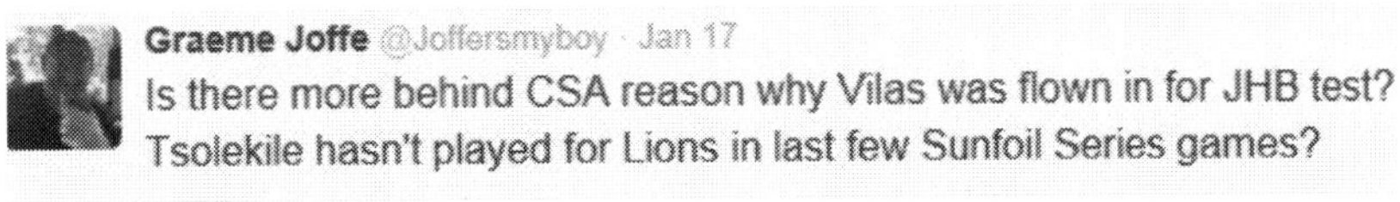
Graeme Joffe @Joffersmyboy · Jan 17
Is there more behind CSA reason why Vilas was flown in for JHB test?
Tsolekile hasn't played for Lions in last few Sunfoil Series games?

Two days later, the Guardian broke the story and Tsolekile's fate was sealed seven months later.

Former South Africa keeper Thami Tsolekile given 12-year corruption ban

The former Test wicketkeeper Thami Tsolekile has been banned for 12 years by Cricket South Africa following a Twenty20 corruption scandal. As revealed by the Guardian in January, Tsolekile was being investigated for allegedly receiving at least R75,000 (£4,200) to improperly influence an aspect of last year's Ram Slam competition. (The Guardian, 8 August 2016)

In January 2016, I was sharing some information with SA investigative news journalist, Angelique Serrao about the corruption in the Department of Sport and Recreation as well as this so-called Gauteng Olympic Bid.

She had just written this expose …

Gauteng Sport's R289m irregular expenditure

The Auditor-General's report into the Gauteng Department of Sport, Arts, Culture and Recreation - which saw the head of the department suspended for allegedly trying to bribe an official at the AG's office - has found there was R289 million in irregular expenditure over the 2014/15 financial year. (IOL, 8 December 2015)

R289 million in irregular expenditure?

Angelique Serrao

Just seems like there's no end until the reserves run out

4h

Yes. Unfortunately.

4h

Sorry you didn't have a media house to back you up. I do these stories all the time and never experienced what you did.

4h

Thanks Angelique, also too many media conflicts

and untouchables in SA sport protected right at the very top!

4h

Sports journalists often face that I have seen. In a way my job of interogating everyone is easier. Although I have had 1 or 2 threats.

4h

Angelique Serrao

The sudden investigation is very political. They wanted the MEC out

4h

All about money in the end and there's so much of it for Sport and Rec

4h

And it is a department that is seldom focussed on unlike education and health for instance and there is still corruption there!

4h

Yip, I dug into all of it as they also had irregular expenditure with fan parks for AFCON 2013 - they didn't have the rights first of all and then paid millions to "contractors" for them for use on one day. While R1.7 million owed to us (Township TV) just disappeared ....

4h

Sounds typical. Really pathetic. And they are exposed and still carry on

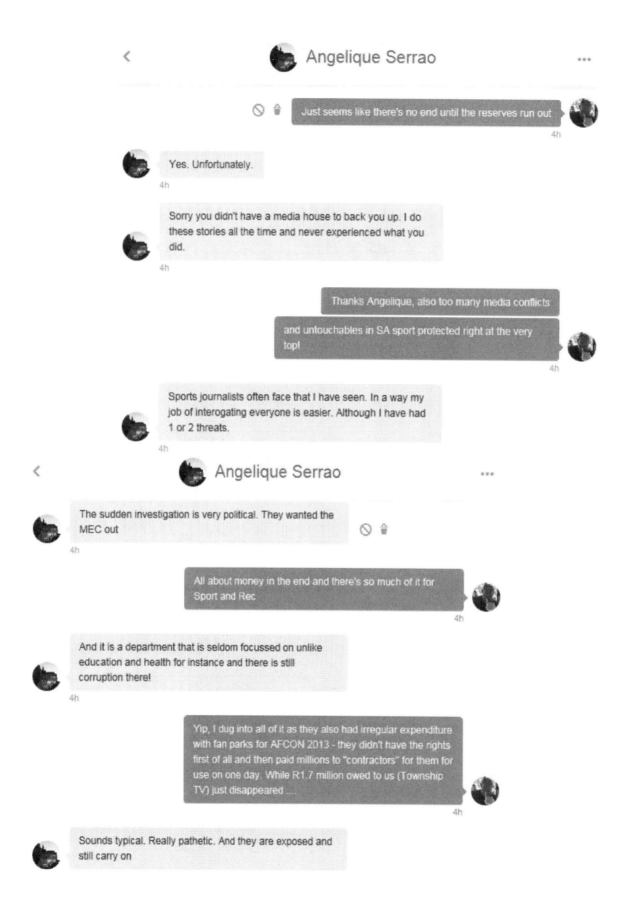

One of the most incestuous relationships in SA sport was that between the Sports Minister and SuperSport. SuperSport (SS) had a 'dedicated' TV camera for Fikile Mbalula. If the then Sports Minister sneezed, SS were there - if you get what I mean and we know how much he loves the camera and publicity.

Fikile Mbalula in his 2nd home at SuperSport

Mbalula loves to be seen and heard.

Hardly, a home Springbok rugby game went by without a live halftime 'political' catch up with Mbalula and how astute it was of SuperSport (Naspers) to employ the former spokesperson for the Sports Ministry, Graham Abrahams to look after the cosy relationship.

Television sports rights have long been an issue in SA and SuperSport had the right guy in their lens and on speed dial.

It's almost nauseating how often Mbalula was on SuperSport.

In most countries, few people would even know the name of their Sports Minister. In South Africa, they call him Fikile "Razmatazz" Mbalula and the twitter celebrity. Over 400 000 twitter followers when I last looked, before I was blocked.

But he's so full of hot air and travels around the world on tax-payers money, thinking he's actually a celebrity.

Just wish I had the photographs from when he was blind drunk and had to be carried out by his bodyguards from back stage after the Floyd Mayweather dinner at Emperors Palace in January 2014.

Mbalula is also a close ally with Imtiaz Patel, who was appointed as SuperSport CEO in 2005 and soccer boss, Irvin Khoza (PSL (whose daughter has a love child with President Zuma). That was Zuma's

20th child.

Almost enough for two football teams.

So, when I started to expose Abrahams in my Finweek (Naspers) column, it wasn't a few weeks later that my column was dropped.

The Acting editor of Finweek, Willem Kempen sent me this email.

> Hi Graeme, I have spoken to Jana Marais, who is to take over as editor on 1 October. We agreed that we do not want to continue with sports copy in Finweek.
>
> While I have been contemplating this possibility for a while, such a decision certainly had not been made before now. Where @samediawatch got the idea that you had been "dumped", I do not know. It certainly wasn't true when it was posted, and the decision is about the idea of having weekly sports copy in Finweek, not about you or your work.
>
> I sincerely regret that this decision has been hastened on because of a nameless comment on Twitter. I did not communicate the possibility of an end to our arrangement to you earlier because it was nothing more than a thought being considered. I also confirm that we have not used your sports copy for the past two weeks simply because we have had specific space constraints due to special features carried in the magazine.
>
> I had indeed been informed about a complaint from Graham Abrahams about a recent reference to him in your copy, but I assure you that is not relevant to this decision.

It was a nice little cover up and it didn't stop there with Naspers.

On the evening of 14 April 2015, I received an irate call from George Mazarakis, the executive producer of Carte Blanche.

Carte Blanche being an investigative news programme on M-Net (Naspers).

George was defiant after I had exchanged several emails with some of his staff, asking for confirmation and access to a PAIA (Promotion of Access to Information Act) document from the Department of Sport and Recreation and Sports Trust that I had spent several hours assisting them with back in February 2014.

They missed their second deadline – so now I am going to submit another version that forces their hand – ugh I hate timely crap! They're just stalling ... - (Sasha Schwendenwein, Researcher Carte Blanche, 21 May 2014)

I had a feeling this investigation wasn't going to go very far due to the conflict of interests.

Carte Blanche is part of the Naspers stable and not as independent as they claim to be.

The Sports Trust is a dirty conduit for the Department of Sport and Recreation. SuperSport is a partner of the Sports Trust.

During the next few months, several of my emails to Sasha to get an update on the PAIA went unanswered but I persisted and almost a year later ...

The department answered the questions and the journalist and producer that dealt with it was satisfied with their answers. - (Sasha Schwendenwein, 8 April 2015)

In other words, no PAIA? Please could I get a copy of the department's answers.

My managing editors have said I'd need a full motivation for what you need it for so that I can discuss it with Gerorge. - (Sasha Schwendenwein)

I was forcing Carte Blanche's hand and George wasn't liking it!

Why couldn't they hand over the answers from the Department of Sport and Recreation? Did they even exist?

There was a history with Carte Blanche in that I had spent hours and hours, assisting them with stories prior to this PAIA.

Stories on SA Rugby, the EP Kings, SASCOC, Lottery corruption and Oscar Pistorius.

I agreed to an interview on Oscar after the murder of Reeva and the Carte Blanche producer asked me to please jot down ten questions for Derek Watts (CB presenter/journalist) to ask the Sports Minister, who he was interviewing in Cape Town the same day.

The Minister was going to be very uncomfortable with my questions which included him to please expand on his statement that it was "a political decision" to send Oscar to the Olympic Games in London.

It was time to put him on the spot.

Bongani Bingwa (presenter/journalist), who was doing my interview, said to me quietly, "don't be surprised if Derek doesn't ask your questions."

That comment caught me a little off guard but made perfect sense as there seemed to be a 'block' on investigating and reporting all the other sports information I had previously given them.

When watching the Carte Blanche programme on Oscar, there was very little of Mbalula and I asked the producers if I could get a copy of his answers from the interview with Derek or if I could view the raw footage.

I'm still waiting!

The call with George turned into a heated exchange as he told me that 'none of my information could be verified by them' and that's why they haven't aired any of the sports corruption exposes.

Really?

What about the tip-off and information I gave them regarding the Cape Minstrels alleged Lottery fraud, which aired on one of the Carte Blanche programmes after my expose?

We didn't get the information from you. - George Mazarakis

Dario Milo who was representing SASCOC in my defamation case also just happens to be the Carte Blanche legal adviser.

Carte Blanche is totally editorially independent of SuperSport and we don't use any information from any source unless we can confirm its accuracy ourselves. Dario and I have not discussed your case. - George Mazarakis

The EP Kings and SASCOC information I gave to Carte Blanche blew up into explosive stories but still no expose.

Maybe, George and company are still trying to confirm the accuracy themselves!

SuperSport themselves, have a problem with conflict of interests.

Some senior staff members at SuperSport are on the "payroll" of TV production companies and other, who in turn use the 'payments' to get their recorded programmes or live events approved and commissioned for broadcast.

Clinton van der Berg is one of those staff members as he acts as a "PR" agent for Rodney Berman's Golden Gloves Boxing Promotions.

Hence, the struggle for other boxing promoters to get a foot in the ring with SuperSport.

Clinton responded on behalf of SuperSport:

The nature of our broadcast contracts is confidential – we do not disclose details to third parties. Our ratings are also confidential, although these may be acquired elsewhere. When staff perform duties beyond SuperSport, it is with the consent of the company. We certainly do entertain proposals from other promoters, who have in the recent past have included Eyethu Boxing Promotions, Rainbow Boxing Promotions, Xaba Boxing Promotions, Barnco Sports Productions, Main Events/Showpony (Mchunu's overseas fights), Real Steel Promotions, Thinus Strydom and Esthebeni.

I wonder if Clinton gets consent from SuperSport for all his trips to Monte Carlo for the big Golden Gloves events?

Did "executive producer," the late Gert Roets get consent for all those years he was on the Trickshot Productions payroll?

And I hear more of the big wigs at SuperSport are still double dipping.

It's freebie city!

The wheels of the "gravy bus" go round and round
8 August 2014

Here we go again.

I remember the hoo-ha in 2010 around the open top bus parade for Bafana Bafana before the World Cup.

A "victory parade" before you've even won a game?

Perhaps, it was based on the friendlies they won before the World Cup, which have since come to light as allegedly fixed.

The Bafana Bafana coach, Carlos Alberto Parreira didn't want the parade and coming from a country that knows how to parade, like Brazil, that was enough said.

But the Department of Sport and Recreation (SRSA) and Lead SA went ahead with the great, big fanfare.

Who was the parade really for? Was it the Bafana Bafana players, the other celebrities or the radio presenters on 94.7 and 702?

As one of the presenters then, I was embarrassed to say the least.

I remember hiding on the second bus and despite being the Commonwealth "knife and fork" champion for many years, I didn't need or want the recognition.

I didn't want to be part of the parade at all.

Lead SA is a Primedia initiative which is very conflicted.

The relationship between SRSA and Lead SA is a very "cosy" one and could explain why the Primedia news arm, EWN doesn't do investigative sports journalism.

Our EWN sports team is very small and seldom, if ever, focuses on investigative sports stories. As much as we'd love to, it's a capacity and seniority issue. - Katy Katapodis (Group Editor-In-Chief: EWN)

Somehow, I don't think the 'business relationships' would last very long if there was a full blown EWN expose on the Department of Sport and Recreation or SASCOC.

You are entitled to your views. However, we will not be dictated to on what to do and not to do. Lead SA will continue to promote national sport and encourage active citizenry. Lead SA is no big "money spinner"as you claim. - Yusuf Abramjee (Lead SA)

Then, it's another open top bus parade through the streets of Sandton to celebrate the success of our

Commonwealth Games athletes.

On parade: Fikile Mbalula and Mark Alexander

The cost of the parade could probably pay for 10 multi-purpose courts in less fortunate areas.

I'm sure the majority of our athletes would forgo this parade for the money to rather go into development and training.

Many top coaches are still working for nothing and some of the Commonwealth Games medallists have not been reimbursed for their OPEX travel expenses since May.

SASCOC's reply to them: "We don't know when you'll be paid."

How can this be right for our athletes that have done SA so proud to be continually fighting to get paid?

How many teams have to represent SA on self-funded tours?

Also, sport at grass root level in South Africa is at a cross roads.

Government and the respective sport Federations have promised South Africans for far too long now that fields and facilities will be built and maintained, equipment will be supplied and structured and well organised coaching programmes will be put in place. This has not materialised and what we are seeing at national level where the quota system is being reinforced is testimony to the failure of the current system and its administrators to implement systems that are well organised and structured that produce results. - Brad Bing (Sporting Chance)

But no, we will rather have another expensive parade through the streets of Sandton for a day of "active citizenry" to paper over the cracks of maladministration and corruption in SA sport.

Standing on top of the medal podium for any athlete has to be the ultimate recognition – it doesn't get much bigger.

Primedia radio presenters have been shouting from the rooftops about Team SA's golden performance in the build-up to the parade and one even labelled it as "SA's best Commonwealth Games ever".

SA got 40 medals in Glasgow, a far cry from our best ever performance.

We got 46 in 2002.

Australia got 137 medals (49 gold) at these Commonwealth Games. They were disappointed and it's back to work.

SA is blessed with incredible sportsmen and women.

If only, we had transparent administration with correct funding procedures, we would be getting at least 80 medals.

Instead, we celebrate 40 as if we've won the World Cup!

***

In February 2013, EWN sports reporter, Cindy Poluta asked me for some information and questions as they were going to investigate SASCOC.

I duly obliged but told her she'd probably be wasting her time as if EWN really wanted to investigate, it would be an assignment for the resourced news team.

Four months later, I asked Cindy if anything came of the SASCOC investigation.

Nope. Nothing came of it.

I knew my customers. There was no investigation!

EWN journalist, Mandy Wiener authored the book "Killing Kebble" which includes anecdotes on the corrupt, murdered mining magnate's relationship with among others, Fikile Mbalula.

Mbalula was then preparing to become (ANC) league president and spent much time at Kebble's home in the upmarket Johannesburg suburb of Atholl. Fikile was here often. He'd come here and in like an hour he'd finish a bottle of Johnny Walker Blue Label. Flat. Flat. They were like children in the house. They'd always be looking for something to eat and would drink only champagne ... They'd be fine when they arrived, but the more they drank, they'd become hooligans. I knew Fikile drank quite a bit. They behaved like absolute hooligans. - 'Killing Kebble'

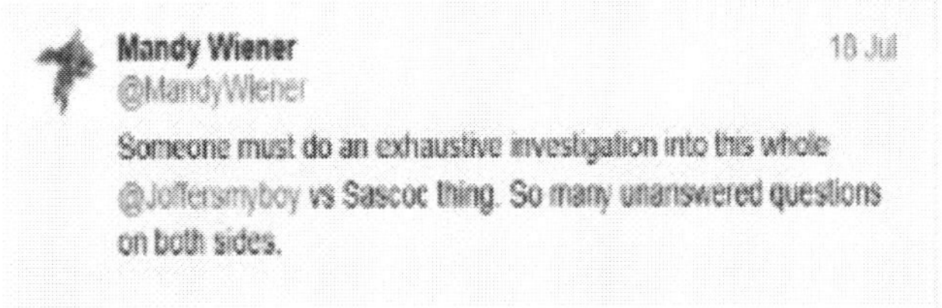

Mandy Wiener
@MandyWiener
18 Jul
Someone must do an exhaustive investigation into this whole @Joffersmyboy vs Sascoc thing. So many unanswered questions on both sides.

Emma Mansvelt
@EmmaMansvelt
Follow

@MandyWiener @Joffersmyboy How bad must things be when one of the top investigative journalists wants "someone" else to investigate a story?

7:57 AM - 18 Jul 2015

Mandy never asked me for my side!

On 12 July 2017, I received an email from EWN/Primedia journalist, Barry Bateman who was working on a story relating to Fikile Mbalula and the Sedgars company.

I need to understand the links between Mbalula, Sedgars and the department. What business does Sedgars or its owners do with the department? Can you help me?

Sure, I can help.

And Bateman's expose was a juicy one.

MBALULA'S R680K DUBAI TRIP BANKROLLED BY SPORTS SUPPLIER SEDGARS

At the time of the trip, Fikile Mbalula was Sports Minister, while the company that sponsored involved was doing business with the Sascoc. An Eyewitness News investigation has established that a sporting goods supplier allegedly paid at least R300,000 – and possibly as much as R680,000 – for a trip to Dubai by Minister Fikile Mbalula and his family last year. While working on the investigation, Bateman adds that Sedgars Sports technically didn't actually pay the money but was funded by a company called Reimon Uniform. "But I've managed to establish that Reimon Uniform is a shelf company and its account is used by Sedgars to facilitate funds to some entity." (Primedia)

After being exposed, Mbalula came up with the alibi that he couldn't afford the trip for R684,000 and he acquired a 'loan' from Sedgars owner, Yusuf Dockrat.

The Public Protector couldn't have had an easier case.

Mbalula was found to have violated the Executive Ethics Act and the constitution by asking a SASCOC supplier to help him pay for his family holiday to Dubai in 2016.

That's if it was even a loan? More like another big lie from Mbalula!

The post trip transactions in 2017 was some fancy footwork from the former Sports Minister and Sedgars …

5.1.13. On **3 February 2017**, an amount of **R150 000** in cash was delivered to Ms Jennifer Baylis' *Munlin Travel* offices on Mr Mbalula's behalf and on the same day, she took the money and deposited it into the bank account of *Munlin Travel*. On **6 February 2017**, two further cash deposits were made into the entity's bank account with an amount of **R75 000** deposited in Hatfield and another **R75 000** deposited in Brooklyn.

5.1.14. On **27 and 28 February 2017** amounts of **R100 000 and R200 000** respectively were deposited into *Munlin Travel* bank account from *Reimon Uniforms* Nedbank account.

(Public Protector report, December 2018)

I asked Bateman if he would also be investigating and reporting on the kickbacks received by SA Rugby president, Mark Alexander from Megapro/Primedia Sport paid through Sedgars?

Our communication dried up.

I guess it would have been a little too close to home to report on the kickbacks!

And these were contents of an email from a well-respected freelance journalist forwarded to me on 29 March 2016.

My attempts at Cape Talk (Primedia station) to resurrect Graeme's story of serious maladministration and apparent threats to his life (that forced him to the US) were stonewalled. Young editors telling me he's discredited. Makes me think of Spotlight and McCarthyism, driven by the multichoice/ naspers connection. As with stories I tried to do on China for George 'u have the right to know' Mazarakis - also directed by Naspers, which for obvious commercial reasons isn't keen. China's relative efforts at capture maybe isn't that far behind Gupta. Q: why did a delegation of 25 fly to NZ for last years commonwealth games host awarding ceremony, when SA was the only applicant city?

The SA sports media is seriously conflicted.

How many journalists have had trips, dinners and other paid for by the likes of SRSA, SASCOC, SA sporting federations and corporates involved in SA sports capture?

Primedia and Carte Blanche (M-Net/Multichoice) were behind the joint venture with the Oscar (Pistorius) Trial Channel.

The greedy people of Primedia and MultiChoice wanted this. Not me. To broadcast criminal trials is stupid. Counter-productive. Court rooms are open for the members of the public if they want to learn how court proceedings work. If they don't have the time they can read the transcript of court proceedings. From day one there were issues with this live broadcasting from the court room. South Africa's low class media imposed this media circus and not the consumers. Look at Dario Milo's (Media Lawyer of South Africa's low class media) tweets and his hash tags #OpenJustice how people try to defend stupidity. I hope this was the first and last criminal trial live on tv and radio (globally) in South Africa. – Hust (Comment Opinion, Mail & Guardian Oct 2014)

David O'Sullivan is a well-respected news and sports journalist in SA but even he was afraid to speak out.

Joffers, don't get me started on the Primedia arrogance, Lead SA etc, ect. My criticism of the attitude has already landed me in hot water, so I now keep my head down. I like my job too much. I understand where your'e coming from on that one. I know I'm not alone. Most of the 702 presenters think along the same lines as I do, but we're all protecting our jobs.- David O'Sullivan

Protecting our jobs?

There are some brave exceptions.

Robert Marawa and Neal Collins often stick their neck out and report without fear or favor.

Marawa, the most popular sports journalist in South Africa, threatened resignation from the SABC if his "room dividers" rugby expose radio programme was canned on request from Mbalula.

The Sports Minister had come under increasing fire on the programme and didn't like it.

The truth always hurts.

Collins himself has been on the receiving end of threats for his sharp criticism and investigations into SA football.

Getting those calls where nobody talks! But you know all about that! Been five years of strange calls and unknown visitors at the estate gate. Used to it now.

I can't comprehend that the public and the greater sporting men and woman have been duped into this autocratic nightmare. SASCOC is hell bent on bullying federations or individuals, running up exorbitant legal costs to obviously make it unviable to pursue, so they can hold onto this giant cash-cow.

The words corrupt, unethical and "player and referee"are intertwined with SASCOC when reading blogs on any site.

The Sports Ministry and SASCOC reward party loyalty, rather than ability and continue to close ranks against any who would speak up against them. They reward only those who sing their highest praises.

Just ask any of the Olympic athletes, who are brave enough to speak up.

Sunette Viljoen @Sunette_Viljoen · 12 Sep 2015
Sascoc has now officially "red-flagged" me for telling the truth about us having to beg them for every single cent. I stand by every word.
247
99
Sunette Viljoen @Sunette_Viljoen · Aug 24
Just to confirm: I am NOT speaking out only for myself but for the hundreds of other talented athletes who never get a cent of support.
247
249
LJ van Zyl @ljvanzyl · Aug 24
@Sunette_Viljoen I had to cell my @samsung gift phone just to help cover some costs for my Rio prep. So don't feel alone.
268
155

Dear Sunette ... I know from my own experience just how much courage it takes to speak up against the system. I know the consequence is to become an outcast, someone they say "Doesn't co-operate". Is ungrateful. Arrogant. Greedy. In my case, being critical was a career-limiting move. For others, it's worse - for instance, consider Graeme Joffe, a journalist who left South Africa because he faced death threats for trying to expose their incompetence and corruption. These people do not play nicely when threatened. - Ross Tucker

These administrators are guilty of the ultimate sporting foul: they play the man and not the ball!

Chapter 22: No Sochi, No Rio…

A 'mampara' is South African slang for a fool or buffoon.

The Sunday Times runs a weekly news column, 'Mampara of the Week' to name and shame a public figure. SASCOC CEO, Tubby Reddy got his turn in January 2012.

Mampara of the Week: Tubby Reddy

It's bad enough that a portly man named Tubby Reddy is in charge of SA Olympic Sports. But it stretches the bounds of credulity when Tubby and his pals jet off en masse to Innsbruck, Austria, where South Africa fielded just one athlete at the Winter Youth Olympics, alpine skier, Sive Speelman. (Sunday Times, 15 January 2012)

The news this weekend that the SA Sports Confederation and Olympic Committee (Sascoc) sent a five-man delegation to Austria to accompany the country's lone participant in the Winter Youth Olympics should not come as a surprise. It is not the first time nor will it be the last. For the Soccer World Cup in Korea and Japan in 2002 Safa sent about 50 officials, including their own security chief. This was more than double the playing squad. And there is more. Those Safa officials who decided not to go on the jaunt were given a cash handout. (EP Herald, 19 January 2012)

Two years later and these very same officials who piggybacked on Sive Speelman to Austria for a 'free holiday' denied the athlete a chance to become South Africa's first black Winter Olympian at the 2014 Games in Sochi.

What a story that would have been for the country!

Sive Speelman on his way to the First Ascent *SA National title at Tiffendell*

Former SA alpine skier, Alex Heath was Speelman's coach and mentor …

Sive is the ultimate Olympic story. He would be the first Black South African Winter Olympian. Sive comes from a humble background, and started skiing through a school ski programme at Tiffindell. Sive took to skiing, and quickly outshone his friends. Snow Sports South Africa identified his talent, and gave him the opportunities necessary to excel. Sive progressed well, and qualified for the Youth Olympics in Innsbruck 2012, where he did SA proud.

The next goal was Sochi. SASCOC, Snow Sports and the IOC signed a contract with IOC Solidarity, giving Sive the chance to train and race to qualify for Sochi. The purpose of the IOC Solidarity grant, is to get athletes to Sochi, and it states clearly that if an athletes qualify, he must go. In November, I found out that Sive was going to go to Donkerskool (initiation). I almost had a heart attack, as the stories of illness and death are common.

We organised a meeting with Sive, his father and the headmaster, where it was agreed that the initiation would be postponed until after Sochi. Sive wasn't overly impressed with the decision, as most of his friends were taking part in that ceremony. We left for Europe on the 2nd of December.

The night before, his best friend died in the initiation. Sive was not in a good place psychologically. In the 2nd race in Austria, his training partner crashed breaking her wrist. She had to fly home for surgery. When this happened, Sive fell ill. He was seen by doctors, and later taken to hospital. The chances of him making his points during December were severely hampered. We returned to South Africa late on Christmas eve.

I drove Sive home on Christmas day. A few days after Christmas, I tried contacting him, to find out when he would be available to go to Europe again, to qualify. I couldn't get hold of him. Eventually, I found out through someone in the community that he had been put into Donkerskool. I almost died. But, what could I do. I just had to say a few prayers.

A couple of days after he came out of initiation, we left for Europe again. It was the 9th of Jan. On the 10th, Tubby (Reddy) sent an e-mail to Snow Sports, stating that they have analysed Sive's performances and have decided that he will not be sent even if he manages to qualify. We were there, so we raced. And Sive qualified. On returning to SA we went to SASCOC House, out of courtesy. They did not have the time to talk to us, only sending one of their junior employees to let us know that they will make a decision tomorrow.

The tomorrow being yesterday, deadline day for the IOC to have entries in. During the morning, we received the e-mail that they sent to the IOC, saying that they were declining South Africa's participation. Not long afterwards, the Secretary General of the FIS (International Ski Federation) called Peter Pilz, SA Snow Sports President to ask why in the world we would be stupid enough to decline.

Anyway, there are endless phone calls going all over the world, and we are doing our best to undo this gross wrongdoing. - Alex Heath, former SA alpine skier

Sadly, the endless calls came to nothing.

SASCOC had come up with all sorts of their usual spin to shatter the Olympic dream of a yet another star athlete.

Speelman fails to meet selection criteria for Winter Olympic Games

Share 0 Tweet 0 Updated January 23, 2014

The South African Sports Confederation and Olympic Committee (SASCOC) has made a decision that Sive Speelman will not be participating in the 2014 Winter Olympics in Sochi, Russia.

This decision was made after recommendation from the High Performance Advisory Committee, which also includes the Chair of the Athletes Commission, who is elected specifically to ensure that the athletes rights and needs are protected, to the SASCOC Board who unanimously endorsed the recommendation received.

The decision was taken due to the following reasons:

In terms of the FIS (International Ski Federation) qualification system;

clause 3.1 specifically refers to an A qualification which relates to athletes who are ranked in the first 500 in the Olympic FIS points list; and
clause 3.2 specifically refers to the B qualification which makes provision that the National Olympic Committee, that is SASCOC, may, should they so desire, take up one allocated slot.

In this regard, Speelman has not met the minimum qualification of 140 in the Olympic FIS points list, having achieved 140,126. It is further noted that the athlete concerned is currently ranked 2, 290th in the world.

After due consideration and taking into account all the facts relating to the matter, SASCOC as the National Olympic Committee, unfortunately will not be delivering him to the Winter Olympic Games, Sochi 2014.

SASCOC will continue to adhere to its selection policies in order to ensure participation at the various multi-coded sports events is of the highest quality.

He did qualify. We have confirmation from the FIS that he qualified. The craziest thing is that we, as the National Federation, were never consulted during their decision making regarding his final participation. – Alex Heath

It would have also been very difficult to get minutes of the High Performance Advisory meeting as a source within confirmed there wasn't one. It was all done via e-mail.

Reddy had sent a letter out on the 10th of January, saying that even if he does qualify, they will not send him.

And then you have journalists aligned to SASCOC who would push the pitiful agenda with blatant misinformation.

Wesley Botton @wesbotton 2m

@123wee3rded @Joffersmyboy @This_Kate The B standard in winter sports doesn't actually exist, and there are free rides. Read the criteria

The B standard doesn't actually exist? Perhaps, Wesley Botton should have read the criteria before defending SASCOC.

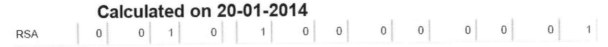

ALPINE QUOTA LIST FOR OLYMPIC GAMES 2014

Calculated on 20-01-2014

RSA	0	0	1	0	1	0	0	0	0	0	0	0	1

RSA 1 = B men, base men and quota (Sive Speelman)

2. ***NOCs' tasks:***

The NOCs perform the following tasks:

2.1 They constitute, organise and lead their respective delegations at the Olympic Games and at the regional, continental or world multi-sports competitions patronised by the IOC. They decide upon the entry of athletes proposed by their respective national federations. Such selection shall be based not only on the sports performance of an athlete but also on his ability to serve as an example to the sporting youth of his country. The NOCs must ensure that the entries proposed by the national federations comply in all respects with the provisions of the Olympic Charter.

Just like the Jamaican bobsled team of the 1988 Olympic Games in Calgary, Sive Speelman would have made the headlines, whether he finished first or last.

South Africa had missed a golden opportunity.

Sochi was the first Olympics since South Africa's readmission that the country's flag was not seen.

Sive Speelman's Olympic Dream
February 7, 2014 ·

"It was painful watching the Opening Ceremony. It would have been my proudest moment in sport to walk behind Sive carrying the flag. It was a long hard road to qualify, and he earned his place...what a tragedy." Alex Heath

Speelman wasn't the only South African skier to have his Olympic dreams shattered.

As Heath recounted, SASCOC board member, Hajera Kajee was responsible for this shameful action when she was chef de mission for the two member SA team that went to the Winter Olympics in Vancouver in 2010.

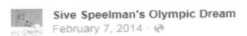

One particular skier was sent home during the 2010 games in Vancouver because he asked an Olympic driver who had been assigned to him to go and fetch his ski boots which he'd forgotten. A SASCOC official needed the driver at the same time to driver her to watch an event where no South Africans were competing. She sent him home for using a driver when she needed him! He now lives in Val d'Isere and

is trying to get an EC passport as he's been banned from competing for SA ever again. He was a very good alpine skier and a potential final 30 contender for Giant Slalom. We have video of the confrontation because he left his camera on while in the room with her. - Alex Heath

I saw the video and was horrified at how Kajee went off at this athlete. She should have been sent home!

It continues …

For the Youth Olympics in 2016, SASCOC got a Lottery grant of R4 million but they refused the athletes any funding for the qualification trip.

One parent paid for four athletes to train in Europe for three weeks.

NATIONAL LOTTERIES DISTRIBUTION TRUST FUNDS		
• Athlete Support – Olympic Preparation	**37 945 335**	17 026 647
• Athlete Support – Paralympic Preparation	**12 000 000**	3 500 000
• Commonwealth Games	**16 000 000**	7 500 000
• Durban 2022 Commonwealth Games Bid	**63 000 000**	-
• All Africa Games	-	1 100 000
• SA Sports awards	-	1 500 000
• Long Term Participant Development	**1 669 507**	1 859 704
• Region V Games	**4 000 000**	1 000 000
• General Assembly and Seminars	-	6 000 000
• African Youth Games	**6 000 000**	1 000 000
• Youth Olympic Games	**4 000 000**	-
	144 614 842	40 486 351

What did SASCOC pay for in the end for the Youth Olympics from a grant of R4 million?

Three airfares and some cheap clothing from Sedgars?

A nice little profit from the Lottery, which SASCOC would have spent on something else (a serious grant violation) whilst the athletes continue to suffer.

Field hockey always seems to get the short end of stick, if you'll excuse the pun when it comes to funding in SA sport.

There is a history with the old Olympic body, NOCSA (National Olympic Committee of South Africa) and it still seems as if there's a stigma attached.

It was one of the biggest selection controversies in SA sport when the men's hockey team qualified for Sydney 2000 Olympics but NOCSA president, Sam Ramsamy denied them the opportunity to compete saying the team was 'too white'.

Ramsamy tried to defend the decision but it only caused more harm and SA sent a baseball team to Sydney instead.

Mark Alexander was the president of SA Baseball at the time and the team, including a 44 year old were hopelessly out of their depth in Sydney.

They won one out of seven games with heavy losses to Cuba (16-0), USA (11-1), Italy (13-0), Japan (8-0) and South Korea (13-3).

Hockey players from that era still say it's still their biggest disappointment and who can blame them as most athletes may only get to one Olympic Games in their careers.

They qualified and should have gone – no ifs and buts and whatever Ramsamy would like to tell you.

In addition, a number of those players had given up day jobs and put their heart, soul and own money into qualification.

15 years on and little has changed.

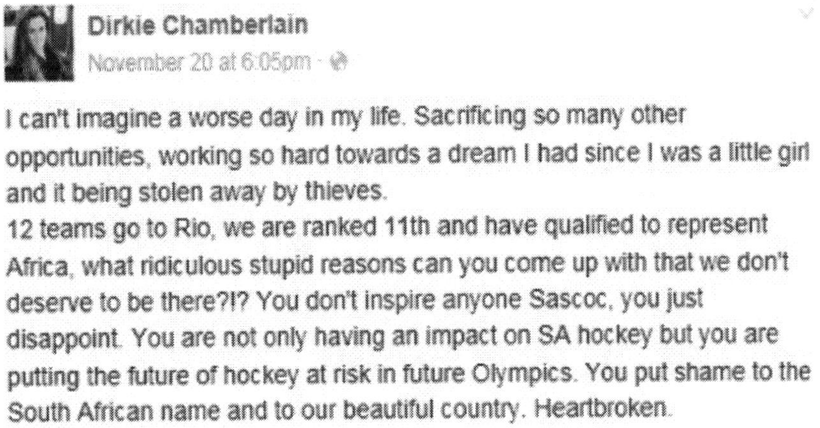
Dirkie Chamberlain
November 20 at 6:05pm ·

I can't imagine a worse day in my life. Sacrificing so many other opportunities, working so hard towards a dream I had since I was a little girl and it being stolen away by thieves.
12 teams go to Rio, we are ranked 11th and have qualified to represent Africa, what ridiculous stupid reasons can you come up with that we don't deserve to be there?!? You don't inspire anyone Sascoc, you just disappoint. You are not only having an impact on SA hockey but you are putting the future of hockey at risk in future Olympics. You put shame to the South African name and to our beautiful country. Heartbroken.

The International Hockey Federation (FIH) qualification for Rio 2016 gives an automatic berth to winners of the African continental championships.

South Africa won the men's and women's continental championship in November 2015 but what the players didn't know is that SASCOC had already made a decision in March that the teams would not be going to Rio.

Notice how the "and" is crossed out in the SASCOC reply to the International Hockey Federation's preliminary entry form below.

FIH

PRELIMINARY ENTRY FORM FOR
THE GAMES OF THE XXXI OLYMPIAD

To be returned to the FIH Lausanne Office on or before
18h00 (Central European Time) Monday 27 April 2015
E-Mail: martyn.gallivan@fih.ch
Fax: + 41 21 641 0607

We confirm that our team(s) WILL take part in the
Qualification Tournaments for ~~and~~
the Games of the XXXI Olympiad

Name: Tubby Reddy
Signature
Position: Chief Executive Officer / Sec. Gen
National Olympic Association: South Africa
Date: 23/03/2015

November 2015
Dear SASCOC

The excitement of qualifying for the Rio Olympics a few weeks ago was short lived and soon replaced with anxiousness as I was watching, listening and hoping on your decision.

The last few days – since that decision was made – felt surreal and the disappointment has just sunk in. The dream is gone...

This decision does not only affect us as players. I asked myself – numerous times – what does the Olympics really mean to me, my family and friends, but mostly our nation.

We all talk about sacrifices, but do we really comprehend the extent of these sacrifices? Passing fitness tests, picking up injuries and long flights are not sacrifices. It is part of what we do. The sacrifice is that we make the sport we love so much part of our lives, which has a direct influence on all the people that are close to us.

I realize that at the age of 32, I am probably close to the end of my career. I have proudly represented my country for the last 9 years. During these 9 years, I was blessed with the most beautiful daughter, now 5 years of age. I have sacrificed a lot of time away from my daughter, missing some of her big milestones that are precious moments for a first time dad, in order to play for my country. I did this with the hopes of her being proud of her dad one day and being able to learn from my career and my journey.

That hope has now been taken away. We are all well aware of the fact that hockey is not played professionally in South Africa. Since 2007, most of the sacrifices stretch further than just our families. I have seen a lot of sacrifices from other team mates too, including:

- *missed job opportunities*
- *-- playing in Europe / UK, making sure that we are improving our hockey skills by playing in top leagues whilst being paid peanuts*
- *delaying University degrees*
- *no personal leave*
- *pressure from employers*
- *pressure from loved ones.*

These sacrifices were taken in our stride, with our eyes on the big picture and life-long dream, not just for us but to give hope and be an inspiration to the rest of our nation and youth.

Our previous performance and participation at the 2012 London Olympics seem to have gone unnoticed.

Our team was a danger to big hockey nations. We came so close to success: we drew against Great Britain after being 2-1 up... GB ended up playing in the Bronze medal match; we beat a hockey playing nation, India, that is currently ranked 6th in the world. We also lost marginally with only one goal in the end against Spain, who was the 2008 Beijing Olympic silver medalist.

This served as great motivation to me personally and showed me that we still had some unfinished business at the 2016 Rio Games. We as players sacrificed another 4 years with the belief that we will have a successful Rio Games.

What gave us even more belief, was seeing teams like Brazil, Canada and Ireland qualifying. Don't get me wrong, I'm not taking anything away from these three teams because they deserve to be there, but history shows that we do beat them more often than not. It was also incredible to see how proud their countries were when they qualified – no talk of rankings, no talk of money. They were just so bloody proud of what their athletes have achieved.

I can continue giving reasons why we deserve and should go to the Olympic Games, but it will make no difference.

It is just very sad and difficult for me to you use the phrase "Proudly South African", when decisions get made and dreams get shattered in the boardroom and not on the playing field...

Regards,
Your goalkeeper – Rassie (Pieterse)

***

SASCOC used the criteria that continental qualification was not good enough.

Amazingly, it was good enough for Banyana Banyana (SA women's football team) to qualify through Africa but not for hockey and SASCOC president, Gideon Sam said:

There was an agreement entered into between both parties (in May 2015 he forgets to add). Hockey President Mike Du Plessis signed it. At the end of this quadrennial, if people feel this cannot be right, let us change it then.

No consideration for the three years of blood, sweat and tears that the players have already put into qualifying which is the minimum that it takes to be a successful Olympic athlete.

The hockey players should have sued SASCOC for every cent they've put in themselves to qualify for Olympics, only to be told in May they're not going. Also, for loss of revenue as the Olympic stage would have given a number of these players the chance to impress scouts from the International leagues.

In spite of the facts, SASCOC has opted to stick to the agreement that was signed, we have opted to "demystify" the said agreement. SA Hockey will now explore any other possible avenues that may be available to us to further advance the possibility of entry for the Rio Olympic Games. - Marissa Langeni. SA Hockey CEO

They did explore other avenues with the assistance of the FIH but there was no joy, even at the IOC level.

Has the IOC forgotten one of the mottos introduced by Pierre de Coubertin on the creation of the International Olympic Committee in 1894?

The most important thing is not to win but to take part.

SAHA MEDIA RELEASE

IOC reject SA Hockey appeal

The South African Hockey Association confirms that the SA Women and Men's Hockey teams will not be going to the Rio Olympic games, this after the IOC reviewed the International Hockey Federation's appeal submitted on behalf of SAHA and found in favour of the national olympic committee of South Africa – SASCOC.

"It is with great sadness that we receive this news," said SAHA CEO Marissa Langeni. "We accept and respect the final decision of the IOC. We will continue our efforts to lobby for the review of the general qualification criteria of SASCOC beyond the 2016 Olympic Games."

No doubt Ramsamy with his lofty position within the IOC had something to say again.

There will always be athletes that will seek greener pastures for the lure of the dollar but for many South African sportsmen and women, it's the lure of fairness and the opportunity just to compete at the highest level that sends them packing.

Hi Graeme

My history of Sam Ramsamy and his cronies goes way back to 1996 Olympics where he kept the men's hockey team (of which I was vice captain at the time) on tenterhooks as to whether we would be allowed to participate , based on his subjective decree, and the interference and maladministration of SA sports has just got visibly worse ever since.

I now live in Vancouver, Canada, I have a nephew that captains Derbyshire county (now as an Englishman) and I have another nephew playing Super Rugby (now as an Australian) .. my story is not unique for South African families I know but, as you alluded to, the drain in talent from SA will ultimately decimate the competitiveness of our national teams. I can only sympathize with how you feel ... I have been in Vancouver for 5 years so less attached nowadays, but did go to world cup hockey in The Hague last year and watched the SA teams underperform, again ... and as you know , not because of the lack of talent but because - to compete at international level (regardless of marquee sport or not) they need cash - which will not be allocated to them while the national administrators feed at the trough, and the federation's respective leaderships are their puppets.

I have read your blogs consistently since been here and admire your hard work and effort ... but can understand that it must often feel like pissing into the wind. I'm glad you are encouraged by the investigative journalists that pursued Armstrong and FIFA respectively.

Your point about 6 medals being an embarrassment to celebrate back in SA is well made but sadly greed and corruption clearly know no logic.

Now that you are back on this continent ... and if you ever head to Vancouver (7s rugby in 2016?), please look me up so we can cry into our collective beer for SA sport... it is very sad.

Cheers
Bodders (Gary Boddington)

***

Hockey people and sports fans vented but it all fell on deaf ears.

We respectfully submit that the baby (SASCOC) – given birth to in good faith by Sporting Federations in SA - has become a monster devouring its parents. It "made itself over" and adopted a "new Constitution" – elevated itself by its own bootstraps and assumed draconian powers to oppress its voluntary members and now wield the "power of God" over its creators. The new constitution of SASCOC affords them every possible right - that can possibly be dreamed up by any narcissist - to overrule, interfere, oppress and dictate and to prescribe to members – who lost any control over the baby. Members expressly have no right to criticize SASCOC – (hence the pseudonym) – explicitly no right to access any of SASCOC's internal bookkeeping records (except for no detailed audited statements if perhaps chosen to present at a meeting). Member Federations have no right to be reported to - or accounted to - on anything by SASCOC. To the contrary oppressed members must in fact now report TO SASCOC on absolutely everything - and may not take any decision about anything - unless first submitted to - and approved by SASCOC first. The new SASCOC constitution makes one cry - and really - no sane person could ever agree to - or subscribe to it. It is not worth it - to hand over one's whole existence to this child. We strongly suggest that someone somewhere in SAGF (SA Gymnastics Federation) take the trouble to READ the new SASCOC Constitution with open eyes (albeit it confusingly riddled with cosmetics and much complicated obscure complications). Please all we ever wanted to do is Sport – not to be chastised for "existing" – or to be turned into mindless minors unable to draw a breath – or beaten down by a sadist with a chip on its shoulder and an itch that could never be scratched to its satisfaction.

SASCOC have satisfied themselves and get caught out in lie after lie.

In a hard-hitting interview with Robert Marawa on MetroFM after the announcement of the SA Olympic team going to Rio, SASCOC president, Gideon Sam was a mouthful of teeth and lied like a rug.

Sam said: The SASCOC board and public didn't want him to go after he said he would fall on his sword if SA didn't get 10 medals in London.

LIE. SA got six and I don't remember the public or SASCOC getting to vote!

Sam said: No athlete had to pay out of their own pocket for Commonwealth Games in Glasgow.

LIE. I can name at least eight who were only reimbursed four months later after begging for their money.

Sam said: The SARU president is to blame for the Women's rugby 7s side not going to Rio.

Sam said: SASCOC sees all member federation's financials.

Really?

He was unaware that SARU have been getting R15 million per annum for the academies. He could only remember R30 odd million five years ago for the academies.

Sam said: The SA Hockey president is to blame for the hockey teams not going to Rio. The Olympic hockey agreement/criteria/qualification was only signed in May 2015.

LIE. Did he conveniently forget about the preliminary entry form SASCOC sent back to the FIH in March?

Sam said: SAFA were responsible for the accommodation issues with the women's football team in Rio?

LIE. No, they weren't. It is SASCOC's job!

Sam said: Tubby Reddy was no longer President of Volleyball SA as of 2015 because it was unconstitutional and said council only brought it up last year because there was a complaint.

LIE. It's been well documented for years that it's unconstitutional. Mokoena is suddenly the new president but not according to SASCOC website and not according to Volleyball SA letterhead in July 2016.

Volleyball South Africa

Share 0 Tweet 0 Updated: January 21, 201

Name: Mr. Anthony Mokoena

Designation: Vice President

Members of the executive committee:
Tubby Reddy (President), Anthony Mokoena (Vice president), Kriba Reddy (General secretary), Vinesh Maharaj (treasurer), Donovan Nair (Media Director), Deva Moodliar (Competitions Director),Michael Makhubela (Development Director) Size Vardhan (Technical Director), William Mojapela (Social Responsibility and Transformation)
Tel 011 402 1703 Fax: 011 4024397
www.volleyballsa.co.za

Sam said: Dr Kevin Subban (a volleyball mate of Reddy) is going to Rio as the Chief Medical Officer and with all the talk of transformation, SA has never had a black CMO at the Olympic Games!

Sam said: SASCOC board member and DA parliamentarian, Kobus Marais is lying if he said he didn't go to games in London. He did and is going to Rio.

Marais **LIED.**

Sam said: OPEX athletes are paid monthly for Olympic preparations

LIE. Is that why Sunette Viljoen hasn't got a cent since February?

Sam said: As for the recent R70 million bailout from the Lottery, we asked for R100m and only got R70m.

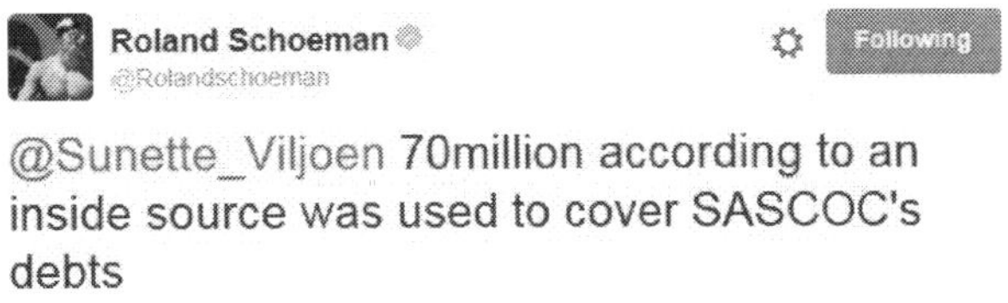

And to pay for non-working officials and family members to enjoy the Games ….

I have just returned from Rio where I was a technical official and I must admit, I learnt a lot and had a bit of exposure to the administrators on the SASCOC gravy train. Still in shock that the same faces are still there and how they lack the passion for sport yet are happy to fall asleep in the stands while our SA 7's men are playing! Disgusting. – Former SA Olympian

It is disgusting and it is also incomprehensible that any athlete, let alone, Olympic 400m gold medallist and world record holder, Wayde van Niekerk would receive treatment of this nature from SASCOC that almost saw him denied selection for Rio.

Wayde's agent, Peet van Zyl wrote on 17 September 2015 (sic) …

Hi Joffers

Well sir let's start with the following in reaction the sascoc statement on Wayde who is an Opex athlete.

Communication - sascoc stance is they refuse to communicate directly with any athlete, coach and agent on individual basis, they only communicate with federations (in our case which needless to say leads to even more chaos).. As an accredited IAAF Athlete Representative the world governing body of our sport recognizes me in my capacity as the persons responsible for managing the careers of top athletes (which is my profession and due to the nature of the business one has to be on top form and deliver at all times to ensure that the one career and chance your client has to reach his/her full potential is delivered upon) thus why I am refused to communicate with the sports body to work with them to ensure all parties are on the same page as to what the plan is for the year with specific goals for this year, which was Beijing 2015 , then longer term goals such as Rio 2016, London 2017 and even looking towards Tokyo 2020 is beyond my comprehension . I have the likes of Wayde van Niekerk , Akani Simbine ,

Ruswahl Samaai , Victor Hogan , Justine Palframan , Orazio Cremona and Rynardt van Rensburg as clients . All athletes with potential to make finals and even win medals at major events, which the likes of Ruswahl with Commonwealth Games bronze did, Akani and Justine with gold medals and Rynardt with his bronze medal at world student games did. Sascoc are not interested to hear from you what you plan for these kids and what are put in place through our own initiatives and not ASA to help these kids achieve.

Communication - back to Wayde . I was sitting in a skype conversation (which sascoc did not know about) between Wayde , his coach Ans Botha and the appointed high performance coach , Frank Dick and the person in charge of Opex , Yoliswa Lumka (whom I heard have resigned and by the way she was axed from Maties athletics club due to her inability to perform her duties but then got the job to have the responsibility of taking care of SA top sports persons) . There were various topics of discussion :

·

> *1. Wayde's preparation for Beijing - to which a full report and feedback were given to sascoc , but it was evident that the previous months progress reports that were submitted were not read and assessed , clear example to proof the test was to submit same reports just change the dates*
>
> *2. Frank Dick strongly suggested Wayde and other world championship finalists of team SA in Beijing should not compete in Brazzaville which we supported as it was a risk so close to Rio with fatigue the main concern after a long season but also things like Ebola , yellow fever etc*
>
> *3. Frank Dick also suggested Wayde does not do any races post Beijing, between myself , coach Ans Botha and Wayde we did not agree , one we had planned to run a specified amount of races prior to Beijing to enable Wayde to be fresh and in best possible shape going into Beijing . In exchange we have negotiated with sponsors ie adidas he will commit to the amount of DL races as per his contract required post Beijing which also served the purpose of allowing Wayde to earn substantial income based on his success in Beijing . I have sent the required info to ASA as they are the federation who supposedly communicate on our behalf with SASCOC to inform them of our plans (emails to follow to proof this)*
>
> *I also put it to the federation that the likes of Akani Simbine and Ruswahl Samaai and my decathlon athlete Willem Coertzen who does not receive a cent from SASCOC or ASA have invites to DL meetings and the Decastar final of decathlon equivalent of DL final, clashing with Brazzaville and being a professional athletes this is how they earn their living . If either SASCOC or ASA are willing to compensate these athletes in exchange to compete in Brazzaville we are more than willing to compete . Needless to say no reply was received accept a very interesting email from Pieter de Jager at ASA (which I will also include)*

Travel - when an athlete is on OPEX the athlete has to submit a list of meetings where he will compete . This was submitted well in advance prior to Wayde's 1st race in Birmingham DL early June . When Wayde asked for his flight ticket to be issued in time to confirm his participation with the meeting director in Birmingham SASCOC refused to issue the ticket . Due to them not communicating with me I asked Wayde's stepdad Steven Swarts to step in on behalf of Wayde and ask when this ticket will be issued . They gave Steven the run around and even then sent email that they now refuse to deal with him as well . I even took it upon myself to speak with Gideon Sam who took my call and looked into the matter for me. The outcome was that this wonderful lady at Opex Yoliswa reckoned Wayde had to undergo a medical first to proof his fitness before issuing his flight ticket (this all 3 days before the Birmingham DL) Apparently according to Yoliswa Wayde was injured as per his coach info supplied (this was also established to be a lie on her side during this self same Skype call between Wayde , Ans Botha , Frank Dick and Yoliswa where she had to admit reluctantly she was in the wrong) A week prior to this debacle Wayde competed in Cape Town at the new athletics stadium in a 200m setting a quality time of 20,56 sec in the rain . So how can he be injured doing this ? Opex personnel did not even bother to confirm his status but rather go on hearsay and make life very uncomfortable for the athlete and his coach

Travel - so with Wayde's ticket issued by Fly Africa travel who also belongs to family of SASCOC personnel . what was very interesting to note on the flight ticket was the return date , 15 Sept 2015 . which means Wayde is only expected back on 16th Sept which in itself shows he will not make it in time for Brazzaville . I changed Wayde's return ticket to 13th Sept which we had to pay for ourselves and accordingly did so Needless to say neither sascoc or fedetaion bothered to enquire from their own travel agent what the travel plans are of Wayde seen as they refuse to talk to me

Media Hype on public welcome to be given to Wayde - Joffers to be quite honest Wayde preferred to arrive back in SA with his close family members , supporters from Grey high school , training mates , university of FS etc to welcome him back as the hero he is in Bloem and not have his achievements being made a political platform as to the success be attributed to ASA or SASCOC as the ones behind him but rather his family , his coach and his university hence the low key arrival , but again , the travel agent of SASCOC knew exactly when Wayde was going to arrive back in SA

Allocation of SASCOC OPEX contracts to athletes - not quite sure what is used as criteria to give OPEX contracts . I have sent to both SASCOC and ASA requests to ask for the likes of Akani Simbine (the most promising sprinter in SA history which he has already proven with his 9,97 sec) who I can also add has been courted by the likes of coach Glenn Mills from Jamaica (Bolt and Blake's coach), Lance Braumann (Tyson Gay's former coach) Matt Kane (US collegiate coach) who all believe he can run a 9,80 sec 100m , Ruswahl Samaai , who last year in his first international year won bronze medal at Commonwealth Games , this year leapt to 8,38m at sea level and is under top 10 in the world rankings and Justine Palframan as one of the a handful of female track stars (she is also been to Jamaica to have stints with coach Mills who is of opinion she can with real development run a 50 sec 400m) to be given support by SASCOC . Needless to say we never received any feedback let alone a cent of support ... Do you blame these guys for then rather going to compete on the circuit where they can earn a substantial income to provide for their families. Same goes for Willem Coertzen who is a married man had great results on the decathlon circuit this year and provides for his family with funds he earns from applying his talent as decathlete . Another example , Victor Hogan in discus throw , was on OPEX in 2013 , had a great world champs in Moscow , loss of form and injuries in 2014 and gets axed from OPEX so what are the grounds and basis and criteria for awarding OPEX contracts ?

Keep up the good work!
Peet

When it comes to travel, SASCOC has an 'exclusive partnership' with a company, owned by their good friend, Nazeer Camaroodeen.

Fli-Afrika offers fully inclusive packages to many of the world's major events, including the Olympic Games, FIFA World Cup, Rugby World Cup, Formula 1 Grand Prix, FA Cup Final, Wimbledon and

Golfing Championships. The aim is to ensure that the traveller derives the most from these remarkable occasions.

What's remarkable is that the SASCOC deal with Fli-Afrika has never gone to tender and any potential competitors are frowned upon.

Loving the columns. Please check out "Fli Afrika". If you think SASCOC is rotten you have no idea how far this cancer has grown. Basically they own the travel agency which has exclusive rights for all Olympic tickets etc. as well as OPEX having to use them. I got taken out big time for trying to arrange a tour for our supporters around Beijing because I didn't use them ...

And the SA supporters were left out in the cold for the Winter Olympics in Sochi as well.

There will be no South African presence, on and off the field, at the Winter Olympic games in Sochi, Russia. This is because not only did the South African Sports Confederation and Olympic Committee (Sascoc) decide not to send a team to compete at the winter games, the Olympic body has also prevented hundreds of other South Africans from travelling to Russia to watch the Olympics live. There were over 400 South Africans who were keen to attend the winter Olympics as spectators but could not get hold of any tickets because SASCOC and its appointed operator Fli-Afrika failed to meet the deadline they were given by Olympic organisers to apply for tickets for the Winter games. - (Weekend Argus, 8 February 2014)

More to ponder …

Since the Ramsamy/NOCSA days, Fli Afrika has been awarded the rights to run the Olympic hospitality programme i.e. they sell packages to supporters for air tickets, event tickets and accommodation. This is really the only way a South African can get to the Olympics given the crack down on black market and re-selling processes. It would be interesting to see if there has ever been an open tender for this. From memory, not.

A little birdie tells me the Sascoc board members pay cash for airline tickets? Why? Trying to hide transactions?

The Fli-Afrika website had glowing references from the likes of Raymond Hack, Imtiaz Patel and Dr Irvin Khoza.

A PSL club, Orlando Pirates holding a press conference at the offices of Fli-Afrika?

Gallo Images - TL_937688.JPG - irvin khoza orlando pirates fli afrika
www.galloimages.co.za/image/irvin-khoza-orlando-pirates-**fli-afrika**/1224641/1
31 Jan 2012 - JOHANNESBURG, SOUTH AFRICA - JANUARY 31, Irvin Khoza during the Orlando Pirates press conference at the **Fli Afrika** Office in ...

(google)

Is Khoza perhaps a silent 'shareholder' in Fli-Afrika and who in SASCOC benefits from this relationship?

Khoza pal in World Cup row

A bruising battle over the sale of World Cup packages is brewing between the South Africa Football Association (Safa) and a company called Fli-Afrika Travel, which is owned by a friend of Irvin Khoza, Nazeer Camaroodien. According to Safa chief executive Leslie Sedibe, at the centre of the dispute is an allegation by Fli-Afrika that it entered into an agreement with Safa that compels the football mother body to buy tickets on behalf of the tour operator from Fifa ...The new Safa executive, headed by Kirsten Nematandani, is not happy with the deal, said to have been signed by the previous leadership of Molefi Oliphant and former chief executive officer Raymond Hack with the sports tour operator. (Mail & Guardian,1 April 2010)

Eight years later and the 'deal" came back to bite South African football.

SAFA suffers costly court blows

Fli-Afrika Travel was awarded on appeal in the Johannesburg High Court an amount of approximately R14 million from SAFA in connection with an unfulfilled agreement relating to the 2010 Socer World Cup in South Africa - with costs set to swell the amount to close to R20 million. (sport24, 30 August 2018)

And a top volleyball player was suspended by a SASCOC legal committee chaired by Raymond Hack at the offices of Fli-Afrika.

Why would a SASCOC legal committee convene at Fli-Afrika offices?

What's the link between SASCOC (Reddy), Khoza, Hack, Patel and Fli-Afrika?

Obviously more than meets the eye!

Interesting how a lot of the same names keep popping up. It's a powerful group of untouchable people controlling sport in South Africa.

They're 'flying' alright!

Hack was the SAFA CEO until he resigned in January 2010. He said he wasn't pushed but many would beg to differ.

After all, he was a strong ally of Khoza who lost out on a bid to become SAFA president to Kirsten Nematandani in September of the previous year. Nemantandani and Hack didn't see eye to eye.

We're well rid of Raymond Hack ...

While in office, Hack was a character cut from a strange cloth, seemingly getting his mojo from going against wave after wave of public opinion. When the pressures of the job, which subjects the incumbent to so much public scrutiny, got to him, you could count on him to dream up some ridiculous excuses that bordered on the incredible. (Timeslive, 11 January 2010)

It's been alleged for years that Hack has been moving funds offshore for Khoza and with all his job titles, he is often in Switzerland.

And in 2017, he was appointed as chairman of FIFA's Players Status Committee.

FIFA, funds and Switzerland? Makes you wonder!

Hack's company directorships are also of an interesting variety and include Soccer City, the stadium, which was built in Johannesburg for the 2010 FIFA World Cup.

His law firm, Rapeport Incorporated was SASCOC's go to for any legal matters and questions around the relationship were not answered very enthusiastically in 2015.

Your request is quite strange and "out of the blue"so to speak. I'm sure you'd agree that it's necessary to find out why you want the information requested and in what capacity you ask for same. This is tantamount to a stranger knocking on my door and asking for the information, which is certainly not in the public domain. Please let me know what this is all about so that I can properly consider your request. As to the amount of our legal bill to SASCOC for the last financial year, this information is confidential and can only be released by SASCOC, so I would suggest you communicate with SASCOC in this regard. - Lawrence Sacke, Rapeport Incorporated

But the million-dollar question is what did Hack know in connection with South Africa's bribe to host the 2010 FIFA World Cup?

He had to have known something.

According to the US indictment, two South African officials were implicated in the $10 million bribe of Caribbean football head Jack Warner, who is the subject of an arrest warrant himself, and a second suspect thought to be his colleague Chuck Blazer ... Given the information revealed in the indictment, the pool of potential suspects is small. The Mail & Guardian narrows it down to just eight people: 2010 bid chief executive (and new Port Elizabeth mayor) Danny Jordaan, 2010 bid chairman and Orlando Pirates boss Irvin Khoza, Naspers chairperson Koos Bekker, sports promoter Selwyn Nathan, lawyer and ENSafrica chairperson Michael Katz, former South African Football Association (Safa) chief executive Raymond Hack, Kaizer Chiefs chairperson Kaizer Motaung and former Safa president Molefi Oliphant. (Daily Maverick, 3 June 2015)

Now Hack is one of FIFA!

Chapter 23: The Political Mix

South Africa was never able to select their strongest teams during Apartheid as non-white players were marginalized.Twenty years into the country's democracy, it's now reverse discrimination.

The buzz word is 'transformation'.

There are official and unofficial quota systems, restricting the number of white players in teams, even at provincial junior school level.

SOUTH AFRICA SCHOOLS ATHLETICS

GENERAL SECRETARY: PEPPI OLEVANO
Tel: ++27 (0)57- 573 1162
Fax: ++27 (0)57- 573 2265
Cell: ++27 (0)82- 550 7032
E-Mail: peppi.olevano@uvss.co.za

S.A. SCHOOLS ATHLETICS
PO BOX 202, HENNENMAN, 9445.
SOUTH AFRICA.
Web Site: http://www.schoolathletics.info

04 February 2019

ATTENTION: All SASA Provinces

In terms of the *TRANSFORMATION OF SCHOOLS ATHLETICS* on all levels of participation the following Quota System must be implemented with immediate effect to reflect the Demographics of South Africa:

A minimum of 40% from the Previous Disadvantaged Communities for all SASA Teams on all levels of Competition, with specific emphases to Girls Athletes.
At least 1 athlete per Event and Age Group must be from the previous disadvantaged community.
Provinces must not exceed the Maximum Number of Athletes allocated as per the National Schools Championships Competition Manual for 2019.

High Schools Athletics Quota System:
A maximum of 3 athletes per event on merit and must qualify; At least 1 athlete per event must be from the previous disadvantaged community which can be the 4th athlete in the event (no qualifying standard needed for this athlete) - A maximum of 4 athletes per event per Province inclusive of the Disadvantaged athlete. In case of 2 or 3 athletes in the event, 1(one) of them must be from the previous Disadvantaged Community.

Primary Schools Athletics Quota System:
A maximum of 2 athletes per event on merit and must qualify; At least 1 athlete per event must be from the previous disadvantaged community which can be the 3th athlete in the event (no qualifying standard needed for this athlete). A maximum of 3 athletes per event per province inclusive of the Disadvantaged athlete. In case of 2 or 3 athletes in the event, 1(one) of them must be from the previous Disadvantaged Community.

We trust you will find this in order.

Peppi Olevano
(General Secretary SA Schools Athletics)

How do you explain to a 9-year-old that they can't compete because of a quota system?

These quotas are a direct result of corrupt sports administrators who don't know how to and are too lazy to implement grass roots development programs!

Politics and sport have never been a good mix.

Sadly, it's a given that politics will always play a destructable role in SA sport.

27 April 2014

Dear Mr. Mbalula

I notice you've had your busiest work month since you took office as Minister of Sports back in 2010.

You've been on the run this April, opening new sports facilities in De Doorns and Limpopo, handing over cheques to winning athletes and re-igniting the good old debate about quotas and transformation in SA sport.

How timely with the national elections just around the corner.

I guess this tweet says it all about your electioneering campaign.

ANC @ANCwcape Apr 25

Handover of sports facilities in De Doorns by Minister Mbalula at 11h00.. ANC Government working for you.. #VoteANC

Did you also have time to hand out food parcels and mattresses to the people of De Doorns?

The fact of the matter is SA sport is in dire straits and you can't fool the sporting public with all your media spin and PR.

From the last six Olympic Games, SA has brought home a total of just 25 medals.

Few can argue we are one of the perennial under achievers on the Olympic stage for what we have in talent, facilities and finance.

The reason why we are under achieving is quite simple: Cronyism, failed administration and abuse of funds.

Between the Department of Sport and Recreation, SASCOC, the Sports Trust and the Lottery, you have found a way to manipulate the system.

There is no accountability and SA sport is being milked dry.

The Lotto is your "go to bank" and it's no surprise that there are major contradictions in grants between the Lotto distribution agency and the sporting federations.

Who is really benefitting?

Even the Lottery has now gone the ostrich route (head buried in the sand) as the questions become too tough to answer.

In 2011, you debated quotas and transformation – why then in 2012, did you not make a stand for Simon Magakwe to be included in the SA Olympic team and in 2014 for Sive Speelman to go to the Winter Olympics? Magakwe could have lined up against Usain Bolt and Speelman would have been our first black Olympic skier.

How big would that have been for SA sport and for youngsters to look up to? You don't need quotas – these guys are good enough on merit.

But instead, you piggy backed onto Oscar Pistorius for the London Olympics, saying quote: It's not really about the athlete; it is a political decision that has been taken."

Why are you preaching transformation and quotas again in 2014?

Electioneering perhaps?

I see you were also very quick to jump on the 'Magakwe bandwagon' when he broke the SA 100m record earlier this month.

"We are going to take care of him so that he does not have to worry about other things except to run great times. We will put him on the Opex programme."

I guess better late than never but why wasn't Magakwe already on the Opex programme?

Perhaps we can have another dinner to debate it.

Ernst van Dyk is also now one of your 'favorite' SA athletes after he won his 10th Boston Marathon title.

But what about his nine previous wins and did you know that van Dyk almost lost his Opex funding in 2013 for legitimately being critical of the SASCOC elections?

Our athletes are being silenced and the majority of the federations just go with the flow in fear of losing their funding.

It's a web that is destroying SA sport.

If you really want a good story to tell, then please make sure that after these elections that SA has a Sports Minister who knows about sport and not one who says:

"If Ntini (Makaya) wasn't brought to the fore & fast-tracked by Steve Tshwete, he wouldn't be the best spin bowler that we have."

Your over is up Mr Mbalula.

You've "spun" us a yarn since 2010 and spent more on awards, dinners, parties and travel than your two predecessors combined.

The "razzmatazz" needs to go and SA sport needs to be cleaned up once and for all.

***

I agree 100% with the fact that 'siphoning off' of funds hinders transformation. But I also think that the 'transformation at all costs and against all logic and the law' is a 2nd way in which nonsensical policies and unfounded political correctness under the guise of good governance are killing SA sport. My concern with this 2nd element is that SA government and the politicians who love to get screen time on the back of these unsophisticated voter-friendly soundbites do not realise the risks they are posing to SA federations and the athletes within the international sports politics community: Lack of money will keep our athletes out of competitions, just as much as potential bans from international competitions because our government is flouting international sports law (Olympic Charter principles etc.) with their rubbish policies. Let's not forget - it was local policies and laws very much like these which brought about the international sports boycott against apartheid sport. – AM Louw

The ANC and Mbalula in particular - continuously cry out about racism in sport, but it's them who are perpetuating that attitude of course kids around the age of 10 are going to resent being dropped from a side because they're not black! Do you then honestly believe those same kids are going to welcome those self-same black players as their friends of course not! I've seen mixed provincial teams, SA representative teams, and I've seen how black and white embrace each other in times of success and glory they can do it if they're left to their own devices - they sure as hell don't need some racist ANC politician or sports administrator interfering! – Adrian Stevens

Transformation's achilles heel. Where did FIFA millions go?
10 June 2016

It took almost an hour for any common sense to prevail in the 702 sports transformation debate on Tuesday afternoon.

Sports Minister, Fikile Mbalula was given the platform for the first twenty minutes to do his usual politicking and to try and explain his reasons for suspending certain federations from hosting international events due to a lack of transformation.

That was followed by some bizarre comments from an out of touch, Willie Basson who has made a living from transformation charters and reports.

Then jackpot …

The CEO of the Gauteng Cricket Board, Greg Fredericks said we need to dig deeper as to why there is a lack of transformation and why a school in Sandton has more cricket facilities than all the township schools in Gauteng combined.

Boom, he hit two nails on the head right there.

No facilities equal no opportunity, which equals no growth of talent, which equals a lack of transformation.

Fredericks also took offence to a couple of Basson's comments, which included the reference to one group for Blacks, Coloureds and Indians when it comes to transformation.

Mbalula got hot under the collar and jumped onto Fredericks for 'grandstanding and playing the man, not the ball'.

How ironic from the Razmatazz!

Mbalula then put his foot in his mouth as he talked about the hundreds, yes hundreds of cricket facilities that Dr. Bacher and company had built in Soweto after the 2003 World Cup in SA but they are now dilapidated due to lack of maintenance.

Mbalula blamed the federations for this state of disrepair but excused government from any accountability.

It would be interesting to see the map for these hundreds of cricket facilities.

But why do we only hear about this now and why hasn't Dr. Bacher or Cricket SA had to answer for it?

Perhaps, because Mbalula and company do exactly the same with the Sports Trust. They drop off multi-purpose courts in townships with no coaches and no maintenance plan and they call it 'grass roots development'.

Quick and easy grandstanding!

Fredericks is on the money.

You need facilities with proper structures (coaching and maintenance) in the townships if you want to see real transformation.

Why is there this lack of structure?

The second nail …

Many of SA's 'high ranking' sports administrators and officials are making money without even having to earn it.

If you can sit on your jack and do nothing and get millions from the National Lottery through misappropriation of funds and false applications (with friends in the distribution agencies) – why would you want to be on a dusty field coaching, doing maintenance or trying to make a difference?

The gross corruption in SA sport starts with the Lottery and these are also largely funds that should be going to grass roots development, Olympic athletes and charities.

There are so many good coaches, officials and former players who would love to get involved but so much of this type funding goes to feed the greed.

Speaking of greed, has anyone seen how the FIFA millions from the 2010 World Cup trust are being allocated to SA football?

SA's good friend and former FIFA secretary-general, Jerome Valcke (who has been banned from football for corruption related activities) and SAFA president, Danny Jordaan were two of the signatories on the account.

Is there another 'diaspora?'

Mbalula said to 702 radio show host, Xolani Gwala 'not to speak as if we don't have facilities at all, like the DRC.'

Oops, he did it again.

Then added that he didn't go for the 'joogular' with the suspensions of the federations!

Basson also made a howler, using SA Bowls as an example, saying they had a real problem because the average age of the players was 74.

Not sure of the transformation relevance here and not to mention, the SA Bowls team won seven medals at the Commonwealth Games in Glasgow.

A top sports administrator was seeking to return to South Africa in 2015 but was warned against it.

*When I was back in May, a senior figure in sport told me to stay away from sport in SA as it is very corrupt " stay the f**k out of sport" were the words. It is disappointing that my experience is similar in international sport where corruption and some dubious practices occur and we wonder why national sports operate similarly.*

Finally, if you want a real debate on transformation in SA sport, do it on a national radio station and not on a station that isn't conflicted as a Sports Ministry/SASCOC beneficiary.

Hope Primedia didn't get paid to host the transformation debate!

***

The corruption and political interference and corruption is at all levels of SA sport and I would have thought the strongest opposition party in government, the Democratic Alliance (DA) would have been interested in trying to change this?

Helen Zille was the leader of the party at the time but the DA was conflicted with their own parliamentarian, Kobus Marais sitting on the SASCOC finance committee.

I wasn't expecting a positive response from Zille and sure enough I didn't get one.

I have been into this in some depth with the various DA people who have investigated. Apparently, you have reported this to the PP (Public Protector), and other institutions; Let us wait for the verdict. Also, if there is a criminal case, please lay a charge at a police station; if there is validity in it, the police will lay a charge, and once Kobus has pleaded, I will be in a position to take action, but not before. If there is a case to be made he must answer; but I can't make him answer to a case that has not been motivated or upheld.- Helen Zille

The DA are quick to run to the Public Protector and lay charges at a police station to expose members from the ruling ANC party but not when one of their own runs foul.

I had already caught the DA and Marais in a cover up when the latter went to Corfu as SA's Powerboating representative.

3 lies and you're out?
24 October 2012

In twitter terms, it was called #thatakwardmoment.

SASCOC President, Gideon Sam admitted to lying while standing before the parliamentary portfolio committee on sports and recreation this week, while asking for R400 million to prepare our Olympic athletes for Rio 2016.

The Mail and Guardian reported that when Mr Sam was asked about his recent comments that "SASCOC was on a sound financial footing" – the reply was:

> *No, we don't have cash. We are battling. It's just that we didn't want to create a scene at the airport. It's not good for our athletes and it's not good for the country. When you get to that place, you sort of ... you know, I mean you are all politicians. Siyazigquma izinto [we cover-up things], we don't pa ha [reveal] in public. We get together in a corner and talk about these things.*

Must be a big corner.

In real terms, it's an absolute disgrace and national embarrassment and not the first time Mr. Sam has been caught with his pants down.

He lied about the SASCOC PR account, a "tender" that never went to tender.

He said he "would fall on his sword" if TeamSA didn't get 12 medals at the London Olympics – when last I looked he was still SASCOC president and now "siyazigquma izinto" – just glad I don't have to pronounce it.

"Cash strapped" SASCOC is because of one reason and one reason only – the gravy train.

Officials, family members and guests flying business class to London, China, Monaco, Corfu and all the other destinations is a costly business but that's how the gravy train rolls.

Just wish we could get a figure on what the SASCOC officials have spent on travel and entertainment in the last year.

It would be staggering.

How many of these officials are only concerned with how they get from point A to point B and don't give a rats' XXX about the sport or the athletes?

So, let me 'rat' on Kobus Marais, the Shadow Minister Public Service & Administration for the Democratic Alliance, SASCOC board member and now Powerboating South Africa (PSA) administrator.

SASCOC and PSA have been involved in an ongoing legal battle, which has resulted in PSA being suspended and the matter is now sub judice.

But that hasn't stopped Mr Marais from travelling all over the world, acting as the PSA spokesperson without locus standi.

He was in London for the Paralympics, made a pit stop in Monaco and was in Corfu last week for the Powerboating UIM.

Who's paying for this?

Amazing that a full time Minister has so much time to travel for other work.

The DA's response courtesy of Victoria Hasson.

The DA has a leave policy administered by the Chief Whip regulating its member's attendance in parliament. As part of this policy members have to apply for leave in advance if they are unable to be present when House is in session. Leave of absence was granted in respect of Mr Marais' travel to the London Paralympics. However, because the powerboat meeting took place over the weekend official leave from the Chief Whip was not required.

Needless to say, the UIM in Corfu was from the 15-21 October and Mr Marais was there from Friday the 19th and only returned to SA on Tuesday the 23rd.

Not another lie?

The DA didn't respond further on the matter.

***

Police leaves investigation to Sascoc

The South African Police Service (SAPS) and the national prosecuting authority (NPA) last year dropped a case of alleged fraud because Sascoc "was already investigating" the matter. The complainant maintains she was never contacted by the investigating officer. Instead, she merely received two SMS's informing her that the case had been dropped months after she lodged the complaint. Despite SASCOC's name featuring in the two SMS's – one of which was "signed" by the investigating officer from the SAPS – CEO Tubby Reddy's office last week denied carrying any knowledge of the matter. The fraud involves the alleged fraudulent issuing of skipper tickets and boat licenses. (Rapport, 22 September 2013)

The SMS's …

S BALL, Hermanus cas 558/02/2012 refres (sic), the prosecuting authority has declined on 2012. 11. 27 to prosecute the case, case was withdrawn, the matter is already being investigated by SASCOC. W/O Coetzee.

S Bali (sic), Hermanus CAS 558/02/2012 the prosecuting authority has declined on 2012. 11. 27 to prosecure (sic) in this matter for the following reasons: the matter is already being investigated by SASCOC.

Sounds all too familiar with my personal case.

It gets bounced around from department to department and then ends with “declined to prosecute”.

It’s strongly alleged that Marais had a hand in this obstruction of justice and didn’t let on to his SASCOC superiors.

Was interfering with an ongoing criminal investigation not abuse of his power as a DA parliamentary member?

I fed information to the DA Shadow Sports Ministers for years, hoping they would take some action.

It needed political clout to root out the corruption in SA sport. They talked a good game, without really making a difference.

The DA would ask questions in parliament but there was seldom a follow up, especially when there were blatant lies from the Sports Ministry.

QUESTION NUMBER 1777. NUMBER 1777 FROM Mr M S MALATSI (DA) TO THE MINISTER F.A. MBALULA: MINISTER OF

SPORT AND RECREATION

(1) **What are the names of the service providers contracted by (a) his department and (b) SA Sports Confederation and**

Olympic Committee for hosting and managing the Ekhaya Facility at the 2014 Commonwealth Games in Glasgow;

(2) **what are the names of the (a) chief executive officer, (b) executive directors and (c) chairperson of each service**

provider;

(3) **for each service provider, what were the (a) services provided, (b) cost of the contract, (c)(i) names of other service providers who competed for the contract and (ii) cost of their bids and (d) reasons for awarding the contract to the successful bidders?**

REPLY

(1) **(a) Sport and Recreation South Africa (SRSA) contracted Corinthian Catering Limited c/o The Trades Hall of Glasgow**

(b) SASCOC M&M Hiring service providers.

(2) **From SRSA (a) is Mr Ian Gilchrist- CEO of "The Trades Hall"**

(b) **n/a (c) n/a. From SASCOC,**

(c) **(i) is David Naidoo – Owner**

(ii) **n/a**

(iii) **n/a**

(iv) **n/a.**

(3) **The contracting was done by the South African High Commission in London for and on behalf of SRSA. This was after comparing the suitability and availability of other venues in Glasgow. The services required were for (a) Venue Hire and Catering and the cost in British Pound Sterling were converted to South African currency was (b) ZAR 1 386 984.50 for the entire duration of the Common Wealth Games.**

(c) **(i) n/a- a reconnaissance visit to Glasgow was done by SRSA officials (Chief Operations Officer and Chief Director: Corporate Services) with assistance of the South African High Commission in London where 4 different venues were assessed (these were the only possible venues still available that might have suited the needs for Ekhaya**

(ii) n/a

(d) **"The Trades Hall of Glasgow" was considered the most suitable to the needs of Ekhaya Hospitality Centre.**

SASCOC did also procure the (a) Venue Branding and Equipment and Freighting within the specifications of the Trades Hall with conditions that the branding and venue dressing had to protect, preserve and ensure damage free to the walls, floors, wooden plating and other building features. This made the venue dressing very costly, but this was mitigated by the largely affordable daily rate for renting the building itself. The other costs drivers were for the

import duties on the freight of the exhibition and the storage fees in respect to all the cargo shipped to Glasgow and its return fare at the cost of (b) ZAR 5 940 000.00. The other companies that quoted SASCOC for the same scope of work was (c) (i) kings Function Hire-ZAR 9 690 000.00.

(d) SASCOC is an Association governed by its Constitution. It implements its own guidelines and processes in regard to the procurement of goods and services. This process is managed through a data-base of preferred service providers as and when the need arises. Such procurement requires quotations on costs for goods and services. These quotations are then assessed by SASCOC management, who subsequently make a final decision relating to the appointment of a successful preferred service provider.

Reply received: October 2014

For weeks, I asked the DA to follow up on this as there was NO tender from Kings Function Hire and Kobus Marais should have known about this as he sits on the SASCOC finance committee.

Please excuse the delayed response. As far as I know, Kobus (Marais) still holds all his positions with SASCOC. With regard to the other question; I will liaise with our research team. I can't recall if we submitted follow up questions.- (Solly Malatsi, DA Shadow Minister for Sport and Recreation, 28 September 2015)

Kings Function Hire is based in Newtown, Johannesburg and owned by Abbas Sayed and these were their responses when I asked them if they tendered for the Ekhaya at the Commonwealth Games and who owns their company?

> On Fri, Sep 18, 2015 at 4:56 AM, Kings Function Hire <info@kingshire.co.za> wrote:
> Why do you need this information and for whom?
>
> > On Thu, Sep 17, 2015 at 11:56 PM, Graeme Joffe <graemejoffe@gmail.com> wrote:
> > So, Kings Function Hire did not put in a tender quote?
> >
> > > On Thu, Sep 17, 2015 at 5:46 PM, Kings Function Hire <info@kingshire.co.za> wrote:
> > > You have contacted the wrong company

And a couple weeks later ...

> **Rukshana Ravat** <rukshana.ravat@gmail.com> 9/30/15
> to me
>
> No we did not but as far as I can remember M&M HIRING MARQUEES asked us for a quote but no response on that we recieved

M&M Hiring, with their political connections got the deal with no tender at an "inflated price" agreed to by owner David Naidoo and SASCOC CEO, Tubby Reddy.

At the same time, I asked the DA to follow up on a Lottery payment of R35 million to the Limpopo Academy of Sport in July 2015?

Not only was the amount of R35 million staggering but the DA had already uncovered this about the same academy in November 2014.

R1,2 million equipment in storage for 8 yrs

Much-needed gym equipment worth around R1,2 million, which was donated to the Limpopo Academy of Sports by the National Lottery in 2006, has never been used and is stored in an office at the academy. This was according to DA Limpopo spokesperson, Solly Malatsi, who said the DA was shocked by the discovery during an oversight visit by the national assembly's portfolio committee on sports and recreation.(Capricorn Voice, 4 December 2014)

Did the DA monitor and follow up? Your guess is as good as mine.

Darren Bergman, the DA Deputy Shadow Minister for Sports and Recreation said nice things after my expose on the Border Rugby Football Union (BRFU) which was in a total shambles and finally suspended by SARU in 2018.

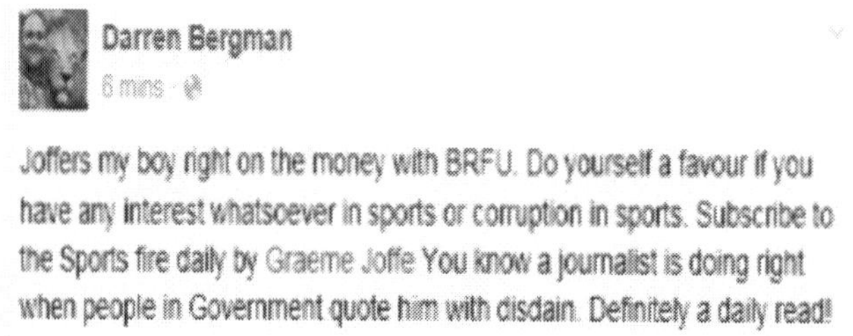

Darren Bergman
6 mins
Joffers my boy right on the money with BRFU. Do yourself a favour if you have any interest whatsoever in sports or corruption in sports. Subscribe to the Sports fire daily by Graeme Joffe You know a journalist is doing right when people in Government quote him with disdain. Definitely a daily read!

But then in the same breath, Bergman would be a VIP guest of SA Rugby at a test match, seated in a suite in front of Fikile Mbalula and Jurie Roux. Hypocrisy?

I was hoping Darren and Solly would be more pro-active than their predecessors.

They left me disappointed.

But then you have a real DA dick like Cameron McKenzie – apologies for the crude language but no other way to describe this politician after his comments on Facebook when I was forced to flee South Africa.

Cameron MacKenzie How about an irrelevant Joffe looking for political asylum in the USA...this is one way to get a green card even though you have no cash or specialised skills#justsaying

Graeme Joffe You are one very sick person Cameron MacKenzie and I hope you or your family never have to experience what I did. Perhaps, you should call the SAPS captain in Sandton and PI before making such idiotic and stupendous statements. It is only a matter of time before you look like a complete fool!

Seeing these comments from Cameron MacKenzie again after many months still makes me very angry.

I had lost my last little bit of respect for SA politicians.

It just seems as if they're all in it for themselves and sadly the colourful, rainbow nation has no chance like such.

There are three things in the world that deserve no mercy, hypocrisy, fraud, and tyranny. - Frederick William Robertson

Chapter 24: Township TV: Making a Difference

At the beginning of 2007, the rumour mill had it that the South African Broadcast Corporation (SABC) was going to lose the local Premier Soccer League (PSL) TV rights to SuperSport.

From free to air (where one only pays a small annual license fee), it was now going to be on a pay channel. For the majority of local football fans, this was a travesty as they would not be able to afford the SuperSport (DStv) monthly fee.

Over lunch, a friend of mine, Cherie Eilertsen suggested the idea of erecting big screen televisions in poorer areas where we could show these football games at no charge.

In other words, TV fan parks.

It was a brilliant idea and I bought into the concept immediately. What a way to give back and uplift the communities.

But where to start?

That same weekend, we took a drive into Diepsloot, which is a densely populated Township in the north of Johannesburg to see if there were open spaces or land that could be used for the project.

It felt like we hit the jackpot on our first drive through.

A City Park situated between the shacks with a kids playground, a sand football pitch and a large open area.

Little did we know how tough it was going to be to do something good for these communities with all the red tape.

The park was owned by the City of Johannesburg (government property) and I set up a meeting with officials from Johannesburg City Parks (JCP) to share our vision for Township TV.

OBJECTIVES

- To provide the Townships of South Africa with a unique form of Entertainment in a Safe and Secure Environment, at no cost to the people
- To install Big Screen TVs in strategic locations within the Township Communities of South Africa
- To give Sponsors and Advertisers an incredible opportunity to reach their target market through Township TV
- To make a meaningful Social Responsibility contribution which will impact on the lives of millions of people

- To showcase the City Councils and Local Governments in their efforts to provide Social Activities for the Communities

- To proactively reduce Crime in our country by creating extra – curricular activities in the communities, and by changing the lives of millions of people in a positive and meaningful way

- To educate with innovative and constructive Programming which will be screened on Township TV

- To ensure that Township TV is officially sanctioned and begins as soon as possible, with a view to 2010 and more importantly, to continue way beyond 2010

- To conduct a comprehensive feasibility study on this exciting project, ensuring long-term sustainability and profitability of Township TV

- To create jobs for the unemployed through the various components of Township TV

- To create business opportunities for Vendors at all Township TV sites

- To grant each community the rights to sell food and refreshments at the sites

Sadly, it was the wrong people we met with up front from JCP in Jenny Moodley and Dee Daniel.

They sounded all excited in the first meeting but after many weeks, they had still not shared our vision with the powers that be to get the ball rolling. I had a feeling they wanted to steal the concept and run with it themselves.

It was only after a chance meeting with the then Marketing Manager of JCP, Fouch Fouche a couple months later that things started to move forward.

Fouch wanted the best for the communities and Township TV was going to change lives with the free education and entertainment.

I shared our project vision with good mate, Warne Rippon and the very next day, he gave me a cheque for a R1 million to get started.

Thanks Rip!

The plan was then to get one of the 2010 FIFA World Cup sponsors to align with us the rest of the way. I was going to drive this project and make it happen even though I had no experience in outdoor media or sales.

But I had the passion to make a difference.

I approached the World Cup sponsors and got a bite from the mobile telecommunications company, MTN.

They wanted 20 Township TV venues across the country for 2010.

What? It was game on.

After months of meetings, getting quotes, looking for contractors, suppliers and staff, we did what most thought would be impossible.

Township TV launched on a cloudy day in Diepsloot on 8 December 2007.

This was one of my most satisfying days ever.

I had tears of joy seeing all the smiles of the Diepsloot residents who had come to the park for the launch.

This was their TV and the community took immediate ownership.

"Thank you Umlungu (white man), thank you for what you're doing for us." - I didn't need to hear any

more.

It became a labour of love.

There was no power in the Diepsloot Park and twice a week, I would drive around 90 minutes to fill the jerry cans with fuel for the diesel generator we bought to run the big screen.

Lewis was our first employee (also his first job) and he was like the pied piper as the kids would follow him from his shack at 2pm, knowing he was on his way to switch on the TV.

Our remote system would only come months later.

Township TV staff

For the next few months, I travelled around Johannesburg and other parts of the country to identify the other nineteen sites.

Word was out about Diepsloot and we started getting requests from all over the country for Township TV.

We could only do so much and funding would ultimately determine the scope of the social responsibility project.

Every month, we would try to put up a new screen and each one gave me a great sense of satisfaction.

Jobs were created for vendors and security staff, kids were being kept off the streets and families could spend time together, watching their favourite teams and TV programmes 365 days a year at no charge.

Township TV was making a difference.

"Big Screens in Parks - Confederation Cup"
Featured in the Sowetan (12 June 2009)

"Township TV ready to thrill crowds during extravaganza"
Featured in the Citizen (11 Jun 2009)

"MTN has joined the Township TV initiative"
Featured on Bizcommunity (22 May 2009)

"Seven Sites for Township TV"
Featured on Bizcommunity (05 Mar 2009)

"Third Screen for Township TV"
Featured on Bizcommunity (26 May 2008)

"TV in the township makes its mark "
Featured on Bizcommunity (14 Feb 2008)

"Township TV hauls fans out of Diepsloot misery"
Featured in the Sunday Times (01 Jan 2008)

"Township TV launches in Diepsloot"
Press Release (13 Dec 2007)

By the time, the 2010 FIFA World Cup came around, Township TV had twenty sites across South Africa.

There were a number of government employees and officials who all of a sudden tried to take credit for the project but that didn't bother me.

Township TV became 'official fan parks' for the 2010 World Cup and even though the tournament was played in the middle of winter, over 600 000 people watched the games in their local parks, free of charge.

FIFA 2010 World Cup in Township TV parks

Keeping the project going after 2010 was of paramount importance.

It had to be a legacy project.

MTN exercised their option for the sponsorship renewal but then reneged on the written agreement at the end of the year, giving us little to no time to get a new sponsor on board.

Most corporates do their budgeting in September and October.

I was devastated.

How on earth could we now take all these screens down and what was I going to tell the people?

Serame Taukobong from MTN was the guy who pulled the plug and it's hard to forget. He gave me the lame excuse that his budget was used up on his new big sponsorship of Lions rugby. Ironically, a deal that was brokered with Eric Ichikowitz and company.

To this day, there are unanswered questions about that rugby "deal" and Township TV was kicked into touch.

I don't remember Serame once coming to any of the parks to see what a difference it was making to these communities.

MTN did some very questionable sponsorships for 2010 and needless to say, the agency, EXP where one of Serame's family relations was CEO, never had problems getting deals done with MTN.

What ever happened to social responsibility and what is right for the brand?

We had to fight for a small cancellation fee from MTN and were on the brink of shutting down before getting short-term sponsorships from DStv, Amalgamated Beverage Industries (ABI) and the SA political party, COPE.

Soweto derby day in Thokoza Park, Soweto

The COPE sponsorship was just ahead of the 2014 election and it gave me hope for the country, having met their leader, Mosiuoa 'Terror' Lekota.

He restored some of my faith and had an aura about him that reminded me so much of the great Nelson Mandela.

Lekota was also one of the struggle fighters who was imprisoned on Robben Island and his nickname 'Terror' supposedly came from his playing style on the soccer field.

We met for the first time at a hotel in Sandton, Johannesburg and after twenty minutes, I had his political party buy-in for Township TV.

He was a man of his word and when we met later in the day at my apartment complex, he greeted all the staff downstairs as if they were long lost friends.

Such was the man, treating everyone as equal.

Before getting to COPE, we had taken another step with a Township TV proposal to offer free educational programming in the parks during the morning for those students who didn't have the means to go to college or university.

I recall our first meeting with the Gauteng Education Department and driving into the basement of their building in downtown Johannesburg and seeing more luxury vehicles than a Mercedes dealership.

Just a little concerning.

We were later introduced to the Gauteng Provincial Department of Education (GPEDU) and they were over the moon with the partnership proposal.

They were desperate for something like this Township TV initiative as more and more students in SA were unable to afford tuition fees.

The programming that would be offered included soft skills courses such as: Business Literacy, First Aid, Report Writing, Time Management, Budgeting and Tourism Management etc.

Free education, free education!

We had the buy in from GPEDU but after more than five months, we heard nothing on the progress of the agreement and were no closer to starting the project.

But my hopes were restored on 4 June 2013 on receiving an email from Elizabeth Thobejane who was heading up GPEDU.

Graeme, please provide me with a letter that you are the only service provider who owns or have rights to township tvs or parks. I will use this to procure your services as a sole provider.

We gave them everything and that was the last we heard from anyone at GPEDU.

I wonder if a brown envelope would have moved things forward.

I wasn't going to change my ethics to find out but from what I had seen and heard - the unwritten language for so many government officials and marketing people who control the purse strings is:

What's in it for me?

The labour of love for Township TV had gone, it was now a daily battle.

Education is the most powerful weapon which you can use to change the world. - Nelson Mandela

Why could these GPEDU officials not see through their rose-tinted glasses and continue the legacy of our former president?

The last straw was the Gauteng Province (Department of Sport and Recreation)/City of Johannesburg failing to pay Township TV the R1.7 million for use of our screens during the Africa Cup of Nations (AFCON) in 2013.

Treasury had in fact allocated R2.5 million to Township TV for AFCON 2013 but it was obviously "used" for something else.

We could not carry the cost.

Township TV initiated legal proceedings to try and recover the owed payment but I didn't have the energy and patience to fight another case against an organisation that had deep pockets with use of our public funding.

They stalled the trial from day one as their advocate was double briefed and attended another trial in Port Elizabeth the same day.

We wasted a whole day in court and he then lied to the Deputy Judge President on day two of the trial. The defendants also withheld discovery despite numerous requests. They were in contempt of court but there's a different set of rules for government departments.

We finally got some discovery at the court on day two.

In black and white, a total of R7.5 million was signed off for the AFCON public viewing sites (three of them belonging to Township TV) – we never got a cent.

I had spent sleepless nights trying to get the public viewing rights for the tournament to make sure we could deliver.

After getting the run around for months, Township TV secured the exclusive fan park rights for AFCON 2013 in SA.

But that didn't stop the Province from paying 'another contractor' over R3 million to set up three unlicensed fanpar ks for just one day. The city and province had no authority but no doubt some of the officials and friends got 'rewarded' financially.

Township TV rewarded for making a difference

After seven years of Township TV, trying to make difference had now become a daily grind.

It pained me to send out a notice of closure as we had formed some special relationships, especially with sites that weren't government owned, like the Ndlovu Care Group in Elandsdoorn.

Graeme, thrive on the success of the last seven years and do not be sad as such. Projects sometimes go like that. You are a captain and a star who have brought many people many hours of joy. - Hugo Tempelman, CEO Ndlovu Care Group

I didn't have the heart to take the screens down and we looked for a buyer to continue the legacy and to keep the project going.

After months of negotiations, we had a sale agreement with a consortium led by Robbyn Burger and Lunga Kepe from Red Cherry Media, who had previous dealings with Johannesburg City Parks (JCP).

Kepe was also part of the ANC Communications team and they had big plans to use the Township TV parks for the upcoming presidential elections in 2014.

The consortium put down a deposit but then reneged on the deal after messing us around for months.

What next?

JCP then started to make life difficult for us, saying Township TV, would have to go out for tender as the rental agreements had expired.

What a cheek. It was our concept and our project!

We had spent millions putting in the infrastructure, made the parks safer with our 24 hour security, uplifted the communities and now we must tender for our own project?

> Johannesburg City Parks undertakes to protect the Township Theatre TV concept and not to disclose any information relating to the third party agreements, negotiations and designs as relates to the Township TV concept/project nor to enter into similar agreements with any other parties for the duration of this project and for a further period of twelve (12) months thereafter.

They didn't care about the people they supposed to be serving and I could no longer fight the system.

JCP has a history of corruption within its corridors and tenders are the easiest way for dirty officials to grease their palms.

Ex Joburg City Parks MD in court for fraud

A former managing director of Johannesburg City Parks has been arrested for fraud and corruption involving R57m, the Hawks said on Tuesday. "He was arrested with another man for fraud and corruption that happened between 2006 and 2012,"spokesperson Captain Paul Ramaloko said. The case related to a contract awarded by City Parks to Jozi Mart to supply trees. According to the Hawks, the company presented itself as a nursery and was subsequently awarded the tender. They presented themselves as a nursery which they are not. They were buying trees from other nurseries for R70 and selling them to City Parks for R700. – (News24, 8 October 2013)

City Parks 'rotten'

A SYNDICATE exploiting opportunities to enrich themselves is operating unhindered, plundering the coffers of Joburg's City Parks department.And a damning report by the Hawks exposing the rot within City Parks was given to the City of Joburg on December 14 – and appears to have gone ignored. – (IOL, 5 March 2012)

Even when we finalized our Township TV agreement with JHB City Parks, their legal secretary asked:

So, when do we get our Mercedes (gift)?

I called him on it the next day, expressing my disgust and he apologized but I should have known then it was going to be a tough road.

Township TV was forced to switch off in March 2014.

We were left with little choice. Staff and security had to be let go. Vendors packed up. The parks became less safe and gone was the free entertainment for so many.

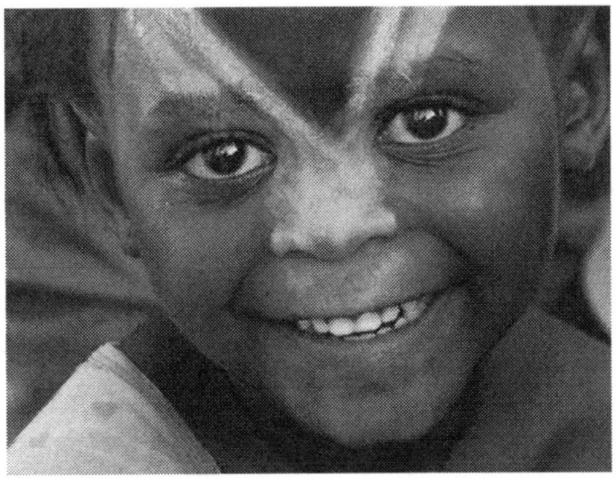

Gone were these smiles.

It broke my heart.

In February 2016, this is what City Parks had to say:

We as JCPZ do not have money to fund Township TV's at all. We have issued a request for proposals as attached twice last year asking for innovative investment in our parks which would include tv's. This means we are looking for a company to fund township tv's. To date we have not received any such response and has thus been unable to implement.

They killed the project with their greed and lack of vision.

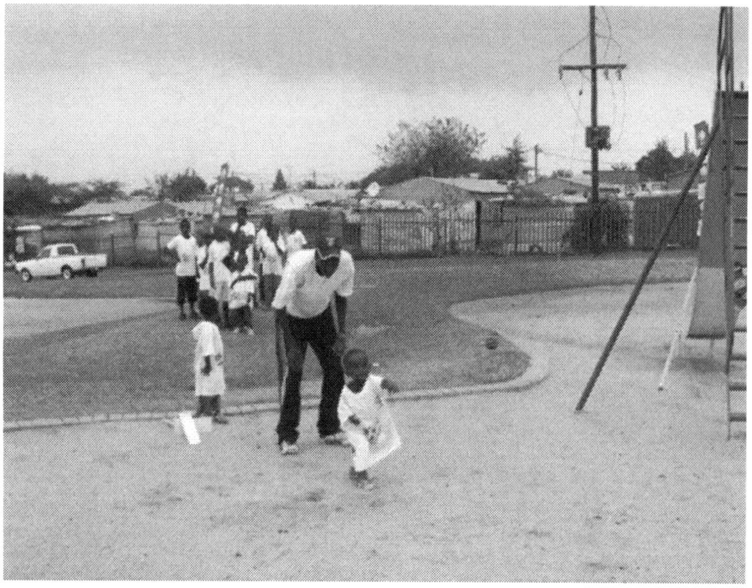

KFC mini cricket clinic in Diepsloot Township TV park

Who knows this could have been the next Proteas fast bowler?

We created these opportunities!

So many people had done their bit to make Township TV a huge success.

My heartfelt thanks goes out to Fouch Fouche, my partners, Warne Rippon, Grant Morris and two very special people who were there with unwavering support from day one, Adine Strashun (DStv) and Sue Eisermann (Ellies).

In May 2016, I was reminded of the good we had done and it is a very sad inevitably what had become of the TV parks.

Fix our fan park!

The Nelson Mandela Peace Park in Motherwell used to attract large numbers of soccer lovers. Now it lies empty as the television no longer works. A worker at the park said: "The television has not been working for a long time now. The speakers were stolen. Criminals have stripped it of all its cables." A resident, Nombulelo Liso (46), said she used to sell food at the park. "I used to make lots of money from selling soft drinks, sweets and fruit to soccer fans. Now I struggle to pay my children's school fees. I wish the municipality would fix the TV," she said. – (Daily Sun, 23 May 2016)

Township TV has been a revelation and a great benefit to both Umlazi and KwaMashu communities. - (Lunga Lamula, City of Durban)

So, why did it have to be so hard when all we were trying to do was make a difference?

Chapter 25: Breaking My Silence

The first few months in Cincinnati were mentally very tough.

I had said little to anyone back in South Africa as I didn't want to jeopardise the criminal case and was hoping the police investigation would flush out those responsible for the threat to my safety.

And maybe I would be able to go back home.

But after three long months and no advance in the criminal case, I decided to break my silence.

Graeme Joffe flees South Africa

Former TV and radio sports presenter - and Sport24 columnist - Graeme Joffe fled South Africa three months ago. Writing on his SportsFire Daily blog on Friday, Joffe spoke of how his life in South Africa changed forever following a late-night phone call earlier this year. (sport24, 17 July 2015)

Graeme Joffe shuts up shop, sings to US officials – here's why

Joffers my boy – a common reference amongst sports lovers listening to the radio. But how times have changed. Graeme Joffe went into hiding and now finds himself living in the US, where he used to work as an international sports anchor for CNN years ago. We carried a Sport 24 report last week in which Joffe expressed gratitude for the extensive public support he received on and off social media. He gave reasons as to why he felt threatened enough to flee. In this heartfelt piece Graeme Joffe talks about life as a South African and what exactly led to his secret getaway. A real loss to South African sport, which affirms the length and depth of corruption in this country. (fin24, 31 July 2015)

The support from readers was heartening …

We all stand helplessly as we see corruption - severe corruption - with every turn we make. Sports, health, construction, transport, wildlfiem ... We shake our head and then get on with our day. What a shame or rather, sham. We need more people like you Graeme. - Nichola Smith

Now I realise I have not heard you for ages. Because you love South Africa, I beg of you Graeme write the Book. The Truth about Sport in South Africa. Please. Good Luck. The very best for the future. - Alicia Louise

The two groups who were identified as being deserving of funding from the so-called "National Lottery"were the various sports' bodies in South Africa and the various charitable organisations such as the homes and organisations that look after the handicapped and the destitute. Because of blatant corruption, from the awarding of lottery rights to the distribution of lottery monies, very, very, very little of the otherwise earmarked money, gets through to these people. One of the greatest indictments against the ANC led government of South Africa, is that they have absolutely no qualms stealing from the poor! The ANC is an absolutely DISGUSTING organisation, led by an ABSOLUTELY DISGUSTING INDIVIDUAL, collectively speaking, of course! - Bruce Rothman

It is sad that whistle blowers must always get the short end of the stick? The moment they point out fraud and corruption immediately they are threatened! - Ryan Zander

This country needs more journalists like you in order for it to reach its full potential, Don't give up keep digging. - C'ya Khubone

This is very sad considering what Joffers has done poor township kids and families. Through his efforts big screen televisions were installed townships around Joburg for families who had no access to television. I probably have the most Highveld Stereo branded clothes than anybody in Soweto. I have sexy cooler box I also won at Highveld Stereo. Not to mention rugby and cricket match tickets. I won all those when Joffers presented sports on Jeremy Mansfield's Rude Awakening. I would send tricky sports quiz questions. If the caller got the answer right, prize would go to him and on the other hand callers got it wrong, prize would to the quiz sender. After those experiences, I felt like I knew Graeme Joffe personally even though I have never met him in person. Your life is more important than anything. This is what this country has come to. We'll miss you. - Richardson Mzaidume

I am sad to hear the plight you have to endure Sir, but having seen what you are capable of, I am sure that you shall indeed prevail. Thank you for exposing the incompetencies of some of our sport 'administrators' and for your tireless, one-man struggle to ensure that sport truly uplifts our nation. Godspeed to you Sir.W e who love South Africa salute you and patiently await your triumphant return one day. - Everton Bouwer

Tragic that Graeme has to flee the country of his birth simply for telling the truth! I salute Graeme for sticking to his guns!! - Paul Cowie

South Africa has lost a true champion of our sports people, who themselves have no voice. Graeme took on all the corrupt sports organisations, without fear or favour, and really rocked their precious boats by exposing their never-ending shenanigans, corruption, nepotism and general skullduggery. I wish Graeme well in the States and hope that he can still continue to question and expose these crooks on behalf of our beleaguered athletes. - Truthseeker

But there will always be the odd exception …

Bye bye Graeme . RSA won't be affected by your departure. Connect well with your original place of your evil ancestors. I wish we have stories like this daily. In that way all these pink guys would eventually disappear without conflicts. - Rudzani Raselabe

Apartheid was never going to have a happy ending and racism will tragically always be rife in South Africa.

The support for what I had tried to achieve was overwhelming and in the back of my mind, I knew I had to fight on.

Emails like this from Wendy Rippon gave me the courage to keep going.

Dear Joffers

I read with a very heart your facebook post of today, and can understand how you must be feeling - sadness, anger, hurt, and a there must be string of emotions to add.

You gave everything and when you thought there was no more to give, you never gave up and you gave even more.... I know that you threw all you had to bring justice and for everyone to have a fair chance in life. There are many people whose lives you did change for the better, so your hard work was not all in vain. I admire you for all that you did expose of corruption, stealing and racism.

We miss you, you have all our support always, and we love you

W xxx

Three independent producers for Carte Blanche made contact with me, wanting to come over to the USA to get my story.

Executive Producer, George Mazarakis blocked it.

The mainstream press were quiet as expected and I did my first interview with Gareth Cliff on cliffcentral.com (one of the few independent radio voices in the country).

Gareth Cliff speaks to sports journalist Graeme Joffe who's in exile in the United States, after death threats. Graeme's harrowing story reveals mass shameless corruption in South African sport.

It was midnight in Cincinnati (early morning SA time) when I did the interview and it opened up a lot of old wounds. I was still very angry but it helped me to get a lot of my chest.

Tony Peter Why should we be surprised by what joffers is saying. We have the master in thief running the show. The shit flows down hill.
Like · Reply · 3 · July 20, 2015 at 6:39pm

Gordon Morrison This gave me the chills. Graeme you lectured me at the Rhodes business school at the beginning of the year. Your story was inspiring and not in vain. I'm certain the youth will follow in your footsteps. Keep at it
Like · Reply · 5 · July 20, 2015 at 4:05pm · Edited

Gert Botha this country is a joke!! one hears of this kinda stuff in every sphere of government and I wonder when it will come to an end. I now understand why they wont leave "white" run sports alone, they want that monies too...
Like · Reply · 4 · July 20, 2015 at 3:40pm

Angela Bondary Nanchou I have goosebumps after listening to this interview
Like · Reply · 1 · July 21, 2015 at 1:02am

Laurinda Carreira Pestana This is so sad...this beautiful country of ours is falling!!!
P.s. If you think we are the only country this is happening too, then you are very mistaken.
Like · Reply · 1 · July 21, 2015 at 2:49am

Martin Smith 'Shorty' Listen Kenny Sloane, scary shit and there's no money available for genuine sportsmen who want to try to give their best....
Like · Reply · 1 · July 20, 2015 at 3:52pm

Pamela Angeline Harvey The rot starts at the top! The so called leadership. How very sad that the greed is so rampant at the top and the sports stars get the crumbs.
Like · Reply · July 21, 2015 at 12:18pm

Facebook comments continued …

Caroline De Bruyn This filters down into provincial sports leagues as well. Tired of paying huge amounts of money for kids to stay in crappy school dormitories, eating crappy food.
Like · Reply · 5 · July 20, 2015 at 3:34pm
1 Reply

Gavin Byl Read about it last week. Fucking Disgraceful. All those useless fat pieces of shit belong in sewers
Like · Reply · 4 · July 20, 2015 at 3:05pm

Amri Theron Worth listening to the conversation... shocking and very sad indeed... Graeme you are an awesome journalist.
Like · Reply · 4 · July 21, 2015 at 1:00am

David Bennett When you think about what he said about SA getting 5 Olympic medals when we should be getting 30, he is actually 100% correct. I've never thought about that. But when you look at how competitive we are in rugby, cricket etc, he is right.
Like · Reply · 3 · July 20, 2015 at 4:03pm

Michell Steyn Gareth love CliffCentral even more, guts to publicise TRUTH! LOVE COMMENTS OF INCOMPETENT SCOUNDRELS! SOUTH AFRICA TIME TO ACT MASSES MARCHING AGAINST CORRUPTION AND THIEVERY OF OUR GOVERMENT ! Take leave at work, stop complaining and act! !! Search o... See More
Like · Reply · 8 · July 20, 2015 at 5:08pm

Ellen Nortje I so hope this will be brought to light!
Like · Reply · 1 · July 21, 2015 at 1:57am

Valerie Margaret Kennaugh Another abuse of funds going to the wrong people's pockets. Why am I not surprised???
Like · Reply · 1 · July 21, 2015 at 5:36am

Joffers, I have been fortunate enough to know you and spend a lot of my memorable sporting days playing alongside you. Despite your current physique, many don't know how talented you are. Whilst at Rhodes University if I am correct you played premier league soccer, cricket, squash and were a fairly useful golfer. Nevertheless despite the fact that you may have not represented sport at the highest level you enjoyed competing and gave so much pleasure to those you played against. Whilst at the peak of your multitude of sports, you were game to take part in any event in the interests of others and sport in general. Who can forget our epic universities cricket match against Jonty Rhodes when post-match you got him to down a beer at the fines meeting a fate never done before I am lead to believe. The legendary Pineapple cricket tour in Port Alfred saw you compete a few times, not necessary because you wanted to, but because you felt you owed it to the people of the area. I furthermore know that you were at the end of the phone to accept the duties of MC at numerous functions at no reward, but purely in the interests of sport. Sport is such a special thing, and it has given my family, friends and opposition so much fun, that we should not allow the corruption that is busy ruining it to continue. I heard your interview with Gareth Cliff last night and this morning with Daronn Mann and can hear your sincere hurt and frustration with regard to the matter and especially the way that it has been handled. As a fellow old Rhodian, can we not begin an old Rhodian campaign to make our voices heard, enough is enough. Be strong my brother and remember the wheel is round! – Andrew McLean

I did a couple more radio interviews and that was it but I couldn't extract myself from continuing to poke the bear on social media.

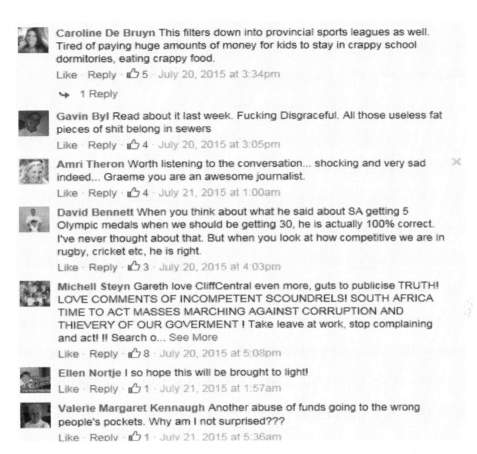

It was hit and miss but kept me in the game.

Over the years, knowing what I knew with all the corruption and politics, I had become less and less patriotic.

I wanted the best for the SA sportsmen and women (that's who I was fighting for) but their success would cloud the reality of what was really going on and the grubby officials would pat themselves on the back.

Members of the public and even friends took issue with me on my waning patriotism but hopefully one day they'll understand where I was coming from.

Before I was forced to flee South Africa, I wanted to write a book on everything that I had uncovered.

I had offers from a couple SA publishers (Jacana & Tafelberg) but never really got stuck into it.

The problem was – where to start?

Not being able to work in the US when I first arrived gave me the perfect opportunity to finally write the book. But for months, I would just lie on my bed, too exhausted to even write a paragraph.

I think they call it post-traumatic stress or was I just simply depressed?

Could have been both.

It took at least eight months for me to start feeling human again and to have the energy and focus to sit down at a desk for five-six hours a day to write.

The writing became therapeutic and it just started to flow. I couldn't believe what I had accumulated over the years but none of it had been forgotten.

I lived it!

But was I now to self-publish or find an international publisher? Who better to get some advice from than the journalist who took FIFA down, Andrew Jennings?

Andrew Jennings <ajdigging@gmail.com> 12/16/15
to me

Advice? Stricken by stroke it must be brief. Take your time. Get other opinions if is clear

I got opinions and took my time.

It was great advice and the SA dirt from and post the Rio Olympics gave me plenty more ammunition.

Investigative journalism had become an addiction!

Chapter 26: Forensic Linguistics

The anonymous author/s of the graemejoffe-exposed.com website had a field day in response to me breaking my silence and did their own little farewell piece.

What an honour to have SA's Olympic Committee media partner, HSM do such a moving tribute with colourful, well captioned photographs.

Where's that sarcasm emoji?

Hamba Kahle (goodbye)
As news broke of Graeme Joffe's permanent exit from South Africa street parties erupted in all corners of the nation. From Phallaborwa to Cape Town cries of delight were heard at the news that the country would not have to endure any longer this 3rd Class journalists rants of fiction. (sic) (graemejoffe-exposed admin, 29 July 2015)

From the word go, I had a strong sense of who was behind the anonymous, defamatory website and I would leave no stone unturned before the forensic linguistics would confirm my suspicions.

Posts on the SA Rugby Magazine Facebook page?

Who controls the page? Highbury Safika Media (HSM) who publish the SA Rugby Magazine.

Joffers My-Boy - www.graemejoffe-exposed.com - Facebook
https://www.facebook.com/sarugbymagazine/posts/866809503340752
www.graemejoffe-exposed.com ... Joffers My-BoySA Rugby magazine · November 24, 2014 · www.graemejoffe-exposed.com · Like · Comment · Share ...

Joffers My-Boy - www.graemejoffe-exposed.com - Facebook
https://www.facebook.com/sarugbymagazine/posts/870424526312583
www.graemejoffe-exposed.com ... Joffers My-BoySA Rugby magazine · December 1, 2014 · www.graemejoffe-exposed.com · Like · Comment · Share ...

Graeme that is an outside post probably from a spam account. By someone who created a Facebook page and linked it to our page. It has not been deleted from google as we have just found it. Whoever did this I imagine is responsible for the web site as well. The fact they have used our site is completely off side to me and I will now try to look into. Simon (Borchardt) assures me he did not see it and we get thousands of posts per day. It was an added post by someone outside this organisation. I have been assured the Mr. Keohane did not have access to Facebook posting in November of last year, so again your sources are wrong. - HSM CEO, Kevin Ferguson

Keohane was fully aware of what was going on and sent out the whatsapp message below to HSM staff in December 2014.

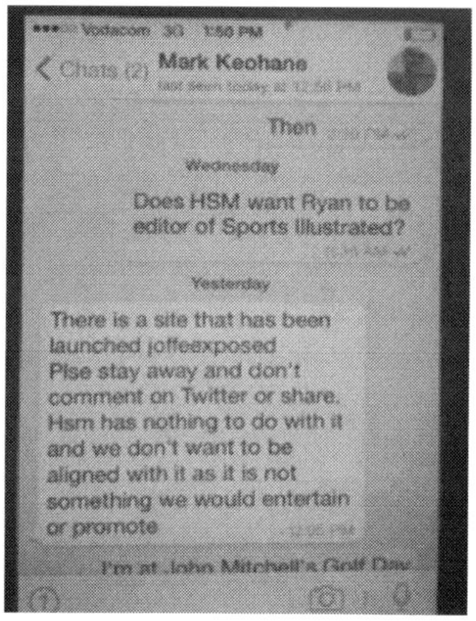

Yes, the same Mark Keohane who resigned from HSM as per media reports and his tweets (below) in 2012 but "we" at HSM don't want to be aligned with it?

Mark Keohane@mark_keohane
Those wishing to get hold of me (markkeo@mweb.co.za) as the keo@hsm.co.za address no longer applies.

Mark Keohane@mark_keohane
I will still be writing the Monday BD col & my freelance services extend 2@SARugbyMag, the Keo website which I founded & BD Col

Mark Keohane@mark_keohane
I resigned from HSM as publishing director & by extension from SASCOC's Olympic Team SA ... have never resigned my opinion on rugby

The fact is, Keohane never left the HSM stable.

On Tue, Sep 3, 2013 at 11:15 AM, Gary Lemke <gazlemke@gmail.com> wrote:
yes. basically hands-on at HSM. in other words, still working for the company, but in a "consultancy" guise. therefore no one can accuse the company of re-employing him. he says that being "away" for 12 months allows him to see things clearly now. "things that one can't see when so involved". smoke and mirrors. he's also personal advisor to TR (Tubby Reddy) and our CEO and some clients etc. advises on who gets increases and who doesn't. and he's "clean for the first time in

years". has a new spiritual side ....zzzzz :)

Thereafter, it was a lot of fishing from Ferguson who suddenly went on the defensive.

As a CEO I will investigate any wrong doing by my employee/s. I would be gob smacked if anyone was involved from HSM, I would be sickened as I believe that type of Journalism is not Journalism at all. I do not have the ability to turn something I did not turn on, off. How have your tech guys not managed this yet? When did that site go live? Graeme what can I do? Please give me the evidence that anyone from this organisation is involved and I will deal with the matter, now expediently. – Kevin Ferguson

Then Ferguson copied the HSM legal in on the next email, saying:

> Hi Tracey I have asked this person to produce evidence against HSM staff for their involvement in his Joffers Exposed Blog, Thus far these are the insults I have been getting from a Mister Joffe, who is clearly not him self, please can you take from here and put this request formally on the record.

I had become used to their legal threats and dirty hidden agendas.

Ferguson also denied that HSM or Keohane had anything to do with the SASCOC defamation lawsuit against me.

> Mark has never discussed the SASCOC case with me and shares my view that it is a complete waste of energy and time, I mean the obvious is there for everyone to see what is the upside to anybody even if they were successful. Our advice to SASCOC as media partners was not to pursue it. That is a fact. Anyone that knows me knows I don't litigate and I certainly would never recommend it.

I don't litigate and Mark has never discussed the SASCOC case with me?

This guy, Ferguson can't lie straight in bed.

> **From:** Gary Lemke [mailto:gazlemke@gmail.com]
> **Sent:** 03 September 2013 10:12 AM
>
> **To:** Graeme Joffe
> **Subject:** Re: FW: Media contacts
>
> hi. MK has flown to Jhb to meet with TR about your document. they have received the charges and going through them. initial feedback is "things are mundane and any questions can be easily explained away".

> **From:** Gary Lemke [mailto:gazlemke@gmail.com]
> **Sent:** 18 September 2013 08:34 AM
> **To:** Graeme Joffe <graeme@butterbean.co.za>
> **Subject:** Re: FW: Media contacts
>
> hello old chap. I was within earshot of MK talking to the CEO about you and the charges .... reckons there's "nothing" to them and all has been explained away ... he doesn't seem concerned ... however, he said that there was 1 issue of corporate governance they were sweating on but it didn't come up ... ? something about TR taking some people (staff?family?) somewhere in Africa.
> and this is the one they seemed most worried about but apparently hasn't been investigated enough.
> cheers

Ferguson himself had also started a twitter account, using the pseudonym, “The Money Man SA” and was happily re-tweeting Wesley Botton’s personal vendetta, trying to discredit me further.

When questioned about this, Ferguson quickly deleted his old tweet with the personal information that he was behind the pseudonym account.

But of course, I already had it captured.

Chris Swart posted a comment on Facebook on 22 July 2015, alluding to the fact that HSM employees were behind the anonymous website.

Shortly after, he got a message from Gary Lemke (HSM), asking him to please delete his post as Keohane and company would think that he was the mole again.

Chris then sent me this Facebook message.

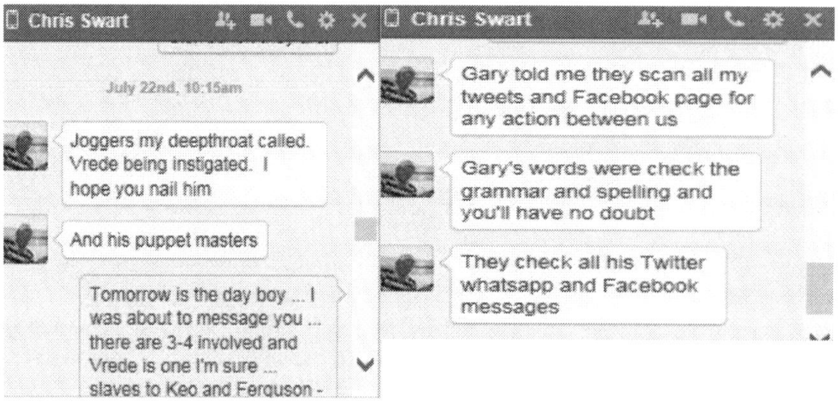

Another member of the HSM staff, Mark Etheridge had told one of my good sources, Wessel Oosthuizen, that Faizal Dawjee was responsible for the defamatory website, knowing that it would get back to me.

Was this just a blatant attempt to re-direct my attention or an opportunity to lay blame on Dawjee who was doing the public relations for the 2022 Commonwealth Games, a contract no doubt HSM would have loved to have?

Recalling the email I received from Etheridge back March 2015 with a sarcastic reference to Kevin Ferguson.

Lovely, lovely chappie isn't he… salt of the earth. Absolutely genuine, no malice, np backstabbing, no narcissistic traits ….

It was real cloak and dagger stuff but I still wanted more concrete evidence to put a whole in these bullet-proof HSM cowards.

Thanks to the research of Lindy, I was able to make contact with a couple experts in the field of forensic linguistics.

Colin Michell who has a MA-Linguistics (University of South Africa) and is in the Faculty of General Education Programme at the Fujairah Women's College in the United Arab Emirates and Isabel Picornell, PhD CFE from QED Limited in Guernsey.

Two people I had never met before and who went out of their way to assist me, for which I will always be extremely grateful.

> *Established in 2001, QED provides forensic linguistic support in the fight against fraud to professional intelligence and investigation organisations. The Principal of QED, Isabel Picornell, is a certified fraud examiner (CFE) with over 20 years experience in investigative research and information analysis. She is also a member of the International Association of Forensic Linguists and is a doctoral researcher with the Centre for Forensic Linguistics (Aston University, UK). QED Limited is a private limited company based in the Bailiwick of Guernsey (British Channel Islands).*

Both requested other writings from the chief suspects of the website for their own, individual analysis. Their reports and findings were very in depth and fascinating.

But to summarize:

> I have been instructed by Graeme Joffe to examine a number of anonymous and questioned blogs (the "**Q texts**") that were posted online on graemejoffeexposed. com to establish the documents' possible origins and to prepare a report on my findings. As of the date of the writing of this report, the website is longer available.
>
> I have been provided with links to online blog postings and Twitter feeds known to have been written by two individuals, Mark Keohane ("**Author A**") and Ryan Vrede ("**Author B**") and

to give my expert opinion on whether either of them is likely to be the author of any or all of the Q texts.

I have compared ten Q texts against:

a. 128 articles known to have been written by Author A (the "**A texts**") on 2 http://www.sarugbymag.co.za/column/category/keo-column;

b. 88 texts known to have been written by Author B (the "**B texts**") on http://www.sarugbymag.co.za/blog/authors/10;

Although the Q texts and the A and B texts are online blogs, the Q texts are written in an informal style which differs from the more formal style of the A and B texts.

For this reason, I have also used the Twitter feeds of Mark Keohane (@mark_keohane – "**Twitter A**") and Ryan Vrede (@Ryan_Vrede – "**Twitter B**") to identify linguistic features associated with their idiosyncratic use of informal language.

CONCLUSIONS

a. Texts Q1, Q7, and Q10 are consistent highly distinctive in style with each other. Texts Q7 and Q8 are consistent distinctive in style with each other. Collectively, these texts are consistent highly distinctive in style with Author B.

b. Text Q2 is consistent distinctive in style with Q1. Both texts share the same inconsistencies with the other Q texts.
c. The stylistic inconsistencies that differentiate texts Q1 and Q2 from the other Q texts may be the products of multiple authorship.

I confirm that I have made clear which facts and matters referred to in this report are within my own knowledge and which are not. Those that are within my own knowledge I confirm to be true. The opinions that I have expressed represent my true and complete professional opinions on the matters to which they refer.

Declaration of Colin Michell in support of Graeme Joffe

I, Colin Michell, declare as follows:

I am a linguistics graduate with a research interest in authorship attribution on social networking sites.

I was approached by Lindy ……. , who was acting in her personal capacity on behalf of Mr Graeme Joffe to analyse the linguistic content of a website (www.graemejoffe-exposed.com) in order to determine the possible authors. The website in question was a direct attack on the character of Mr Joffe by alluding to personal and professional indiscretions.

My task was to perform a complete forensic stylistic analysis of the linguistic content of the website (www.graemejoffe-exposed.com) against the known writings of three potential authors of the website, namely: Ryan Vrede, Mark Keohane, and David Isaacson. The three potential authors are well known to Mr Joffe, as they all harbour personal and professional grievances against Mr Joffe.

The linguistic content of the website totalled 2,670 words and was compared to the contents of the writing done on the social networking site Twitter of Ryan Vrede (3,252 words), Mark Keohane (2,549 words), and David Issacson (2,776 words). My task was to analyse the internal linguistic structure of the website vis-à-vis the known Twitter writings of Vrede, Keohane and Isaacson, with the aim of identifying or excluding the possible authors of the website.

To achieve this goal I have taken a stylistic approach to the analysis to reach my conclusions regarding the authorship of the website. Stylistics is concerned with the patterns of variation in written language. In other words looking for the idiosyncratic language use by an individual and then describing the individual language usage of that individual. When stylistics is used in a forensic linguistic context, the goal is to determine a possible author of a text, or to exclude a potential author. In the case of a disputed text, such as the website in question, the linguist analyses and then describes the style of the texts known to have been authored by one or more potential authors, and the compares and contrasts their internal linguistic patterns to those of the questioned text. The result of this analysis can help attribute or exclude potential authors, and in some cases may even prove inconclusive due to the nature of the texts.

This approach to authorship attribution is well researched and documented peer-reviewed articles, and is guided by two fundamental principles. Firstly, every author has his or her own unique way of using language, often referred to as an idiolect. Secondly, these patterns can be identified through empirical and careful analysis.

Even though people from similar socio-economic backgrounds may use the same dialect of a language, each individual within that group will exhibit their own idiosyncrasies. Exactly why one language user uses one form of a linguistic item, whereas another user may use a different form can be attributed to two reasons. Firstly, how well an individual knows the language, and secondly, how the individual uses the language. Differences in writing styles especially on social media, and/or Internet Based Communication can often be due to the choices available from a large pool of acceptable linguistic alternatives, and the writers own idiosyncratic usage which have become habit. The analysis of the specific habits of writers are known as style markers, and it is this analysis of style markers which forms the basis of forensic stylistic analysis.

Method

The following texts were used for the analysis:

Known: The website www.graemejoffe-exposed.com (2,670 words)

Questioned: Twitter postings from (a) Ryan Vrede (3,252 words)

(b) Mark Keohane (2,549 words)

(c)David Issacson (2,776 words)

I analysed the linguistic features used the questioned website against the linguistic features found in the three Twitter accounts to see if any of the linguistic features used by the three potential authors matches the linguistic features exhibited on the website. In order to perform this task, I did the following: I mined the known writing for features (style markers) that appeared to be idiosyncratic. I looked for similar style markers in the three sets of Twitter feeds.

The following style markers were chosen:

Style Marker	Example
Multiple exclamation marks	This is absolute gold !!!!
Multiple question marks	What do I do now????
Double quotation marks	''Joffers my booooooooiiii''
Brackets	(Drunk in love)
Hyphens	Demi-celebrity
Dashes	Fated adventures – Township TV
Capitalisation	PUBLIC SERVICE ANNOUNCEMENT
Capitalisaion+exclamation marks	THAT IS A FACT!!!
Word+no space+elliptical dots	Real name – Colin Webster……….
Word+space+elliptical dots	Last minute …. Is this an Omen

It should be noted that even though that the language of blogs and the language used on Twitter are both examples of Computer Mediated Communication, they are slightly different genres and the writing styles can be different. Each Tweet can be a maximum of 140 characters, whereas, blogs are composed of full paragraphs. Despite that, the writing styles of the analysed texts shared similar features, and were for the most part spontaneous and unedited, and conversational in style. All the chosen style markers are commonly found in Tweets and blogs, where the non-standard use of punctuation is common and deliberate. The table below shows the chosen style markers and how often they occurred.

Feature	Website	Vrede	Keohane	Isaacson
Multiple exclamation marks	14	19	0	37
Multiple question marks	1	0	0	7
Double quotation marks	11	3	0	4
Brackets	2	5	3	5
Hyphens	7	2	11	12
Dashes	6	6	9	28
Capitalisation	7	3	0	0
Capitalisan+exclamation marks	3	3	0	0
Word+no space+elliptical dots	4	4	1	1
Word+space+elliptical dots	0	0	0	31

Even though all three potential authors used most of the style markers, there are two that stand out for closer scrutiny, namely *Capitalisation+exclamation marks* and *Word+no space+elliptical dots*. These two constructions are quite unusual and the fact that Vrede used both of them indicates the possibility of him being one of the authors of the defamatory blog.

I reserve the right to amend this declaration, if additional evidence is presented to me.

Colin Michell

20 February 2016

Fujairah, United Arab Emirates

***

Vrede was always my chief suspect.

Toegther with Keohane, they would always play the man and not the ball. They needed to deflect from the truth.

They couldn't help themselves.

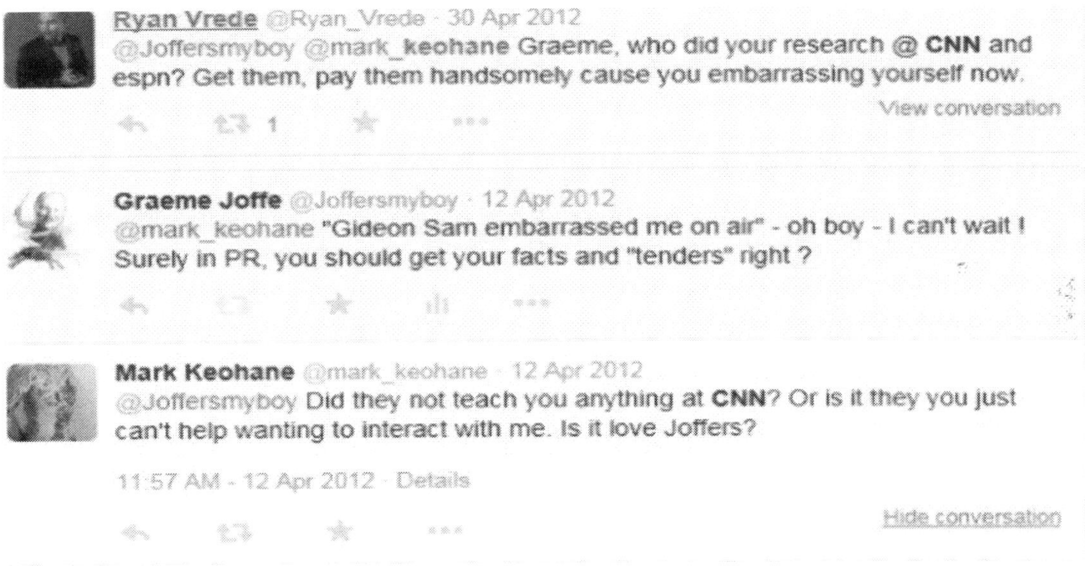

Ryan Vrede @Ryan_Vrede · 30 Apr 2012
@Joffersmyboy @mark_keohane Graeme, who did your research @ CNN and espn? Get them, pay them handsomely cause you embarrassing yourself now.
View conversation
1

Graeme Joffe @Joffersmyboy · 12 Apr 2012
@mark_keohane "Gideon Sam embarrassed me on air" - oh boy - I can't wait !
Surely in PR, you should get your facts and "tenders" right ?

Mark Keohane @mark_keohane · 12 Apr 2012
@Joffersmyboy Did they not teach you anything at CNN? Or is it they you just can't help wanting to interact with me. Is it love Joffers?
11:57 AM - 12 Apr 2012 · Details
Hide conversation

The irony is the love Vrede has for Keohane and still very loyal to his mentor, posting this on twitter after the Boks upset the All Blacks in New Zealand in 2018.

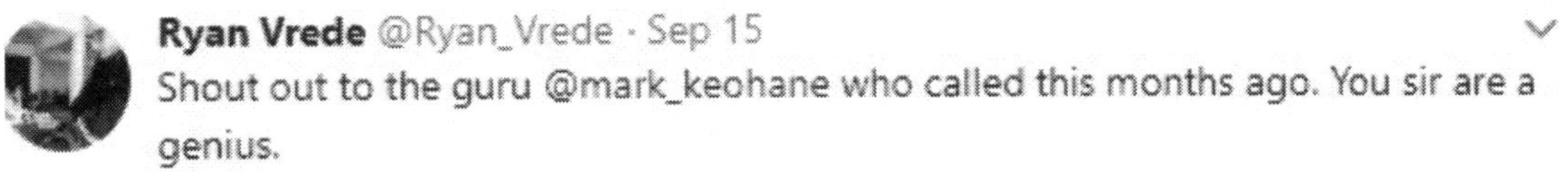

Ryan Vrede @Ryan_Vrede · Sep 15
Shout out to the guru @mark_keohane who called this months ago. You sir are a genius.

Throw in arrogance personified when confronted with a difference of opinion.

Ryan Vrede @Ryan_Vrede · Nov 8
1. I'm employed because I have words. All the words. 2. I'm happy to field different views to my own. You however haven't watched or listened to what we said and then attack our competency based on that. So either rewatch or shut up.

> **Pieter Henderson** @capi2274
> This is the reply I get from Ryan.
>
> I just want to say this is an example of an inability to handle opinion you do not like....

The SA sports media is much the poorer with these type individuals.

As of January 2019, Vrede was the editor of Man magazine and still a senior sports journalist at Highbury Safika Media.

"He has all the words!"

Don't confuse confidence with arrogance. Arrogance is being full of yourself, feeling you're always right, and believing your accomplishments or abilities make you better than other people. People often believe arrogance is excessive confidence, but it's really a lack of confidence. Arrogant people are insecure, and often repel others. Truly confident people feel good about themselves and attract others to them. - Christine Hartman

I would love to sue the pants off HSM for defamation and hopefully that day will still come!

Chapter 27: Defamation Insurance

On going the freelance journalism route, I decided to take out some personal indemnity insurance coverage. Who would have thought a couple years later, it would come in handy for the SASCOC defamation case against me.

But was it in my best interests?

I approached my brokers, Barker Insurance with whom I had been a client with for over twelve years. They referred my SASCOC defamation case to Etana (who had been bought out by Hollard) and who were the underwriters of the policy.

It was back and forth for a few weeks as Hollard had asked their attorneys at Norton Rose Fulbright to evaluate if I did in fact have coverage.

After all, R21.1 million was a big number and it would have been cheaper to find a loophole in the policy.

I had good friend, Chris Watson who is in the insurance game himself, to have a look at the contract and fine print.

RISK DETAILS ***PROFESSIONAL INDEMNITY***

A SPECIALIZED RISK

Professional Indemnity	*DESCRIPTION*
Specialized Section	Professional Indemnity
VAT RULES ON INCOME	VAT Inclusive
PLACEMENT RULES ON INCOME	Placement is subject to standard commission rules
Placement Fee or Commission Percentage	20.00
Schedule Sum Insured	10,000,000.00
Schedule Periodic Premium Amount	22,500.00
Pro-Rata Adjustment General Class (Debit or Credit)	NOT Required
Schedule Pro-Rata Premium Amount	0.00

4. **Defamation**
The **Insurer** will pay on behalf of any **Insured** all **Damages** resulting from any **Claim** for libel or slander committed unintentionally by an **Insured**.

Chris made it clear to the insurers in a meeting that there was no grey area with my policy, which had an annual premium of over R20 000.

After three weeks, I finally got confirmation from Etana that I was indeed covered for the claim, up to R10 million with a R25 000 deductible.

The insurers appointed Norton Rose Fulbright (Kathryn Gawith) to file a Notice of Intention to defend and they in turn had briefed Tremayne Dalrymple and John Campbell SC as "my" defamation counsel.

I say "my" as I soon realized that the case was no longer mine but now that of the insurers and my legal needs were going to be secondary.

I was constantly reminded by Kathryn:

Your insurance policy is there to act as a shield rather than a sword. We will take instruction from Hollard concerning your requests.

What about me, the client and my livelihood while the case dragged on and on?

My first meeting with the entire team (legal and insurers) was in August 2013, where I handed over two files of the information and evidence from all the exposes that I had written up until then.

SASCOC are the masters of delay tactics when it comes to legal proceedings and they use public funds to fight the cause.

They drag it out in hope the individual will lose patience, give up or run out of funds.

Yes, the personal indemnity was a nice to have at this stage ,but I was of the opinion in our meeting that we needed to fight fire with fire and get them into court as soon as possible.

But in Kathryn's words: "Be careful what you wish for!"

I already had more than enough evidence and SASCOC would have had nowhere to hide once we got 'discovery' of some bank accounts (individuals, companies and conduits) as well as contracts and minutes of meetings.

I had already prepared a list for discovery.

The legal team had other ideas and decided to go the exception route.

After fourteen months of legal wrangling over the exceptions and great expense, the first court date.

15 October 2014 in the Johannesburg High Court, Judge Francis, a former labour court judge heard the exceptions.

I cut a lone figure in the third row of the courtroom.

Rather strange that the Olympic body were suing a journalist for R21.1 million but no-one from SASCOC or the media were in attendance.

The "partial" judgement came out almost two months later and SASCOC thought they had won a gold medal.

TEN YEAR ANNIVERSARY CELEBRATION

MEMORANDUM

SASCOC

To: **ALL BOARD MEMBERS, and MEMBERSHIP OF SASCOC**

From: **CHIEF EXECUTIVE OFFICER**

Date: **12.12.2014**

Re: **GRAEME JOFFE**

As you are no doubt aware, Graeme Joffe has been engaged in continuing to defame and attack the good name of SASCOC and its Board, as well as various Members.

Arising out of this, the Board took a decision to institute a defamation suit against Graeme Joffe, which was duly done in July 2013, as a result of a series of online articles, and a tweet published by Mr Joffe. Rather than responding to the Summons and substantiating his defence, Mr Joffe lodged a series of technical objections to the claim.

This matter was held today, before Judge Francis of the Gauteng Local Division of the High Court of South Africa, and all 131 of exceptions to the claim which SASCOC and certain Board Members brought against Mr Graeme Joffe, were dismissed with the costs of two Counsel.

It is interesting to note that paragraph 5 of Judge Francis' Judgment clearly stated that: "this is a clear waste of the court's time and resources. The exceptions raised by the Defendant (Joffe) are the worst form of nit picking that I have ever seen in my 13 years on the bench".

SASCOC is presently drawing and taxing a bill of costs to recover same from Mr Joffe. Once Mr Joffe's substantive defence to this claim is received, I will update you all.

Kind regards,

Tubby Reddy

The "good name" of SASCOC?

Reddy must have his own definition for good.

I mentioned "partial" judgement as Judge Francis had failed to rule on the leave to amend and only did so ten months later.

Yes, ten months later!

What took him so long to make this simple ruling and why?

According to Chris MacRoberts …

Whilst the outcome of the judgment is not a surprise, our view is that it contains a number of gratuitous and inaccurate statements. That it is now 10 months since the matter was argued has not helped. It is strange that the judge has taken this long to resolve this issue in the face of repeated requests.

The objection to the proposed amendment fitted with the exception. It would have been inconsistent to do the one and not the other. This fact is not given credence in the judgment.

Once the exception was dismissed, the major ground of objection went with it – however, as the judge did not deal with this in hios exception judgment neither we nor Webber Wentzel assume that leave to amend was granted. The argument that the amendment was brought in bad faith was because the notice of intention to amend was served well after we have served our second excpetion but the proposed amendment did not cure any of the substantive grounds of exception. It dealt only with the 131 ground of exception.

The point and timing of our objection was based on the fact that the exceptions had already been taken and proposed amendments did not cure any of those defects.

The comment in the paragraph you refer to is not a criticism of the fact that you have not pleaded. It means that you cannot say the amendment is brought late when you have yet to plead.

The case had already dragged on for two years.

I just wish the legal team had debated the merits of my opinion to enter a plea, get discovery and get SASCOC into court as soon as possible.

131 exceptions?

I looked like the idiot and all the legal minds I spoke to about this were stunned and not surprised we lost.

One lawyer in Grahamstown asked me if we were trying to "introduce new law" with all the exceptions and another said: "I will tell you one thing, your lawyers in the case have been talking bullshit technical points."

A couple months after the "graemejoffe-exposed.com" came out, I thought we now had another golden legal opportunity to put a major dent in SASCOC's case as their media partners, Highbury Safika Media (HSM) were involved with the highly defamatory website and were also committing cybercrime.

Mark Keohane would no doubt have been bragging to Reddy about it over some muffins and coffee even though he was 'no longer' an HSM employee.

I requested Norton Rose Fulbright to address a take-down notification concerning the website and obtain a court order to seize HSM computers and documents?

What was I thinking?

We have taken instructions from Hollard concerning your requests. Hollard have declined to fund the requested actions. We are instructed to remind you of your duty under the policy to co-operate with the insurer in respect of your defence and not to take any steps which may prejudice the defence. Failing to do so may cause Hollard to review its coverage position under the policy. Practically, this means that you must render all assistance that we have requested to finalise the plea without delay. That means producing the concise and certain evidence that can be pleaded to support the statements made in your articles. - Chris MacRoberts

My relationship with the legal team was severely strained in February 2015.

I was asked to come to Johannesburg at my own expense to meet with Counsel to go through the plea. The meeting was all over the place and got heated at times. I was under the impression they had been through most of the evidence that I had given them and we were there to dot the i's and cross the t's on the plea.

It wasn't and I was annoyed at having to waste my time and money (airfare and hotel) for a rather meaningless meeting.

Not living in Johannesburg any longer wasn't making matters easier and I asked the insurers if it would be possible to appoint a legal team in Grahamstown.

As far as your request is concerned, we can unfortunately not agree to it. Should you wish to take over your defence, you need to formally withdraw the claim. Albeit very expensive, we believe you have to best possible attorneys and counsel on your side. Insurers accepted you are entitled to indemnity under the Policy and will defend your legal liability as far the claim is concerned. So strictly speaking, whilst you remain the Insured, Hollard is Norton Rose Fulbright's (NRF) client since they obtain all instructions from us and we pay their fees. All actions taken by NRF will always be in your best interest considering the claim at hand. - Willie Jansen van Rensburg (Hollard)

To be perfectly honest, I didn't think the actions being taken were in my best interests and over a R1 million had already been spent.

At the meeting in Johannesburg, I was asked to put another dossier together in respect of all SASCOC claims.

I spent four solid days over the Easter weekend, putting it all together, making sure I left no stone unturned.

Unfortunately, that wasn't good enough.

It is difficult to follow in its present form and we will need to work at distilling the factual evidence relevant to each allegation from the supporting emails, documents and articles.

We attach a further version of the draft plea sent to us yesterday by counsel. Please look at the covering comments by counsel. In particular please confirm:

whether you generated the headline(s) for the articles that you submitted to Sport24;
whether the factual allegations were in fact widely reported in the media in South Africa (other than by

you). Please indicate where this is not the case.

I also attach your working document with our comments and questions. Once you have addressed those we will then need to work towards consolidating the information that you have provided into the draft plea.

Lastly, I was concerned to read your tweet yesterday about completing the dossier for your legal team to enable you to plead. It is not sensible to put that information in the public domain because, at the very least, it invites the plaintiffs to place unwelcome pressure on us to plead. - Chris MacRoberts

It just seemed as if I was doing all the work and what was "unwelcome pressure on us to plead"?

SASCOC should have been in the dock two years ago.

It was a couple weeks later that my safety was threatened and I was forced to flee South Africa.

I wasn't in a good space but remained in contact with Chris to keep him abreast of what was happening.

We then had a tele-conference a few months later to discuss the plea again.

Again, we didn't seem to achieve much as I was of the opinion that some of the strongest evidence was being left out.

27 September 2015
Re: SASCOC/plea

Dear Chris and Kathryn

I cut my trip short by a couple days to address this with the matter of urgency that it requires and am available for the tele-conference on Monday 28 September as discussed.

Firstly, I am not sure if you can appreciate what I have been through in the last four years and especially the last five months.

The lonely crusade of exposing all the corruption has been a very stressful one and with it, came the threats, anonymous blog and then the threat to my personal safety, which forced to me flee South Africa.

So, I am disappointed Kathryn's disgruntled comment during our last tele-conference on 10 September 2015, saying: "we have never had a client like this" ...

How many clients have you had that have had to flee South Africa due to a threat to his/her personal safety?

It still surprises me that there is no mention of my criminal case, SAPS statement, the Private Investigator (PI) recording or whatsapp messages from Tim Marsland in the plea.

The PI refers to the imminent arrest of the SASCOC CEO, Tubby Reddy (third plaintiff in our case) as well as three other sports officials including SASCOC's legal ally, Raymond Hack.

Tim Marsland confirms this in his whatsapp messages.

I strongly believe this information (which is in your possession) plus the fact that the criminal case has bounced around from Sandton SAPS to Randburg Magistrates Court and is now in the hands of the Provincial Investigation Unit is of vital importance to our case.

It also disappoints me that during our last tele-conference (10 September 2015) Kathryn still needed to ask who Tim Marsland was after all these months?

The fact that the arrests didn't happen as promised and that there may be a complete cover up by the SAPS should be brought to the fore in our case.

My phone was tapped, my emails were hacked and my life was threatened forcing me to flee the country.

Surely, that is strong evidence for our case?

I was also given no assistance from any authorities including the SAPS, MTN, SANEF, PP and the radio interview that was conducted by Advocate Paul Hoffman (re: lack of protection for a whistle-blower in my case) is also very strong back up evidence for our case and I strongly believe it should be included in the plea.

There is also no mention in our plea of the anonymous, highly defamatory blog which attempts to defame and discredit me.

I have enough evidence to show that SASCOC's media partners are directly linked to set-up and content in the blog and I have now engaged with a professional MA in Linguistics to try and source the writer/s.

Your email of 09/04/2015 states:

"You are fortunate that Hollard is supportive of the defence but as you are aware, their funding does not extend to pursuing the perpetrators of this website. The fact that it has reappeared suggests that your efforts to close it down may have encouraged them."

What a load of garbage and to say I am fortunate that Hollard is supportive of my defence is concerning. I have had an insurance policy for years, which covers defamation. I was and still am a paying client.

Also, the defaming website was only down for four days while Enom requested he (anonymous) change his personal particulars. It has been up and running again for over three weeks. So, to say that my efforts to close it down is fact for its re-appearance is again of great concern to me.

I often get the feeling from your emails that Hollard is the client and not myself, who is mentioned as the defendant in the summons. The plea has also become very confusing for me with all the changing drafts.

Regards
Graeme

***

I was not happy with the plea and pressurized to sign it but I was not the client! And a day after signing the plea, Christopher MacRoberts was gone.

MacRoberts, Christopher <Christopher.MacRoberts@nortonrosefulbright.com> 9/30/15
to me, Tremayne, jcampbell, Kathryn, De, ETA167

Dear Graeme

We **attach** the signed plea that has been sent for service on Webber Wentzel and filing at court in accordance with your instructions.

An additional plea along the lines suggested in your email below has not been included at this stage for the reasons set out in the **attached** memorandum prepared by Tremayne Dalrymple.

Please note that today is my is my last day with Norton Rose Fulbright. This matter will continue to be handled by Kathryn Gawith and you should correspond with her going forward.

Marais De Vaal will arrange to send you a copy of the recording of yesterday's call via Dropbox or similar and you will hear further from us in due course.

Kind regards

Then Kathryn was gone.

Dear Graeme

SASCOC and others

I trust that you are keeping well. I note that you have forwarded various articles to us for inclusion in your file and Maxine has arranged this.

The purpose of this letter is to advise you that I will shortly be leaving Norton Rose Fulbright and joining Webber Wentzel. In the light of the fact that Webber Wentzel represents SASCOC in this matter, it would obviously be inappropriate for me to remain involved. It obviously goes without saying that I would not discuss this matter with Dario Milo, who represents SASCOC in this action. I have been in communication with the insurers on what they would like me to do having regard to this issue. Willie Jansen van Rensburg of Hollard suggested, and I believe that it is the most appropriate solution, that the file should be transferred to Chris MacRoberts who is now a senior associate at Clydes. As you are well aware, Chris has an intimate knowledge of the details of this action and was involved in all the heavy lifting prior to his departure from Norton Rose late last year. Willie has spoken to Chris about it and I myself have spoken to him as well. He is happy to take the matter over and we will take steps to arrange for the file to be transferred to Clydes. When I spoke to Chris earlier today, he had already been contacted by Willie in relation to taking the matter over and confirmed to me that he is aware of all your recent publications as he continues to follow you on Twitter.

My personal view is that SASCOC are unlikely to take steps to set this matter down for trial and it remains inappropriate for your legal representatives to take a proactive role as long as you are out of the country.

Please contact me if you have any queries. I would like to take the opportunity of wishing you well for the future.

Yours sincerely

Kathryn Gawith
Director
Norton Rose Fulbright South Africa Inc

Yes, gone to the opposition legal firm (who were representing SASCOC) along with her associate, Maxine Smith who had been doing all our filing after the departure of Chris.

I didn't know whether to laugh or cry.

23 August 2016 …

I met with Hollard this morning and we have been instructed to take over the defence of this matter following Kathryn Gawith's departure from Norton Rose Fulbright. I am making arrangements for us to come on record formally and to receive the Norton Rose Fulbright files. - Christopher MacRoberts

Chris was back on the job with his new legal firm.

There was no movement in the case for eleven months from October 2015 to August 2016 and then all of a sudden with the change in my legal team, SASCOC request discovery and more particulars in the space of ten days.

And they want to streamline the case!

3. The plaintiffs propose that the issues taken to trial be streamlined before the parties begin the discovery process and preparation for trial.

4. To this end, the plaintiffs advise that they intend to concentrate their case at trial only on the most significant defamatory allegations made by your client.

5. This approach will reduce the volume of documents required to be discovered by each party, the length of the trial, the number of articles and statements at issue, and the scope of any requests in terms of Rule 21 or 35 of the Uniform Rules.

6. The plaintiffs therefore advise that they intend to focus exclusively on the claims with defamatory statements of and concerning our clients that are per se defamatory and that give rise to the following imputations:

6.1 "The plaintiffs engage in corruption".

6.2 "The plaintiffs engage in election rigging".

It was never going to trial but was SASCOC or their legal team were now in a hurry?

Sascoc still under investigation – Madonsela

An investigation into allegations against the SA Sports Confederation and Olympic Committee (Sascoc) remains ongoing, according to the Public Protector Thuli Madonsela, more than three years after it was launched. "We are interacting with respondents and requesting information on some of the issues critical to the probe," Madonsela's spokesperson Oupa Segalwe said this week. While the office of government watchdog said it had expected a draft report on the investigation in December 2014, it revealed early last year the process had been delayed due to resource constraints. - (The Citizen, 2 September 2016)

I was never called by the Public Protector's office to share any information.

In 2016, SASCOC finally started to feel some heat from other members of the media with stories that were nothing new to me.

Corruption allegations against Gideon Sam come back to life

In the midst of preparing the South African Olympic Team for the Rio Games, the South African Sports Confederation and Olympic Committee (Sascoc) is now holding high-level meetings to discuss the future of its president, Gideon Sam, amid renewed allegations of corruption. (Groundup, 13 July 2016)

Athletes must 'pay' own way to Rio

Despite a windfall of R70 million, South Africa's medal hopefuls will have to cough up thousands of rands just to get to this year's Olympic Games in Rio de Janeiro.With just more than four weeks to go until the Games get under way, at least three of the country's top athletes do not know if their coaches will be allowed to accompany them to Brazil. (City Press, 9 July 2016)

Why SA sport is so rotten

When Fikile Mbalula announced on April 25 that he was banning four sporting codes from hosting and bidding for major international tournaments as punishment for inadequate transformation records, the irony was blatant ... It does not help that we have an increasingly pliant sports media, who too easily sign up to the mundane messages being peddled by the sporting bodies. Often those journalists who fall out of line are bullied by the organisations and cast out of the pack. (Financial Mail, 5 May 2016)

MP's pricey Olympic splash

Parliament's sports portfolio committee chairperson, Beauty Dlulane, has extracted a free ride to the Rio Olympics from one of the organisations the committee oversees – without the approval of the national legislature. City Press has seen a letter from the SA Sports Confederation and Olympic Committee (Sascoc), the controlling body for all high-performance sports in South Africa, confirming that Dlulane and two other MPs would be "guests to join Team SA" for 10 days out of the 17-day sporting jamboree. (City Press, 3 May 2016)

The DA Shadow Minister of Sport, Solly Malatsi was also invited on the junket but declined SASCOC's offer.

We also find it ironic that SASCOC, which often bemoans the lack of funding for struggling to support our athletes as extensively as it wants to, can somehow afford to bankroll 3 MPs to Rio. - Solly Malatsi (Sunday Times, 8 May 2016)

Hockey folly: Shame on SASCOC

With Rio 2016 a mere three months away, the South African Sports Confederation and Olympic Committee (SASCOC), has still not budged with regard to our men's and women's hockey teams and both will unfortunately not be participating in the coveted and prestigious Olympic Games. Having met both the International Hockey Federation's (IHF) as well as the International Olympic Committee's (IOC) qualifying criteria by both being crowned champions of Africa, SASCOC simply does not have faith in these teams. The red tape of SASCOC's strict qualifying criteria will no doubt have serious repercussions and consequences down the line. Short- sighted, petulant and self-serving - this seems the only way I can describe the above-mentioned sporting body. (sport24, 5 May 2016)

Was the R10m for not fighting their Olympic exclusion legally? If so, SAHA has sold their own players out.

Unfortunately, they (SAHA) did not have an appetite for an international arbitration. - Dean Moulder, lawyer

Mind Games: What else is Graeme Joffe right about?

In August 2013 presenter and columnist Graeme Joffe published an article on his SportsFire website that contained perturbing allegations involving SA Rugby Union (Saru) CEO Jurie Roux ... Now further investigations by reporter Pieter du Toit for News24 have brought to light a report by auditing firm KPMG that supposedly confirms Roux's skulduggery. ... This provides whistle-blower Joffe with gratifying justification of his tenacious crusade to expose graft in South African sport ... In time, Joffe became a megaphone for disaffected sports bodies and sportspeople who relayed allegations of maladministration, bad treatment or misappropriation of funds to him, as they feared victimisation if they were to speak out themselves. Joffe became a figure of disparagement. Sports administrators detested his revelations and, sadly, members of the media turned on him. (City Press, 31 January 2016)

Top firm to probe R17m sports spend

Buffalo City Metro has roped in forensic investigators KPMG to probe the dodgy spending of R17.3-million in sports events, some of which never took place, including a R250000 "egg-and-spoon" race tournament. (Daily Dispatch, 30 July 2016)

Must have been some very expensive eggs!

But so often these stories would just disappear without a follow up and no accountability or consequences!

Why? And why was I still being sued?

As of February 2016, my defamation insurance had already paid out over R1.6 million in legal fees.

I can only imagine what SASCOC has paid Webber Wentzel from public funds, which should be going to the athletes.

Is SASCOC also paying for the board members who are plaintiffs in the case?

Is SASCOC even properly constituted after changing from a Section 21 company to an Association?

Why the change? Have they followed the Companies Act? Who were the liquidators, if any?

Not in the plea?

And on 9 September 2016, I received this letter from Chris MacRoberts.

SASCOC and Others / Graeme Joffe

1 We refer to our email to you dated 7 September 2016 in which we cautioned you about the content of a tweet you had published, which read:

> *"Pres & VP of corrupt ASA, ex SASCOC/cricket/rugby officials (dirty hands) & ex pres of corrupt BSA – all on Lottery distribution agency?"*

2 The basis for our email was to reiterate that you must be careful and circumspect in what you publish, particularly where it has the potential to fan the flames in your case, antagonise the plaintiffs or potentially aggravate the damages they are claiming because the content could be viewed as defamatory of the plaintiffs.

3 We have conveyed this request to you on numerous occasions in the past.

4 We emphasised that the captioned tweet is precisely the kind of publication that must be avoided and asked that you refrain from publishing similar comments in order to comply with your obligations under the policy.

5 Hollard have brought a further tweet dated 7 September 2016 to our notice which reads:

> *"When are Mbalula, Moemi & co going to be exposed? Just stepped on another land mine/dirty conduit of SRSA with abuse of Lottery funding."*

6 We are instructed that Hollard is not prepared to condone tweets of this nature given their potential to aggravate the issues in dispute and compromise your defence, irrespective of what the public interest may be.

My freedom of speech was now being curtailed?

By the end of 2016, SASCOC had not only streamlined the case but had also cut their plea/summons in half.

In essence, they had admitted 'half guilt' already but Hollard were now going to make a 'business decision' and settle the claim.

10 April 2017 …

Hollard has, following our recent engagement with the plaintiffs' attorneys, mandated us to make a settlement offer to the plaintiffs, in full and final settlement and without admission of liability, of R1.3 million plus costs on the party and party scale as taxed or agreed. This does not require an apology or acknowledgement of wrongdoing by you and is a purely commercial settlement to put an end to the action. 16 In terms of the policy, Hollard requires your written consent to settle the matter on this basis and we accordingly request this from you, such that if the offer is accepted by the plaintiffs the settlement can be made effective. We draw your notice to the fact that if you withhold consent to such settlement, Hollard's liability for all Loss on account of your Claim shall not exceed the amount for which it could have settled such Claim, plus Defence Costs incurred as of the date such settlement was proposed in writing by Hollard. - Chris MacRoberts

So as to ensure that you understand the consequences of consenting or not consenting to the proposed settlement, we advise you that: 10.1 Should you furnish the consent requested, Hollard will conclude the settlement agreement. If you have consented by signing the proposed settlement, it will not be necessary for Hollard to sign it. Either way, Hollard will comply with the terms of the proposed settlement vis-à-vis the plaintiffs. This will constitute a full and final settlement of the action against you. 10.2 If you decline to consent to the proposed settlement, or fail to revert to us by the time referred to above, Hollard will not conclude the settlement agreement. This s because Hollard cannot conclude the settlement agreement without your written consent.

The litigation will thus continue. 11 In the event of what is set out in the immediately preceding paragraph transpiring: 11.1 Hollard will terminate our mandate to act on your behalf; 11.2 We will immediately withdraw as your attorneys of record; 11.3 You will be free to defend the action in your personal capacity or to appoint new attorneys to deal with the matter and who will act solely on your instructions and at your own cost. 11.4 Should you not inform the plaintiffs' attorneys of an address within 15 kilometres of court at which you will accept service of documents, or not appoint new attorneys within ten court days of our withdrawal, the plaintiffs will not be obliged to notify you of any further steps in relation to the litigation. It is likely that they will proceed to set the matter down for default judgment against you. 11.5 Hollard's ultimate liability to you under the policy will be limited to the amount of R1 300 000.00. - Tony Hardie & Christopher MacRoberts Clyde & Co

In other words, if I didn't consent to the settlement, Hollard would have paid me out R1.3 million to continue to fight the case on my own.

What a joke!

The policy limit was R10 million.

R1.3 million would have been gobbled up in legal fees before even going to trial.

Or I would face a default judgement. Hollard had now boxed me into a corner. My insurance policy had failed me. Was there a conflict of interests?

Hollard has long been a major sponsor of South African rowing and is thus a partner to SASCOC.

Paolo Cavalieri is one of the Hollard top brass (former CEO and managing director) and is still very involved with SA rowing at the highest level.

It's ironic that a few years back he wanted to privatize SA rowing as he was concerned that the Hollard sponsorship funding was being mismanaged by the sporting officials.

He knew the SASCOC antics.

When I asked for a meeting with Cavalieri at the very first meeting with Hollard, they chose to ignore my request. Hollard acted in a disgraceful manner with my case, no backbone and failed to adhere to the policy on numerous occasions.

The big corporate bullying tactics, lack of transparency and conflict of interests was shameful!

Hollard's 'top notch' legal team also got it horribly wrong with so much of the defence including the reason for not appealing the exceptions ruling.

Chris told me for Constitutional Court authority on the general principle that the dismissal of an exception is not appealable and referred to a legal case not even relating to defamation.

Baliso v Firstrand Bank Ltd. (04 August 2016)

I gave him a legal case where the exceptions ruling was appealed in a defamation case.

Khumalo and Others v Holomisa (CCT53/01) [2002]

No response.

But four years later and the criminals of SA sport get a settlement!

If one wants to clear your name, you want to get to court as soon as possible.

Not SASCOC, they wanted to bully, cripple and silence me and they were allowed to do it.

I only consented to the settlement so I could move on with my life but had Hollard stuck to the policy and paid out the remainder of the limit, I would have continued the fight for justice.

Had the legal team taken instruction from me, this case would have ended years ago and I wouldn't have been chased out of the country.

I can only hope that no other individual who tries to make a difference, suffers the same fate.

It was a malicious prosecution!

And this is how some in the SA media covered the settlement …

Graeme Joffe settles SASCOC legal battle

Sascoc has welcomed the request by lawyers for Graeme Joffe for a settlement in the long-standing legal case. Joffe's insurers Hollard Insurance proposed a settlement to pay Sascoc R1.3 million. Sascoc has agreed to the terms of the offer. (EWN, 18 July 2017)

SASCOC, Graeme Joffe reach out-of-court settlement

The settlement offer is a clear indication that, despite Joffe's numerous allegations and challenges to SASCOC, he was unable to substantiate or provide evidence that would have stood up in court. Hence the offer to settle is an acceptance of his misconduct. (sport24, 18 July 2017)

There was no byline for the sport24 story but no doubt my 'good friend', Mark Keohane had some input.

So, I had to set the record straight again, which was published in BizNews.

Sports journalist Graeme Joffe has made a name for himself by scrutinising corruption in South African sport. He previously started asking uncomfortable questions around the Guptas close links to local sports federations, a fact that has since emerged in the controversial Gupta email leaks. His exposes and tough questions seemingly caused such a stir that he was forced to leave South Africa to ensure his safety. He has always been outspoken and now he's speaking out following a decision by his insurers, Hollard Insurance, to pay a proposed settlement to Sascoc of R1.3 million. The settlement centres on a defamation claim, launched by Sascoc in July 2013, against the sports journalist following a series of online articles and tweets published by Joffe concerning the sports body and its board members. Joffe tells his side of the story here. – Gareth van Zyl

18 July 2017

Dear fellow South Africans:

I would like to take this opportunity to set the record straight after all the factually incorrect and misleading media reports which were mostly copied and pasted from a SASCOC press release and the SASCOC website.

Not one sports journalist even called or emailed me for a comment or to confirm or deny the SASCOC PR spin. So, for the record:

I did not settle with SASCOC, I did not pay them one cent and there was no apology or retraction.

I will never ever apologize for telling the truth!

Everything I have reported on was factually correct and the truth will all one day prevail.

SASCOC is a totally corrupt organization!

Hollard Insurance took a business decision to settle with SASCOC which I was vehemently opposed to.

And this despite, "our" legal counsel saying we would more than likely win the case.

Hollard took over my defence, they appointed the legal team and run the case as they saw fit from the very beginning.

I wanted SASCOC in court as soon as possible and did not agree with the exceptions route but it wasn't my case any longer.

The legal team took instruction from Hollard.

After four years, there was still had no discovery from SASCOC despite my numerous requests to Hollard and the legal team.

But SASCOC twice requested the same discovery from me (another delay tactic) and after the first round, they reduced their summons in half, knowing I had too much evidence.

SASCOC suing me in my personal capacity for R21.1 million was just a blatant attempt to bully and silence me and cripple me financially.

They didn't know I had defamation insurance when they sued.

So, they kept the case going for four years to try and make a point and not to embarrass themselves further.

According to SASCOC, they wanted to clear their "good name" – really?

If you wanted to clear your good name – wouldn't you want the defendant in court as soon as possible?

Not SASCOC because their name is anything but good!

SASCOC were never coming to court and we probably would have waited another four years to get discovery from them.

One has no idea how investigative journalism consumes your life and becomes an addiction but I have no regrets, especially knowing in a couple years-time or however long it takes, you will all be able to say Graeme Joffe was right.

I exposed the Gupta capture in SA sport last March – I was right without having access to the GuptaLeaks.

http://www.biznews.com/thought-leaders/2016/03/26/graeme-joffe-have-guptas-also-captured-sa-sport-certainly-looks-like-it/

I could go on and on …

My phone wasn't illegally tapped for nothing, my emails weren't hacked for nothing.

SASCOC's media/PR company didn't create a fake website on a server in Panama to defame and discredit me for nothing.

I wasn't followed from Melrose Arch after a breakfast meeting for nothing.

The criminal case I opened up wasn't swept under the carpet for nothing.

I didn't receive a threat to my safety for nothing.

The corrupt have too much to lose and they got what they wanted, to get me out of the country and for me to stop my digital publication which was naming and shaming corrupt sports officials as well as exposing the blatant theft of National Lottery funds.

There is a mafia running SA sport aided by a seriously corrupted National Lottery and a conflicted media.

SASCOC and many of the other big SA sporting federations hand select journalists to go on 'freebie' tours and trips and these are many of the very same journalists who would only be too happy to see me go down.

Not one of them even reported on the fact when SASCOC cut their summons in half after getting discovery.

I guess there was no press release from SASCOC on that.

The gravy train journalists love to stay in SASCOC's good books and will copy and paste whatever the Olympic body sends out, even if it's ten days after the fact, like in this case.

Head of News24 sport, Garrin Lambley said:

> Hi Graeme, article a 'copy and paste' from SASCOC press release sent earlier today. Also available on the SASCOC website. Should you disagree / differ from what was sent, and wish to have something published, please email a statement to mysport@sport24.co.za

Let's see if they publish my response without editing.

Sport24 reporter, Mark Keohane is still a 'SASCOC consultant' and likes to cover for his buddies and paymasters, Tubby and Gideon.

Primedia reporters will also do their best to try and discredit me after I exposed Primedia Sport in a kickback scandal for a SA rugby commercial contract renewal.

Also, they haven't been able to answer any of my tough questions about LeadSA and how they benefit financially from all the sports parades and airport welcomes and send offs for SA Olympic teams.

Ironically, the lawyer representing SASCOC in my defamation case was Dario Milo who just happens to do work for both News24, Primedia and many other media houses.

Hollard's business decision makes me sad for SA's sportsmen and women as this was the one chance to expose the rot in SA sport.

My fight was for them.

Gideon Sam, Tubby Reddy and company should have had their day in court three years ago even though they would have withdrawn at some point, if the case ever got close to going to court.

The Hollard settlement made it ever so simple for SASCOC to withdraw.

I can now finally get on with my life after having this devious case with conflicted interests hanging over my head for four years and after devoting six hard and lonely years, exposing the corruption and maladministration in SA sport.

But again, I have no regrets!

I have my ethics and integrity as a sports journalist.

Best regards
Graeme

Chapter 28: Joining the Dots (Part 1)

In July 2017, things started to really unravel for the South African Olympic Committee (SASCOC).

The CEO, Tubby Reddy was suspended on charges of sexual harrassment and governance related issues. There had been another major fallout between Reddy and the SASCOC president, Gideon Sam and the board was split.

In January 2018, the suspension led to Reddy's dismissal as well as that of the SASCOC CFO, Vinesh Maharaj and manager, Jean Kelly.

Game over for disgraced SASCOC CEO sex-pest Reddy

Explosive details have emerged which led to the immediate sacking of SASCOC CEO Reddy, as well as the organisation's chief financial officer (Maharaj) and executive manager (Kelly) following a disciplinary hearing last month. (sport24, 11 January 2018)

The disciplinary report was 27 pages and explosive.

Advocate Anton Myburgh SC, an independent senior advocate and member of the Johannesburg Bar chaired the hearing.

> I have found Mr Reddy guilty of a wide range of charges relating to sexual harassment, Don Chen, M&M, SS Griffin, PCS, the ASA / SASCOC dispute, and BSA. In numerous instances, Mr Reddy acted dishonestly and betrayed the duty of good faith and trust and confidence that he owed to SASCOC and its board – conduct that is incompatible with the position of CEO. To exacerbate matters, his conduct brought SASCOC into disrepute, which has (as Mr Sam testified) negatively affected its ability to obtain funding and sponsorships. According to Mr Sam, the trust relationship between the parties has been irreparably destroyed, with this being borne out, in my view, by the severity of Mr Reddy's misconduct and the nature of his position. In the circumstances, despite Mr Reddy's length of service (12 years) and clean record, I recommend his summary dismissal.

> Turning to Mr Maharaj, I have also found him guilty of a wide range of charges relating to BGA / Fli-Afrika, M&M, SS Griffin, PCS, KSS, and BSA. In a number of instances, he acted dishonestly or committed financial irregularities, striking at the core of his duties. Overall, his conduct is incompatible with the position of CFO. According to Mr Sam, the trust relationship between the parties has been irreparably destroyed, with this being borne out, in my view, by the severity of Mr Maharaj's misconduct and the nature of his position. In

> the circumstances, despite Mr Maharaj's length of service (12 years) and clean record, I recommend his summary dismissal.
>
> Finally, in relation to Ms Kelly, although I found her guilty of only two charges (pertaining to SS Griffin and the ASA / SASCOC dispute), her misconduct was severe. In both instances, she acted dishonesty or in breach of her duty of good faith, and colluded with Mr Reddy against SASCOC. As mentioned above, the SS Griffin report caused SASCOC embarrassment and reputational damage – and Ms Kelly played a part in it. To my mind, her conduct is incompatible with the position of executive manager, which is also a senior position within the organisation. According to Mr Sam, the trust relationship between the parties has been irreparably destroyed, with this being borne out, in my view, by the severity of Ms Kelly's misconduct and the nature of her position. In the circumstances, despite Ms Kelly's length of service (ten years) and clean record, I recommend her summary dismissal.

The only reason why they had "clean records" was because no-one was prepared to dig and expose them.

It had to come from within and there is a decade of SASCOC dirt to still to be uncovered.

Reddy and Maharaj had run SASCOC like their own business for almost ten years.

In the guilty verdicts from the hearing …

Tubby Reddy

Guilty of sexual harassment. He emailed an erotic calendar to SASCOC employee, Desiree Vardhan and asked her to "identify her birthday position." Also, he repeatedly asked for neck and shoulder massages during working hours.

* (I had previously exposed his affairs and disgusting treatment of staff)

Guilty for failing to disclose to the SASCOC board his relationship with a Hong Kong based marketing company, Double Edge who were the agents for the controversial Chinese Olympic kit supplied to Team SA. On 1 April 2015, Don Chen sent an email to Reddy re: the agreement for the kit to be supplied at $900 (R11 000) per set and asked: "Let me know if we shall put the price up a bit or not, OK?" Then on June 8, 2016, Chen emailed Tubby's son, Mushed saying he was 'Tubby's friend and partner in China' and he should pass on the email which proposed "projects" between SASCOC or relevant companies under SASCOC adding "of course all these projects don't have to be real projects ... what we need is to create these opportunities and cash flow between SASCOC and the Chinese sports agency side."

* (I had already exposed his irregular trips to Hong Kong and questioned the Chinese clothing deal on numerous occasions)

Guilty for failing to disclose a conflict of interests with the controversial Ekhaya and SA bid exhibition at the 2014 Commonwealth Games in Glasgow. Reddy was a personal friend of David Naidoo whose marquee hiring company, M&M got the job without a tender and were paid R9 million for the set up despite the Service Level agreement showing they should only have received R5.94 million.

* (The Ekaya and irregular payments to Naidoo was one of my big exposes back in 2014)

Vinesh Maharaj

Guilty for getting the SASCOC service provider, Fli-Afrika to pay R90,000 for renovations to his home. According to the disciplinary report …

43.1 Both Fli-Afrika and Brad's Glass and Aluminium (BGA) are service providers to SASCOC.

43.2 On 25 January 2016, BGA submitted a quotation to Mr Maharaj for renovations at his home – the quotation being for some R90 000.

43.3 On 2 March 2017, Fli-Afrika addressed a letter to BGA advising that it had erroneously paid R535 310.20 into Fli-Afrika's bank account, and that the amount that should have been paid was R50 000. A refund of the balance (R485 310.20) was thus requested. (Seemingly it was duly effected.)

43.4 On 23 August 2017, Fli-Afrika addressed a further letter to BGA concerning the retained R50 000. The letter records:

> "We hereby formally request a refund of the amount paid to you during February 2016, <u>in respect of aluminium works that were supposed to have been carried out for Mr Vinesh Maharaj</u> (who is employed at SASCOC) at his flat in Rosebank, which works never took place.
>
> You will recall that Vinesh had spoken to Gasant to refund the monies to us, as <u>we had done the payment on his behalf</u>. However, the matter cannot simply be forgotten and we hereby request immediate refund of the sum of R50 000 into our bank account … ." (Own emphasis.)

The SS Griffin story was Reddy's concocted idea it backfired spectacularly.

Reddy missed a staff meeting address in February 2017 and construed that Sam was going to bug/tap the SASCOC offices.

He hired SS Griffin to debug the SASCOC offices and his own personal home.

On request of Reddy, Kelly asked Maharaj to pay R171 850 to SS Griffin for debugging and it was paid from the account of Volleyball South Africa.

Another payment to SS Griffin for R28 700 was made from the SASCOC account.

SS Griffin turned out to be a 'mystery' company and their report into the so-called bugging was altered by both Reddy and Kelly.

The SASCOC waters had now been severely muddied and in August 2017, the new Minister of Sports, Thulas Nxesi announced there would be a Ministerial Commission of Inquiry into the affairs of SASCOC.

The inquiry into Sascoc was in response to numerous and serious allegations of poor governance, financial mismanagement and non-adherence to the Sascoc constitution, and the Sascoc board's failure to respond to these matters. Some of these matters had been reported in the media, and others were directed to his office from individual board members, federations and aggrieved individual. In the light of these serious allegations, I have decided to appoint a committee of inquiry – consisting of a retired judge, two additional members and a team leader for leading evidence. - Thulas Nxesi

I had taken a back seat from poking the bear on social media but Alec Hogg from BizNews suggested with SASCOC now under the microscope, this would be a good time for me to remind people about my story.

January 16, 2018

#JoiningTheDots: The SA sports mafia – Graeme Joffe. MUST READ!

JOHANNESBURG – Former Finance Minister Pravin Gordhan famously coined the phrase 'Join the dots', when referring to the Gupta family's involvement in State Capture. And below former CNN International and 94.7 sportscaster Graeme Joffe does just this. He weaves together a piece that exposes what he calls South Africa's sports mafia. And in it he implicates what many could soon refer to as the 'usual suspects'. Hogan Lovells, whom Peter Hain yesterday accused of a white-wash in a so-called independent investigation into shenanigans at the South African Revenue Service. Even the former CEO of Steinhoff Markus Jooste is thrown amongst the sports pigeons, having contributed to the controlling mafia, funnelling money for personal benefit rather than to the areas where it is so needed, development. Joffe fled South Africa previously because his life was in danger, these allegations are likely to keep him there a little longer until the dirty laundry gets aired. A must read. - Stuart Lowman

(BizNews)

THE SA SPORTS MAFIA …

SA Rugby (SARU) president, Mark Alexander was one of the two SASCOC board members who voted "NO" for the dismissal of SASCOC CEO, Tubby Reddy, CFO, Vinesh Maharaj and Executive manager, Jean Kelly.

The SASCOC board members who supported the recommendations for immediate dismissal:

> Gideon Sam, Barry Hendricks, Merrill King, Jerry Segwaba, Dr Debbie Alexander, Lwandile Simelane and Kobus Marais

Mark Alexander (SA Rugby president) and Khaya Majeke (Bodybuilding SA vice-president) did not support the recommendations (voted against the immediate dismissals)

IOC/SASCOC members, Sam Ramsamy and Anant Singh did not respond in writing and in person by the due date, as prescribed (chose not to express an opinion)

Hajera Kajee (SA Table Tennis vice-president), Les Williams (Korfball SA) and Natalie du Toit abstained and chose not to express an opinion

The disciplinary report from a senior advocate was so damning with the numerous charges ranging from sexual harassment (against Reddy), corruption (against Reddy and Maharaj) and collusion.

Alexander chose to be loyal to his "bad buddies" and turned a blind eye to the sexual harassment and corruption.

Why? He is one of the SA sports mafia!

In April 2010, SARU renewed a very lucrative contract for Megapro to be their official, exclusive commercial agent.

The Primedia Group were the majority shareholders of Megapro at the time of the deal and the company was run by George Rautenbach.

But how did Megapro get the deal done without it going to tender as other companies had also put in proposals?

The answer …

Then SARU deputy president and Chairman of SANZAR, Mark Alexander was promised R500.000 per year of the five-year contract to push the renewal through and he went along with it.

A "kick-back" of R2.5 million!

Two of the five payments went from Megapro to the clothing manufacturers, Sedgars to Alexander.

The Sedgars invoice descriptions were: "Consulting fees on Marketing" and "Consulting Fees on Rights INC SA Rugby" - not bad for clothing manufacturers!

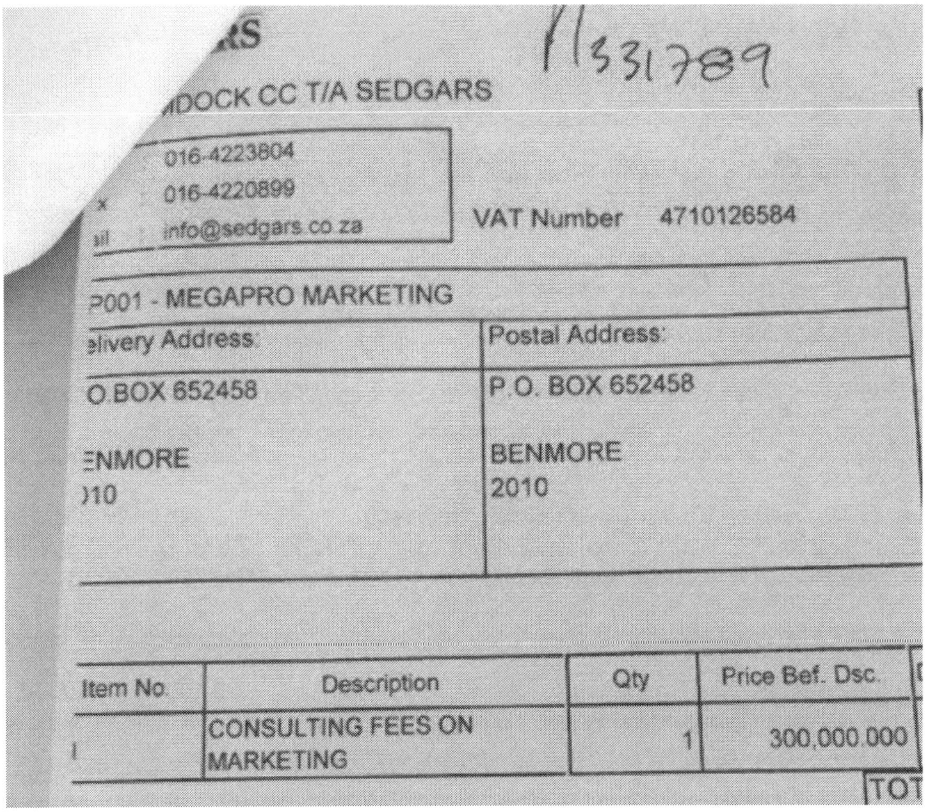

rS

11331789

DOCK CC T/A SEDGARS

016-4223804
x 016-4220899
il info@sedgars.co.za

VAT Number 4710126584

P001 - MEGAPRO MARKETING

elivery Address:	Postal Address:
O.BOX 652458 ENMORE)10	P.O. BOX 652458 BENMORE 2010

Item No.	Description	Qty	Price Bef. Dsc.
1	CONSULTING FEES ON MARKETING	1	300,000.000

TOT

And two payments went through a company called "Ambro".

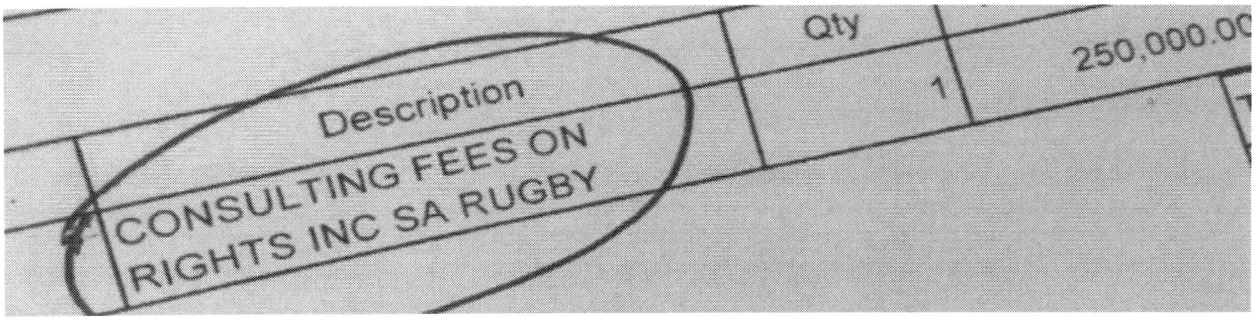

Description	Qty	
CONSULTING FEES ON RIGHTS INC SA RUGBY	1	250,000.00

The payment through Sedgars in 2012 was flagged by Deloitte's in the Primedia group audit.

Primedia got concerned and sold shares back to Megapro in early 2013.

Rautenbach and Steinhoff's Markus Jooste are very close friends and it's believed the money to buy the Megapro shares back from Primedia came from Jooste.

Megapro did the SA Rugby/Steinhoff sponsorship deals and Jooste got Megapro into the SA Horse racing scene with the SANSUI Summer Cup.

When I asked Alexander if he had ever received a commission or any payment, any benefit or perk from Megapro.

He replied: "Please deal with Andy our media person."

SARU's media person, Andy Colquhoun told me I'd be "wasting my time" by emailing him.

Rautenbach told me that Imtiaz Patel (the then CEO of SuperSport) had told him to give back to SA sport and by giving the funds to Sedgars, they would then look after a development team with kit and equipment.

Nothing about consulting.

What happened after the payment to Sedgars and who was the sponsored team?

Rautenbach couldn't tell me.

Sedgars answered me with legal threats from their lawyer, Nazir Kathrada. But I wasn't the only sports journalist who knew about the kickback scandal.

As far as Mark A is concerned, the story is that he managed to persuade the SARU executive to renew the Megapro deal, despite the fact that Andy Marinos was keen to put it out to tender. For his troubles, he received a kickback from George Rautenbach, although it was channelled through Sedgars, the sportswear manufacturers down in Vereeniging. Imtiaz Patel is also involved, apparently, although I'm not sure how or in what capacity. - Luke Alfred, sports journalist

Patel from Multichoice/SuperSport is very involved and he too was a benefactor of 'cash/commission' from the dirty conduit, Sedgars when MEGAPRO did the Engen sponsorship for SuperSport United.

The commission was R300 000 (another invoice from Sedgars to Megapro) and Patel also received cash for every year of the Engen deal.

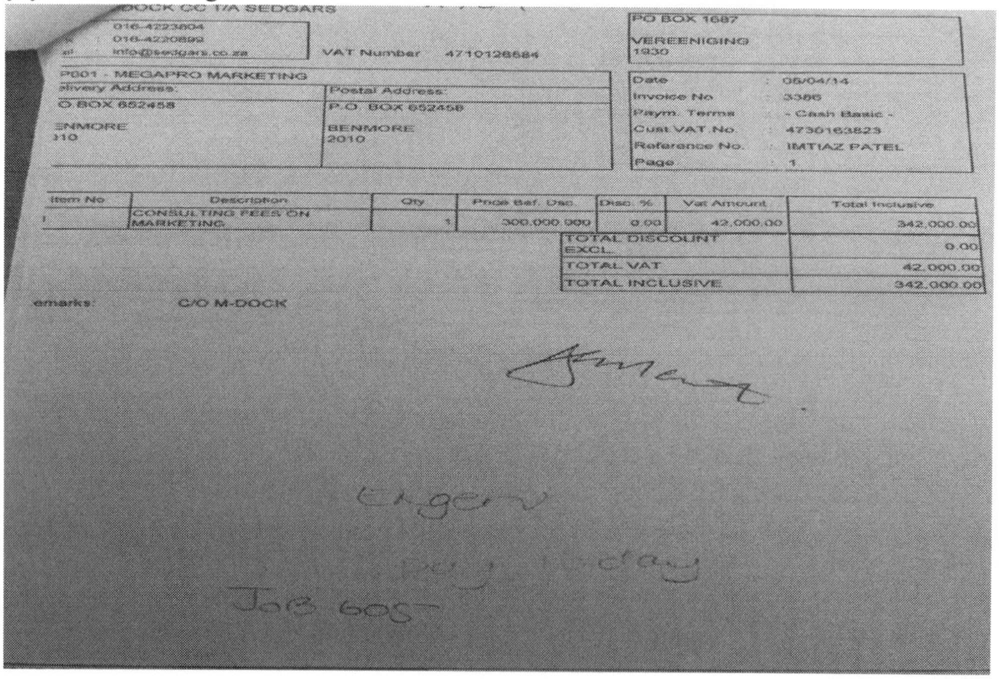
DOCK CC T/A SEDGARS

016-4223804
016-4220899
info@sedgars.co.za

VAT Number 4710128584

PO BOX 1687
VEREENIGING
1930

P001 - MEGAPRO MARKETING

Delivery Address: O BOX 652458 ENMORE 110

Postal Address: P.O. BOX 652458 BENMORE 2010

Date: 05/04/14
Invoice No: 3386
Paym. Terms: - Cash Basic -
Cust VAT No.: 4730163823
Reference No.: IMTIAZ PATEL
Page: 1

Item No	Description	Qty	Price Bef. Disc.	Disc. %	Vat Amount	Total Inclusive
1	CONSULTING FEES ON MARKETING	1	300,000.000	0.00	42,000.00	342,000.00

TOTAL DISCOUNT EXCL.	0.00
TOTAL VAT	42,000.00
TOTAL INCLUSIVE	342,000.00

Remarks: C/O M-DOCK

Engen

Reference no: "Imtiaz Patel"
Payment terms: "Cash basic"

Engen could have done the deal themselves but Patel got Rautenbach involved to grease all their own palms with the 'commission'.

Rautenbach requested a meeting with me after I started the rugby expose back in 2014.

He started by telling me that I was making so many enemies with my work and what happened to the old Joffers that everyone used to love?

And this is how South Africa is and I wasn't going to be able to change anything.

He then went on his fishing expedition to see how much I knew about the kickbacks but I kept the cards close to my chest.

Patel called Rautenbach whilst we were sitting at the coffee shop in Morningside, probably thinking the meeting was over.

He was no doubt desperate to see how things went.

On 24 September 2014: I received a text message from a former Megapro employee saying:

Go you good thing Joffers on the MegaPro skulduggery!!Just be sure to watch your back with Rautenbach. When ……. and I left MegaPro he had us followed. Especially now that you've got dirt on him.

Sure enough and but it was a lot more than just being followed.

Megapro paid R75,000 to their lawyer, Brian Biebuyck from Hogan Lovells for me to be spied on.

They used the forensic specialists, Basileus Consilium.

It was soon after that my phone was illegally tapped, emails hacked and I was followed from a meeting in Melrose Arch.

It was getting scary as I was working on my own as a freelance journalist with no luxury of any group to back me up.

I opened a criminal case with the Morningside SAPS which bounced around between Randburg SAPS and Gauteng Provincial before being swept under the carpet.

In April 2015, a private investigator identified a threat to my safety and after four days underground in Johannesburg, I returned to the USA, where I had spent seven years as an International Sports Anchor with CNN.

Alexander's business record is also pretty revealing.

He had been a director of seven companies that had gone into voluntary liquidation since 2000.

And despite all of this, he was elected unopposed as SARU president in 2016!!

SARU's blind eye and silence with the Jurie Roux affair is just as deafening.

How do you extend the contract of a CEO, who is under a Hawks investigation for allegedly misappropriating R34 million while he was working at Stellenbosch University?

The KPMG report couldn't be more damning.

Roux is also top of the invite list for overseas trips with Megapro and went with them to the Masters at Augusta in 2015 and the British Open last year.

Also, let's not forget that Sedgars are bed fellows of SASCOC as well as a number of sporting federations and paid for one of the then Sports Minister, Fikile Mbalula's family vacations in Dubai.

Alexander is close to Mbalula through his SASCOC links and was Chairman of the Durban 2022 Commonwealth Games Bid.

The Games were embarrassingly taken away from South Africa after R100 million that we know of, was spent on the bid. Durban was the only bidding city.

Megapro were official hospitality providers for the 2010 FIFA World Cup in South Africa and it's alleged that Danny Jordaan also benefitted handsomely from a briefcase of cash.

It's just part and parcel for the SA sports mafia!

***

Brian Biebuyck left Hogan Lovells in March 2017 under a cloud and the law firm covered up for him with my spying case.

Dear Sir

YOURSELF// MEGAPRO// HOGAN LOVELLS

1. We refer to your mail of 23 January 2018.

2. As we have previously mentioned, we have examined the content of our file. As you are well aware, we not in a position to release legally privileged and confidential client information in the absence of an abandonment of privilege by Megapro. Suffice to state, and without disclosing legally privileged confidential client information, your allegations of 'payments having been made to Brian Biebuyck, spying, tapping of phones, hacking of emails and following of you' is not borne out by the contents of our file.

3. In the circumstances, we now regard this matter as being finalised.

Yours faithfully

HOGAN LOVELLS (SOUTH AFRICA) INC

Not so fast Hogan Lovells.

What about the Hogan Lovell's invoice (I35164) for R75,000 which was sent to Megapro with "Graeme Joffe" as the subject line and another invoice (referencing I35164) which shows Hogan Lovells paid R50,000 plus tax to Basileus Consilium to spy on me?

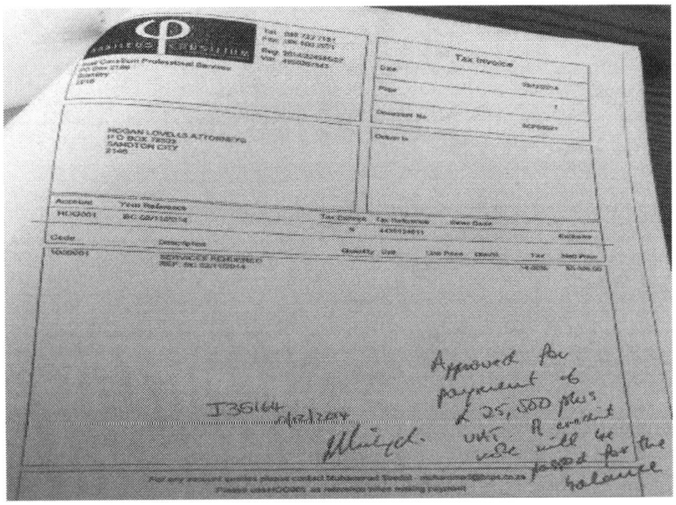
Tax Invoice

HOGAN LOVELLS ATTORNEYS
SANDTON CITY

SERVICES RENDERED

I35164

Approved for payment of £25,500 plus VAT. A credit note will be passed for the balance

And in January 2019, the dirty dealings of lawyer, Brian Biebuyck were further exposed as he was implicated in the state capture testimony.

Law firm 'appalled' that former partner implicated in state capture testimony

Hogan Lovells South Africa said it was appalled and shocked by allegations made by former Bosasa executive Angelo Agrizzi at the Zondo commission of inquiry on Thursday which linked one of the firm's former partners to Bosasa's corrupt payments to government officials. Agrizzi implicated Brian Biebuyck, a former lawyer at Hogan Lovells who left the firm at the end of March 2017, in his testimony before the commission. (news24, 18 January 2019)

The mastermind behind the corrupt payments was the CEO of Bosasa, Gavin Watson, the brother of former EP Rugby president, Cheeky Watson.

The apple doesn't fall far from the tree.

Meanwhile, Alexander didn't enjoy being in the limelight again for his corrupt activities and went on the bully offensive.

SA Rugby boss calls for sports journo Joffe's arrest

A Rugby president Mark Alexander wants to see sports journalist Graeme Joffe arrested once he sets foot in South Africa. Alexander has laid a criminal defamation charge with the police against Joffe following the latter's allegations that the SA Rugby boss was involved in corruption .... I expect him to visit South Africa sometime in future and I want him to be arrested on criminal defamation charges,"Alexander said in a sworn statement. (sport24, 22 February 2018)

The lawyer for Alexander and SARU, Frikkie Erasmus also made up some cock and bull story as to why I left SA to try and discredit me.

They like to play dirty when they get exposed for what they really are.

My response was simple.

The truth obviously hurts. It's high time that Alexander admits his transgressions and resigns from his position at SA Rugby. I'm also curious as to why he didn't act earlier when I first broke the story more than three years ago.

Alexander was probably concerned I would be coming back to SA to give evidence at the SASCOC Commission of Inquiry and that's the last thing any of them would have wanted.

I sent the Commission loads of written evidence but deep down I had a feeling it was going to be a waste of time.

A criminal defamation threat wasn't going to stop me.

A few days later, I sent an email to Alexander, copying in Roux and Colquhoun.

28 February 2018
Dear Mr. Alexander

We are busy with a couple follow up stories and kindly request your answers to the following questions before close of business Thursday 1 March 2018.

1. As per the attached invoice and others in our possession, SARU (if not before) is now fully aware of the
fraudulent activity of its commercial partner, Megapro;
1.1 Will SARU be cancelling their contract with Megapro?
1.2 If not, why?

2. On the day Megapro were at SARU offices for discussions around the contract renewal, Mr Hoskins said
Megapro would not be able to get the contract renewal without a tender process.
Can you explain;
2.1 How the deal was done the very next day?
2.2 Why SAIL were not given an opportunity to tender?
2.3 Why this was not included in the SARU minutes?

3. Mr Rautenbach told Megapro staff the payments to Sedgars were for the SARU contract.
3.1 Do you have a comment on this?

4. Did you at any point consider getting your own personal office space at Megapro?
5. In December 2010, you went on a trip to the UK to meet with Brian Mujati;
5.1 Please can you detail the reasons for the trip?
5.2 Who paid for the trip?

6. The second attachment is a list of some current and past companies you've been involved in.
6.1 Please could you furnish details as to the reasons for all the liquidations
6.2 Who the liquidators were?

***

No response from them as expected, the rugby bullies had gone quiet!

In the meantime, Rautenbach's 'big buddy/investor,' Markus Jooste had landed himself in some real hot water.

Steinhoff reports former CEO to South African police

Steinhoff has reported its former chief executive Markus Jooste to South Africa's elite Hawks police unit over suspected corruption, its acting chairwoman told a parliamentary committee hearing on Wednesday. The South African retailer, whose more than 40 brands include Britain's Poundland, revealed accounting irregularities in December, causing an 85 percent fall in its share price that wiped more than $10 billion off its market value.(Reuters, 31 January 2018)

Steinhoff Ex-CEO Told Friends to Sell Stock Before Collapse

Former Steinhoff International Holdings NV Chief Executive Officer Markus Jooste advised friends to sell the South African retailer's shares days before the stock collapsed, according to a mobile phone text message seen by Bloomberg. The message, sent around Nov. 30 to at least two people, told recipients there was impending, unspecified bad news coming. At the time, Steinhoff was in discussions with Deloitte LLP about the viability of its accounts. On Dec. 5, the company said it had uncovered accounting irregularities and that Jooste had quit, causing the shares to plunge 63 percent in a single session. (Bloomberg, 10 October 2018)

Two sources informed me they had heard that Rautenbach was contacted by Jooste to sell off his Steinhoff shares.

But I don't think Rautenbach took a liking to my line of questioning.

15 February 2018

George, we have a new story under consideration and kindly request your responses to the following:

1) Do you still have Steinhoff shares?
2) Did you short or sell any Steinhoff shares before the big Steinhoff news broke on 6 December 2017?
3) Who owns Megapro?
4) A R500 000 'gift' was given to Kirsten Nemantandani on request from Danny Jordaan - did those funds came from a Megapro or Steinhoff account?
5) Did Megapro tender for any of its contract work in SA Horse racing eg. Sansui Summer Cup?
6) Have you or Megapro ever given any payments (cash or through a conduit) in return for favours from Mark Alexander, Danny Jordaan, Ali Bacher, Imtiaz Patel and others?
7) Have you ever settled a sexual harassment claim?

Please if we could get your response before close of business Friday 16 February.

George Rautenbach <george@megapro.co.za> Fri, Feb 16, 10:21 AM
to me

Graeme,
In response to your questions.
1,2&3- none of your business , 4&6- these questions have been asked and answered repeatedly since 2014. 5- really not question for me to answer.

Very evasive and no comment on question 7 regarding the sexual harrassment claim, which I have confirmation of.

Rautenbach is a sick, corrupt predator!

When SA rugby was in the midst of losing sponsors in 2015, Rautenbach got Steinhoff to lift the financial gloom.

Megapro Brokers Steinhoff Sponsorship For Springbok Sevens

The Springbok Sevens team topped off their winning form with the announcement that Steinhoff International – the integrated retailer with operations in Africa, Europe and Australasia – had agreed a three-year partnership to sponsor the national team. (Megapro, 15 December 2015)

Wonder what the commission was and who got paid what?

Both Rautenbach and Jooste were quoted in the Megapro press release and it was business as usual.

Until the Steinhoff bubble burst towards the end of 2017.

SA Rugby confirms Steinhoff no longer Blitzboks sponsors

SA Rugby confirmed on Monday that it had received notification from Steinhoff International that the company was withdrawing from all sponsorship activities. (sport24, 15 January 2018)

My column, "SA Sports Mafia" touched a lot of nerves and brought me into contact with people I hadn't heard from in a long time.

Graeme – Imagine my surprise when I receive a call from Brandon Foot at SuperSport last night about your recent article about the "sports mafia" on Biznews ... Imtiaz (for reasons you can divine) is very sensitive at the moment; so is Brandon ... It beggars belief that something I may have written to you in a private capacity a long time ago is now hauled up as part of your conspiracy theories ... There was a subtle but threatening sub- text to BF's conversation with me last night. I can only hope good sense prevails and this goes no further. - Luke Alfred, Journalist

'A subtle but threatening sub-text'?

I had corresponded with Foot (SuperSport's chief legal officer) during my exposes of the Sports Trust with SuperSport being one of their major partners. He got short with me then and didn't engage with me on this latest scandal.

My reply to Luke …

Luke, no where in your email did you say not for publication and you are welcome to publish any of my emails to you and the content thereof. I am not scared of the truth and it concerns me that you knew about this Alexander/Patel story and haven't dug further or reported on it in three years. What was holding you back?

Hopefully, not the editors who held you back in the SASCOC story and my legal case? Or the SA Football Museum? "My conspiracy theories"? Not another SA sports journo who wants to discredit me? Used to it - so, it's okay! There are a number of big, prominent South Africans just waiting to pounce on the SA sports mafia. And I can assure you Imtiaz has a lot of reasons to be sensitive at the moment. Not just from the Multichoice/ANN7 deal and the corrupt dealings with Megapro/Sedgars! I am also still waiting for replies to my emails sent to you with regards the HSM directors in February 2015 (not sure if that was info to try and mislead me) and then Kelvin Watt (SAHA director?) on 14 September 2016. Maybe, those are conspiracies.

I never got a reply from Luke.

Then I received a phone call from Selwyn Nathan (Nates) who I hadn't heard from since the 2010 World Cup scandal broke.

He congratulated me on the 'SA sports mafia' expose and wanted to stay in contact.

Nathan was the Sunshine Golf Tour Executive Director and Patel was on the board of the tour.

I suspected the call had another purpose.

Then, it was a call from the SuperSport United CEO, Stan Matthews, who I had known for a long time.

Stan said he did the deal with Engen through Megapro and knew nothing about a "commission" paid to Patel.

He said the club board wanted answers from him regarding the Engen deal and that they were considering taking legal action against me.

I told him they were welcome to take action and there was a much bigger story to come.

Imtiaz Patel is a very dirty player.

Chapter 29: Joining the Dots (Part 2)

When an individual or company are exposed, it seems to give strength to other whistle-blowers to come forward.

Patel and SuperSport were now firmly on the radar and sources provided me with a bombshell.

It was in relation to the South African Premier Soccer League (PSL) television rights deal done in 2007, which was suspicious from the get-go.

SABC: Soccer deal a sham

Johannesburg - The Premier Soccer League (PSL) have concluded a deal worth well in excess of a billion rand over five years with SuperSport International, giving the pay channel exclusive TV rights on all their fixtures. The bombshell announcement was made by PSL chairperson Irvin Khoza at the League's Parktown offices on Thursday and is the culmination of a simmering war with SABC who have held the TV rights since the League's inception nine seasons ago.- (news24, 14 June 2007)

PSL money spat too hot to handle

The rumpus revolves around the R1,5-billion TV deal that the PSL has entered into with SuperSport over the next five years and the R30-million each earmarked for the five members of the PSL's sponsorship committee—Trevor Phillips, Irvin Khoza, Kaizer Motaung, Peter Mancer and Mato Madlala—for the roles they played in helping to secure the massive largesse. - (Mail & Guardian, 18 August 2007)

Eleven years later, the shocking allegations from my sources …

The PSL first appointed an agency to do the tender process for the PSL broadcast rights. Irvin Khoza then decided to fire the agency and that a PSL committee will oversee the tender. Khoza chaired this. Before the tender was adjudicated, Imtiaz Patel paid the PSL R50 million for the 'Mobile broadcast rights'. This money definitely never made its way to the PSL. On the day of the tender, Khoza opened the SABC tender and gave Patel the amount.

Imtiaz then adjusted the SuperSport tender to R2,1 billion and of course SuperSport got it.

The PSL deal was the most important thing for SuperSport, without that they will lose many thousands of subscribers.

Imtiaz was adamant that Koos Bekker would fire him if he lost it. The implication was: do whatever. The question to ask is around the Mobile rights. That was not public and was a bribe.

Scary!

And just reading who the role players were made me nervous.

As in the past, I couldn't sit on the information and emailed Alec Hogg to see if Biznews had an appetite for what could be the biggest scandal in SA sport.

Just think about the millions and millions of SA soccer fans who have been denied access to their national sport because they didn't have the financial means to get in on a pay channel.

Alec was keen initially and sent an email outlining the allegations to Imtiaz Patel and copied in Koos Bekker (the chairman of the Naspers group, which owns SuperSport).

Imtiaz replied the same day, asking Alec for a suitable time to talk, adding:

In the interim, please be assured that I emphatically deny the allegation of a bribe and reserve my rights should the person concerned persist with this allegation. The PSL's mobile rights are dealt with as part of its public tender process.

Two days later, Alec had a telephonic conversation with Imtiaz Patel and Branden Foot and sent me an email saying:

Have just had a long telephonic chat to Imtiaz and Branden. It seems we will have a serious problem proving the allegations that SS/Imtiaz bribed Khoza - something they vigorously deny btw.

The tender process is public and the winning bidder (in this case SS) is awarded the contract on the basis that its funds are paid directly to the PSL. It is an identical process to the way sports rights are handled elsewhere in the world. Were there some deal within the PSL to enrich any of its directors or split a commission three ways as you mentioned for "swinging" the deal, it would be an internal decision that the PSL sanctioned or not. One cannot blame SS/Imtiaz for something which may have happened within the PSL and over which they had no control.

In effect, you will need to provide documentary proof that SS paid Khoza separately. Is this what you believe happened? Or were he and his accomplices paid by the PSL?

Secondly, Imtiaz is furious at the allegation that he took a kickback as alleged in the Alexander/Rautenbach story. As a matter of huge urgency, please send me the evidence you have to back this - if it is not available we'll need to remove the offending sentence.

I'm flat out in Davos, but am copying Stuart so that he can action everything from here on. Please keep me in the loop.

Of course, they would deny it all and of course Imtiaz would be furious about the allegation he took a kickback.

There is no denying the kickback.

The smoking gun was the first Sedgars invoice for R300 000 for Imtiaz and then cash was paid the following years.

The Engen sponsorship was R12 million and commission was 2.5% for each year.

There was no need to remove the 'offending sentence' - sorry Imtiaz!

A couple days later, I got another call from Selwyn Nathan asking me to please email Imtiaz and tell him I'm not the one digging into the PSL story.

Nathan said innocent people are involved here and Khoza for one, doesn't need the money.

There was never going to be an email to Imtiaz, but I played it down saying I wasn't going to dig any further as this story made me worry about my saftey again.

But my sources were strong and I was always going to follow through with the expose.

Imtiaz is heading into a shit storm. This whole thing about ANN7 and SABC being paid to lobby government is not going away. And it is the truth and he was heavily involved. I wonder who is the innocent people? ... The other 2 must have been on the PSL board at the time. Our understanding was that they were mandated by the PSL to do the tender process. We are sure with this last round of bidding for the broadcast rights it was cooked again. Vodacom was bidding for it as far as we understand. They obviously had no chance. Imtiaz was overheard saying that Irvin screwed the other 2 and that the split of the R50 million was changed heavily in favor of himself. If this goes public Irvin will lose his hold on the PSL. They will do anything to make sure it never comes out. But it is a culture at Naspers. Koos won't get his hands dirty and will never admit knowing anything, but he knows everything and he manipulated a lot of guys to do dodgy things. Imtiaz included.

Patel/Multichoice/Naspers were under pressure to explain the ANN7 deal but it was all swept under the carpet.

MultiChoice and ANN7: So many questions still left unanswered

On Wednesday, the Naspers-owned pay TV company MultiChoice announced that it would not be hosting ANN7 on its DSTV channel from August 2018, following an internal investigation into its relationship with the channel. The #GuptaLeaks emails had previously revealed large payments made to ANN7 during the period when MultiChoice was lobbying government to make a decision on digital migration to benefit the company. MultiChoice says its investigation revealed "mistakes" in the handling of ANN7, but "no corruption". They are not releasing the "commercially sensitive" full investigation report – so inevitably, questions remain. Why did MultiChoice CEO Imtiaz Patel lie to the media in 2013? After it was announced that a Gupta-owned 24-hour news channel would air on DStv from August 2013, then-MultiChoice CEO Imtiaz Patel told Tech Central: "I can confirm that we are not paying for this channel and we are merely providing space on our bouquet." We know that this was untrue – MultiChoice initially paid ANN7 R50-million per year, before upping this to R141-million annually from 1 April 2016. It also paid ANN7 a once-off amount of R25-million at this time. (Daily Maverick, 1 February 2018)

Imtiaz has a lot to answer for ...

Graeme, your untrue and defamatory story regarding me allegedly taking a kickback has already been published by you (and others) without regard to the most basic tenet of journalism- not affording me an opportunity to respond to those allegations. The damage has been done and to seek my comment after the fact serves no purpose. The provision of this document takes the matter no further and is not proof of the wrongdoing you allege. Similarly, your allegations about my conversation with Alec are simply untrue. I have proof of that. All rights insofar as you and other publishers are reserved. - Imtiaz Patel

"Allegations about my conversation with Alec are simply untrue? I have proof of that."

Can't wait to see proof of that!

I wasn't too familiar with the PSL operations and reached out to a couple football journalists in South Africa, to which one replied:

Wasn't aware of the specifics but Imtiaz also consumed a lot of SuperSport Utd cash with Stan Matthews. The give-and-take between SS and Khoza is vast and longstanding ... Mobile TV rights are the new-fangled way to make money, selling to mobile phone companies after TV rights holders. So much I could add but I've had tangible evidence of Khoza's legal and physical defence... deeply unpleasant. Pirates income R300m a year, don't buy players or pay top dollar. Cash being funneled to mining in DRC and CAR... no PSL clubs ever submit SARS DOCUMENTS, PSL exec (Khoza led) take R70m out of the game every year, previous boss Abdul Bhamjee jailed for taking far less "commission." Weird thing is SuperSport don't really have any rivals for PSL coverage, they're all just handing each other money which could/should go on to development... Keep fighting. Incredible nobody listens or even asks questions in SA sports journalism. And more and more media doors shut in your face the more questions you ask.

Matthews was the CEO of the PSL for a seven-month stint in 2011/12 before returning to SuperSport Utd.

Irvin Khoza, Imtiaz Patel and Selwyn Nathan are all very close.

In July 2018, Nathan's name appeared in a hard-hitting expose by AmaBhungane, 'an investigative journalism organization focusing primarily on exposing political corruption in South Africa and neighboring countries.'

Was he the "boss" behind the investment manager, Integrated Capital Management (ICM) which had links to the Guptas and state capture?

Nathan hired criminal lawyer, Billy Gundelfinger to help defend the allegations.

AmaBhungane: The 'Gupta Minyan' and the R647m Transnet scam

We went after a trail left by Gupta lieutenant Salim Essa. What we found was a group of Jewish businessmen who complain of being shunned by their community because of their association with the Guptas. Our investigation suggests the community called it right. Essa extracted R76-million from a Transnet relocation project – but not without the assistance of a fake company with a stolen identity and a ghost director to help drive up the price Transnet was willing to pay ... Gundelfinger told us the association with Essa began in 2014 when Selwyn Nathan introduced Essa as "a credible BEE businessman and potential client". It is worth flagging Nathan before he exits the stage. He is a former golf-pro turned sports marketer who hit the big time with Vodacom's sponsorship arm. He served on the 2010 World Cup local organising committee and has strong business and political connections, mostly golf-related. If he only made the introductions, we asked ourselves, why was he even legally represented? Clues to that might be found in whispers about Nathan being "the boss" behind ICM. Back in 2015 he was listed prominently on the ICM web page as the "non-executive chair". - (Daily Maverick, 26 July 2018)

Where there's smoke, there's normally fire.

Khoza is undoubtedly one of the most powerful men in SA sport and seldom has anyone been able to stand up to him. But the owner of the PSL club, Black Leopards has confronted him head-on, in what will be a very interesting case to follow.

'Release the PSL from capture'

In what could shake South African football to its core, embattled Black Leopards boss David Thidiela has launched a scathing attack on PSL chairperson Irvin Khoza ... "The PSL is completely captured. Individuals, structures of the NSL, match officials, etc are manipulated for the self-interest of one man, or a few who surround or are appointed by him, to wage personal battles; to maintain the exercise of unfettered control or authority over PSL; to ensure self- or enrichment of the selected few – an inevitable compelling call for a commission of inquiry into the NSL." (City Press, 13 December 2018)

The NSL trades as the PSL.

It was tough for me to dig further into the TV football rights scandal from a distance, but I just hope someone local asks a lot more questions about what appears to be a very "off-sides" deal.

Millions of fans have been cheated!

The public were also cheated of an open, transparent, full Ministerial commission of inquiry into the dealings of SASCOC.

From the outset, the commission lacked professionalism, there was no live streaming and one of the committee members was very conflicted.

Former cricket boss, Dr. Ali Bacher has strong links to SuperSport and is also alleged to have received kickbacks from Megapro when the Indian Premier League (IPL) came to South Africa in 2009.

The commission extracted very little that I hadn't already exposed in the previous six years but it was some vindication for me to now see it all in black and white.

Explosive revelations on first day of the committee of inquiry into Sascoc

The SA Sports Confederation and Olympic Committee (Sascoc) was dysfunctional, the ministerial committee of inquiry into governance issues at the umbrella body heard on Monday. Desiree Vardhan, in charge of coaching at Sascoc, told the inquiry the environment at work was "very toxic and threatening" and innovation was shunned. - (Times Live, 12 February 2018)

Analysis: Sascoc Inquiry scratches the surface of corruption, but misses transparency mark

There have been two days of testimony in the Zulman Inquiry into alleged maladministration of the South African Sports Confederation and Olympic Committee (Sascoc), but already a clear picture is starting to emerge: Corrupt, more corrupt, most corrupt, with the names of high-ranking officials likely to replace each word in the degrees of comparison. (Daily Maverick, 16 February 2018)

Sascoc inquiry: 'It sounds to me like a whole bunch of corrupt activities'

Committee members probing SA Sports Confederation and Olympic Committee (Sascoc) governance matters have branded as corrupt the "common practice" of board members and staff seeking favours

·om service providers. (Times Live, 9 March 2018)

ascoc inquiry: Gideon Sam accused of sheltering allegedly corrupt 'friend'

ascoc president Gideon Sam has been accused of highly improper, grossly irregular and negligent ehaviour to shelter a friend by ignoring a report into a member federation. (IOL, 15 February 2018)

nside the rot at Sascoc

tartling revelations, accusations and counter-accusations went into overdrive when the fired Sascoc ·io of Tubby Reddy (chief executive), Vinesh Maharaj (chief financial officer) and Jean Kelly (executive ianager) took the stand in the past week. They accused Sam of "double-dipping" on allowances, onflict of interest by chairing companies that do business with Sascoc and his alleged disregard for HR nd financial policies. (Sunday World, 11 March 2018)

'ormer Sascoc CEO Tubby Reddy accused of interfering and dishonesty

'ubby Reddy, the former CEO of the SA Sports Confederation and Olympic Committee (Sascoc), has een accused of interfering in Athletics SA (ASA), attempting to influence the outcome of an inquiry and 'ishonesty. (Times Live, 27 February 2018)

'ascoc Inquiry: Perks For Spouses, Sexual Harassment And Fictitious Companies

'he spouses and partners of the SA Sports Confederation and Olympic Committee (Sascoc) board iembers were given allowances of R2,400 a day during the 2016 Rio Olympics, The Citizen reported. 'his while Sascoc reportedly claimed it could not set up a proper training camp for the Olympic team. Iearings into governance problems at Sascoc are currently underway, and allegations from financial iismanagement to corruption and sexual harassment have emerged. (HuffPost, 9 March 2018)

SASCOC: Reddy accused of 'fraud' for altering report

'ubby Reddy's failure to disclose to the Sports Minister that he altered the Griffin Report was 'tantamount to fraud" the disgraced former Sascoc chief executive heard yesterday. (IOL, 9 March '018)

'ascoc deputy president quits in protest over money transfers

'A Sports Confederation and Olympic Committee (Sascoc) deputy president Hajera Kajee on Monday aid she had resigned from the body's investment arm because she didn't want to be implicated in ·ertain money transfers ... Kajee said she had recently resigned as a director of Gride, Sascoc's nvestment arm which owns shares in gaming outfit Phumelela and was worth nearly R100-million. Times Live, 5 March 2018)

Inalysis: Sascoc Inquiry highlights grotesque arrogance and disregard for SA athletes

'he ministerial inquiry into Sascoc's shenanigans concluded last week and while few, if any, of the llegations raised were earth-shattering, it once again highlighted that those tasked with a duty of care o South Africa's top athletes are too busy fighting with each other to deliver a successful high-performance programme that should make the country one of the world's top athletics nations. (Daily Maverick,. 22 March 2018)

The inquiry ended in the middle of March, but the findings/report wasn't released to the public until December. That in itself should have raised eyebrows.

The minister has requested the IOC members to facilitate the report to the IOC. They have agreed and have now distanced themselves from the report discussions. (Sam) Ramsamy is responsible for past atrocities and equally responsible for the apathy toward exposing corruption and "lackadaisical" attitude by abstaining during votes on these issues. - SASCOC board member

But there were some tactical leaks of the report and these were some of the bigger talking points.

* SASCOC's award of national colours to athletes through its executive management and or the CEO, is irregular and unlawful;

* There is a significant lack of corporate governance in the management of SASCOC and especially in the management of its financial affairs;

* SASCOC's failure or refusal to consider the Pullinger report is inexplicable and irrational;

The Pullinger report, which came out in mid-2015, was led by advocate Alex Pullinger in 2013. Pullinger found that there had been intimidation of minors, manipulation of scores in competitions, discrimination, inappropriate awarding of national colours a corrupt relationship between SA Sports and Fitness Federation office bearers and maladministration of funds, of which the senior national officials were aware. (IOL, 13 February 2019)

* SASCOC's internal dispute resolution process is inappropriate;

* There is a complete mismanagement of funds used for costs associated with international travel for members of the Board and senior management;

* In light of the factionalism within the Board, it is a Board that is essentially dysfunctional;

* The SASCOC policies of the procurement of services are woefully inadequate;

* CEO Tubby Reddy's conduct in relationship to the Griffin report was unethical, dishonest and amounts to a fraudulent misrepresentation and the payment to SS Griffin (from his monies and Volleyball SA) appears to be inappropriate and irregular;

* CFO Vinesh Maharaj's conduct is using SASCOC's service providers for personal favors for himself and for other members of the board, constitutes conduct akin to corruption;

* President Gideon Sam's mode of operation, function and leadership style is highly inappropriate and not suitable for a public institution like SASCOC, almost dictatorial in nature;

* SASCOC should undertake a complete and thorough audit of its financial transactions for the last five years including travel and other benefits and procurement of services and that any irregular or wasteful expenditure is dealt with and possibly recovered

I wouldn't hold my breath!

ıe Sports Minister simply agreed with the recommendations of the Inquiry and told SASCOC to ıplement the changes by April 2019.

. other words, allowed them to mark their own exam papers.

o forensic audit, no criminal action and no heads rolled!

'hat the commission really needed was for the likes of Fikile Mbalula (former Sports Minister), Mark lexander (SASCOC board member and SA Rugby president), Imtiaz Patel (SuperSport), Mohammed ıd Yusuf Dockrat (Sedgars), Nazeer Camaroodeen (Fli-Afrika), George Rautenbach (Megapro), embers of the National Lottery distribution agency for sport and respective auditors from Deloitte and PMG to be grilled.They have a lot to answer for in the capture of SA sport!

he commission of inquiry was just the tip of the iceberg but it did open taps for more dirty running ater.

Graeme Joffe @Joffersmyboy · Sep 7

In **SASCOC** books, 3 flights to **Kuwait** for Int Court of Arbitration seminar in 2014 - all different amounts - one being R389,952.00 & that person never even went! Why was this not interrogated at Ministerial COI? Did Deloitte auditors turn a blind eye? Who got the dirty R389k?

he flight to Kuwait for R389,952,81 were in the name of Mubarak Mahomed who never went to the eminar.

'he other two flights were just over R35,000 and three per diems for R10,877,32 were also paid out om the SASCOC account.

2014/06/05	Tubby Reddy PerDiem Kuwait ICAS Seminar 2-6June	GLO002-RCP10876	10 877,32
2014/06/05	Mubarak Mahomed PreDiem Kuwait ICAS Seminar 2-6June	GLO002-RCP10876	10 877,32
2014/06/05	Raymond Hack PerDiem Kuwait ICSA Seminar 2-6June	GLO002-RCP10876	10 877,32

ʌystery over R390,000 a ticket in SASCOC debacle

ɪn air ticket to Kuwait for nearly R390,000 is one of several anomalies uncovered on a travel schedule or the SA Sports Confederation and Olympic Committee (Sascoc) ... 'All I know is the three of us were upposed to have gone.' – Tubby Reddy - (TimesLive, 16 September 2018)

Iack confirmed in the story that he was the only one who attended the seminar on instruction of ASCOC and he received no allowances.

o, around R450,000 on just this trip is unaccounted for?

But that's a small number in comparison to the Lottery funding that often goes unaccounted for.

In September 2018, Gideon Sam goes before the Sports Portfolio committee and claims that SASCOC got no funding from the National Lottery in the lead up to the 2016 Rio Olympics.

A few months before the Rio Olympics SASCOC received R70 million. This seemed like a huge amount of money to people. What they did not take into consideration is that the preparation of a team happens over a four year period. Over this four year period SASCOC did not get money from the NLC and SASCOC had to steal from Paul to pay Peter. - Gideon Sam

I guess Sam just forgot about these National Lottery payments to SASCOC:

2013: R75 million
2014: R110 million
2015: R65 million
2016: R190 million

SASCOC vice president, Barry Hendricks promised me answers with a full breakdown of the Lottery spend during those four years.

I am at the office today and will request the information. Please note that some of the new board are only discovering these issues now. (via twitter, 2 October 2018)

I'm still waiting for the information.

But Hendricks likes to play the good cop …

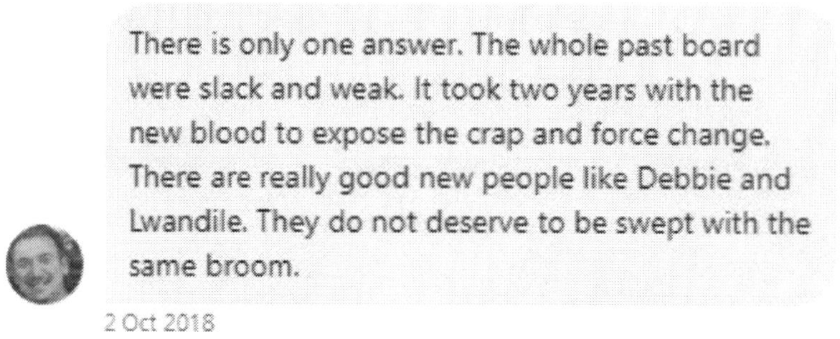

There is only one answer. The whole past board were slack and weak. It took two years with the new blood to expose the crap and force change. There are really good new people like Debbie and Lwandile. They do not deserve to be swept with the same broom.
2 Oct 2018

Why then in 2019 are the 'good new people' silent when SASCOC is hopelessly insolvent but are paying a sponsorship consultant (Qondisa Ngwenya) R50 000/month before he even secures a sponsor, R60 000/month for a part-time financial consultant from Durban (Ravi Govender) and millions more to Sedgars for SA team attire with no proper procurement?

Worst of all, silence in the SASCOC 'cover up' of sexual harrassment, racial abuse and consumption of alcohol in the Olympic Village at the 2018 Summer Youth Games in Buenos Aires.

SASCOC manager of operations and events, Clifford Cobers was the central figure in the eight page incident report filed by SA team doctor, Karen Schwabe.

> Firstly, I did not want to report the incidents, but for the honor of our country and respect for future medical and Olympic colleagues, I feel it my duty to report the poor conduct of the acting chef de mission Mr. Clifford Cobers and add the unacceptable behavior of Alroy Dixon of athletics. I have discussed this matter with various colleagues at the recent games and of previous games and have been asked to do this.
> This is the first time in my career as a Sport and Exercise Physician, I need to report anything. I am exposed to various levels of sport, from being the Springbok 7's team physician for a few years, running a trauma unit for 12 years , to head of medical at Western Province Rugby now. Other charity included working for the Red Cross Air Mercy Service for many years.

The sexual misconduct allegations against Cobers were also corroborated by SA team physiotherapist, Narayani Pillay.

> On numerous occasions he had said the physiotherapist room looks like a bordello.
> He repeatedly asked if he can come get a 'happy ending' – ongoing as if that was a joke. This was not appreciated at all.
> He presented to physio a few times for his back, making these statements again in front of Narayni.
> Alroy Dixon was in the physio room on many nights till late.

Cobers denied all the allegations in the eight page report and SASCOC gave him a little slap on the wrists.

Noting that Dr Schwabe has withdrawn the case and therefore this matter can't be pursued further, we are however of the view that based on the above three points raised together with him being the head of delegation on behalf of both SASCOC and the country, we recommend that he is given a written warning. This will be in his personal record for six months and if found guilty of a similar offence during the six months period, he will face a disciplinary inquiry as guided by the SASCOC HR Policy.

But according to a SASCOC insider:

The good doctor was called by SASCOC and asked to present herself to SASCOC for questioning. When she refused, as she was not on trial, they advised her that she should be careful in making unfounded accusations. They also said that if she knew what's good for her and if she wanted to continue working with SASCOC, she should drop the charges. She maintains that she did not withdraw the charges even though SASCOC stated publicly that she withdrew the letter.

How can anyone on the SASCOC board remain silent about this behaviour?

I met Hendricks at a lunch squash meeting some years ago. He arrived late, no apology and was quick to tell me how much money he was getting for Squash SA from the Lottery.

Not a good first impression.

We would run into each other at squash events after that and I was very circumspect. For good reason.

Hendricks is another one of those well connected, power hungry administrators with his own personal agenda.

Barry Hendricks is the pretender to the SASCOC throne! He has carefully crafted a plan to ascend to the position of President. And he believes he is almost there. If Hendricks is elected, SASCOC will be going from "the frying pan into the fire". Hendricks will not solve the challenges facing the sports movement in our country, but rather, he will abuse the leadership position. Bear in mind that he receives the bulk of his income from Sascoc and from his crooked friend Yaseen Lombard who he has entrenched as Secretary General of Gauteng Sports Confederation, of which Barry is President. He also runs training programs for sports people and gets paid to train volunteers for the Arnold Classic event, whose funds are facilitated by his long-time friend, Ivor Hoff of the Department of Sport Gauteng. The position of President needs an individual with integrity. A starting point would be to request Hendricks to subject himself to a lifestyle audit and a forensic audit into the books of Gauteng Sports Confederation. - SASCOC insider

The fact that there wasn't a vote of no confidence in the SASCOC board by the member federations following the Commission of Inquiry is a tell-tale sign of just how deep the systemic corruption is in SA sport.

And the numbers don't lie …

> ***Cricket South Africa forecasts R654m loss over 4 years***
> *Cricket South Africa (CSA) told the parliamentary sports portfolio committee that they project a loss of R654 million in their next four-year financial cycle. (EWN, 31 October 2018)*
>
> ***SA Rugby almost bankrupt, records loss of R62 million in 2017***
> *The South African Rugby Union (SARU) is on the verge of financial collapse after recording a net loss of R62 million last year. (The South African, 29 August 2018)*
>
> ***Safa on the brink of collapse***
> *The SA Football Association's (Safa's) finances are in tatters, the point where its regions are facing closure owing to non-payment of monthly grants. Mounting lawsuits – amounting to millions of rands – against Safa are adding insult to injury, and the football association has been left struggling to hang on to its assets. (City Press, 9 September 2018)*
>
> But there's no accountability and the administrators will continue to enrich themselves at the expense of the sport and the athletes.

It stretches across the board.

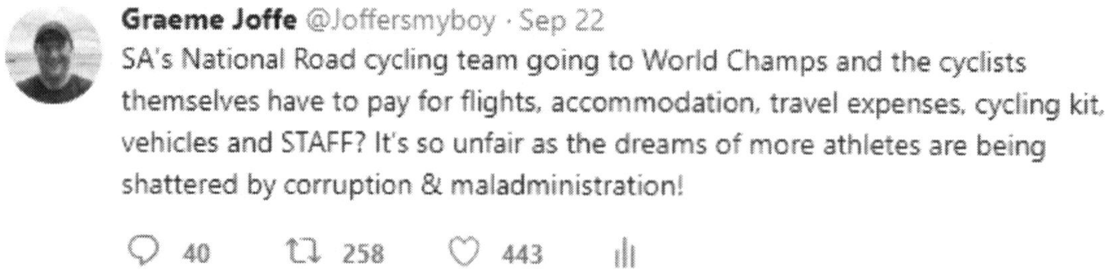
Graeme Joffe @Joffersmyboy · Sep 22
SA's National Road cycling team going to World Champs and the cyclists themselves have to pay for flights, accommodation, travel expenses, cycling kit, vehicles and STAFF? It's so unfair as the dreams of more athletes are being shattered by corruption & maladministration!

40 258 443

Rodger Warren @RodgerWarren · Sep 22

Replying to @Joffersmyboy

Same with the SA team that went to the World Equestrian Games, and they had to take their horses and support teams. My kid was part of a SA gymnastics team to Switzerland, I paid. She got a bladder infection there, team managment did nothing for her. SA sport bodies useless.

ZwemZa @ZwemZa · Sep 23

Replying to @Joffersmyboy

Its not only in cycling Joffers My Boy - Team SA to recent FINA Jnr World Open Water Swimming Championships had to pay 40K each to compete, yet those who went to Africa Championships in Algeria received a 10k subsidy! Despite this 15 kids withdrew from Algeria team

And this was a Facebook post of mine from December 2018 …

For two straight nights, the females of the South African swim team at the U20 Youth Games in Botswana had to sleep on a floor with no pillows and no showers. The first night was after a 10 hour bus ride and there was no toilet paper either at their disposal. The Olympic Committee of SA (SASCOC) and Swimming SA wouldn't put them up in a hotel or B&B for the two nights! These young girls have been through so much just to make the team and then they get treated like this by SASCOC whose board members still get paid salaries in contravention of the International Olympic Charter (IOC) charter. My heart bleeds for these young future stars and their parents. This is why I cannot give up the fight. SA sport needs change more now than ever!

The 2017/2018 SASCOC financials make a sorry sight for sore eyes – the Olympic Committee of South Africa is hopelessly insolvent!

Over R3 million in salaries paid to the board?

The CEO, Tubby Reddy got R2.5 million in 2016/2017 and just over R2 million in 2017/2018 before his suspension.

The highest paid board member was the SASCOC president, Gideon Sam who got R331 000 in 2016/2017 and the same again in 2017/2018.

(Source: SASCOC financials 2017/2018)

3a Salaries

Board Members		
Mr H Kajee	268 727	268 727
Mr M Alexander	224 237	224 237
Mr L Williams	224 237	253 897
Mr SJF Marais	224 237	224 237
Mr SG Sam	331 014	331 014
Mr MM Mohamed	-	149 491
Mr J Naidoo	-	149 491
Mr SJJ Segwaba	224 237	224 237
Mr TS Hlasho	-	149 491
Mr EE Smith	-	149 491
Mr MSI King	224 237	224 237
Mrs MR Keikabile	-	149 491
Mr TA Skhosana	79 640	47 878
Mrs DG Alexander	224 237	74 597
Miss LZ Simelane	224 237	74 597
Mr BE Hendricks	268 727	89 427
Miss N Du Toit	268 933	47 257
Mr K Majeke	224 237	74 597
TOTAL	**3 010 936**	**2 906 394**
Other Employee Benefit Expenses		
Chief Executive Officer	2 017 210	2 575 321
General Manager High Performance	1 367 762	1 391 360
Chief Operating Officer	1 555 873	1 588 760

And the IOC charter clearly states …

> *National Olympic Committees must be completely independent and autonomous and entirely removed from political, religious or commercial influence.*
>
> Because of the importance of National Olympic Committees which are in complete charge of the Olympic Movement in their countries, great care must be exercised in choosing members, who should be men of good standing, upright character, sound judgement, independent mind, and a knowledge and belief in Olympic principles.
>
> **Members of National Olympic Committees shall accept no salary or fee of any kind because of their position. They may, however, accept reimbursement for transportation, lodging and other proper expenses incurred by them in connection with their duties.**

But there is just no accountability!

The sad part in all of this failed system is that more and more SA sports teams are now selected on wealth and not merit. Athletes often have to pay their own way with the majority of federations in financial turmoil

It also kills any chance of real transformation.

Four time Olympian and SA swimmer Roland Schoeman has long been fighting for change and hasn't given up the fight.

Roland Schoeman @Rolandschoeman · Sep 20
Such a sad state of affairs for South African athletes. Careers & lives are being ruined by a select few because of their own greed. How many more champions could we have? How much better could our teams be? We can all take a stand against this. Now is the time we need to.

echo your sentiments 'Rollie' but tough to take a stand against the sports mafia unless it's mass action.

he athletes need to stand together!

he systemic corruption in SA sport is a betrayal to the country, the public and aspiring sports men and omen.

orruption is widespread in world sport and the milllion dollar question is ...

as sports betting aided this scourge of corruption?

s a blatant missed call in a key game a genuine mistake or something more sinister?

s a last minute dubious penalty award, just part of the game or part of a different game?

s an untypically lethargic display by a star player just par for the course or a sign he is on the take?

Vith legalized betting, will coaches and players be able to resist the lure of making millions of dollars n a missed foul shot or penalty in a meaningless game?

nd what about eating a pie during the game?

ecalling one of the most bizarre betting stories involving the English part-time goalkeeper, Wayne haw who was suspended for eating a pie during the FA Cup match between Sutton United and Arsenal n the 2016/2017 season.

here were betting odds laid against 'the pie eating Shaw' and he was captured on live television ating the pastry on the substitutes bench in the 82nd minute. He was alleged to have influenced betting narkets.

he betting pie is very big with spread betting!

he bizarre story raises a very important aspect of betting. Most of the fixing of matches of all sorts oesn't come from match results, but specific events within the game. So, it's not did the favorites win, ut rather were they up at half-time, or scored within the first ten minutes, or were offside twice in the irst-half.

oes legalized sports betting tempt players and officials to fix games? What about all the illegal online ookmakers?

Betting on sports is legal from Australia to western Europe (the U.K. has the biggest legal market), but *flourishes globally even when it's outlawed. Sportradar AG, a Switzerland-based data company that monitors betting markets for fraud, estimates that 1.5 trillion euros ($1.8 trillion) in wagers are placed worldwide annually, with the majority going through unregulated markets. In the U.S., where a 1992 law had limited the practice almost exclusively to Nevada, annual illegal sports wagers are estimated at $50 billion to $150 billion. That compares with Nevada's record $4.8 billion of sports bets in 2017. The landscape is about to shift, though, after the U.S. Supreme Court in May struck down the 1992 law, freeing New Jersey to legalize sports gambling and other states to follow. (Washington Post, 18 May 2018.*

The pros and cons of sports betting is a book on its own.

Chapter 30: New Beginnings

ıst as well for the television series, 'WKRP in Cincinnati' otherwise, I'm not sure many would ave known which country I was in. Even when I re-connected with my US friends, most of them ould say - "why Cincinnati"?

Iy standard reply, 'don't knock it until you've tried it'.

he Ohio city grew on me fast thanks to the great, friendly people, the ease of getting around and of ourse, the chicken wings even though it's known for its chili.

ut how permanent was my move back to the USA going to be?

had to try get the thought out of my head that I could go back to South Africa to finish what I started. Ioving on was hard plus I had to start the legal process all over again of getting to work and stay in the .S. Political asylum was the most obvious choice or I could have gone the "Vegas route" and married or a green card.

hat's if anyone would marry me?

t 46 years of age, having never been married and often being told 'I've got a face for radio', the Vegas oute may have been a stretch.

n asylum application?

ounds very drastic and it is for millions of people around the world who are displaced.

learned about these hardships during my initial meeting with Cincinnati Immigration Lawyer, Doug Veigle, who had done hundreds of asylum cases. The asylum application process could take years but vithin eight months of applying, I could be granted worth authorization which would be valid for a year nd renewable.

t would be a waiting game.

Vithin the first couple months of being in Cincinnati, I was introduced to Dick Weiland, a well nown lobbyist. Through all his political connections, he wanted to assist me and his words echoed loud: "We need to keep this South African in the country".

Vhat a character Dick Weiland was.

he first two-hour meeting at his apartment is hard to describe. You had to be there. But I'll try my best.

he 84-year-old greeted my sister and myself at the entrance to his apartment in a wheelchair and uickly spun around on route to the lounge. We followed.

he walls were covered with pictures (a lot of them black and white) of Dick himself with past US presidents, Governors, Marilyn Monroe (who he said he had a date with) and others.

It was an impressive Wall of Fame.

We sat down and I told him my story in between hearing about his very interesting life and tennis, which was still his passion.

After about an hour, he asked me to give him all the business cards that were somehow hidden in the gap of the couch.

The dust came up with them but Dick knew what he was looking for.

Within 15 minutes, he had called five or six different people and told them: "We need to keep this South African in the country".

This South African didn't know whether to laugh or cry but Dick was keeping us royally entertained.

Suddenly, the wheelchair spun around again and he was off to get a close up of the TV screen to see how the financial markets were doing.

Back again for a couple more calls and then he wanted to show us around the impressive Walls of Fame.

The only photo that was upside down was that of Hilary Clinton as Dick was unhappy with Hilary's stance on Israel.

That's politics for you.

The visit ended after two hours and if anything, it was going to be good for my book but Dick wasn't done.

A few days later, he called my sister and told her to get me a tie and jacket and we must pick him up on Friday around 4pm.

We were going to a Republican function downtown.

A tie and jacket, you kidding me?

Those weren't in my suitcase.

But I did as was told and there I was at the Marriott Hotel downtown Cincinnati on a late Friday afternoon.

I was the only person without a name tag, amongst a number of politicians including the then Speaker of the House, John Boehner.

I had never seen Boehner before.

When the well-tanned (orange) gentleman got up to speak, I thought it was the Master of Ceremonies, who looked more like a used car salesman.

Obviously, I didn't say that aloud.

It was John Boehner and my first real live entrée into how dirty US politics is.

The Speaker didn't mince his words and President Obama was mostly on the receiving end.

I didn't really understand the animosity or the difference for that matter between the Republicans and Democrats, but I was slowly getting a taste of it.

There was no fluff from Boehner.

He was direct and to the point. "The Republicans need to take back the White House. Obama and the Democrats are destroying this country of ours."

I remember thinking, I wonder what Boehner would say if he lived in South Africa under President Zuma or in Zimbabwe under Robert Mugabe.

Talk about destroying a country!

Before and after Boehner's talk, Dick introduced me to a couple of the aides as well as the owner of the Cincinnati Reds Baseball team, Bob Castellini.

Within seconds, Dick was a man on a mission. "Hey Bob, we need to keep this South African in the country. Will you write a letter?"

I remember the puzzled look on Bob's face.

He had no idea what Dick was talking about and I tried to rescue the situation by giving Bob the elevator version of why I was in the US.

We had a good chuckle and said he'd be happy to assist if he could.

I wanted to know what time I could throw out the first pitch at the next Reds game – yeah right!

Dick also introduced me to Boehner who was just as friendly. I wish I knew he was a golf fanatic and I would have dropped some names, although not my style.

The function was an experience and real eye opener.

Dick Weiland knew most of the people at the function and the ones he didn't, it was the immortal words of, "got a business card?"

And I'm thinking, he's going to have to buy another couch to host the new cards.

A couple weeks later, an email arrived from the Republican office in Cincinnati saying they would keep an eye on my case. Despite the fact I wasn't even a citizen of their country, they were willing to go the extra mile to make me feel welcome.

Graeme, in regards to your case, we will continue to service it even after Congressman Boehner has resigned. No worries! I recently sent an inquiry to USCIS requesting a status update on your case. As soon as I receive it, I will let you know. Have a great week! Respectfully, Ben Thaeler, Office of Representative John A. Boehner

Each week was a challenge in the beginning but something good would happen every week to lift my spirits.

Early on, I had gone to a neighbour's house for coffee and after sharing my story, I was invited to do a Cincinnati TEDx talk. I didn't realize what a big deal TEDx was.

But it helps when the neighbour, Jami Edelheit is the main organizer of TEDx Cincinnati.

Within a couple days of the invite, I was assigned a coach, Michael R Davis and it was off to the training.

Michael opened my eyes to so many different angles for my talk, more specifically who was responsible for who I am today.

It was my late dad, who was a true gentleman and who taught us all about fair play.

As kids growing up, he spent hours and hours with me on the tennis court, on the squash court and nothing was ever too much for him. He never wanted to kill a point, he wanted to keep the rally going and to make sure whoever the opposition was, they were having a good time. Some tennis shots would be hitting the back fence but he would volley it just to keep the point going.

Frustrating if you were his doubles partner but they were some very valuable life lessons.

It's not all about winning.

I also recall Michael's first words after seeing the anonymous Joffers-exposed blog. "You must be doing something right, if they writing about you and trying so hard to defame you."

We met a couple times to fine tune my rehearsed talk as I only had five minutes to get in my whole story. I was very fortunate to have this opportunity and didn't want to mess it up. July 9th 2015 was the big day.

I was more nervous for this than any other prior speaking engagement.

It had more to do with the fact I had become so accustomed to just speaking off the cuff but this was different.

I had to memorize word for word of my five minute talk and this was also the first time I would be sharing my story with a large audience.

The stage was big and the speakers were unbelievable.

I was inspired.

I delivered my talk in the second half of the evening and it went off okay. It didn't feel like I was able to really get into it, trying to remember every word in the five-minute cram. I guess we are always our own harshest critics but if I had an opportunity to speak again, I would do it straight off the cuff. It is more me. Regardless, the whole experience was very special and I met some remarkable people who do amazing things.

Thank you TEDx Cincinnati!

One of the biggest sporting events of the year in Cincinnati is the ATP/WTA Masters Series in August and what an event.

It has the feeling of a Grand Slam and it gave me the opportunity to get out and enjoy the world class tennis. I used to be able to do that with my job but that all changed once I became an enemy of the "sporting state" in South Africa.

Whilst at the tennis in August 2015, I got a call from good friend, Ricci Roberts who was Ernie Els's long-time golf caddie. He put Ernie on the phone and the golf legend, known around the world as the "Big Easy" told me to come to Greensboro for the PGA event, starting on Thursday that week as it would be good to catch up and I needed some time with the boys.

It meant a lot to me coming from one of SA's greatest sporting ambassadors.

I had known Ernie for a long time, since my days of reporting from the Masters for CNN and later back in SA, being the TV producer for the Ernie Els Invitational.

I couldn't miss the opportunity to see the SA boys again and it was four of the very best days. We ate, drank, partied, laughed very hard and even watched some golf.

It took my mind off everything else.

.

The Big Easy wasn't in contention on the weekend and we started the party in the hotel pub on the Saturday afternoon. The locals loved it.

Ernie is a hero to millions around the world and I lost count of the people (including the Mayor of Greensboro) that came up to him in the hotel pub to thank him, not just for his golf but for what he was doing for Autism awareness.

The party was rolling and after a few drinks Ernie told me I wasn't going back to Cincinnati on the Sunday but rather going back with them to his house in Jupiter, Florida.

I wasn't sure if he would remember in the morning, but he wasn't taking no for an answer.

We left the hotel in convoy after the final round on Sunday, drove onto the tarmac of the private airport and boarded Ernie's private jet. Destination – West Palm Beach.

Sunday night at Ernie's home in Jupiter was one of those nights I will never forget. My cheeks were hurting from all the laughter.

Ricci and I pulled off the big upset at on the pool table as we accounted for Ernie and fellow PGA Tour professional, Branden Grace.

The $10 bet - my first pay day back in the USA.

Sorry Ernie and Gracie!

I spent three unforgettable days with Ernie, Liezl and their family in Jupiter.

It was a stark realization to how much life I had been missing during all the years of chasing the next big expose.

Ernie threatened a tennis challenge while I was there but it never materialized. It probably saved me from giving back the $10.

Ernie was born in South Africa on 17 October 1969. As a youngster, he was outstanding in cricket, rugby and tennis. At the age of 13 he won a significant regional tennis event, the Eastern Transvaal Junior Championships. A year later aged 14 and playing off scratch, Ernie won the World Junior Golf Championship in San Diego, California, beating Phil Mickelson into second place. Ernie was just 16 years old when he formally competed against professional golfers. He was awarded his Junior Springbok colours in 1984, the State President Sports Award in 1987, and in 1988 his full Springbok colours. – ernieels.com

I was very touched by their son, Ben who has autism and to see the Ernie Els Autism Centre which opened in 2015. If you ever get to that part of the world, it's a must see.

It will blow you away.

When my nephews were small and watching golf on television, they would see Ernie and say, "look there's uncle Graeme."

Just slightly different golf swings and few zeroes difference in our bank accounts!

But hey, I did get to play Augusta.

My very first trip down Magnolia Lane was with CNN in 1997 and boy was it an eventful reporting debut.

The late CNN sports anchor, Jim Huber was my mentor and there couldn't have been a better educator to learn the ropes from. I was very green, if you'll excuse the pun. I was in front of the clubhouse, interviewing Fuzzy Zoeller along with a couple of other TV crews, when he made the controversial remarks about Tiger Woods, serving "friend chicken and collard greens" at the champions dinner.

I didn't know what collard greens were and thought nothing of the throw away comment until the producer was going through the tape that afternoon. The storm brewed fast and I think Fuzzy is still paying for his ill-advised comments to this day.

It was a very good lesson to learn early on in my journalism career.

I will also never forget my very first live crossing from the first fairway during the practice round on the Tuesday. I was as nervous as anything but the ice was broken by a couple South African fans who walked by after a few cold ones and said: "Look, there's Graeme Joffe - he doesn't look too bad with make-up on."

The night life in Augusta was good and my initiation was drinks with Ernie's caddie, Ricci Roberts in one of the locals.

I thought I handled it fairly well only to get back to CNN in Atlanta on the Tuesday after the tournament to find a photograph of myself, holding up the cigarette vending machine in the pub from fatigue.

Needless to say, I was a little embarrassed.

I only got back on the Tuesday as I got to play the course, yes Augusta National on the Monday after the tournament. Yes, I know a lot of golfers are now hating me right now.

It's been a Masters tradition for years that they do a media lottery during the tournament and around 50 journalists get to the play the course on the Monday.

There was 'Joffers' on the first tee at Augusta National on the Monday, hoping to win the green jacket.

First hole. Par 4: topped the drive 160m down the left, second shot a 5-iron into the trees on the left, third shot a punch to the front of the green and a 3-putt for a double bogey six.

92 blows later, my green jacket dreams were smashed.

It was an unbelievable experience just to play the course and even more amazing is that I can remember all 92 shots. That's what makes Augusta so special is every hole is worth remembering even if you're making a big number.

The club tees are a lot further forward than the tournament tees but we still had the Sunday pin positions.

My shot of the day: From the right bunker on the par-3, 16th to within a couple feet for par. (I gave myself the putt).

Remember it like yesterday.

Through sport, you make friends who will always be there, no matter how long you've been away.

My world had changed significantly in 2015 but spending time with Ernie, his family, Ricci and good mate, Stuart 'Cuzzie' Swanepoel was very therapeutic.

Later that year, I was also fortunate enough to be a guest when Ernie received the Payne Stewart Awar in Atlanta.

The Payne Stewart Award is presented annually by the PGA TOUR to the player who best exemplifies the values of character, charity and sportsmanship.

It was another special night that ended around 3am but not before "Cuzzie" and I had smashed a "breakfast" with another golfing legend and real gentleman, Nick Price at a 24-hour diner in downtowr Atlanta.

I hadn't seen Nick since the beach party at the Nedbank Golf Challenge at Sun City a few years back where we chatted about South Africa and how it was going in the same direction as Zimbabwe.

Nick is a native of Zimbabwe and his insight then now makes so much sense.

That's what I was missing about South Africa more than anything else. The familiar faces and friends wherever I went, whether it be at a sports event, dinner, function, corporate or charity golf day.

The charity golf days were very close to my heart, especially, "Reach for a Dream."

Sporting celebrities would give up their day to play in a four-ball to give back to a charity which fulfils the dreams of children with life threatening illnesses.

I was often the Master of Ceremonies and would joke around at the expense of the celebrities.

There was no airs and graces. It was all about the great cause.

Among the celebrities that never seemed to miss the day of 'giving back' were the late SA cricket great Clive Rice who always managed to win the free haircut and blow prize (Ricey was balder than me - I miss you Ricey), former Bafana Bafana players, Neil Tovey and Mark 'super sub' Williams, Mark 'I played for almost every PSL club' Batchelor, former England International, Terry Paine who must be about 97 now, former Bok flyhalf, Naas Botha (who still hasn't made a tackle), SA cricketer/shot put champion, Hugh Page (sorry Pagey) and boxing legend, my good mate, Corrie Sanders, who was urdered in September 2012.

RIP Corra"
September 2012

woke out of a deep sleep at 4am on Sunday morning and was browsing through twitter on my one to see who was leading the Tour championship in the U.S but was side-tracked by a tweet garding a very good friend and one of our boxing greats.

ur friend, the legendary CORRIE SANDERS is fighting for his life after being shot in an armed bbery! PLEASE PRAY!

elt helpless, who do I call at 4am to find out what's happening?

ore tweets followed and an hour later, the worst was confirmed:

A singer, Kurt Darren tweeted:

k is hartseer, my golf partner en n baie goeie man met n reuse hart, Corrie Sanders, is Hemel toe moggend. Rus in vrede Corra. (I am heart sore, my golf partner and a very good man with a uge heart has gone to heaven this morning. RIP Corra)!

put down the phone and cried like a little boy. My heart was broken. Another senseless murder in outh Africa.

orrie had been through so much, life had thrown him a number of curve balls but he was slowly getting ack on his feet.

t 46, he still had so much to give.

chatted to Corrie on the phone a few weeks ago. We talked about life, golf, rugby and he gave me remedy for my gout. We laughed like the old times but both of us were disillusioned about what as happening in South Africa.

ow, one of our sporting heroes is just another statistic of a cowardly act in a country where crime is piraling out of control.

Many fond memories (most of them on the golf course), of this gentle giant with a like sized heart. single figure handicap who could hit the little white ball as hard as he hit his opponents in the ring.

e loved his golf except for the snap hook off the tee.

Many charities benefitted from his presence and even at 6ft 4, he made everyone feel taller.

or years, I had a regular midweek monthly golf game with Corrie.

We shared so much laughter until one day we were caught off guard when Corrie received a summons n the golf course. I couldn't believe a clerk of the court would go this far, let alone know which nine e were on.

Hope he paid for the golf cart!

But Corrie took it in his stride, he trusted everyone, which was probably one of his only downfalls in life.

The summons led to more laughter but at my expense.

Having never been on a golf course, when someone was issued with a summons, I suggested to Jeremy Mansfield and Darren Simpson that they set up something similar again with Corrie as a prank for their MNet TV programme, "Laugh out Loud".

What I didn't anticipate was that Darren would secretly meet with Corrie the night before the prank and would turn it around, that I became the target.

We arrived at Royal Johannesburg for our monthly game and I made as though nothing was unusual. I chatted to the TV producer and cameramen as if they were other golfers and the plan was to make it all happen on the 17th tee box.

By the 15th hole, the game was over, Corrie was on the losing end and I was a little nervous to go through with the prank in case it would add insult to injury. But Corrie knew otherwise and I had no idea that he had turned the prank around.

Needless to say, we got to the 17th tee, Darren was dressed up as a clerk of the court and making as though he had never met Corrie, he issued him with a summons.

Corrie "lost it" and went after Darren as both went tumbling to the ground.

I was now mumbling, it had gone all wrong. Darren got up with blood all over his face (I hadn't seen him put on the fake blood from his pocket) and I was now at loss for words.

Darren told Corrie it was "my idea" and Corrie came after me.

It felt like 20 minutes but it was probably only 30 seconds that Corrie had me in a head lock on the ground.

The caddies had run for the hills, scared of what was about to happen and our playing partners were pleading with Corrie not to hurt me.

Only after some heavy breathing, did I get the sucker from Darren to say: "You've been pranked on Laugh out Loud!"

It was one of the scariest days of my life and I will never forget how strong Corrie was. Even one of his little southpaw jabs in the ribs left you with a bruise for weeks.

Who will ever forget March 2003, our boy Corrie beating Wladimir Klitschko in the 2nd round in Germany to become the WBO heavyweight champion.

outh Africa had a new heavyweight champion, we had tears of joy.

emember him telling me how his final fight, the first round defeat to Osborne Machimana in 2008 hurt ore than any others, as he was booed out of the ring by those that had supported him for all those ars.

oxing is tough in and out the ring but Corrie never held a grudge. He was grateful for what he was ven and for what he achieved and boy, did he achieve.

icknamed 'The Sniper', Corrie had 46 professional fights, winning 31 by knockout and only losing four nes. He was one of our boxing greats.

have some anger inside of me as to why "Corra" is no longer with us and maybe his life could have een spared. They allegedly wouldn't treat him at a private hospital in Brits on the night of the murder ecause he didn't have medical aid and a hospital in Pretoria also refused to admit him because he was ot outside of Tshwane province.

hose one or two hours could have been crucial. Surely, when it's a matter of life and death, it's the osest hospital?

here is still a numbing sense of disbelief. I think of Corrie's daughter, 15 year old Marinique who will member every day of her life that her dad died trying to protect her.

he damage is never limited. Families become silent casualties.

urder, rape, poverty is destroying SA and it all starts with corrupt officials and we have less than no nance if media doesn't expose them.

orra, you made us all "laugh out loud" when you pranked me, now you've got us all "crying out loud."

IP boxing legend!

***

orrie's murder was just another senseless act in a country where crime and corruption has spiralled out f control.

guess I was just lucky to get out in time to have a chance to box on.

incinnati was very good to me.

did some Olympic reporting on the Rio Games for the radio station Q102 and taught tennis to inner ity kids.

Through sport, there is always an out.

It was whilst selling membership at Harper's Tennis Club that I felt the need to up skill and do more than sit behind a desk.

I enrolled for the Total University Tennis course at the Van der Meer academy in Hilton Head.

Over the years, I had heard so much about the coaching legend, Dennis van der Meer and how much he had done for South African players.

Unfortunately, I never got to meet Dennis as he wasn't well but the course was remarkable, a true testament to the man himself.

After a week on the island of Hilton Head, I said pick me!

I went back to Cincinnati and looked on indeed.com every day for any possible job opportunities on the island.

Sea Pines Racquet Club shop attendant popped up. Not quite what I was looking for but it was a foot in the door.

I am now living a boys dream – teaching tennis and caddying on an island, voted by readers of Travel + Leisure magazine as the "Best Island" in the continental United States in 2018 for the third year in a row.

I've been extremely fortunate to have the tennis legend, Stan Smith as a mentor. Not many get the opportunity to rub shoulders and learn the trade from a winner of two grand slam singles titles, US Open (1971) and Wimbledon (1972).

And also got to hold the trophies!

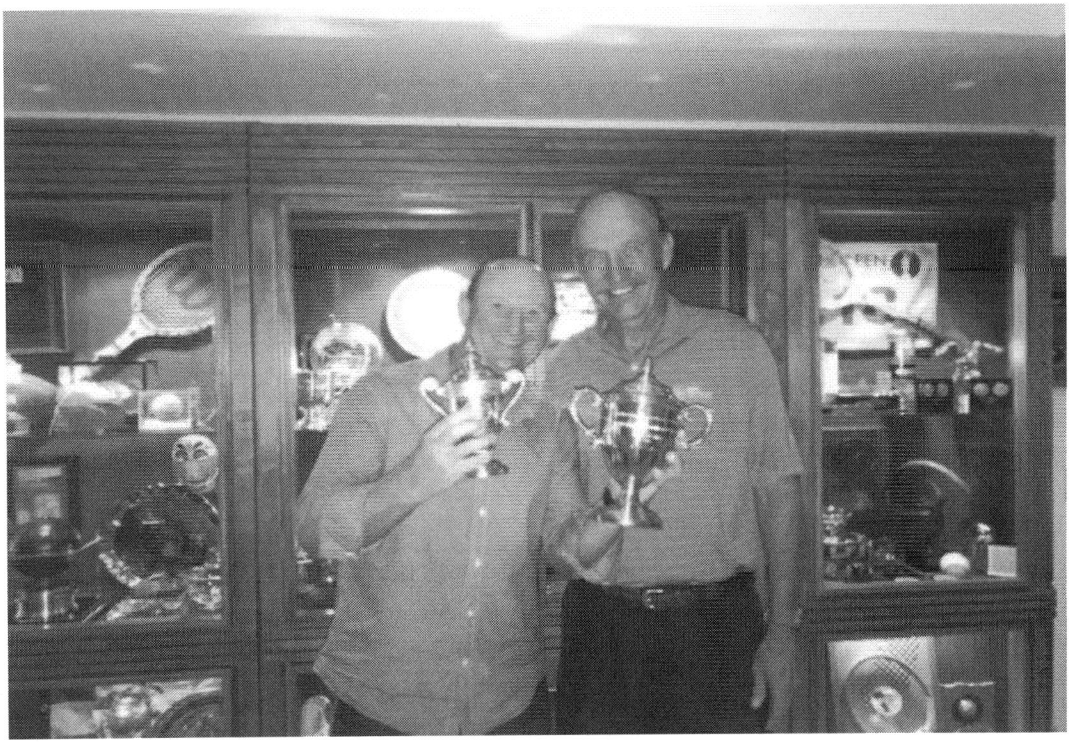

Now I just need to get my name on a pair of those Stan Smith shoes!

The island has had a calming influence on my life – it was desperately needed!

I've met more amazing people and I'd be amiss not to mention the Bocce boys led by the 'ambassador', Dr. Wayne Johnson who have given me great advice, friendship and so many laughs since landing on the island.

Beach Bocce is the real deal!

I get asked this question a lot - will I ever go back to South Africa?

Once you have Africa in your blood, it never goes away.

Sadly, I may never be allowed back and I wouldn't know who to trust. It's no fun looking over your shoulder the whole time.

But I have no regrets for doing what is right and telling the truth.

On 25 July 2014, I was invited to speak at the Johannesburg Sportsman's Club lunch at the Wanderers.

They asked me for a 'teaser' for my talk.

For two years, I have been fighting a lonely battle in exposing the corruption and maladministration in SA sport. I have nothing to gain but as a sports journalist, I feel an obligation to expose what is really going on. Our sportsmen and women deserve so much better and for what we have in talent, finance and facilities, we are perennial under achievers on the Olympic stage. My fight is for the athletes as they are silenced while I continue to fight a R21 million defamation lawsuit from SASCOC. I will not be silenced!

"It is not often that our speakers get a standing ovation; you have certainly given us food for thought." – Dave Penrose, Honorary Secretary (Johannesburg Sportsman's Club)

I remember that lunch like it was yesterday!

It's all out there now for someone else to take the baton and run with it, if they really want to see SA sport and the country change for the better.

Graeme Joffe, you are my hero!! At last, someone is prepared to stand up to this seemingly despicable corruption that exists at the top of our sports 'governing' bodies. We need to get to the bottom of this as it has been going on for far too long, and our athletes are suffering as a result of this blatant greed. - Annette Cowley-Nel, SA Olympic swimmer

Joffers! Soooooo sad to hear of this sick ordeal. I just had a feeling something had happened man! I'm sending you the hugest hug over the miles, and super proud to know a Man with such morals and a hunger for truth and justice! You go Boy! – Sue Coombs

Dear friend, comrade and fellow countryman. It is people like you who are real South African liberators. Tata Mandela wherever he is, is proud of you. You are the true son of the soil. We need more people like you in this country. Corruption is sickening and some have accepted it as a norm. You are doing a sterling job and do not back down. Your contribution might be a drop in the ocean, taking into account corruption that is going on in other government departments, but to many of us you are doing a wonderful job. You have contributed in the the liberation of this country. Your contribution is huge and it is much appreciated. I thank you very much and may the almighty grant you courage, wisdom and strength to fight this evil. You have proven that you love your country and your country needs you more than before. I thank you. - Khehla Momi

I admire Graeme for his investigative sports journalism. I really didn't expect him to endure such a harrowing experience which resulted in him having to leave our shores. What he touched on, in my humble opinion is just the tip of the iceberg. This is evident in ALL codes of sport in our country. It's just unfortunate that it will take so long to bring the culprits to book and by then another few will surface. - Neelesh Bhana

I hope, with you, that the wheel will turn and the criminal scum can get their just desserts someday. May it be soon. I am just sad that their voting constituency are unaware or don't care about the danger that i ultimately holds for them as well. – Anthony Gould

Dear Graeme, Sad you had to leave SA to continue your noble crusade on behalf of all our sports people. So scary that your life is threatened. Unacceptable! I admire your courage and dedication. Vasbyt. - Stuart Scheffer

I cannot express how deeply pained I am of the trying moments you have been succumbed to. It is with great respect that I admire your work and courage to stand up for the truth and nothing else but the truth. Sport plays a vital role in our lives and to discover how undermined or should I say silenced athletes become when they have to be financed by the board in charge of distributing sporting funds it's painful. The hard work they harness in the fields should not go un-noticed. Everyone in our country knows how corrupt we are from the president down to the civil worker especially on national security and the judicial system. It's a losing battle what we need as a country is to overhaul the whole government and appoint according to merit. A lot of people hold key positions that they do not know how to sustain it is time for change. I admire your work. If need be to carry it on in your absence, I can gladly be your acquaintance and complete your story as you would want it published. - Mbuliso Jonas

What do I hope to achieve with the book?

* A better future and fair chance for all SA sportsmen and women
* Justice and an end to the gravy train
* A message of never giving up and standing up for the truth
* A culture of investigative sports journalism in South Africa
* Vindication and closure

It took a long time to accept my fate but can now look back and safely say, the corrupt who had a hand in chasing me out of South Africa actually did me a big favor.

I would never have left SA if not fearing for my safety and don't think I would made it to 50.

The old 'Joffers my boy' is now back, loving life again and 30 pounds lighter!

The further a society drifts from truth the more it will hate those who speak it.'- George Orwell

THANKS

A heartfelt thanks to my sister and brother-in-law, Glynnis and Glenn for looking after their new 40 year-old child.

Words cannot express my gratitude enough.

But I did do a lot of household chores e.g. mow the lawn, get the mail, feed the fish and run the dishwasher to pay for the free 'Michael Jordan' suite.

To the other members of my family who gave me the support and strength to carry on when things looked very dark.

Thank you to my mom, Hazel, Mandy, Loren, Neil, Elana and all my special nephews and nieces.

I love you all!

To the family, friends and public who supported me in my crusade - just your words were enough.

I can't thank you enough.

To all my sources, you know who you are - my heartfelt thanks for your bravery and time.

To my new friends in Cincinnati and Hilton Head, you kept me alive. Great, great people!

Dr. Howard Rankin, who assisted me in this endeavor, my sincere gratitude. You inspired and pushed me to deliver.

Last but not least, to my late dad, Claude who taught me how to be a gentleman and how important it was for everyone to be given a fair in chance in life.

I dedicate this book to you Dad!